Managing
Your
Business
With
MULTIPLAN®

UPDATED
for
Version 3

Microsoft®
PRESS

Managing Your Business With MULTIPLAN® RUTH K. WITKIN

UPDATED
for
Version 3

**Practical Business Solutions
Using Microsoft's Award-Winning
PC Spreadsheet**

PUBLISHED BY
Microsoft Press
A Division of Microsoft Corporation
16011 N.E. 36th Way, Box 97017, Redmond, Washington 98073-9717

Library of Congress Cataloging in Publication Data
Witkin, Ruth K.
Managing your business with Multiplan.
Includes index.
1. Multiplan (Computer program)   2. IBM Personal Computer—Programming.
3. Electronic spreadsheets.   4. Business—Data processing.   I. Title.
HF5548.4.M74W57   1987   005.36′9   87-7773
ISBN 0-914845-94-2

Printed and bound in the United States of America.

1 2 3 4 5 6 7 8 9 MLML 8 9 0 9 8 7

Distributed to the book trade in the
United States by Harper & Row.

Distributed to the book trade in
Canada by General Publishing Company, Ltd.

Distributed to the book trade outside the
United States and Canada by Penguin Books Ltd.

Penguin Books Ltd., Harmondsworth, Middlesex, England
Penguin Books Australia Ltd., Ringwood, Victoria, Australia
Penguin Books N. Z. Ltd., 182-190 Wairau Road, Auckland 10, New Zealand

British Cataloging in Publication Data available

IBM® is a registered trademark and PC/XT™ and PC/AT™ are trademarks of
International Business Machines Corporation.
Microsoft® and Multiplan® are registered trademarks of Microsoft Corporation.

Dedication

To a man who first saw a computer in action at age 85, who couldn't wait to get his hands on it, who wasn't awed or apprehensive the way some people are, who was fascinated by this crazy machine that could do such wonderful things—my dad, Ben Weissman, in memoriam.

Contents

3

Using Multiplan to the Fullest

Acknowledgments

From an author's point of view, things have changed since those early, hectic days when *Managing Your Business With Multiplan* was on the first Microsoft Press list. Now, three years and two Multiplan versions later, the familiar voices on the phone have been replaced by others that have become just as familiar. The deadlines are still there, but they are not quite so close-to-impossible to meet. And a calmer atmosphere prevails. Some things didn't change. The people of the Press were—and remain—professional, bright, and generous with their talents.

At Microsoft Press, special thanks to Ron Lamb for honchoing this second edition and fine-tuning my words and ideas; Mike Halvorson for putting the spreadsheets through their paces and detecting the quirks that drive users mad; Roger Shanafelt for rushing the latest Multiplan disks to me with rock-solid reliability; Chris Kinata for sitting at the other end of the modem; Dave Laraway for reviewing my Multiplan 2.0 manuscript and offering his kind words; and the editorial, design, and production staff, without whom all of this would be only sky-writing: Darcie Furlan, Russell Steele, Jane Bennett, Ruth Pettis, Debbie Kem, Kristen Laine, and Susanne McRhoton. Also, thanks to Theresa Mannix and Karen Meredith for publicizing the existence of this book so that you, the reader, will rush to buy it.

At Microsoft Corporation, I offer my appreciation to Dale Christensen, Multiplan marketer extraordinaire, for his early help in moving this project along, and to Dave Moore for answering my macro questions and getting much of my wish list into Multiplan 3.0.

In my acknowledgments to the first edition, I noted the contributions of some special people who are no less deserving of mention here. I continue to be indebted to my friend Bob Nissen for his unflagging support of my efforts in revising this book and for his willing ear at even the oddest hours. My deep appreciation to Stanley Malaga, C.P.A, whose efforts on the original manuscript have well withstood the test of time. Stanley expertly applied the new tax laws to the examples in this edition. Many thanks to Gil Freeman whose keen mind got a seemingly impossible formula off the ground.

I am grateful to my husband, Burt, for his patience during the time of re-creation, and to my children, Karen and David, who finally got around to acknowledging, "Hey Mom, you're an author!"

Ruth K. Witkin
Plainview, New York
June 1987

Introduction

Welcome to the world of Multiplan, one of the friendliest and most powerful of electronic spreadsheet programs. If you are already using Multiplan, this book will expand your mastery of the program. If you are a first-time user, you're in for a treat. This book is tailored for business people who need practical spreadsheets for a variety of tasks, who have little or no programming or technical background, and who want to be working with Multiplan in the shortest possible time.

Why do you need Multiplan? Because whether you manage a small department, a major division, or your own company, you work with numbers every day. Numbers are the language of business. Multiplan replaces the traditional tools—ledger paper, stubby pencils, worn-out erasers, desktop calculators, and bottles of aspirin—with a management tool that is light-years ahead in speed, accuracy, and capability. Multiplan helps you with financial planning, analysis, forecasting, and recordkeeping. Best of all, it gives you a method of examining the implications of endless "What if?" situations—the tough alternatives you face in running your business profitably.

- What if you project a sales increase of 15 percent over the next six months, but sales increase only 5 or 10 percent?

- What if you give your employees a 4 percent raise, or 7 percent, or 10 percent? How does each increase affect cash flow next year and the year after?

- What if you depreciate your capital equipment over 3, 5, or 10 years? Which is the tax-wise term and method?

- What if you take that discount for a volume purchase? Will the immediate savings offset the long-term storage costs?

■ What if you rent those larger offices at a 15 percent rent increase. Is it smarter to look for something in the 8 to 10 percent range?

■ What if you borrow more at a lower rate for a longer term? Does it give that new operation a better chance or an intolerable burden?

What's the net effect of all these decisions—the impact on the bottom line? Multiplan can help answer these questions and can lead you to better business management and greater profits.

WHAT'S THE BEST WAY TO USE THIS BOOK?

Begin by reviewing the contents page, then browse around the opening chapters and flip through the spreadsheet instructions in Part 2 and the in-depth explanations in Part 3. When you have a feel for what's in the book, start by reading Chapter 1, "Getting Acquainted with Multiplan." This chapter describes the Multiplan screen, discusses cursor movements, commands, and keystrokes, and explains how to use a mouse.

Then go to Chapter 2, "Creating a Spreadsheet," which describes the steps to take in creating your own spreadsheets and gives you the theory behind these steps in nontechnical terms. This is not just theory for theory's sake. When you are at the point of creating your own spreadsheets, you'll find Chapter 2 an excellent reference. Then skim through Chapter 18, "Making Macros Work for You," which will make the macros you create in the spreadsheet chapters more understandable. A macro is a series of keyboard instructions that cause Multiplan to perform spreadsheet tasks. Macros let you automate repetitive operations you would otherwise have to perform yourself.

Since the best way to learn a program is to use it, Part 2 (Chapters 3 through 14) contains 12 business-oriented spreadsheets of varying size, scope, and complexity. Each chapter begins with business concepts and takes you, step by step, through formatting, formulas, and printing. Several figures in each chapter show the spreadsheet at important stages of development. If you are a first-time user eager to create a spreadsheet, start with a simple one, such as the business start-up analysis in Chapter 3. If you're experienced with Multiplan, the choice is yours. A summary of commands and formulas at the end of each chapter lets you create spreadsheets without following step-by-step instructions.

Part 3 explains how to use Multiplan to the fullest. Chapter 15 tells you about Multiplan's functions—the built-in routines that perform mathematical, search, and logical operations. Chapters 16 and 17 take you on in-depth tours of the IF and LOOKUP functions. Both chapters contain mini-spreadsheets that you can readily adapt to your own business applications. Chapter 18 discusses macro command codes, key codes, and the exciting "follow-me" feature, which tells Multiplan to record your keystrokes and then play them back as a macro. Chapter 19 describes how to track down and correct errors in formulas; it also covers the audit feature, available with Multiplan 3.0, which lets you easily examine formula relationships. Chapter 20 covers the specifics on printing your own spreadsheets and provides solutions that can help if you have difficulty printing the spreadsheets presented in this book.

WHICH MULTIPLAN VERSION CAN I USE?

The instructions and explanations in this book, originally written for version 1.2 of Multiplan, have been updated to the capabilities of version 3.0, which is larger, faster, and smarter than its predecessors—and it's loaded with new features. Using this book with anything but version 3.0 can be confusing at best and, in some cases, impossible. If you don't already own Multiplan version 3.0, contact your dealer.

Multiplan version 3.0 supports networking, which allows network users to access each other's spreadsheets on their own computers. This makes it easy, for example, to get the most current figures from anyone on the network for use in your own calculations. Since Multiplan lets you split the screen into eight windows, you can see the spreadsheets of as many as eight network users at one time. You must have DOS version 3.1 or later to use Multiplan on a network. Refer to the Multiplan manual for further information.

Multiplan version 3.0 easily runs in the Microsoft Windows operating environment, either by filling the entire screen or by running in one window of a multi-window screen, which allows it to share the screen with other Windows applications. Your Multiplan and Windows manuals can provide more information about this capability.

ANYTHING ELSE I SHOULD KNOW?

One of the difficulties of writing a how-to book about a computer program is that the text in the book is not always the same as what you see on your screen or on your keyboard. The following are the conventions used to present the material in this book:

What the Italics Mean

Certain words and phrases are shown in italics. This makes it easy for you to distinguish information that might otherwise get lost in the surrounding text.

Here are the kinds of things you will find in italics:

■ Your keystrokes. For example, to specify cell locations: Type *R49:54C6* and press Enter. To tell Multiplan to store your spreadsheet: Type *TS* (Transfer Save) and press Enter. Keeping typed-in characters away from periods and commas (which mean something special to Multiplan) wasn't always possible in writing this book. So, you will sometimes find italics followed by a period that ends the sentence, such as: Type *Y.* Type the Y but not the period. A bit of Multiplan experience will quickly dispel any confusion.

■ Spreadsheet titles in the middle of text. For example: Type *Cash Funds Available* and move the cursor to the next cell.

■ Words that Multiplan displays on the screen, such as: Multiplan displays *COPY FROM cells: R9C4*, the cell to copy from.

■ Multiplan command fields. For example: Type *:R1C7* and move the cursor to the *area* field.

What the Columns Contain

You'll find two columns of information in the step-by-step instructions. The column on the left explains what you are about to do or which cell to move the cursor to. The column on the right tells you which keys to press or how the cursor movements will look on the screen.

Which Names and Characters Appear in Uppercase

To distinguish them from the rest of the text, the names of Multiplan functions (IF, LOOKUP, SUM, and so on) are in uppercase letters. Macro key codes (*'RT, 'TB, 'SP,* and so on) are shown in uppercase and italic letters. You can type anything in either uppercase or lowercase—it doesn't matter to Multiplan.

Which Keys Do What

The keys mentioned in this book are available on the keyboard used with the IBM PC, XT, AT, and 100-percent-compatible computers. Multiplan runs on many other computers. If you are using a different computer or terminal, you can still create all the spreadsheets, but first refer to your Multiplan manual for a translation of the keyboard differences, especially the action of the function keys (no relation to Multiplan functions). For example, on the IBM PC, pressing the F4 function key recalculates the spreadsheet. On a Tandy 2000, the exclamation point key (!) serves the same purpose.

How Keys Are Shown

The names of keys used in the text are as you see them on the IBM keyboard, with these exceptions:

■ The keys marked Del, Esc, Alt, and Ctrl are referred to as Delete, Escape, Alternate, and Control.

■ The two keys with the thick arrow pointing up are called Shift.

■ The key with opposing arrows is called Tab.

■ The key with the broken arrow is referred to as Enter.

■ The key in the top row with the arrow pointing left is called Backspace.

■ The arrow-marked keys in the numeric keypad at the right of the keyboard are referred to in the text as Left Arrow, Up Arrow, Right Arrow, and Down Arrow.

Keys joined by a hyphen, such as Shift-F1, mean that you hold down the first key, then press the second key. All these keys and their actions will become quite familiar to you after a short while.

HOW DO I GET STARTED?

To run Multiplan, you need to set up Multiplan for your computer and have a supply of formatted data disks on which to store your spreadsheets. If you are using a hard disk, you still need formatted data disks to back up your spreadsheets and protect you against calamity if something happens to the hard disk. You'll find details on setting up Multiplan for your computer in your Multiplan manual and information on formatting data disks in your MS-DOS manual. After you've set up your system to run Multiplan 3.0, at the system prompt (typically A> for a system with floppy-disk drives and C> for a system with a hard-disk drive) type *MP* and press Enter to bring up the Multiplan screen.

And now, let's get acquainted with Multiplan.

PART 1

Concepts,
Commands,
and Keystrokes

1

Getting Acquainted with Multiplan

First impressions are important, so let's begin at the beginning with the Multiplan screen shown in Figure 1-1. Multiplan gives you a wealth of information before you even press the first key. Since you must be able to understand what happens on the screen to create efficient, working spreadsheets, this chapter describes each part of the Multiplan screen by explaining what they are and what they tell you.

A, the blank area, is your workspace. It is a window to the computer's memory through which you view and manipulate your spreadsheet. The Multiplan spreadsheet is a rectangular grid 4095 rows down and 255 columns across, or more than seven thousand times the area you see on the screen. Because the spreadsheet is so large, you can see only a portion of it at one time, much as you can see only a portion of a scene when you look through the viewfinder of a camera. By moving the Multiplan window, your viewfinder, you can see all the spreadsheet, one screenful at a time.

B, the highlighted #1 in the top left corner, is the number of the window on your screen. Multiplan always starts with window #1 open. You can open up to seven more windows to see eight areas of a spreadsheet simultaneously— even see parts of eight different spreadsheets at the same time, one in each window. Chapter 14 explains how to open and use windows.

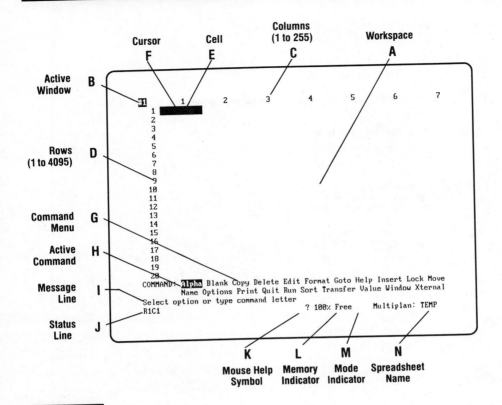

FIGURE 1-1.
The Multiplan screen

C, the numbers 1 through 7 across the top of the screen, are the numbers of the columns visible at this time. (Imagine vertical lines between the numbers, separating one column from the next.)

D, the numbers 1 through 20 down the left side of the screen, are the numbers of the rows visible at this time. (Imagine horizontal lines running between the numbers, separating one row from the next.)

E, the rectangle formed by the intersection of the imaginary row and column lines, is a cell. Multiplan refers to a cell by its row and column numbers. Thus, R1C1 is the cell at the intersection of row 1 and column 1 and R9C12 is the cell at the intersection of row 9 and column 12.

F, the movable highlight within the window, is the cursor. The location of the cursor determines the active cell, the one that can accept information. You make a cell active by moving the cursor to it with the keyboard keys, which will be discussed shortly.

G, in the lower part of the screen, is the command menu from which you choose the task you want Multiplan to carry out. The command words are alphabetized from Alpha to Xternal and describe what they do, which makes them easy to recognize and remember. You can start a command any time you see the command menu on the screen.

H, highlighting the word *Alpha* in the command menu, indicates that Alpha is the active command, the one selected if you press Enter. To select a different command, you type the first letter of the command (for example, *T* to select the Transfer command). You will learn more about selecting commands later in this chapter.

I, below the command menu, is Multiplan's message line. The message line is where Multiplan proposes the next action for you to take or tells you if you have made an error.

J, at the bottom of the screen, is the status line. The left side of the status line displays both the location and the contents of the active cell. When you start a new spreadsheet, the cursor is on R1C1, as shown on the status line in Figure 1-1. Because R1C1 contains no information, the cell contents area to the immediate right is empty.

K, in the center of the status line, is a question mark—the mouse help symbol. It is displayed, along with the mouse pointer (a flashing square), only if you have a mouse installed. To get help while using the mouse, click either mouse button when the mouse pointer is on the question mark.

L, in the center of the status line, is the memory indicator. It displays the amount of computer memory remaining for this particular spreadsheet. The memory indicator has nothing to do with available disk space, so don't confuse the two. When you start a new spreadsheet, the indicator displays *100% Free*. As you enter information, the amount of free memory decreases, as shown by the memory indicator.

M, to the right of the memory indicator, is where Multiplan can display a two-letter code that indicates the special keyboard mode you've activated (for example, *RM* when you are in the Record Macro mode). The keyboard is in standard mode now, so this area is empty.

N, at the right end of the status line, is the spreadsheet name. Until you assign a name, Multiplan gives the spreadsheet the name *TEMP*, for Temporary.

MOVING AROUND YOUR SPREADSHEET

You can move around your spreadsheet by using the direction keys to step the cursor along one cell at a time or by using special keys that move the cursor rapidly in large increments to specific cell locations.

Direction Keys

The direction keys—Up Arrow, Down Arrow, Left Arrow, and Right Arrow—are in the numeric keypad on the right side of the keyboard. (Computers equipped with the IBM enhanced AT keyboard have four additional direction keys to the left of the numeric keypad. These perform the same operations as the direction keys on the numeric keypad.) When you press an arrow key, the cursor moves one cell in the direction of the arrow. If you hold down the arrow key, the action repeats. If you have Multiplan on your screen now, try using these keys. You won't hurt anything.

When you move the cursor past the right or bottom edge of the screen, the row or column numbers start to change. You are moving your window over areas of the spreadsheet that were not visible before. If you continue to move the cursor to the right, you will eventually see the 255th column of the spreadsheet. If you continue to move the cursor down, you will eventually see the 4095th row. This window movement is called scrolling.

Rapid Movement Keys

When cells are at a distance from each other, using the rapid movement keys to jump the cursor from cell to cell is far more efficient than pressing the arrow keys. Figure 1-2 shows the active area of a spreadsheet. The beginning cell, R1C1, is in the upper left corner of the rectangle. The ending cell, R8C7, is in the lower right corner. Even though R8C7 is empty, it is the ending cell, because that's where the last row and column of information intersect.

Let's say you want to move to the first cell in the spreadsheet, R1C1. To do so, you press the Home key, and the cursor jumps to R1C1. When you press the End key, the cursor jumps just as quickly to R8C7.

Pressing the PgUp (page up) or PgDn (page down) key causes the cursor to jump 20 rows (the size of the window) up or down. When you hold down the key, the movement repeats rapidly.

Two key combinations jump the cursor horizontally: When you hold down the Control key and press the Right Arrow or Left Arrow key, the cursor jumps seven columns (one page) to the right or to the left. To jump the cursor by pages repeatedly, hold down Control and the Right Arrow or Left Arrow key. Holding

```
Beginning
Cell R1C1
              1          2         3         4         5         6         7
          1  |_____|  BUDGET 1987
          2  ========================================================================
          3  Month        July     August   September  October   November  December
          4  ------------------------------------------------------------------------
          5  Mfg          15       12        19        18
          6  Admin        18       18        20        21
          7  Sales        13       15        14        14
          8  Service      12       12        12        13              |_____|
          9
         10                                                             Ending
         11                                                             Cell
                                                                        R8C7
```

FIGURE 1-2.
The active area of a Multiplan spreadsheet

down the Control key and pressing the Home key jumps the cursor to the upper left cell in the current window.

The Goto command lets you jump the cursor to any cell in the spreadsheet.

Function Keys

The function keys (imprinted with the letter F and a number), on the left side or top row of the keyboard, move the cursor in special ways. (For example, when you open more windows on your spreadsheet, the F1 key enables you to jump the cursor to the next open window.) You will learn how these keys work in the step-by-step instructions for building spreadsheets in Chapters 3 through 14.

USING MULTIPLAN COMMANDS

A command is a task you tell Multiplan to do. For example, you use the Blank command to tell Multiplan to erase the contents of cells, the Copy command to copy the contents of cells, and the Insert command to insert empty rows or columns between rows or columns that contain information.

A command may have two or more options, or subcommands, you can choose from, and each option may offer further options, called fields. Think of the Multiplan command structure as a road map: a command is a major highway, an option is a road branching off the highway, and a field is a local street.

You can start a command only when you see the command menu on the screen. At first, the highlight is atop the command name *Alpha*. You can select Alpha or any other command in one of several ways:

■ If the highlight is on the command you want, simply press Enter.

■ If the command you want is to the left of the highlight, press the Backspace key until the highlight is atop that command, and then press Enter.

■ If the command you want is to the right of the highlight, press the Spacebar or the Tab key until the highlight is on that command, then press Enter.

■ Type the first letter of the command name.

I recommend that you always type the first letter of the command name, even if the highlight is on the command you want. That way, you won't have to check the location of the highlight, ponder which direction you want it to travel, or decide which key to use and how many times to press it. Typing the first letter simplifies matters.

Selecting an Option

When you start a command, the command menu is replaced by the name of the command you're in. If the command has options (subcommands), the highlight is on the first one, and the message line asks you to make a selection. Again, even if the option you want is highlighted, typing the first letter (not simply pressing Enter) is a good habit to develop, because you have less to remember. All you have to know is the name of the option, not both the name and where the highlight appears. After you work with Multiplan for a short time, the commands and options will be as familiar as your face in the mirror, and typing the first letter will become automatic.

Working in the Fields

When a command or an option has several fields, the highlight appears in the first field, and the message line tells you what to do next. Some fields need a number, so the message line asks you to type a number. Others need a cell location. You can type cell locations, or you can move the cursor to the cell to cause Multiplan to type for you. Still others need a Yes or No (you type Y or N). And still others offer a collection of choices from which you can select by typing the first character.

Multiplan starts with standard settings (called defaults) and retains as standard some of the settings you later make. Parentheses enclose the current setting, the one you can choose by pressing Enter. If you have something else in mind, all you have to do is follow the prompts and make your changes.

Pressing the Tab key moves the highlight from one field to the next. If you overshoot a field or if you decide to change something you already entered, you can press the Tab key a few times to move the highlight full circle or you can press Shift-Tab to move the highlight backward one field.

Executing a Command

The way you execute a command depends on the command you're using. For most commands, you press Enter after making your option and field selections, and Multiplan carries out the command. Some commands need further confirmation. For example, if you change something on your spreadsheet and don't save the changes before selecting the Quit command to exit the program, Multiplan asks you to *Enter Y to save edits, N to lose edits, or cancel,* so you type *Y* or *N,* or you press the Escape key to cancel. A few commands are carried out when you choose them. If you save your work before you choose Quit, for instance, Multiplan exits without asking any questions.

At times you won't want to confirm a command. If you start the wrong command, select the wrong option, or make the wrong response in a field, it's easy to get out of it. Just press the Escape key to cancel the action and to return the command menu to the screen.

An Illustration: Using the Copy Command

Let's assume you want to copy the contents of a cell into the five cells immediately below it. The cursor is on the cell you want to copy from, the command menu is on the screen, and the message line tells you to *Select option or type command letter.* Here are the steps to follow:

1. Type *C* to start the Copy command. The command menu disappears, and you are in the Copy command.

2. Now you see the command line containing the command name and three options:

   COPY: Right Down From

The highlight is on the word *Right* (Multiplan always highlights the first option) and the message line again tells you to *Select option or type command letter.*

Since you want to copy down, you type *D.*

3. The options are now replaced by two fields:

   COPY DOWN number of cells: *starting at:*

This time the message line tells you to *Enter number.*

4. You type the number 5, which appears in the *number of cells* field. In the *starting at* field, you see the cell location of the cursor, so you don't have to do anything else. Simply press Enter to tell Multiplan to carry out the Copy command. Multiplan then copies the contents of this cell into the five cells below it, just as you told it to. Whatever is in the cell you copied from remains unchanged. Simple.

Saving Keystrokes

Before you start a command, you move the cursor to the cell you want to work on or, if you want to work on several cells, you move to the top left cell in the group. Multiplan enters that cell location at the proper place in the command, which saves you keystrokes and eliminates the possibility of a typing error. For example, in our Copy illustration, the cell the cursor was on when you started the Copy command appeared in the *starting at* field. You didn't have to press Tab to move to the field and then type in the cell location.

In certain commands or the options of some commands, such as Transfer Save, it doesn't matter where the cursor is located when you start the command, because you are working with the entire spreadsheet, not with specific cells. These distinctions will become second nature to you after a short time.

When you create a spreadsheet, you repeat many actions. In certain commands, Multiplan "remembers" the last action you took and proposes it as your next action. You can save many more keystrokes by making use of these proposed responses.

In our Copy illustration, you copied the contents of a cell into the five cells below it. Now, suppose you want to copy down into five cells again, but from another cell. When you get to the *number of cells* field after starting the Copy command, Multiplan proposes the number 5. You don't have to retype the number. You can simply press Enter to accept the proposed response and confirm the command. If you don't want the proposed number, type another number. This new number, in turn, becomes Multiplan's proposed response to the next Copy command.

Multiplan retains certain responses, not only within a spreadsheet, but also from spreadsheet to spreadsheet. In the Print command, for example, the margins you create on one spreadsheet become the proposed responses for the next one you create, until you change the settings. Again, to change a proposed response, simply type a new number.

CELL RANGES AND UNIONS

To make your work even easier and faster, Multiplan lets you use either a colon (:) or a comma (,) to group cells you want to handle in the same way. You'll use both the colon and the comma a great deal in Chapters 3 through 14. Since each has a different meaning to Multiplan, here's a summary of what they do and how you use them. You can also see their uses illustrated in Figure 1-3. In all of these examples, note that the cell locations, colons, and commas are never separated by blank spaces.

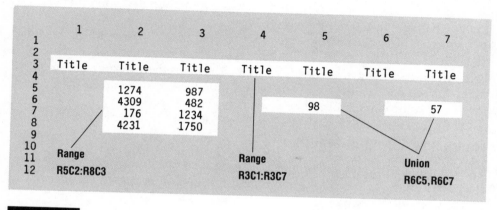

FIGURE 1-3.
Ranges and unions of cells

The Colon

The colon, called the range operator, is used to group contiguous cells—those that are all next to one another. A range can contain anywhere from two cells to as many cells as you wish. You can insert the colon by pressing Shift and the colon/semicolon key, or merely by pressing F6 to save one keystroke. In Figure 1-3, you see two ranges of cells: titles in row 3 and numbers in columns 2 and 3. Suppose you want Multiplan to center each of the seven titles within each cell. To center the contents of a cell, you use the Format command. You start with the cursor on R3C1 (the first cell in the range) and type *FC* to start the Format command and to select the Cells option. Multiplan has already entered the cell location R3C1, so all you do is press F6 to produce a colon (the range operator) and then move the cursor to R3C7 (the last cell in the range). The result appears as *R3C1:R3C7*, the range of cells from R3C1 to R3C7. Now press Tab to move to the *alignment* field, type *C* to select the *Ctr* option, and press Enter. All the titles are centered.

You can group the range of cells from R5C2 to R8C3 in the same way, as you'll see in a moment.

The Comma

The comma, called the union operator, is used to group cells that are separated from one another but which you want Multiplan to act on as a group. Figure 1-3 shows two separate cells in row 6. One cell is in column 5 (R6C5) and the other is in column 7 (R6C7). Suppose you want both numbers shown as dollar amounts (also handled by the Format command), and you don't want to include R6C6, the cell between them.

You start with the cursor on R6C5 and type *FC* (for Format Cells). Multiplan enters *R6C5* in the *cells* field. Now type a comma, and move the cursor to R6C7. The result appears as *R6C5,R6C7*. You press the Tab key twice to move to the *format code* field, type *$*, and press Enter. Cells R6C5 and R6C7 are now formatted for dollars, and cell R6C6 is not.

Ranges and Unions Together

You can use ranges and unions of cells in the same command. Simply move the cursor to the cell locations and type colons or commas at the proper places to identify which is which.

Using the examples in Figure 1-3 again, suppose you want to show the range of cells from R5C2 through R8C3 and the two single cells in R6C5 and R6C7 as dollar amounts. Start with the cursor on R5C2 (the first cell in the range, because it is in the upper left corner of the group) and type *FC* (Format Cells). Multiplan has already entered *R5C2* in the *cells* field, so you press F6 to insert a colon. Move the cursor to R8C3 (the last cell—that is, the cell in the lower right corner of the group). Then type a comma to separate the range from the next cell location, move the cursor to R6C5, type another comma, and move the cursor to R6C7. The result on the command line is *R5C2:R8C3,R6C5,R6C7*. You can now format all these cells in one step by tabbing to the *format code* field, typing *$*, and pressing Enter.

Cell-Entry Shorthand

Using the cursor whenever possible is basic to using Multiplan efficiently. Multiplan keeps track of cursor movements and enters cell locations at the proper places in commands. The instructions in this book, however, would be endless if they described every cursor movement. Therefore, you are asked to type the cell locations until you feel comfortable enough to move the cursor on your own. To keep the typing to a minimum, these locations are shown in Multiplan shorthand.

Let's suppose you are working with a range of cells in row 3 from columns 1 to 5, another range in rows 23 to 28 in column 10, and a single cell in R35C21. If you entered these locations with the cursor and typed only the colons and commas, you'd have a total of 30 characters, and here's how they would look:

R3C1:R3C5,R23C10:R28C10,R35C21

Using the short form, this book would show the locations of these cells in 23 characters:

R3C1:5,R23:28C10,R35C21

To be sure everything works properly, type every character exactly as shown. After you gain experience with one or two spreadsheets, let Multiplan do the work. Just move the cursor to the cell locations and type only the commas and colons. By all means, try it. Moving the cursor is a whole lot faster, easier, and more accurate than typing.

You will sometimes see a notation such as R2 or C3, which indicates an entire row or column (row 2 or column 3). You can't use the cursor to enter this kind of notation—you must type it.

USING THE MOUSE WITH MULTIPLAN

Using the Microsoft Mouse (or a compatible) is an alternative way to start commands, move the cursor, and enter information in a spreadsheet. Instead of typing command letters or pressing direction keys, you have the mouse do it. Every key on the keyboard, even with an active mouse, is still available for manual entry and movement.

The Multiplan Mouse Screen

When you install a mouse, you see the mouse pointer (shaped like a flashing square) and the question mark to the left of the *memory indicator* mentioned earlier in this chapter. The question mark is a gateway to Multiplan's Help instructions. Clicking a mouse button when the pointer is on the question mark works the same as typing *H* to start the Help command or pressing the Alt-H key combination when you are in a command, and provides easy and immediate access to help wherever you may be.

The Mouse Anatomy

The mouse is a sleek little plastic device with two buttons on top and a ball underneath. Clicking the buttons produces different results, depending on the action you are about to take. For example, if you're working with a command, clicking the left button takes you to the next command level, clicking the right button carries out the proposed command on the lowest command level, and clicking both buttons cancels the command. With cursor movements, clicking a button jumps the cursor to the location of the pointer.

The ball controls the movement of the mouse pointer. When you slide the mouse across a desktop, the computer translates the rotation of the ball into direction and distance. This rolling action combined with clicking the mouse buttons moves the cursor through the spreadsheet in much the same way as do the direction keys and the rapid movement keys (Home, End, PgUp, PgDn, Control-Right Arrow, and Control-Left Arrow).

Unlike the cursor, which moves from cell to cell, or the highlight, which skips through the command menu, the mouse pointer can move anywhere on the screen—to cells, to the command area, to the row and column numbers.

The Mouse Language

The mouse lexicon is colorful. Here are definitions of mouse terms:

■ *Clicking:* Pressing and quickly releasing one or both mouse buttons.

■ *Dragging:* Holding down a mouse button and moving the mouse pointer and cursor across the spreadsheet. In essence, the pointer is dragging the cursor with it.

■ *Thumbing:* Jumping the cursor in large increments by clicking the left or top border of the Multiplan window with both mouse buttons. It's as if you were thumbing through the pages of a book to jump many pages at a time.

MAKING MOUSE CALLS

The following practice session will help you get acquainted with your mouse. To work best, the mouse needs a flat surface about five inches in diameter. If you run out of space before the pointer is where you want it on screen, or if sliding the mouse becomes uncomfortable or inconvenient, pick up the mouse and place it somewhere else. Since the ball isn't rolling, the position of the pointer won't change until you slide the mouse again.

If you're eager to get started, bring up the Multiplan TEMP screen (the screen you first see when you start Multiplan). Spend a few moments sliding the mouse so that you can get an idea of how the pointer behaves. Wander into different areas—the column numbers at the top, row numbers at the left, command menu, question mark, and spreadsheet filename. It may feel a bit awkward at first, but only for a short while. Now let's explore how the mouse handles cursor movements.

Moving the Cursor Short Distances

This first exercise demonstrates how to jump the cursor to visible cells, in this case the lower right portion of the screen. The cursor should still be on R1C1. If it isn't, press the Home key. Now slide the mouse so the pointer is in R20C7 (a bit above *Move* in the command menu). Click the left or right mouse button, and the cursor jumps from cell R1C1 to R20C7. That was easy enough. Let's try another, this time jumping the cursor to the top of the screen. Move the mouse pointer to R1C7 (a bit below the column number 7) and click the left or right button. And here's the cursor in R1C7.

Scrolling the Spreadsheet Window

Next, let's scroll the spreadsheet window to cells that aren't visible right now, keeping the cursor in the same relative position in the window. Move the mouse so the pointer is on the column number 7. Click the right button. Column 13 appears with the cursor below it. Click the right button twice to see columns 19 and 25. To return to column 19, click the left button once. Each click of the right button moves the window to the right; each click of the left button moves the window to the left. The cursor remains in the last column on the screen. The number of columns in each incremental jump depends on which column number the pointer is on when you click the button: The farther the pointer is from the left margin, the greater the jump. For example, if the pointer is over the middle column, the window jumps fewer columns than if it were over the far right column.

To scroll vertically by rows, place the pointer on a row number at the left edge of the screen and click the right button. The right button scrolls the spreadsheet down, and the right button scrolls it up. The number of rows in each incremental jump depends on which row number the pointer is on: The farther the pointer is from the top of the screen, the greater the jump.

Dragging the Cursor

This exercise scrolls the pointer and cursor together. Slide the mouse so the pointer is on R10C4. Hold down one of the buttons. Now slide the mouse forward and back several times, then side to side. As the pointer moves, it drags the cursor with it. Move the pointer to the right edge of the screen and hold it there. You can see new columns come into view. As soon as column 20 appears, release the button. With the cursor in column 20, hold down one of the mouse buttons while you slide the mouse so the pointer moves downward and new rows come into view. When the cursor is in R40C20, release the button.

You need an active area for the next exercise, so type *12345* (or any value you like) and press Enter.

Thumbing to Distant Areas

This final exercise thumbs the cursor to distant areas of the active spreadsheet. Our sample spreadsheet is now R1C1 to R40C20. You thumb through a spreadsheet by positioning the mouse pointer in the left margin (to move vertically) or top margin (to move horizontally) and clicking both buttons. The distance you travel per click depends on where in the margin you place the mouse pointer.

Let's try it.

Press the Home key to jump the cursor to R1C1. Now slide the mouse so the pointer is atop the row number 11, or about the middle of the left margin. Click both buttons. The cursor zooms down to R20C1, the vertical middle of the active spreadsheet.

Now place the pointer atop the number 4 above column 4, the middle of the top margin, and click both buttons. The cursor zooms to R20C9, the horizontal middle of the active spreadsheet.

Commands and the Mouse

The other major mouse activity is working with commands. You start a command by placing the pointer on the command name and clicking a button. Clicking the left button takes you to the next command level of options. Clicking the right button executes the proposed response on the last level—a dandy shortcut for an experienced Multiplan user. If you're still getting up to speed, however, your best bet is to stick with the left button, wending your way through each command level.

Four spreadsheets from this book are already on your Multiplan Template disk, each with the extension .MOD after the filename. Let's move to the Multiplan directory and use the mouse to load AMOR.MOD from the directory, then take the more conservative (left button) approach.

Step 1: Place the mouse pointer on *Transfer* in the command menu. Click the left button. You now see the names of the Transfer options—*Load, Save, Clear, Delete, Options, Rename,* and *Import*—on the command line.

Step 2: Place the pointer on *Load*. Click the left button. Multiplan now displays *TRANSFER LOAD filename:* with a rectangular highlight after the colon.

Step 3: Place the pointer on the rectangular highlight. Click the right button. This brings up the files in the current directory, just as if you pressed a direction key.

Step 4: Move the pointer to *AMOR.MOD*. Click the left button to highlight the filename. Or, with the pointer on *AMOR.MOD*, click the right button (instead of pressing Enter) to select the file and confirm the command. AMOR.MOD appears on your screen.

Unlocking a Cell and Entering Information

Let's suppose you want to change the title from *LOAN AMORTIZATION ANALYSIS* to simply *LOAN PAYMENTS*. In the process, you'll use three commands. We'll take the more adventurous (right button) approach in the following exercise.

Step 1: The cursor is in R1C1. Place the pointer on the word *LOAN*. Click either button. The cursor moves to R1C2.

Step 2: Before you can make any changes, you have to unlock R1C2, which is handled by the Lock command, Cells option. Place the pointer on *Lock* in the command menu. If you clicked the left button now, Cells (the one you want) would be the proposed response, and you would have to click the left button again to select it. You can skip that step by clicking the right button now over *Lock,* which brings you directly to the Lock Cells subcommand level. This shows that R1C2 is locked. (*Locked* is in parentheses in the *status* field.)

Step 3: Place the pointer on *Unlocked*. Click the right button. This action also bypasses a command level, because Multiplan not only switches from Locked to Unlocked, but carries out the command in the same step.

Step 4: Place the pointer on *Alpha* in the command menu. Alpha is a single-purpose command with no options, so click either button. Now type *LOAN PAYMENTS*. Click the right button to confirm the command and to enter the title in R1C2 (or, since your hands are on the keyboard, simply press Enter).

Step 5: You want to keep the original version of the spreadsheet intact, so you need to remove this new version of AMOR.MOD without saving your changes. This final step lets the changes disappear. Place the pointer on *Transfer* in the command menu and click the left button. Next, click *Clear* with the left button, then *All* with the left button. Multiplan now asks if you want to save the edits, lose the edits, or cancel. Clicking either button has the same effect as typing Y to save the edits. Clicking both buttons cancels the command. You don't want to save or cancel, so unhand that mouse and type N. This clears the screen and presents you with a new, empty spreadsheet.

These exercises demonstrate basic cursor movements and commands. The best way to master the mouse is to experiment on your own. Now let's move on and see how to create a spreadsheet.

2
Creating a Spreadsheet

Creating a spreadsheet from scratch can be smooth sailing or a stormy voyage, depending on your approach. The key to success is advance planning. Your best approach is to start on paper before you even turn on your computer. You don't need to write down every detail and every number, and you don't need to make any calculations—that's why you have Multiplan. You do need to know what you want your spreadsheet to do. Don't start out with some vague idea and spend a lot of time drifting in different directions. Experiment, if you will, as you develop the spreadsheet—some great spreadsheets result from experimentation—but know the purpose before you begin. Have a good idea of what your titles will be and where they will go, how your numbers will relate to each other in formulas, and which commands will make your ideas and your spreadsheet work best for you.

Then, with these major concepts clearly in mind and a preliminary layout on paper, fire up your computer.

DEVELOPING YOUR SPREADSHEET

As you turn your plan into reality, try to follow a logical sequence of steps that can help you avoid backtracking or repeating the same operation several times. It is more efficient, for example, to adjust the widths of the columns before you type the titles, format the cells for dollars before you enter the numbers, and name all the cells that need to be named before you build the formulas. A consistent, logical approach will speed you on your way to a working spreadsheet.

The sequence of steps in Figure 2-1 can guide you in developing your own spreadsheet. The second column describes what you want to do; the third and fourth columns show the name of the command and what to type to start the command; and the fifth and sixth columns show the name of the option and what to type to select the option. This sequence is by no means universal—after all, each spreadsheet has a character of its own—but, in general, you will find that following this sequence saves you time and produces a finished spreadsheet in the most direct way.

This chapter explains how and when to use each of these steps. Reading this book while you have Multiplan on your computer screen helps, but isn't absolutely required. You can still get a good feel for Multiplan even if you're reading this book on a train, on a plane, in bed, or anywhere else. Don't be concerned if all the details don't sink in at the first reading. It would be unusual if they did. The step-by-step instructions in Chapters 3 through 14 will ease you into their use, and at that time, these concepts will fall neatly into place.

If you have a computer handy, try the commands as you read, look at the options and fields, make up and enter some titles and numbers, and experiment with simple formulas. Relax and enjoy. You won't break anything. If you hit a snag, press Escape and Multiplan will return the command menu to the screen.

STEP 1: Turn Off Automatic Recalculation

When automatic recalculation is active, Multiplan recalculates your spreadsheet every time you enter something in a cell. At first, recalculation is quick, but it takes longer and longer as you enter more information. To save time, you can turn off automatic recalculation before you make any entries or at any stage of the development process. When you want to see the calculations, simply press the F4 key. Even with recalculation turned off, Multiplan recalculates the spreadsheet before storing it on disk, so stored information is always current. The recalculation status—yes or no—is saved with the spreadsheet and becomes the proposed response on the next spreadsheet you create.

STEP 2: Adjust the Column Widths

After you plan your layout, you should have a reasonably good idea of how many columns you will use and how wide you want them to be. Multiplan starts with columns that are 10 characters wide, but you can change the width of one column, several columns, or all the columns to anything from 0 to 64 characters. The 0-character setting lets you conceal a column of information on the screen and on the printed page.

Step	Description	Command	Type	Option	Type
1	Turn off automatic recalculation	Options	O		
2	Adjust the column widths	Format	F	Width	W
3	Enter the titles	Alpha	A		
4	Enter the long lines using the REPT function	Value	V		
5	Format the titles	Format	F	Cells	C
6	Format the number cells	Format	F	Cells	C
7	Name the cells	Name	N		
8	Save and name the spreadsheet	Transfer	T	Save	S
9	Enter the test or real numbers	Command menu or Alpha/Value			
10	Enter the formulas	Value	V		
11	Copy the formulas	Copy	C	Right	R
				Down	D
				From	F
12	Lock the formula cells	Lock	L	Formulas	F
13	Save the spreadsheet	Transfer	T	Save	S
14	Enter the real numbers	Command menu or Alpha/Value			
15	Enter the transient text	Alpha	A		
16	Set the print margins	Print	P	Margins	M
	Set the print options (and save the spreadsheet again)	Print		Options	O
17	Print the spreadsheet	Print	P	Printer	P
	Print the formulas	Print		Options	O
18	Exit Multiplan	Quit	Q		

FIGURE 2-1.

Steps in developing a Multiplan spreadsheet

One of the goals in adjusting the column widths is to produce a well-spaced spreadsheet that is easy to read and pleasing to the eye. If you have a column filled with long titles, for example, increase the column width; if a column contains only one- or two-digit numbers, reduce the column width. Adjusting the widths also gives you some leeway in the amount of information you can print across a page. It can even let you keep the full width of a small spreadsheet on the screen—a nice convenience.

STEP 3: Enter the Titles

Titles identify information on a spreadsheet, just as they do on any hand-written document. They can be at the tops of columns, down the left side in rows, or anywhere else you want them to be. Because you start a command by typing a letter, you must tell Multiplan you intend to enter a title by first typing *A* to start the Alpha command. Otherwise, Multiplan will interpret the first letter of the title as the start of a command, and you'll end up in a command you don't want or, if no command starts with that letter, with the error message *Not a valid option.*

Once you are in the Alpha command, however, you can continue to type titles without starting the command again, as long as you move the cursor to another cell after each title instead of pressing Enter. If you do press Enter, the command menu returns to the screen, and you again have to type *A* (for Alpha) before typing the next title.

The Alpha and Value commands have a meaningful relationship. When you move the cursor, Multiplan displays *ALPHA/VALUE* on the command line. The next character you type selects the proper mode—a letter selects Alpha and a number selects Value. This lets you move the cursor from cell to cell, typing titles or numbers to your heart's content, until you press Enter to indicate you are through.

As an alternative, you can keep Multiplan in an alpha/value mode (accessed from the Options command), which bypasses the command menu. Then even if you press Enter between titles, you don't have to restart the Alpha command. If you want to use a command other than Alpha or Value while in this mode, press the Escape key to bring up the command menu. After you complete your entries, you can turn off the alpha/value mode as easily as you turned it on.

If you make a typing error, press the Backspace key (not a direction key) to back up the highlight and erase the character before it. If the mistake is at the beginning of the title, press one of the editing keys (F7 through F10) to move the highlight along the command line without erasing. Figure 2-2 shows what these keys do. Holding down an editing key causes the action to repeat rapidly.

With the highlight at the proper place, you can type a missing character or press the Delete key to delete an unneeded character. If you notice a mistake

F7	Highlights the next word to the left
F8	Highlights the next word to the right
F9	Moves the highlight one character to the left
F10	Moves the highlight one character to the right

FIGURE 2-2.
The keys that move the highlight for editing

in a title already in its cell, you need to use the Edit command to place the title on the command line before you can correct it.

STEP 4: Enter the Long Lines

Lines across a spreadsheet help to separate areas that serve different purposes and that make the information easier to read. A simple way to create lines is to use the REPT function to repeat a minus sign (when you want a single line) or an equal sign (when you want a double line). In one cell, you enter a REPT formula that repeats the sign enough times to fill the widest cell on the spreadsheet. That way, when you copy the formula across the spreadsheet there will be no gaps in the line. Using a REPT formula often is more efficient than typing a lot of minus signs or equal signs. You'll learn how to use this function in Chapters 3 through 14.

STEP 5: Format the Titles

Multiplan left-justifies a title (the first letter is at the left edge of the cell). You can change this alignment to centered or right-justified.

If a title is too long to be displayed completely in one cell and you don't want to increase the width of its column, simply format the title cell and the empty cells to its right as continuous. This lets the title extend across several cells. A title that occupies more than one cell can only be centered or right-justified if you indent by using spaces before typing it.

STEP 6: Format the Number Cells

Multiplan right-justifies numbers, placing the last digit one character from the right edge of the cell. This allows room for a close parenthesis if it's a negative dollar amount or for a percent sign if you format for percentage. If you want numbers aligned with the titles in the cells above, you can change the standard alignment so that numbers are centered or left-justified.

Unless you give different instructions, Multiplan displays numbers exactly as you type them, as long as they fit within the confines of the cell width. When a number is too long to fit in a cell, Multiplan displays it in scientific notation. You can code the cells so that numbers are displayed as:

- Dollar amounts (with a leading $, with or without decimal places)

- Percentages (with or without decimal places, followed by %)

- Fixed, or fixed point, numbers (with decimal places)

- Integers (without decimal places)

Numbers in a dollar, percent, or fixed format can have from 0 to 15 decimal places.

When you tell it to, Multiplan inserts commas in large numbers that have a dollar, percent, integer, or fixed format. Commas don't appear in any numbers you leave at the *Def* (default) setting—the setting Multiplan uses when you start a new spreadsheet.

Multiplan also lets you display numbers in foreign currency formats, including pounds, kroner, lire, and pesetas, and even lets you define your own currency formats.

STEP 7: Name the Cells

Names are a convenient way of referring to cells. You can use plain English words, such as SALES or COSTS, to make your formulas easy to build and immediately understandable to others. You can even name a group of cells, then use that name in a command to affect all the cells in the group. For example, you can use the Blank command to erase the contents of a group of named cells in one step, or you can use the Print command to print a named area of your spreadsheet.

Naming the cells that you plan to use in formulas before you start entering the formulas can prevent a slew of error messages. You can name cells for blanking or printing at any stage. It's good practice, however, to name all these cells at one time, so you establish a regular routine.

Names must start with a letter and can contain from 1 to 31 characters, including numbers, periods, and underscores. You cannot use the letters R or C as cell names, or names that look like cell references, such as RC1, since they could be confused with row and column numbers. When you name cells, use words that describe their purpose.

You can see a list of all the names you've entered by starting the Name command and pressing a direction key. Pressing the Down Arrow key highlights each name in turn and shows the cell locations. To delete a name, simply tab to the *to refer to* field, press Delete to erase the cell locations, and press Enter.

STEP 8: Save and Name the Spreadsheet

Up to this point, everything you've done on your spreadsheet is stored only in the computer's working memory, not on disk. If you turn off your computer without saving your spreadsheet or if you run into an emergency situation such as a power outage, all your work will be lost. So save your spreadsheet! Saving it now and at frequent intervals takes only a few seconds and can save you hours of lost time.

When you save your spreadsheet the first time, you give it a filename that Multiplan writes in the disk directory. This filename can be up to eight characters long, followed by a period and up to three more characters. It's wise to have the filename appear on the printed spreadsheet, too, so you don't have to rely on your memory. You can enter the filename directly on the spreadsheet or make it part of a header or footer that Multiplan prints at the top of each page.

STEP 9: Enter the Test or Real Numbers

Before you create any formulas, enter some numbers (test or real) for the formulas to work with. If you are experimenting, use simple test numbers. You'll find it a lot easier to check your formulas if you use 12 plus 8 instead of 1278.69 plus 876.04.

You can type a number any time you see the command menu or *ALPHA/ VALUE* on the command line. Simply move the cursor to the desired cell and type the number. As with text, don't bother to press Enter after each number. Move the cursor to the next cell that will contain a number, type it, and continue in this way until you type the last number. Then press Enter.

STEP 10: Enter the Formulas

Formulas do your calculations, and they make all your efforts worthwhile. Since every spreadsheet you create will have its own concepts and its own requirements, only you can determine what calculations your formulas should perform and, therefore, what form they should take.

To build a formula correctly, you need to know how Multiplan refers to the cells on your spreadsheet, and you need to know how Multiplan uses the contents of those cells in its calculations. This section gives you the foundation you need to build not only the formulas in this book but all those you will create on your own.

Formulas calculate by using the contents of cells and arithmetic operators, such as + and −. Let's suppose you have the number 1 in one cell and the number 2 in another cell. In a third cell, you build a formula to add the two numbers. Your spreadsheet calculates 1 + 2 and enters the result, 3, in the formula cell. In its simplest form, this is a formula—but you probably had something more interesting in mind when you decided to use Multiplan.

Formulas can also use Multiplan functions to produce rapid, accurate answers to both simple and sophisticated mathematical problems. A function is a shortcut built into the Multiplan program to perform a particular kind of calculation. If you include the SUM function in a formula, for example, you can add up a list of numbers by simply telling Multiplan the cell locations of the first number and the last number in the group. This is very different from using pencil and paper or a calculator to add each number individually.

You can include many other types of functions in a formula. You will see some of them when you go through the spreadsheets in Chapters 3 through 14. You'll find an explanation of each of them in Chapter 15, "Multiplan's Built-In Functions."

Cell References

A formula must know which cells to refer to for its calculations, so you include cell references in the formula. These references can be either relative or absolute. Think of a relative reference as something like giving directions by saying a house is so many blocks north and so many blocks east of where you are, whereas an absolute reference is like saying a house is at 123 XYZ Street.

Relative Cell References: A relative cell reference gives the location of a cell in terms of direction (above, below, left, and right) and distance (number of rows or columns away) from the formula cell. Multiplan displays relative direction and distance in a special way called Multiplan notation. This notation plays an important role in your formulas, and you should have a good grasp of it before trying to develop any spreadsheets—your own or the ones in this book.

In Multiplan notation, relative cells above or to the left of the formula cell are indicated by a minus sign; relative cells below or to the right of the formula cell are indicated by a plus sign. The distance is shown as the number of cells away. Both the direction (+ or −) and the distance (a number) are enclosed in brackets. For example, a relative cell that is one cell above or one cell to the left of the formula cell is shown as [−1], and a relative cell one cell below or one cell to the right of the formula cell is shown as [+1].

Since we have both rows and columns to deal with, the letters R (Row) and C (Column) tell us which is which. For example, R[−1]C is a relative cell that is one row above the formula cell, and RC[−1] is a relative cell that is one column to the left of the formula cell. You can see relative cell locations diagramed in Figure 2-3.

	C[−2]	C[−1]	C	C[+1]	C[+2]	C[+3]
R[−4]						R[−4]C[+3]
R[−3]						
R[−2]						
R[−1]			R[−1]C			
R		RC[−1]	Formula			RC[+3]
R[+1]						
R[+2]						
R[+3]	R[+3]C[−2]					

FIGURE 2-3.
Some relative cell locations

To help you become familiar with relative cell references, here are some of the ways they look on the screen:

■ RC[+3] is a cell three columns to the right of the formula cell.

■ R[−4]C[+3] is a cell four rows above and three columns to the right of the formula cell.

■ R[+3]C[−2] is a cell three rows below and two columns to the left of the formula cell.

Now for the good news. You don't have to type any of these letters, brackets, numbers, or symbols. When you are building a formula, Multiplan generates the notation as you move the cursor.

Absolute Cell References: An absolute cell reference is a target cell for a formula and is indicated by a specific row and column number, such as R5C7, or by a name given to a specific cell, such as PROFIT.

As with a relative cell reference, you don't have to type the row and column numbers of an absolute cell reference. You simply move the cursor. Up to this point, the screen shows brackets, symbols, and numbers, just as for a relative cell reference. With the cursor on the cell, you tell Multiplan you want to treat it as an absolute cell reference by pressing the F3 key. The relative cell notation immediately changes to row and column numbers. When you include a named cell in a formula, you don't have to move the cursor at all. You simply type the name at the proper place in the formula.

Now here's the bottom line to these differences: Your choice of whether to use relative or absolute cell references is important only if you intend to copy the formula to other cells. Relative cell references refer to different cells, depending on where the formula is copied to. Absolute cell references always refer to the same cells, regardless of where the formula is copied to.

Order of Calculation

Arithmetic operators tell Multiplan what kind of calculation to perform with the numbers in the cell references. The addition operator is the standard +, subtraction is −, and percent is %, but some of the others may not be as familiar to you. Multiplication is *, division is /, and exponentiation, or raising to a given power, is ^.

If you remember your high school algebra, you remember that you had to write an equation with the operators in a particular order so the equation would produce the correct result. This operator priority also applies to Multiplan formulas. A negative value has the highest priority and is calculated first, followed, in this order, by %, ^, * and /, and + and −, which share the lowest priority. If you have more than one operator of the same priority level (for example, + and −) in a formula, Multiplan works on them as it finds them, from left to right.

You can change the normal order of calculation by placing parentheses around calculations you want Multiplan to handle first. For example, in the formula $10 + 6 * (9 - 5)^2/4$, the $(9 - 5)$ portion is calculated first because it is in parentheses. Then the result of that calculation is raised to the power of 2, that result is multiplied by 6, that result is divided by 4, and, finally, the 10 is added. The answer to the formula is 34.

Building a Formula

Value is the formula command. You start with the cursor on the cell that will contain the formula and type *V*. You then move the cursor to each cell location you want included in the formula. If you want an absolute reference to a cell, press F3 while the cursor is on the cell and Multiplan converts the relative notation to a row and column number. In building a formula, then, you have to type only the function names, cell names, text, numbers, and symbols. When the formula is complete, press Enter.

(When you look at the formulas in this book, you can easily distinguish among function names, text, and cell names: Function names, such as SUM, are followed by an open parenthesis. Text, such as "Due Company", is enclosed in quotation marks. Cell names, such as TOTAL, are neither followed by an open parenthesis nor enclosed in quotation marks.)

If your formula begins with a number or a symbol that Multiplan recognizes as the start of a formula, you don't have to type *V* to start the *Value* command. These symbols are: (, =, +, −, ., and ". (The comma is not one of the characters.) Except for the equal sign, the number or symbol you typed becomes the first character in the formula.

Formulas are the heart of a spreadsheet. The harder they work, the easier your work will be. In developing your spreadsheet, build the obvious formulas; then look for places where a formula can do even more of the work for you. You'll frequently find at least one potential formula just waiting for you to discover it.

A Formula Example

To give you a taste of Multiplan formulas, the daily sales summary mini-spreadsheet in Figure 2-4 contains two simple addition formulas. Formula 1 uses the plus sign (+) and two relative cell references. Formula 2 uses the SUM function and the colon (:) range operator to add the contents of six relative cell references.

	1	2	3	4
1		DAILY SALES SUMMARY		
2	===			
3		Cash	Charge	Total
4	Department	Sales	Sales	Sales
5	---			
6	Tires	$296.60	$327.78	$624.38 ❶
7	Batteries	$176.54	$98.70	$275.24
8	Parts	$156.68	$367.90	$524.58
9	Accessories	$84.75	$234.67	$319.42
10	Labor	$137.42	$221.40	$358.82
11	Other	$76.20	$147.85	$224.05
12		---------	---------	---------
13	Totals	$928.19 ❷	$1398.30	$2326.49

Formula 1: RC[−2]+RC[−1]
Formula 2: SUM(R[−7]C:R[−2]C)

FIGURE 2-4.
Daily sales summary mini-spreadsheet illustrating addition

Formula 1, in the total sales column at R6C4, adds the cash sales and charge sales and appears as RC[−2] + RC[−1]. This translates as follows: Add the contents of the cell that is two columns to the left of the formula cell to the contents of the cell that is one column to the left of the formula cell. Multiplan's Copy command copies Formula 1 down column 4, so it adds the cash sales and charge sales for each department.

Formula 2, in the cash sales column at R13C2, adds the numbers in column 2 and appears as SUM(R[−7]C:R[−2]C). This translates as follows: Add the entries from seven rows above the formula cell to the entries two rows above the formula cell. This time, the Copy command copies Formula 2 to the right into columns 3 and 4, where it totals the entries in each column.

STEP 11: Copy the Formulas

The Copy command makes it easy to copy a formula to another cell, a row or column of cells, or a rectangle of cells. If the formula you copied contains absolute cell references, the formula in the new location uses the same cells for its calculations. If the formula you copied contains relative cell references, the formula uses different cells related to its new location.

STEP 12: Lock the Formula Cells

After you enter all your formulas, you should protect them from inadvertent change. If you accidentally overtype a formula with a number or text, the formula is lost. You can always reenter it, of course, but why spend the time if you don't have to? Locking is a convenience, not an irreversible condition; you can always unlock the cells.

You have two options in the Lock command: Formulas and Cells. When you use the Formulas option, all the cells containing formulas are locked, but so are all the cells containing text, including your titles. You can't lock one without locking the other. If you find this inconvenient because you plan to enter text (billing dates, employee names, and so on) that you'll update regularly, enter it later, after locking. If you use the Cells option, you can lock cells selectively, but this is time-consuming when you have formulas throughout the spreadsheet.

It's best to use the Formulas option and afterward (in Step 15) enter the text you regularly change. Numbers that are not generated by formulas—those you type in yourself—remain unlocked, so you can change them at any time without unlocking any cells.

STEP 13: Save the Spreadsheet

If you haven't been saving your formulas as you create them, lock them now and then store them on disk. Because you saved the spreadsheet in Step 8 and gave it a filename at that time, the filename will appear in the *filename* field. You don't have to retype it, you simply press Enter.

At this point, however, Multiplan is determined to protect you from yourself and asks if you want to overwrite the earlier version of the spreadsheet. Although it's easy to type *Y* for *Yes*, take a moment to ask yourself if this is really what you want to do. If you have any doubts at all, save the new version under a different filename. You can always go back later and erase the old file from the disk. Train yourself to avoid automatically typing Y. You'll be glad you did.

STEP 14: Enter the Real Numbers

If you entered real numbers in Step 9, skip to Step 15. If you entered test numbers in Step 9, read on.

If your formulas are working properly with your test numbers, now is the time to enter the real numbers. If you have any question about which cells contain test numbers and which contain formulas (they both show up as numbers on the spreadsheet), hold down the F2 key. The cursor will jump to the unlocked cells. When you move the cursor around the spreadsheet, you can also see the test numbers and formulas on the status line at the bottom of your screen.

You don't have to blank out any test numbers, unless you feel you might overlook a few. Simply overtype them. If automatic recalculation is turned off, press the F4 key after you enter the last number to tell Multiplan to recalculate your spreadsheet.

STEP 15: Enter the Transient Text

Transient text is text you intend to change regularly, such as employee names, company names, or dates. Now that the formulas and titles are locked, you can enter this text in the same way you entered the titles earlier. As an alternative, you might want to enter transient text with the titles, then unlock the cells you want to change.

STEP 16: Set the Print Margins and Options

The print settings let you customize the appearance of your printed spreadsheet. In Margins, you select where the spreadsheet is positioned on the page. In Options, you define the print area and type styles (pitch or character size, boldface, italic, and so on). You also use Options to tell Multiplan whether to print row and column numbers and whether to print the formulas. The margins and formatting codes you specify on one spreadsheet become Multiplan's proposed responses on the next one you create. To simplify matters, all the spreadsheets in this book are printed in 12-pitch type. The margins change from spreadsheet to spreadsheet.

It's a good idea to store your spreadsheet on disk immediately after you make the print settings and before you print, so you don't forget to do it. This way, you'll have the correct settings the next time you print the spreadsheet.

STEP 17: Print the Spreadsheet and Formulas

With the print settings stored on disk, print your spreadsheet. First, turn on your printer. Then start the Print command and select the Printer option (a matter of two keystrokes—*PP*).

It's a good idea to print your formulas, too, particularly when you have invested a good deal of time in creating them. You need change only one setting in the Print command to have Multiplan print this behind-the-scenes information that makes your spreadsheet what it is. Then if something unexpected happens, you can always re-create your spreadsheet from the printout.

STEP 18: Exit Multiplan and Copy the Spreadsheet

To end a Multiplan session, use the Quit command. If all your work is stored on disk, Multiplan exits directly. If you made any changes since the last time you saved the spreadsheet, Multiplan prompts you to *Enter Y to save edits, N to lose edits, or cancel.* When you type Y, Multiplan asks if you want to overwrite the existing file if one exists under that name. If you type Y again, Multiplan overwrites the earlier file, and exits. If you type N, Multiplan exits without saving the changes. Pressing Escape cancels the Quit command.

When you stop work on a spreadsheet—even for a short while—take the time to copy it to a backup disk. Floppy disks are reasonably hardy, but accidents can happen. Coffee spills, dust, fingerprints on exposed surfaces, or catastrophes such as sitting or stepping on disks or exposing them to magnetic fields can destroy your data. Protect your work by making a copy. If you are working with a hard disk, you know that hard disks sometimes crash. So be sure to keep the latest version of your spreadsheet on a floppy disk, too.

When All Else Fails, Read the Help Instructions

When you're setting out on an ocean voyage, it's comforting to know there are lifeboats on board. Multiplan has many lifeboats. If you have difficulty at any step, this is how to get immediate on-screen help:

■ When you see the command menu on your screen, type *H* (for Help) to bring up Multiplan's extensive explanations and instructions about applications, commands, editing, formulas, keystrokes, and macros.

■ When you are in a command, press Alt-H to replace the spreadsheet on your screen temporarily with information about the command.

When you find the answer to your question, press Escape to return the spreadsheet exactly as you left it.

WHAT WAS THAT NUMBER?

Multiplan and numbers are inseparable companions—not only the numbers you enter on your spreadsheets, but the numbers you need to know to enter filenames, set column widths, name cells, and so forth. And then there are the mathematical symbols you use in building your formulas. When you need such numbers or symbols, you often can't quite remember where you saw them. So, to help you in your work with Multiplan, all the numbers and mathematical symbols you need on a day-to-day basis are in Figure 2-5. You may want to keep a copy of Figures 2-1 and 2-5 near your computer.

THE SPREADSHEETS IN PART 2

Now you're ready to create the spreadsheets. Each spreadsheet in Part 2 contains complete step-by-step instructions, starting with the comparatively simple business start-up analysis and ending with the comparatively complex cash flow analysis. Most of these spreadsheets stand alone, but some are related. Financial analysis begins with the balance sheet in Chapter 8, which grows to include the income statement in Chapter 9 and financial ratios in Chapter 10. The cash disbursements spreadsheets in Chapter 12 depend on the check ledger in Chapter 11, so you must create the check ledger first.

Completeness has its pluses and minuses. On the one hand, you can start with whichever spreadsheet you choose, knowing you won't have to skip around the book in search of scattered instructions. On the other hand, it does make for some degree of repetition. Bear with it. There's enough variety and excitement in each spreadsheet to offset the dry spells.

Four spreadsheets from Part 2—business start-up analysis, price volume analysis, loan amortization analysis, and depreciation analysis—are already on your Multiplan Templates Disk. If you need quick answers right now, by all means use the files on the disk. If you really want to learn how to use Multiplan, you're wise to create these spreadsheets from scratch. With that in mind, turn to the chapter of your choice and let's begin working with Multiplan.

Multiplan Numbers

Maximum number of columns	255
Maximum number of rows	4095
Total available cells	1,044,225 (use depends on your computer's available random access memory, or RAM)
Default column width	10 characters
Available column widths	0 to 64 characters (column numbers inhibited if width is less than 3 characters)
Maximum user characters displayed on an 80-character screen	75. Five character spaces are allotted to row number (4 digits) and space between row number and first user-available character
Numeric value storage	14 digits of precision
Available windows	8 (displays up to 8 areas on one spreadsheet, areas on up to 8 spreadsheets, or a combination of both)
Space used by a window border	2 screen lines and 2 screen columns
Length of filenames	Up to 8 characters, plus a decimal point followed by up to 3 characters
Length of cell names	1 to 31 characters. Name must start with a letter. Any single letter except R or C may be used for a name
Decimal exponent range	-307 to $+307$
Maximum entries in a function list	5. Each item can represent any number of cell references
Maximum sheets able to be linked in disk files	Limited to available memory
Maximum sheets able to be listed by Xternal List	8

FIGURE 2-5.
Multiplan numbers and symbols

Default print margins:

Left field	5 characters
Top field	6 lines
Print width field	70 characters
Print length	54 lines
Page length	66 lines
When running Run Report, minimum width of print area	40 characters
Maximum characters accumulated in each cell during macro record	64
Maximum length of a macro message	78 characters
Maximum subroutines in a macro	16
Maximum width of user-defined currency symbol	20 characters
Maximum length of password	15 characters
Maximum length of custom date and time formats	32 characters
Maximum number of date or time formats	19
Default screen height	25 lines
Available screen heights	11 to 43 lines

In cross-reference reports:

Default indents	4 characters
Available indents	0 to 8 characters

Multiplan Symbols

Arithmetic		Comparison		Other	
%	Percentage	=	Equal to	:	Range
^	Exponentiation	<	Less than	,	Union
*	Multiplication	>	Greater than	(space)	Intersection
/	Division	<=	Less than or equal to	&	Concatenation
+	Addition				
−	Subtraction	>=	Greater than or equal to		
		<>	Not equal to		

PART 2

The
Spreadsheets

3
Business Start-up Analysis

If you're thinking about starting your own business, chances are you've worn out many an eraser on planning and projections. You have to consider carefully the type of business to go into, where to locate your business, who your customers will be, what your sales strategy will be, and what type of competition you're up against. But the most important consideration is money. How much capital do you need for start-up, and how will you finance ongoing operations? Many new businesses fail because of unrealistic assessments of cash requirements.

The twin dangers you face are undercapitalization and overcapitalization. Starting with inadequate resources means you will have to cut back on expenditures that can be vital to success. Borrowing too heavily means your resources will be spent on repayments instead of operating expenses. Both problems can be avoided by careful planning.

The business start-up spreadsheet shown in Figure 3-1 lets you replace guesswork with facts. When you enter your estimated expenses and income, the formulas calculate your cash flow during the critical first months of operation. You can experiment with endless combinations, print as many versions as you wish, evaluate them side by side, and find the one that suits you best. If you need a loan or a bank line of credit, you can then approach a lending institution. You may even have a better chance for a favorable decision if you hand a copy of your detailed business plan—your spreadsheet—to the loan officer.

	1	2	3	4	5
1	Sep 15, 1987 2:53 PM	BUSINESS START-UP ANALYSIS			
2	===				
3	Cash Funds Available				
4	Owner's Funds		$35,000		
5	Bank Loan		$60,000		
6			---------		
7	Total Cash Available			$95,000	
8				=========	
9	Organizational & Pre-Operating Expenses				
10	Advertising for Opening		$1,250		
11	Deposits-Phone & Utilities		$1,167		
12	Decorating & Remodeling		$4,500		
13	Fixtures & Equipment		$2,500		
14	Licenses & Permits		$275		
15	Professional Fees		$1,800		
16	Rent-2 months security+1 month rent		$2,925		
17	Other Expenses		$1,500		
18			---------		
19	Total Org'l & Pre-Operating Expenses			$15,917	
20				---------	
21	Cash Balance Available for Operations			$79,083	
22				=========	
23	===				
24	Operations	January	February	March	Totals
25	---				
26	Projected Cash Available				
27	Beginning Cash	$79,083	$55,121	$44,519	
28	Cash Sales	$5,000	$8,000	$14,000	$27,000
29		---------	---------	---------	
30	Total Cash Available	$84,083	$63,121	$58,519	
31					
32	Operating Expenses				
33	Owner's Draw	$2,000	$2,000	$2,000	$6,000
34	Employee Salaries	$1,500	$2,200	$3,000	$6,700
35	Payroll Taxes	$300	$440	$600	$1,340
36	Medical Insurance	$0	$0	$475	$475
37	Advertising & Promotion	$400	$550	$550	$1,500
38	Insurance	$1,600	$0	$0	$1,600
39	Inventory	$20,000	$10,000	$10,000	$40,000
40	Loan Repayment	$1,427	$1,427	$1,427	$4,281
41	Materials & Supplies	$35	$35	$35	$105
42	Professional Fees	$0	$250	$250	$500
43	Rent	$975	$975	$975	$2,925
44	Repairs & Maintenance	$50	$50	$50	$150
45	Telephone	$125	$125	$125	$375
46	Utilities	$200	$200	$200	$600
47	Other Expenses	$350	$350	$350	$1,050
48		---------	---------	---------	---------
49	Total Cash Outlay	$28,962	$18,602	$20,037	$67,601
50		=========	=========	=========	=========
51	Cash Balance	$55,121	$44,519	$38,482	
52		=========	=========	=========	

FIGURE 3-1.
The completed business start-up analysis spreadsheet

The new business in our practice example is a small retail store, Clara's Dress Shoppe. The spreadsheet lists the total cash available for start-up and itemizes the estimated expenses before the doors open, including a contingency cushion of $1,500 in the category of *Other Expenses*. After these expenses are deducted, the cash remaining becomes the beginning cash for the first month. The spreadsheet then details the projected sales and expenses for each of the first three months of operation. The cash balance at the end of each month becomes the beginning balance for the following month.

The expenses in this example include monthly payments on a five-year loan of $60,000 at 15 percent interest, which the owner took out to finance the operation. I calculated the loan repayment of $1,427 on the loan-amortization spreadsheet in Chapter 5. Be patient; you'll soon be doing the same. For now, simply enter the amount shown.

Later in this chapter, we'll modify the business start-up spreadsheet to make it a budget that helps track and control cash flow during three months of actual operations. An easy-to-write macro does most of the updating for you. You'll find complete information about macros in Chapter 18. You will benefit most from this session if you have some familiarity with key codes, command codes, and how Edit Macro works.

If you prefer to create this spreadsheet without following the step-by-step instructions, refer to the summary at the end of this chapter.

SETTING UP YOUR SPREADSHEET

Bring up the Multiplan screen. If you turned off automatic recalculation to speed up data entry on your last spreadsheet, fine. Otherwise, to make data entry faster, leave the cursor on R1C1, type O to start the Options command, type N for no recalculation, and press Enter. Now let's make your spreadsheet look like the one in Figure 3-2.

Adjusting the Column Widths

When you start a new spreadsheet, each of Multiplan's columns is ten characters wide. With only five columns of information on this spreadsheet, we can increase the width of each column and still keep all five columns on the screen—a nice convenience. Let's give the titles in column 1 more room.

Leave the cursor on R1C1:	Type or press:
Start the Format command	F
Select the Width option	W
Specify the number of characters in the column	27
Execute the command	Enter

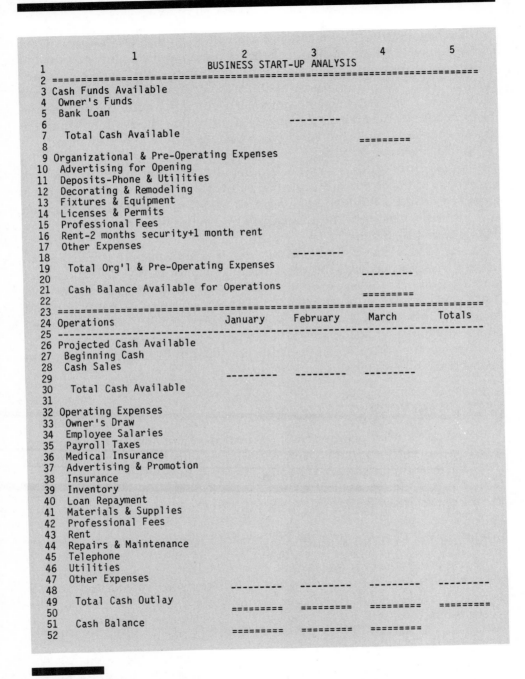

```
                    1              2          3         4         5
1                            BUSINESS START-UP ANALYSIS
2  ==================================================================
3  Cash Funds Available
4   Owner's Funds
5   Bank Loan
6                                     ---------
7     Total Cash Available
8                                                        =========
9  Organizational & Pre-Operating Expenses
10  Advertising for Opening
11  Deposits-Phone & Utilities
12  Decorating & Remodeling
13  Fixtures & Equipment
14  Licenses & Permits
15  Professional Fees
16  Rent-2 months security+1 month rent
17  Other Expenses
18                                    ---------
19    Total Org'l & Pre-Operating Expenses
20                                              ---------
21    Cash Balance Available for Operations
22                                              =========
23 ==================================================================
24 Operations              January   February    March     Totals
25 ------------------------------------------------------------------
26 Projected Cash Available
27  Beginning Cash
28  Cash Sales
29                         ---------  ---------  ---------
30    Total Cash Available
31
32 Operating Expenses
33  Owner's Draw
34  Employee Salaries
35  Payroll Taxes
36  Medical Insurance
37  Advertising & Promotion
38  Insurance
39  Inventory
40  Loan Repayment
41  Materials & Supplies
42  Professional Fees
43  Rent
44  Repairs & Maintenance
45  Telephone
46  Utilities
47  Other Expenses
48                         ---------  ---------  ---------  ---------
49    Total Cash Outlay
50                         =========  =========  =========  =========
51    Cash Balance
52                         =========  =========  =========
```

FIGURE 3-2.

Titles and lines on the business start-up analysis spreadsheet

To accommodate the large dollar amounts, increase the widths of columns 2 through 5 to 12 characters each.

Place the cursor on R1C2:	**Type or press:**
Start the Format command	F
Select the Width option	W
Specify the number of characters in each column	12
Move the highlight to *through*	Tab Tab
Select columns *2 through 5*	5
Execute the command	Enter

Entering the Titles

The next step is to type the titles you see in Figure 3-2 (but not the lines; you'll enter them later). The titles in column 1 are indented in a stair-step fashion, as follows:

■ A title that falls under a general heading, such as *Owner's Funds* in R4C1, is indented one space. Press the Spacebar once before typing each of these titles.

■ A title that identifies a total, such as *Total Cash Available* in R7C1, is indented two spaces. Press the Spacebar twice before typing each of these titles.

The title you type will appear on the command line. If you make a typing error, press the Backspace key (not a direction key) to back up the highlight and erase, or use the F7 through F10 keys to edit the title. Some of the long titles won't appear completely in their cells when you enter them. Don't be concerned. We'll take care of that shortly when we format the titles.

When you have many titles, it's an advantage to keep Multiplan in a constant input-to-the-spreadsheet mode. Then, if you happen to press Enter after typing a title, you don't have to type *A* (Alpha) to prepare the cell for the next title. To activate this special mode, leave the cursor on R1C2 and then type O (Options). Press the Tab key four times to move the highlight to the *alpha/value* field. Type *Y* to select *Yes* and press Enter. *ALPHA/VALUE* now replaces the command menu and will reappear after you enter each title.

Now, start entering the titles: Leave the cursor on R1C2 and type *BUSINESS START-UP ANALYSIS* (the spreadsheet title). Use the Down Arrow and Left Arrow keys to move the cursor to R3C1, the next cell that will contain a title. When you move the cursor, the spreadsheet title disappears from the command line, and the beginning of the title appears in its cell. *ALPHA/VALUE* reappears on the command line.

Type *Cash Funds Available* and move the cursor to R4C1. Now press the Spacebar to indent the text a space. Type *Owner's Funds* and move the cursor to R5C1. Press the Spacebar again. Type *Bank Loan* and move the cursor to R7C1. Press the Spacebar twice and type *Total Cash Available*. Move the cursor to the next cell and type the next title. Continue in this way, and after you type the last title, press Enter.

Now exit the alpha/value mode: Leave the cursor where it is and press the Escape key. Type O (Options) and press the Tab key four times to move the highlight to *alpha/value*. Type N to select *No* and press Enter.

Entering the Lines

Next, let's use the REPT function and an equal sign to enter a double line across row 2. The quotation marks around the equal sign tell Multiplan the sign is text, not an arithmetic operator. To be sure no gaps appear in the line, we'll repeat the equal sign enough times to fill even the widest cell in row 2.

Place the cursor on R2C1:	Type or press:
Start the Value command	V
Repeat an equal sign 27 times	REPT(" = ",27)
Execute the command	Enter

Now copy the REPT formula into the columns to the right.

Leave the cursor on R2C1:	Type or press:
Start the Copy command	C
Select the Right option	R
Specify the number of cells to copy into	4
Execute the command	Enter

The double line now extends to the right through column 5. We want row 23 to contain the same kind of line, so the next step is to copy from row 2. The colon before the number 5 in the following instructions is the *range* operator (which you'll be seeing a good deal of). Pressing the F6 key is easier than using the Shift and Colon keys.

Leave the cursor on R2C1:	Type or press:
Start the Copy command	C
Select the From option	F
(Multiplan displays *COPY FROM cells:* *R2C1*, the first cell to copy from)	
Specify the last column to copy from	:5
Move the highlight to *to cells*	Tab
Specify the first cell to copy into	R23C1
Execute the command	Enter

Move the cursor to row 23, and you can see that the entire line was copied, although you identified only the first cell to copy into. This is because Copy From took the start-to-end information from columns 1 through 5 in row 2 and duplicated it in row 23.

Now let's use the REPT function and a minus sign (used as a text character) to enter a single line across row 25.

Place the cursor on R25C1:	Type or press:
Start the Value command	V
Repeat a minus sign 27 times	REPT(" – ",27)
Execute the command	Enter

Use Copy Right again, this time to copy the single line formula across the row: Leave the cursor on R25C1 and type *CR*. In the *number of cells* field, you now see the number *4*. Multiplan is proposing the same number of cells into which you copied the double line formula. This number is correct, so simply press the Enter key. The single line now extends from columns 1 through 5.

Next, let's use a minus sign to enter the short line in R6C3. We want it to align properly with the numbers that will be in the cells above and below, so we'll indent the line two characters from the left edge of the cell and stop it one character shy of the right edge.

Place the cursor on R6C3:	Type or press:
Start the Alpha command	A
Indent two spaces	Spacebar Spacebar
Enter nine minus signs	– – – – – – – – –
Execute the command	Enter

Copy this line to the other cells that need it.

Leave the cursor on R6C3:	**Type or press:**
Start the Copy	C
Select the From option	F
(Multiplan displays *COPY FROM cells:* R6C3, the cell to copy from)	
Move the highlight to *to cells*	Tab
Specify the cells to copy into	R18C3,R20C4,R29C2:4, R48C2:5
Execute the command	Enter

Now enter a short double line in the same way.

Place the cursor on R8C4:	**Type or press:**
Start the Alpha command	A
Indent two spaces	Spacebar Spacebar
Enter nine equal signs	= = = = = = = = =
Execute the command	Enter

Copy this line to the other cells.

Leave the cursor on R8C4:	**Type or press:**
Start the Copy command	C
Select the From option	F
(Multiplan displays *COPY FROM cells:* R8C4, the cell to copy from)	
Move the highlight to *to cells*	Tab
Specify the cells to copy into	R22C4,R50C2:5,R52C2:4
Execute the command	Enter

Move the cursor down to see all the lines on your spreadsheet, exactly as shown in Figure 3-2.

Formatting the Titles

Now let's have Multiplan display the titles that are too wide for their cells by extending them into the cells to their right.

Place the cursor on R1C2:	Type or press:
Start the Format command	F
Select the Cells option	C
(Multiplan displays *FORMAT cells:* *R1C2*, the first cell to be continuous)	
Specify the other cells to be continuous	:4,R9:21C1:2
Move the highlight to *format code*	Tab Tab
Select *Cont* (continuous)	C
Execute the command	Enter

Now center the titles in row 24 of columns 2 through 5.

Place the cursor on R24C2:	Type or press:
Start the Format command	F
Select the Cells option	C
(Multiplan displays *FORMAT cells:* *R24C2*, the first cell to format)	
Specify the last cell to format	:5
Move the highlight to *alignment*	Tab
Select *Ctr* (center)	C
Execute the command	Enter

Formatting the Number Cells

All the numbers on this spreadsheet are dollar amounts. There's no need to plan to the last penny, so let's set a standard (default) format of dollars with no decimal places.

Leave the cursor where it is:	Type or press:
Start the Format command	F
Select the Default option	D
Select the Cells option	C
Move the highlight to *format code*	Tab
Select *$*	$
Move the highlight to *# of decimals*	Tab
Specify the number of decimals	0
Execute the command	Enter

Inserting Commas in the Large Numbers

This spreadsheet contains some large numbers. To make them easier to read, let's tell Multiplan to insert commas.

Leave the cursor where it is:	Type or press:
Start the Format command	F
Select the Options option	O
(The highlight is on *No* in the *commas* field)	
Select *Yes*	Y
Execute the command	Enter

That's it. You have now completed formatting your spreadsheet.

Saving and Naming the Spreadsheet

This is a good time to store your spreadsheet on disk with the titles, lines, and formats, and give the spreadsheet its own filename. If you need to tell Multiplan which drive contains your data disk or which directory to store the file in, type the drive letter and press F6 (to produce a colon) or type the pathname before you type *STARTUP*, the filename.

Leave the cursor on R24C2:	Type or press:
Start the Transfer command	T
Select the Save option	S
(Multiplan displays the drive letter and *TEMP*, the proposed filename)	
Name the spreadsheet	STARTUP
Execute the command	Enter

ENTERING THE FORMULAS

Figure 3-3 shows the locations of the formulas that perform your calculations. They use relative cell references only.

The left column in the following instructions contains the locations of the cell references and other elements in the formula. The column on the right and the line immediately below the formula heading show the finished formula. To build a formula, move the cursor to each cell shown in the left column (Multiplan will produce the relative notation) and type everything else—operators, symbols, and function names. When you type a character, the cursor returns to the formula cell so that you can type another character, move the cursor to another cell, or enter the formula.

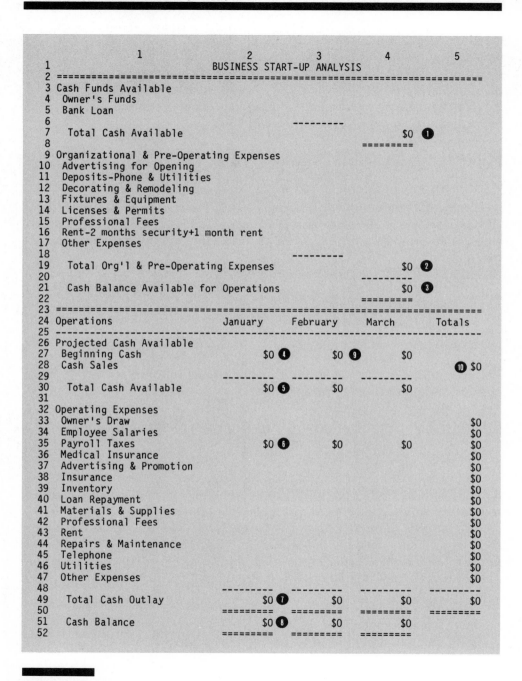

FIGURE 3-3.
Business start-up spreadsheet formula locations

When your formula agrees with the instructions, press Enter. If Multiplan then displays *Not a valid formula*, check each character in the formula. Use the F7 through F10 keys to move the highlight, and correct the problem by typing missing characters or by pressing the Delete key to delete unwanted characters. If you prefer to start the formula from scratch, simply press the Escape key to begin again.

FORMULA 1: Total Cash Available

$R[-3]C[-1]+R[-2]C[-1]$

Formula 1 adds the owner's funds (R4C3) and a projected bank loan (R5C3) and enters the total cash available in R7C4. The bank loan, at this stage, is an estimate until the owner evaluates the overall operations and required funding.

Place the cursor on R7C4:	Type or move the cursor:
Start the Value command	V
Enter the formula: R4C3 + R5C3	$R[-3]C[-1]+R[-2]C[-1]$
Execute the command	Enter

The zero in R7C4 indicates that a formula is in the cell. The status line at the bottom of the screen shows the formula.

FORMULA 2: Organizational & Pre-Operating Expenses

$SUM(R[-10]C[-1]:R[-1]C[-1])$

Formula 2 adds the organizational and pre-operating expenses (R10C3 to R17C3). It includes the empty cell in R9C3 and the line in R18C3 for this reason: When you have a formula that adds a list of numbers, it's a good idea to include the cells above the first and below the last numbers in the list, providing they don't contain anything that will affect the calculation. Then you can later insert rows anywhere between these cells, and Multiplan will adjust the formula to add the new items along with the old.

Place the cursor on R19C4:	Type or move the cursor:
Start the Value command	V
Enter the formula: SUM(R9C3:R18C3)	$SUM(R[-10]C[-1]:$ $R[-1]C[-1])$
Execute the command	Enter

FORMULA 3: Cash Balance Available for Operations

$$R[-14]C - R[-2]C$$

Formula 3 subtracts the total organizational and pre-operating expenses (R19C4) from the total cash available (R7C4) and enters the cash available for operations in R21C4.

Place the cursor on R21C4:	Type or move the cursor:
Start the Value command	V
Enter the formula: R7C4 – R19C4	$R[-14]C - R[-2]C$
Execute the command	Enter

FORMULA 4: Beginning Cash—Month 1

$$R[-6]C[+2]$$

Formula 4 copies the amount of cash remaining after the organizational and pre-operating expenses are deducted (R21C4) into the beginning cash cell in January, the first month of operation (R27C2).

Place the cursor on R27C2:	Type or move the cursor:
Start the Value command	V
Enter the formula: R21C4	$R[-6]C[+2]$
Execute the command	Enter

FORMULA 5: Total Cash Available

$$R[-3]C + R[-2]C$$

Formula 5 adds the beginning cash (R27C2) and the projected cash sales in the first month (R28C2) to get the total cash available (R30C2).

Place the cursor on R30C2:	Type or move the cursor:
Start the Value command	V
Enter the formula: R27C2 + R28C2	$R[-3]C + R[-2]C$
Execute the command	Enter

FORMULA 6: Payroll Taxes

R[−1]C＊20%

Formula 6 calculates the payroll taxes (R35C2) at 20% of employee salaries (R34C2). This rate approximates the amount an employer pays for mandated employee benefits, including social security, federal and state unemployment insurance, and disability insurance.

Place the cursor on R35C2:	Type or move the cursor:
Start the Value command	V
Enter the formula: R34C2＊20%	R[−1]C＊20%
Execute the command	Enter

FORMULA 7: Total Cash Outlay

SUM(R[−17]C:R[−1]C)

Formula 7 adds the operating expenses (R33C2 to R47C2) to produce the total cash outlay in January (R49C2). Again, we'll include the empty cell in R32C2 and the line in R48C2 in the formula so that you can later insert rows anywhere between these cells.

Place the cursor on R49C2:	Type or move the cursor:
Start the Value command	V
Enter the formula: SUM(R32C2:R48C2)	SUM(R[−17]C:R[−1]C)
Execute the command	Enter

FORMULA 8: Cash Balance

R[−21]C − R[−2]C

Formula 8 subtracts the total cash outlay (R49C2) from the total cash available (R30C2) and enters the cash balance for January (R51C2).

Place the cursor on R51C2:	Type or move the cursor:
Start the Value command	V
Enter the formula: R30C2 − R49C2	R[−21]C − R[−2]C
Execute the command	Enter

Copying the Formulas in Groups

We can use some of the same formulas we built for January to calculate the numbers for February and March, so let's copy Formulas 5, 6, 7, and 8. We can copy the formulas because they contain relative (not absolute) references.

Place the cursor on R30C2:	Type or press:
Start the Copy command	C
Select the From option	F
(Multiplan displays *COPY FROM cells:* R30C2, the first cell to copy from)	
Specify the last cell to copy from	:R51C2
Move the highlight to *to cells*	Tab
Specify the first cell in each column to copy into	R30C3:4
Execute the command	Enter

FORMULA 9: Beginning Cash—Month 2

R[+24]C[−1]

Formula 9 doesn't calculate anything. It simply copies the cash remaining after the first month of operation (R51C2) into the beginning cash cell in February, the second month of operation (R27C3).

Place the cursor on R27C3:	Type or move the cursor:
Start the Value command	V
Enter the formula: R51C2	R[+24]C[−1]
Execute the command	Enter

You want the same calculation for the beginning of the next month, March, so copy Formula 9 into R27C4.

Leave the cursor on R27C3:	Type or press:
Start the Copy command	C
Select the Right option	R
Specify the number of cells to copy into	1
Execute the command	Enter

FORMULA 10: Totals

SUM(RC[− 3]:RC[− 1])

Formula 10 adds the projected cash sales in January, February, and March (R28C2 to R28C4) and enters the total projected sales during the first three months of operation in R28C5.

Place the cursor on R28C5:	Type or move the cursor:
Start the Value command	V
Enter the formula: SUM(R28C2:R28C4)	SUM(RC[− 3]:RC[− 1])
Execute the command	Enter

Now copy Formula 10 into the other cells in column 5, where it can calculate the total for each expense during the first three months.

Leave the cursor on R28C5:	Type or press:
Start the Copy command	C
Select the From option	F
(Multiplan displays COPY FROM *cells: R28C5*, the cell to copy from)	
Move the highlight to *to cells*	Tab
Specify the cells to copy into	R33:47C5,R49C5
Execute the command	Enter

Locking the Formulas

To avoid accidental alteration to your formulas, lock them.

Leave the cursor where it is:	Type:
Start the Lock command	L
Select the Formulas option	F
(Multiplan displays *Enter Y to confirm*)	
Execute the command	Y

Saving the Formulas

Now store all the formulas safely on disk. Because you saved the spreadsheet before, Multiplan now asks you to confirm your intention to overwrite the earlier version.

Leave the cursor where it is:	Type or press:
Start the Transfer command	T
Select the Save option	S
(Multiplan displays the drive letter and *STARTUP*—there's no need to retype)	
Execute the command	Enter
(Multiplan recalculates the spreadsheet and displays *Enter Y to overwrite file*)	
Confirm the overwrite	Y

ENTERING THE PRACTICE NUMBERS

Figure 3-4 contains the projected income and expenses for this new business. You can type a number any time you see the command menu on the screen or *ALPHA/VALUE* on the command line. Simply place the cursor on the cell and type the number, which then appears on the command line next to the word *VALUE*. When you move the cursor to another cell, the number moves into the cell where it belongs. Because you formatted the cell earlier, Multiplan will enter the dollar signs and commas for you. Here's the most efficient way to enter the numbers:

1. Start with the cursor on R4C3 and type the numbers in column 3, rows 4 through 17.

2. Move the cursor to R28C2. Type all the numbers in column 2 for the first month of operation and then press Enter.

Many of the numbers for February and March are the same as those for January. Instead of retyping each one, copy them as follows:

1. Move the cursor to R33C2, type *CR* (Copy Right), type 2 as the number of cells to copy into, and press Enter.

2. Now move the cursor to R40C2 and type *CR* again. In the *number of cells* field, Multiplan proposes the number 2, so press Enter. Continue in this way to copy the numbers in rows 41, 43, 44, 45, 46, and 47 from column 2 into columns 3 and 4.

3. To finish up, move the cursor to R28C3 and type the remaining numbers in columns 3 and 4. After you type the last number, press Enter.

```
Clara's Dress Shoppe   Header appears here
Filename: Startup
Page 1                /Date and time
                    1             2         3         4         5
 1 Sep 15, 1987 2:53 PM    BUSINESS START-UP ANALYSIS
 2 =========================================================================
 3 Cash Funds Available
 4  Owner's Funds                      35000
 5  Bank Loan                          60000
 6                                   ---------
 7   Total Cash Available
 8                                             =========
 9 Organizational & Pre-Operating Expenses
10  Advertising for Opening             1250
11  Deposits-Phone & Utilities          1167
12  Decorating & Remodeling             4500
13  Fixtures & Equipment                2500
14  Licenses & Permits                   275
15  Professional Fees                   1800
16  Rent-2 months security+1 month rent 2925
17  Other Expenses                      1500
18                                   ---------
19   Total Org'l & Pre-Operating Expenses
20                                             ---------
21   Cash Balance Available for Operations
22                                             =========
23 =========================================================================
24 Operations              January   February    March     Totals
25 -------------------------------------------------------------------------
26 Projected Cash Available
27  Beginning Cash
28  Cash Sales               5000       8000     14000
29                         ---------  ---------  ---------
30   Total Cash Available
31
32 Operating Expenses
33  Owner's Draw             2000       2000      2000
34  Employee Salaries        1500       2200      3000
35  Payroll Taxes
36  Medical Insurance           0          0       475
37  Advertising & Promotion   400        550       550
38  Insurance                1600          0         0
39  Inventory               20000      10000     10000
40  Loan Repayment           1427       1427      1427
41  Materials & Supplies       35         35        35
42  Professional Fees           0        250       250
43  Rent                      975        975       975
44  Repairs & Maintenance      50         50        50
45  Telephone                 125        125       125
46  Utilities                 200        200       200
47  Other Expenses            350        350       350
48                         ---------  ---------  ---------  ---------
49   Total Cash Outlay
50                         =========  =========  =========  =========
51   Cash Balance
52                         =========  =========  =========
53
54 &LClara's Dress Shoppe   Header is entered here
55 &LFilename: Startup
56 &LPage &P
```

FIGURE 3-4.

Business start-up practice numbers, header, and current date

Now—the moment you've been waiting for. Press the F4 (recalculate) key to see the result of all your work. The numbers on your spreadsheet should now look like those in Figure 3-1, at the beginning of this chapter.

If something is awry, first check your numbers, then compare your formulas, character by character, with the instructions. Correct any errors. If that doesn't do the trick, refer to the section in Chapter 19 that explains how to correct a formula.

Now use Transfer Save to store the spreadsheet on disk: Leave the cursor where it is. Type *TS* and press Enter. Type *Y* to overwrite.

CREATING A HEADER

You can have Multiplan print an informational header at the top of each page. Let's create a header that contains the name of our new business, the filename of this spreadsheet, and a page number, as shown in Figure 3-4. Since Multiplan routinely centers a header, we'll put a special code on each line that left-justifies it instead.

Place the cursor on R54C1:	**Type or press:**
Start the Alpha command	A
Enter the left-justify code and the business name	&LClara's Dress Shoppe
Move the cursor to R55C1	Down Arrow
Enter the left-justify code and the spreadsheet filename	&LFilename: Startup
Move the cursor to R56C1	Down Arrow
Enter the left-justify and page codes	&LPage &P
Execute the command	Enter

The next step is to tell Multiplan where to find the header information.

Leave the cursor on R56C1:	**Type or press:**
Start the Print command	P
Select the Heading option	H
(The highlight is in the *header* field)	
Specify the header location	R54:56C1
Execute the command	Enter
Exit the Print command	Escape

GENERATING TODAY'S DATE

When you print this spreadsheet, you'll want to include today's date and the current time so that later you can distinguish one version from another. Your computer's clock generates this information, which reflects the date and time you enter at the DOS prompt when you power up or the settings kept by a battery powered clock. Multiplan stores the times and dates as serial numbers (see Chapter 15), so first enter the Multiplan function that produces the serial number of the current date.

Place the cursor on R1C1:	**Type or press:**
Start the Value command	V
Enter the formula: NOW()	NOW()
Execute the command	Enter

The format in effect causes a dollar sign and comma to appear in the serial (date and time) number. The next step is to format the cell to display the date and time properly. Since the cell is wide enough, let's create a custom format that displays the date as a three-letter month, one- or two-digit day, and four-digit year, and the time as a one- or two-digit hour, two-digit minute, and either AM or PM.

Leave the cursor on R1C1:	**Type or press:**
Start the Format command	F
Select the Time-Date option	T
Select the Cells option	C
Move the highlight to *format*	Tab
Specify the custom format	MMM D, YYYY H:MM AM/PM
Execute the command	Enter

After a brief delay while Multiplan, in effect, busily flips calendar pages, your computer's date and time appear. These numbers will change each time your spreadsheet is recalculated. Now left-justify the cell contents: Leave the cursor on R1C1 and type *FC* (Format Cells). Press Tab to move the cursor to *alignment.* Type *L* to select *Left* and press Enter.

PRINTING YOUR SPREADSHEET

This spreadsheet is 80 characters wide, including the 5 characters Multiplan uses for row numbers and a space. It is printed in 12-pitch type on one sheet of 8½-by-11-inch paper.

Setting the Print Margins

The first step before printing is to set the margins around your spreadsheet.

Leave the cursor where it is:	Type or press:
Start the Print command	P
Select the Margins option	M

Type the following numbers in the margins fields. Tab past any fields that already have the proper settings. If you overshoot a field, press Shift-Tab to back up one field at a time or press Tab a few times to move full circle through all the fields. The highlight is in the *left* field.

To do this:	Type or press:
Specify the number of characters	8
Move the highlight to *top*	Tab
Specify the number of lines	3
Move the highlight to *print width*	Tab
Specify the number of characters	102
Move the highlight to *print length*	Tab
Specify the number of lines	60
Move the highlight to *page length*	Tab
Specify the number of lines	66
Execute the command	Enter

Setting the Print Options

You are still in the Print command. The next step is to set the print options. These settings are the same for all the spreadsheets in this book: Print the entire spreadsheet, print it in 12-pitch type, and print row and column numbers. The row and column numbers will help you compare your results with the illustrations. You can find the printer code for 12-pitch type in your printer manual.

Now type O to select the Options option. Type in the following responses. (Tab past any fields that already have the proper settings.) The highlight is in the *area* field.

To do this:	Type or press:
Define the print area	R1:4095
Move the highlight to *setup*	Tab
Enter your printer code for 12-pitch type	(your code)

Move the highlight to *formulas*	Tab Tab
Select *No*	N
Move the highlight to *row-col numbers*	Tab
Select *Yes*	Y
Execute the command	Enter
Exit the Print command	Esc

Before you print, save the spreadsheet with the print settings: Leave the cursor where it is. Type *TS* and press Enter. Type *Y*.

Printing the Spreadsheet and Formulas

Now turn on your printer and print a copy of your spreadsheet.

Leave the cursor where it is:	**Type:**
Start the Print command	P
Select the Printer option	P

And there's your spreadsheet. Printing your formulas is just as easy—and useful, too, for reference. All you have to do is change one setting.

Leave the cursor where it is:	**Type or press:**
Start the Print command	P
Select the Options option	O
Move the highlight to *formulas*	Tab (three times)
Select *Yes*	Y
Execute the command	Enter
Select the Printer option	P

The header identifies and numbers each page of the formula printout. You now have two printouts—one showing the spreadsheet results and the other the formulas. A third version—one you could give to a bank or other financial institution—excludes the header entries in rows 54 through 56 and restores the standard settings in the *formulas* and *row-col numbers* fields.

Leave the cursor where it is:	Type or press:
Start the Print command	P
Select the Options option	O
Define the print area	R1:53C1:5
Move the highlight to *formulas*	Tab (three times)
Select *No*	N
Move the highlight to *row-col numbers*	Tab
Select *No*	N
Execute the command	Enter
Select the Printer option	P

INSERTING ROWS AND COLUMNS

Suppose you need four more rows for organizational and pre-operating expenses. Here's how to insert them: Place the cursor on the line in R18C3 and type *IR* (Insert Row). Type *4* and press Enter. Four new rows await your entries. Let's insert six rows for operating expenses. First press the PgDn key. Now place the cursor on the line in R52C3 and type *IR*. Type *6* and press Enter.

Remember when you included that line in each of your SUM formulas? This is where your foresight pays off. Multiplan adjusted the cell references in all the formulas to include the rows you just inserted. All you would have to do now is make your new entries and press F4. The formulas would do the rest. But don't make any changes yet, because this spreadsheet is about to be reborn as a budget.

An easy way to get rid of the rows you inserted is to reload the spreadsheet without saving the changes. Leave the cursor where it is and type *TL* (Transfer Load). Now press a direction key to display the directory. The highlight is on ∗ *STARTUP,* so press Enter. Multiplan asks you to *Enter Y to save edits, N to lose edits, or cancel.* Type *N* to lose the edits (the inserted rows), and the original spreadsheet reappears.

CONVERTING THE START-UP SPREADSHEET TO A QUARTERLY BUDGET

Figure 3-5 shows the business start-up spreadsheet converted into a budget that covers three months of operation. (The time span, of course, can be whatever you want it to be, in months or in years.) You can create it in a few simple steps.

```
Clara's Dress Shoppe
Filename: Budget
Page 1
                1              2           3          4          5
 1 Sep 15, 1987 3:32 PM    QUARTERLY BUDGET
 2 =====================================================================
 3 Operations              January    February    March      Totals
 4 ---------------------------------------------------------------------
 5 Projected Cash Available
 6   Beginning Cash        $79,083     $55,121    $44,519
 7   Cash Sales             $5,000      $8,000    $14,000 OLD $27,000
 8                        ---------   ---------  ---------
 9   Total Cash Available  $84,083     $63,121    $58,519
10
11 Operating Expenses
12   Owner's Draw           $2,000      $2,000     $2,000     $6,000
13   Employee Salaries      $1,500      $2,200     $3,000     $6,700
14   Payroll Taxes            $300        $440       $600     $1,340
15   Medical Insurance          $0          $0       $475 OLD   $475
16   Advertising & Promotion  $400        $550       $550     $1,500
17   Insurance              $1,600          $0         $0     $1,600
18   Inventory             $20,000     $10,000    $10,000    $40,000
19   Loan Repayment         $1,427      $1,427     $1,427     $4,281
20   Materials & Supplies      $35         $35        $35 OLD   $105
21   Professional Fees          $0        $250       $250       $500
22   Rent                     $975        $975       $975     $2,925
23   Repairs & Maintenance     $50         $50        $50 OLD   $150
24   Telephone                $125        $125       $125       $375
25   Utilities                $200        $200       $200       $600
26   Other Expenses           $350        $350       $350     $1,050
27                        ---------   ---------  ---------  ---------
28   Total Cash Outlay     $28,962     $18,602    $20,037    $67,601
29                        =========   =========  =========  =========
30   Cash Balance          $55,121     $44,519    $38,482
31                        =========   =========  =========
```

FIGURE 3-5.
The business start-up spreadsheet converted to a quarterly budget

STEP 1: Make a Copy of STARTUP

Save the business start-up spreadsheet under a different filename so you can modify one copy while preserving the original: Type *TS* (Transfer Save), type *BUDGET* preceded by a drive letter and colon if you are saving it to a drive other than the default or type the pathname if you are storing it in a directory other than the current one, and press Enter. You now have two identical spreadsheets stored under different names, and BUDGET is on the screen.

STEP 2: Unlock the Cells

Let's unlock three cells so you can change their contents: Place the cursor on R1C2 and type *LC* (Lock Cells). Type *,R55C1,R27C2* and press Tab to move the highlight to *status*. Type *U* (Unlocked) and press Enter.

STEP 3: Enter the New Titles

Next, replace the old titles: Leave the cursor on R1C2 and type *A* to start the Alpha command. Type *QUARTERLY BUDGET* and press Enter. Now press the End key, and move the cursor to R55C1. Edit the filename in the header: Type *E* (Edit). Press the F7 key twice to highlight *Startup*. Press Delete to delete *Startup*. Now type *Budget* and press Enter.

STEP 4: Convert a Formula to a Value

Cell R27C2 contains a formula that copies the cash balance produced by the formula in R21C4. When you delete row 21, you will want to keep the cash balance to avoid a *#REF!* error message. You do this by converting the formula to a value: Place the cursor on R27C2, type *E* (Edit), press F4, and press Enter.

STEP 5: Delete the Start-up Rows

You don't need them, so you need to delete the rows in the organizational and pre-operating section: Place the cursor on R3C1 and type *DR* (Delete Row). Type *21* (the number of rows to delete) and press Enter.

STEP 6: Save the Spreadsheet

Save this version of the spreadsheet on disk: Type *TS* (Transfer Save) and press Enter. Type *Y* to overwrite the earlier version.

A MACRO FOR UPDATING THE BUDGET

The budget spreadsheet helps you keep track of past activities and plan ahead, which means you will need to update it regularly. When the first month is past, you'll want to shift the information in the second and third months one column to the left, thereby freeing up a column for a new month. When another month is past, you'll want to do the same thing all over again. This is the kind of repetitive activity that a macro can perform far faster (and with far less drudgery) than if you did it manually. The macro, entered in cells on the spreadsheet, causes Multiplan to perform these tasks automatically, just as if you were typing from the keyboard.

Figure 3-6 shows the update macro in cells R7C7 through R13C7. Don't be alarmed—the macro contains three prompt messages, making it look longer than it really is. The macro is split into seven parts to make it easy to enter. The 'QU (quit) command code that is needed to end the macro doesn't appear until the very end, so Multiplan will run one part after the other as if the entire macro were in one cell. R6C7 contains a description of the macro and its run code.

In cell:	Type:
R6C7	Update the spreadsheet (Alt-UP)
R7C7	'HMLCR3:14C2:4'TBU'RTCFR3C3:4'TBR3C2'RT
R8C7	'ALType new month and press Enter'R3C4'
R9C7	'VAType number shown in R6C3 and press Enter'R6C2'
R10C7	CFR7:26C3:4'TBR7C2'RTBOLD,PRINT'RT'RCLFY
R11C7	'VAType print number (yes = 1 no = 0) and press Enter'PRINT'
R12C7	'IF(PRINT = 1)'PP
R13C7	O'TBN'RT'HM'LK'LK'QU

FIGURE 3-6.
The macro that updates the budget spreadsheet

The macro copies the February entries into column 2, thereby overwriting the January entries, and then copies the March entries into column 3, thereby overwriting the February entries. It then blanks out the amounts in column 4 that tend to vary from month to month and leaves the other amounts intact, which saves you the bother of retyping.

We'll look at how to write this macro a little later, but first we need to make a few preparations.

Naming the Cells the Macro Blanks Out

The amounts that vary from month to month are cash sales, medical insurance, advertising and promotion, insurance, inventory, materials and supplies, professional fees, repairs and maintenance, telephone, utilities, and other expenses. (Your business may have other fluctuating expenses.) To make it easy for the macro to blank out these cells, let's name all of them OLD, as follows:

Place the cursor on R7C4:	Type or press:
Start the Name command	N
Name the cells	OLD
Move the highlight to *to refer to*	Tab
(Multiplan displays *to refer to:R7C4*)	
Specify the other cells to name	,R15:18C4,R20:21C4,R23: 26C4
Execute the command	Enter

Naming and Formatting the Print/No Print Cell

During its run, the macro will look at a cell whose contents tell it whether to print the spreadsheet. First, name this cell: Place the cursor on R5C7 and type *N*. Type *PRINT* and press Enter.

Next, change the cell format so that its contents are left-justified and appear as an integer (without the dollar sign): Leave the cursor on R5C7. Type *FC* (Format Cells) and press Tab to move the highlight to the *alignment* field. Type *L* to select *Left* and press Tab again, this time to move the highlight to the *format code* field. Type *I* to select *Int* and press Enter.

Increasing the Column Width

Ordinarily, you wouldn't bother to increase the width of a column just to display a macro. When you're new to macros, seeing it completely does make it easier to understand. So place the cursor on R7C7 and type *FW* (Format Width). Type *56* and press Enter. This completes the preparations.

Writing the Macro

Now it's time to write the macro. The left column in the following instructions, with one exception, shows the action the macro takes during its run. That exception is the reference to the Edit Macro mode, which alters the standard operation of the keyboard so that Multiplan types in the keycodes for the keys you press. It has nothing to do with what the macro does. The column on the right shows your keystrokes. Type each cell location (no cursor movements) exactly as shown, and pay particular attention to the apostrophes.

There's no need to rush, so take your time. If you make a typing error, press the Backspace key to erase the character. If you're in the Edit Macro mode at the time (you'll see *EM* to the right of the memory indicator), be sure to press F5 first so that Multiplan doesn't enter the keycode for Backspace in the macro. After you correct the mistake, press F5 again and continue from where you left off. You'll find additional information about writing a macro in Chapter 18.

PART 1

'HMLCR3:14C2:4'TBU'RTCFR3C3:4'TBR3C2'RT

Part 1 jumps the cursor to R1C1 (which gives you a good view of the action while the macro is running), unlocks the cells in rows 3 to 14 (columns 2 to 4), and copies the titles now in R3C3 and R3C4 into R3C2 and R3C3. Place the cursor on R7C7 and type *A* to start the Alpha command. Then press F5 to activate the Edit Macro mode.

Macro Action:	**Type or press:**
Jump the cursor to R1C1	Home
Start the Lock Cells command	LC
Specify the cells to unlock	R3:14C2:4
Move the highlight to *status: (Locked) Unlocked*	Tab
Specify *Unlocked*	U
Execute the command	Enter
Start the Copy From command	CF
Specify the cells to copy from	R3C3:4
Move the highlight to *to*	Tab
Specify the first cell to copy into	R3C2
Execute the command	Enter

Press the F5 key to exit the Edit Macro mode. Now press the Down Arrow key to move the cursor to R8C7, and Multiplan enters Part 1 in its cell. You now see *ALPHA/VALUE* on the command line, which means you can continue entering the macro without starting the Alpha command again.

PART 2

'ALType new month and press Enter'R3C4'

Part 2 contains the interactive command code 'AL and a prompt. An interactive command code lets you communicate with the macro during its run. When the macro finds 'AL, it will pause and display *Type new month and press Enter*. It will then enter the month you type in R3C4. The cursor is on R8C7.

Macro action:	Type or press:
Insert the Alpha command code	'AL
Define the prompt for the message line	Type new month and press Enter
Specify the cell that receives what you type	'R3C4'

Press the Down Arrow key to move the cursor to R9C7, and Multiplan enters Part 2 in its cell.

PART 3

'VAType number shown in R6C3 and press Enter'R6C2'

Part 3 contains the interactive command code 'VA and a prompt. When the macro finds 'VA, it will pause and display *Type number shown in R6C3 and press Enter*. It will then enter the number you type in R6C2. This number, the beginning cash in February, is generated by a formula. If you had the macro copy the formula, the cell reference would be wrong, and things would go haywire. The cursor is on R9C7.

Macro action:	Type or press:
Insert the Value interactive command code	'VA
Define the prompt for the message line	Type number shown in R6C3 and press Enter
Specify the cell that receives what you type	'R6C2'

Press the Down Arrow key to move the cursor to R10C7, and Multiplan enters Part 3 in its cell.

PART 4

CFR7:26C3:4'TBR7C2'RTBOLD,PRINT'RT'RCLFY

Part 4 copies the numbers from rows 7 to 26, columns 3 and 4, to column 2. It then blanks out the information in the cells named OLD (those entries in column 4 that vary from month to month) and PRINT (R5C7), recalculates the spreadsheet, and relocks the formula and text cells.

If you wonder why we blank the PRINT cell, here's the reason: During the macro's run (the next step, Part 5), you are asked to type a number (1 or 0) for the PRINT cell. The number 1 sends the spreadsheet to the printer; a 0 tells Multiplan to ignore the print command. Although the number from a prior run may still be valid in the current run, Part 4 blanks it. That way, you're not tempted to press Enter, thinking that doing so accepts the existing number. Pressing Enter would blank out the cell and leave the macro nothing to work with. The cursor is on R10C7.

Macro action:	Type or press:
Start the Copy From command	CF
Specify the cells to copy from	R7:26C3:4
Activate the Edit Macro mode	F5
Move the highlight to *to*	Tab
Specify the cells to copy into	R7C2
Execute the command	Enter
Start the Blank command and erase contents of cells BOLD and PRINT	BOLD,PRINT
Execute the command	Enter
Recalculate the spreadsheet	F4
Exit the Edit Macro mode	F5
Start the Lock Formulas command, Y to confirm	LFY

Press the Down Arrow key to move the cursor to R11C7, and Multiplan enters Part 4 in its cell.

PART 5

'VAType print number (yes = 1 no = 0) and press Enter'PRINT'

Part 5 contains the interactive command code 'VA and a prompt. When the macro finds 'VA, it pauses and displays *Type print number (yes = 1 no = 0) and press Enter.* The number you type tells Multiplan whether or not to print the spreadsheet. The cursor is on R11C7.

Macro action:	Type or press:
Insert the Value interactive command code	'VA
Define the prompt for the message line	Type print number (yes = 1 no = 0) and press Enter
Specify the name of the cell that receives what you type	'PRINT'

Press the Down Arrow key to move to R12C7 and to enter Part 5 in the cell.

PART 6

'IF(PRINT = 1)'PP

Part 6 contains the conditional command code 'IF followed by a test that directs the macro to one of two paths. If the number in R5C7 (the cell named PRINT) is 1, the macro continues to the next element, 'PP (Print Printer), and sends the spreadsheet to the printer. If the number is 0, the macro skips the printing and moves to the next cell down (R13C7). The cursor is on R12C7.

Macro action:	Type or press:
Insert the IF command code and condition	'IF(PRINT = 1)'
Start the Print Printer command	PP

Press the Down Arrow key to move the cursor to R13C7, and Multiplan enters Part 6 in its cell.

PART 7

O'TBN'RT'HM'LK'LK'QU

Part 7 makes sure your computer's audible alarm is on, then beeps to alert you that the macro has ended. The cursor is on R13C7.

Macro action:	Type or press:
Start the Options command	O
Activate the Edit Macro mode	F5
Move the highlight to *mute*	Tab
Select *No*	N
Execute the command	Enter
Jump the cursor to R1C1	Home
Bump the cursor into the left margin twice	Left Arrow (two times)
Exit the Edit Macro mode	F5
Insert the Quit command code	'QU
Enter the macro	Enter

Now compare the macro on your screen with the one in Figure 3-6 to be sure that every character is correct. If something needs changing, place the cursor on that cell and type *E* (Edit). Then press the F7 to F10 keys to move the highlight through the macro. Type a missing character or word or use Delete to remove a character or word, then press Enter.

Naming the Macro

Naming a macro and assigning a run code (the keys you use to run the macro) makes it easy to locate one macro among many. Although this spreadsheet has only one macro, let's name it anyway. It's a good habit to get into.

Place the cursor on R7C7:	Type or press:
Start the Name command	N
Name the cell	UPDATE
Move the highlight to *macro: Yes (No)*	Tab Tab
Select *Yes*	Y
Move the highlight to *command key(s)*	Tab
Assign the run code	UP
Execute the command	Enter

So that you don't have to rely on memory, enter a description of the macro and its run code: Place the cursor on R6C7 and type *A* (Alpha). Type *Update the spreadsheet (Alt-UP)* and press Enter. Store all your work on disk: Type *TS*, press Enter, and type *Y*.

Running the Macro

Now turn on your printer. Keep a watchful eye on the screen, because things will happen quickly. Hold down the Alternate key and type *UP*. The macro jumps to R1C1, then goes about its task of shifting the entries. At the pause, Multiplan displays *Type new month and press Enter.* Type *April* and press Enter. Your response appears in R3C4.

The macro continues its short run and pauses again with the prompt *Type number shown in R6C3 and press Enter.* Type *55121* and press Enter. Your response appears in R6C2. The macro continues its run. At the next pause, which prompts *Type print number and press Enter,* type *1* to print. The macro sends the spreadsheet to the printer, then beeps good-bye as it ends its run.

When the budget returns to the screen, the January entries are gone, February and March are shifted one column to the left, and April is ready for your new entries. If you're eager to try it again, just reload the budget by typing *TL* (Transfer Load), then hold down Alternate and type *UP*. For a change this time, type *0* when the macro asks for a Print number.

And here's to success in your new business venture!

SPREADSHEET SUMMARY: BUSINESS START-UP ANALYSIS

General: The completed spreadsheet is shown in Figure 3-1. Use Value to enter REPT(" = ",27) and REPT(" – ",27) for the long lines. Indent one space for titles under general headings, two spaces for totals titles. Use Lock Formulas to lock the formulas.

Column Width: Use Format Width as follows: Set column 1 to 27 characters wide. Set columns 2 through 5 to 12 characters wide.

Format: Use Format Cells as follows: Continue R1C2:4 and R9C1:R21C2. Center R24C2:5. Left-justify R1C1. Use Format Default Cells to format all cells for dollars with 0 decimals. Use Format Options to insert commas in the large numbers.

Date-Time: Use Value to enter NOW() in R1C1, then use Format Time-Date to assign the custom format MMM D, YYYY H:MM AM/PM.

Print: Business Start-up Analysis is 80 characters wide, including Multiplan row numbers. Set Print Margins for 8½-by-11-inch paper and 12-pitch type, as follows: *left* 8, *top* 3, *print width* 102, *print length* 60, and *page length* 66. *Indent* 0. Use Print Options to set the print area for R1C1:R52C5 so that the header input doesn't print, and enter your printer's code for 12-pitch type. Use Print Heading to locate the header at R54:56C1.

Formulas: Formulas use relative cell references only.

1	R7C4	Total Cash Available	$R[-3]C[-1]+R[-2]C[-1]$
2	R19C4	Organizational and Pre-Operating Expenses	$SUM(R[-10]C[-1]:R[-1]C[-1])$
3	R21C4	Cash Balance Available For Operations	$R[-14]C-R[-2]C$
4	R27C2	Beginning Cash—Month 1	$R[-6]C[+2]$
5	R30C2	Total Cash Available	$R[-3]C+R[-2]C$
6	R35C2	Payroll Taxes	$R[-1]C*20\%$
7	R49C2	Total Cash Outlay	$SUM(R[-17]C:R[-1]C)$
8	R51C2	Cash Balance	$R[-21]C-R[-2]C$
9	R27C3	Beginning Cash—Month 2	$R[+24]C[-1]$
10	R28C5	Totals	$SUM(RC[-3]:RC[-1])$

SPREADSHEET SUMMARY: QUARTERLY BUDGET

General: The completed spreadsheet, adapted from the business start-up spreadsheet, is shown in Figure 3-5. Use Format Width to increase the width of column 7 to 56 characters.

Name: R7C4,R15:18C4,R20:21C4,R23:26C4 are named OLD. R5C7 is named PRINT. R7C7 is named UPDATE and defined as a macro.

Macro: The macro, split into seven parts, updates the budget. To run the macro, press Alt-UP.

1	R7C7	'HMLCR3:14C2:4'TBU'RTCFR3C3:4'TBR3C2'RT
2	R8C7	'ALType new month and press Enter'R3C4'
3	R9C7	'VAType number shown in R6C3 and press Enter'R6C2'
4	R10C7	CFR7:26C3:4'TBR7C2'RTBOLD,PRINT'RT'RCLFY
5	R11C7	'VAType print number (yes = 1 no = 0) and press Enter'PRINT'
6	R12C7	'IF(PRINT = 1)'PP
7	R13C7	O'TBN'RT'HM'LK'LK'QU

4
Price-Volume Analysis

The highest price you can get for a product is not necessarily the most profitable price. If the price you set is too high, sales volume can plummet. If your price is too low, you may sell in greater quantity, but you may not be able to cover your costs. The best selling price is high enough to keep pace with costs, but low enough to attract customers and build sales volume. Price-volume analysis can help you strike the right balance.

In setting prices, your goal is to maximize profit. The ingredients of profit are costs, selling price, and sales volume, each properly proportioned and weighed in terms of market conditions, production capacity, and the financial operation of your business.

Figure 4-1 shows a completed price-volume analysis spreadsheet. The numbers in rows 3 through 8 are your "What if?" playground. You enter the projected starting price of a product, the price decrease, the starting volume, the amount you estimate that price decrease will increase volume, and the fixed and variable costs. The formulas in rows 12 through 22 calculate the fixed costs per unit, total variable costs, sales income, cost of goods sold, total profit, and profit per unit in each of five price-volume tests. You can examine any other combination of price and volume by simply typing in new numbers.

If you're familiar with Multiplan and prefer to create this spreadsheet without following the step-by-step instructions, refer to the summary at the end of this chapter.

```
                1               2           3           4           5           6
                                        PRICE-VOLUME ANALYSIS                    PRICE
 1
 2  ===================================================================================
 3  Selling Price per Unit                  $10.00
 4  Projected Price Decrease                  $1.00
 5  Sales Volume in Units                    10,000
 6  Projected Volume Increase                 2,000
 7  Total Fixed Costs                       $10,000
 8  Variable Costs per Unit                   $3.00
 9  ===================================================================================
10  PRICE-VOLUME RESULTS        TEST 1      TEST 2      TEST 3      TEST 4      TEST 5
11  -----------------------------------------------------------------------------------
12  Selling Price per Unit      $10.00       $9.00       $8.00       $7.00       $6.00
13  Volume in Units             10,000      12,000      14,000      16,000      18,000
14  Fixed Costs per Unit         $1.00       $0.83       $0.71       $0.63       $0.56
15  Total Fixed Costs           $10,000     $10,000     $10,000     $10,000     $10,000
16  Total Variable Costs        $30,000     $36,000     $42,000     $48,000     $54,000
17
18  Sales Income               $100,000    $108,000    $112,000    $112,000    $108,000
19  Cost of Goods Sold          $40,000     $46,000     $52,000     $58,000     $64,000
20                            ----------  ----------  ----------  ----------  ----------
21  Total Profit                $60,000     $62,000     $60,000     $54,000     $44,000
22  Profit per Unit              $6.00       $5.17       $4.29       $3.38       $2.44
23  ===================================================================================
```

FIGURE 4-1.
The completed price-volume analysis spreadsheet

SETTING UP YOUR SPREADSHEET

Bring up the Multiplan screen. If you turned off automatic recalculation on your last spreadsheet, you're ready to start. Otherwise, to make data entry faster, leave the cursor on R1C1, type O to start the Options command, type N for no recalculation, and press Enter. Now let's make your spreadsheet look like the one in Figure 4-2.

Adjusting the Column Widths

This is a new spreadsheet, so each column is 10 characters wide. To give the wide titles the space they need, increase the width of column 1 to 25 characters.

Leave the cursor on R1C1:	Type or press:
Start the Format command	F
Select the Width option	W
Specify the number of characters in the column	25
Execute the command	Enter

To accommodate the numbers, increase the width of columns 2 through 6 to 12 characters each.

```
                  1              2         3        4         5        6
 1                                   PRICE-VOLUME ANALYSIS
 2 =================================================================================
 3 Selling Price per Unit
 4 Projected Price Decrease
 5 Sales Volume in Units
 6 Projected Volume Increase
 7 Total Fixed Costs
 8 Variable Costs per Unit
 9 =================================================================================
10 PRICE-VOLUME RESULTS        TEST 1    TEST 2   TEST 3    TEST 4   TEST 5
11 ---------------------------------------------------------------------------------
12 Selling Price per Unit
13 Volume in Units
14 Fixed Costs per Unit
15 Total Fixed Costs
16 Total Variable Costs
17
18 Sales Income
19 Cost of Goods Sold
20                        ----------
21 Total Profit
22 Profit per Unit
23 =================================================================================
```

FIGURE 4-2.
The titles and lines in the price-volume analysis spreadsheet

Place the cursor on R1C2:	Type or press:
Start the Format command	F
Select the Width option	W
Specify the number of characters in each column	12
Move the highlight to *through*	Tab Tab
Select columns 2 *through* 6	6
Execute the command	Enter

Entering the Titles

The next step is to enter the titles (but not the lines) shown in Figure 4-2. Ordinarily, before you type the first title, you type *A* (Alpha) to prepare the cell to receive text. You then type the title and, instead of pressing Enter, you move the cursor to the next cell that contains a title. When you move the cursor, Multiplan enters the title you just typed and displays *ALPHA/VALUE* on the command line, which means you can type the next title without typing *A* again. If you press Enter instead, you have to type *A* again before typing the next title.

When you have many titles, it makes sense to keep Multiplan in the alpha/ value mode. This gives you more freedom while you type. If you happen to press Enter, Multiplan is ready to accept the next title without your having to type *A* first. To activate this mode:

Leave the cursor where it is:	Type or press:
Start the Options command	O
Move the highlight to *alpha/value*	Tab (four times)
Select *Yes*	Y
Execute the command	Enter

ALPHA/VALUE now replaces the command menu and will appear each time you move the cursor. If you mistype a title, use Backspace to back up the highlight and erase the error.

Now place the cursor on R1C3. Type *PRICE-VOLUME ANALYSIS* and move the cursor to R3C1. The first part of the title appears in the cell. We'll display it fully when we format the titles. Type *Selling Price per Unit* and move the cursor to R4C1. Type *Projected Price Decrease* and move the cursor again. Continue in this way—typing a title and moving the cursor—until you type all the titles shown in Figure 4-2. After you type the last title, press Enter.

Now press Escape to return the command menu to the screen. To deactivate the alpha/value mode, leave the cursor where it is and type O (Options). Press the Tab key four times. Type *N* and press Enter.

Entering the Lines

Next, let's use the REPT (repeat) function and an equal sign to put a double line across row 2. Start by entering a line in R2C1. Column 1 (the widest column) is 25 characters wide, so repeat the equal sign 25 times.

Place the cursor on R2C1:	Type or press:
Start the Value command	V
Repeat an equal sign 25 times	REPT(" = ",25)
Execute the command	Enter

Now copy the REPT formula into the columns to the right.

Leave the cursor on R2C1:	Type or press:
Start the Copy command	C
Select the Right option	R
Specify the number of cells to copy into	5
Execute the command	Enter

The line now extends through column 6. Rows 9 and 23 contain the same kind of line, so tell Multiplan to copy from row 2. Use the F6 key to produce the colon shown in the column on the right in the following instructions.

Leave the cursor on R2C1:	Type or press:
Start the Copy command	C
Select the From option	F
(Multiplan displays COPY FROM cells: R2C1, the first cell to copy from)	
Specify the last cell to copy from	:6
Move the highlight to *to cells*	Tab
Specify the first cell in each row to copy into	R9C1,R23C1
Execute the command	Enter

Let's create another REPT formula and this time use a minus sign to enter a single line across row 11.

Place the cursor on R11C1:	Type or press:
Start the Value command	V
Repeat a minus sign 25 times	REPT(" – ",25)
Execute the command	Enter

Now copy this formula into the columns to the right.

Leave the cursor on R11C1:	Type or press:
Start the Copy command	C
Select the Right option	R

Multiplan "remembered" your last copy instruction and now proposes 5 as the number of cells to copy into. This is correct, so simply press Enter. The single line now extends through column 6.

Now create a short line in R20C2. To align it with the numbers that will be in the cells above and below, start the line one character from the left edge of the cell and stop it one character before the right edge.

Place the cursor on R20C2:	Type or press:
Start the Alpha command	A
Indent one space	Spacebar
Type ten minus signs	– – – – – – – – – –
Execute the command	Enter

Formatting the Titles

Let's continue the spreadsheet title *PRICE-VOLUME ANALYSIS* in R1C3 into the next cell to the right, so you can see it completely.

Place the cursor on R1C3:	**Type or press:**
Start the Format command	F
Select the Cells option	C
(Multiplan displays *FORMAT cells: R1C3,* the first cell to be continuous)	
Specify the last cell to be continuous	:4
Move the highlight to *format code*	Tab Tab
Select *Cont* (continuous)	C
Execute the command	Enter

Now we'll right-justify the cell that will contain the spreadsheet filename, PRICE, and the test titles in row 10.

Place the cursor on R1C6:	**Type or press:**
Start the Format command	F
Select the Cells option	C
(Multiplan displays *FORMAT cells: R1C6,* the first cell to format)	
Specify the other cells to format	,R10C2:6
Move the highlight to *alignment*	Tab
Select *Right*	R
Execute the command	Enter

Formatting the Number Cells

As you can see in Figure 4-1, most of the numbers are dollar amounts, with and without decimal places. Those without decimal places are in the majority, so let's first format every cell for dollars without decimals. We'll take care of the numbers with decimals in the next step.

Leave the cursor where it is:	**Type or press:**
Start the Format command	F
Select the Default option	D
Select the Cells option	C

Move the highlight to *format code*	Tab
Select *$*	$
Move the highlight to *# of decimals*	Tab
Specify the number of decimals	0
Execute the command	Enter

Now format the cells that need two decimal places: selling price per unit (R3C3), projected price decrease (R4C3), variable costs per unit (R8C3), selling price per unit (row 12), fixed costs per unit (row 14), and profit per unit (row 22). Instead of specifying cell locations, specify entire rows, which takes fewer keystrokes and won't affect the appearance of the titles in column 1 included in the group.

Place the cursor on R3C3:	**Type or press:**
Start the Format command	F
Select the Cells option	C
(Multiplan displays *FORMAT cells: R3C3,* the first cell to format)	
Specify the rows to format	,R4,R8,R12, R14,R22
Move the highlight to *format code*	Tab Tab
Select *$*	$
Execute the command	Enter

Next, give the cells that show quantities the integer code. These cells will contain the sales volume in units (R5C3), the projected volume increase (R6C3), and the formulas that calculate the projected volume in units (row 13). Again, just identify the rows.

Place the cursor on R5C3:	**Type or press:**
Start the Format command	F
Select the Cells option	C
(Multiplan displays *FORMAT cells: R5C3,* the first cell to format)	
Specify the rows to format	,R6,R13
Move the highlight to *format code*	Tab Tab
Select *Int* (Integer)	I
Execute the command	Enter

Inserting Commas in the Large Numbers

To make the large numbers easy to read, tell Multiplan to insert commas throughout the spreadsheet.

Leave the cursor where it is:	**Type or press:**
Start the Format command	F
Select the Options option	O
(The highlight is on *No* in the *commas* field)	
Select *Yes*	Y
Execute the command	Enter

You have now completed formatting your spreadsheet.

NAMING THE CELLS

When you name cells, you can use everyday English words in your formulas instead of row and column numbers, making the formulas easy to understand. The unshaded area in Figure 4-3 shows the locations of the named cells. Let's start by naming R3C3, the selling price per unit, PRICE.

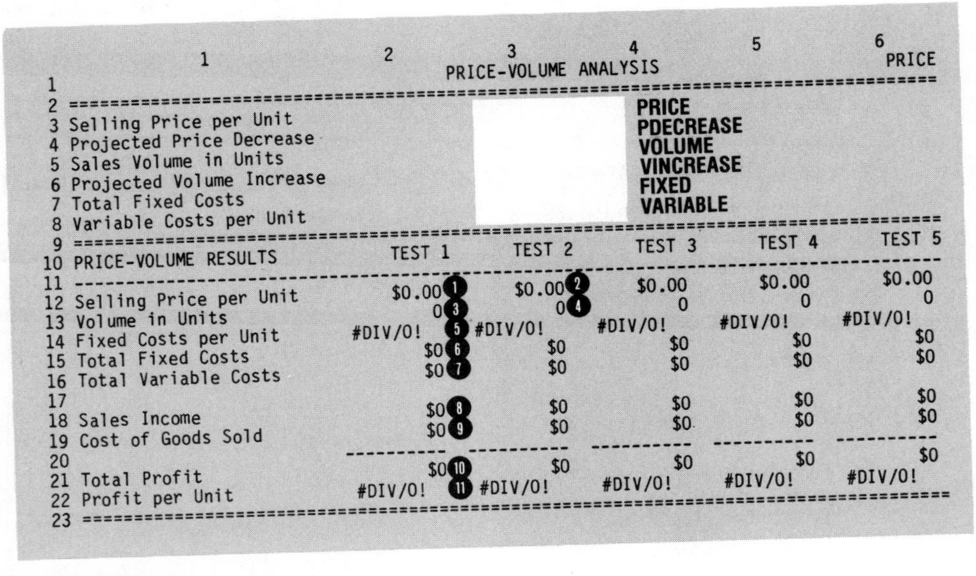

```
            1                      2            3           4           5           6
                                     PRICE-VOLUME ANALYSIS                        PRICE
 1
 2 ===============================================================================
 3 Selling Price per Unit                                PRICE
 4 Projected Price Decrease                              PDECREASE
 5 Sales Volume in Units                                 VOLUME
 6 Projected Volume Increase                             VINCREASE
 7 Total Fixed Costs                                     FIXED
 8 Variable Costs per Unit                               VARIABLE
 9 ===============================================================================
10 PRICE-VOLUME RESULTS          TEST 1       TEST 2      TEST 3      TEST 4      TEST 5
11 -------------------------------------------------------------------------------
12 Selling Price per Unit         $0.00 (1)    $0.00 (2)   $0.00       $0.00       $0.00
13 Volume in Units                    0 (3)        0 (4)       0           0           0
14 Fixed Costs per Unit         #DIV/0! (5)  #DIV/0!     #DIV/0!     #DIV/0!     #DIV/0!
15 Total Fixed Costs                 $0 (6)       $0          $0          $0          $0
16 Total Variable Costs              $0 (7)       $0          $0          $0          $0
17
18 Sales Income                      $0 (8)       $0          $0          $0          $0
19 Cost of Goods Sold                $0 (9)       $0          $0          $0          $0
20                            ----------   ----------  ----------  ----------  ----------
21 Total Profit                      $0 (10)      $0          $0          $0          $0
22 Profit per Unit              #DIV/0! (11) #DIV/0!     #DIV/0!     #DIV/0!     #DIV/0!
23 ===============================================================================
```

FIGURE 4-3.
Price-volume analysis named cells and formula locations

Place the cursor on R3C3:	Type:
Start the Name command	N
Name the cell	PRICE

Now look at the next field to the right. In the *to refer to* field you see R3C3. Since this cell location is correct, all you do is press Enter.

Use this same procedure to name the following cells. (PDECREASE stands for price decrease and VINCREASE stands for volume increase.) Be sure to press Enter after you type each name:

Place the cursor on:	Name the cell:
R4C3	PDECREASE
R5C3	VOLUME
R6C3	VINCREASE
R7C3	FIXED
R8C3	VARIABLE

SAVING AND NAMING THE SPREADSHEET

Now store your spreadsheet on disk with the titles, lines, cell formats, and cell names, and give the spreadsheet its own filename. If you need to specify which drive contains your data disk or which directory you want to store the file in, type the drive letter or pathname and press F6 (to produce a colon) before you type *PRICE*.

Leave the cursor where it is:	Type or press:
Start the Transfer command	T
Select the Save option	S
Name the spreadsheet	PRICE
Execute the command	Enter

ENTERING THE FORMULAS

The cells in column 3 (rows 3 through 8) are your testing ground, where you can experiment with price, cost, and volume to see which combination offers the greatest profit potential. Given these numbers, the formulas in rows 12 through 22 calculate the incremental price decreases, volume increases, unit costs, variable costs, sales income, cost of goods sold, and, finally, profit.

These formulas use relative and named cell references. The left column in the following instructions shows the locations of the relative references, the names of named cells, and other elements in the formula. The column on the right and the line before the formula description show the finished formula.

To build a formula, you move the cursor to each cell location shown in the left column (Multiplan produces relative notation automatically) and type everything else—operators, symbols, function names, and cell names. When you type a character, the cursor returns to the formula cell so that you can type another character, move the cursor to another cell, or enter the formula.

When your formula agrees with the instructions, press Enter. If Multiplan then displays *Not a valid formula,* check each character. Use the F7 through F10 keys to move the highlight, and correct the problem by typing missing characters or pressing the Delete key to delete unwanted characters. If you prefer to start the formula from scratch, simply press the Escape key and begin again.

FORMULA 1: Starting Selling Price

PRICE

Formula 1 doesn't calculate anything. It copies the amount from R3C3 (PRICE) to R12C2, the unit selling price in Test 1. To start the tests with a selling price of $10 per unit, you would simply type *10* in the PRICE cell. Type the one-word formula.

Place the cursor on R12C2:	Type or press:
Start the Value command	V
Enter the formula: PRICE	PRICE
Execute the command	Enter

The formula has nothing to work with, so zeros appear.

FORMULA 2: Decrease in Selling Price

RC[– 1] – PDECREASE

Formula 2 reduces the unit selling price in R12C2 by the amount of the price decrease (R4C3, PDECREASE) and enters the result in R12C3, the unit selling price in Test 2. Let's suppose you start with a selling price of $10 per unit. If you wanted to test the effect of price decreases in increments of $1, you would enter *1* in the PDECREASE cell.

Place the cursor on R12C3:	Type or move the cursor:
Start the Value command	V
Enter the formula: R12C2 – PDECREASE	RC[– 1] – PDECREASE
Execute the command	Enter

Later, when you copy Formula 2 into Tests 3 through 5, it will calculate successive incremental decreases of the amount you enter in the PDECREASE cell.

FORMULA 3: Starting Volume

VOLUME

Formula 3 copies the amount from R5C3 (VOLUME) to R13C2, the volume in units in Test 1. To start the tests at 10,000 units, you would enter *10000* in the VOLUME cell. Type the one-word formula.

Place the cursor on R13C2:	Type or press:
Start the Value command	V
Enter the formula: VOLUME	VOLUME
Execute the command	Enter

FORMULA 4: Increase in Volume

RC[− 1] + VINCREASE

Formula 4 increases the projected volume in Test 2 (R13C2) by the amount in R6C3 (VINCREASE). Let's suppose you start with 10,000 units. You estimate that you will sell an additional 2,000 units each time you reduce the price of the unit. So you would type *2000* in the VINCREASE cell.

Place the cursor on R13C3:	Type or move the cursor:
Start the Value command	V
Enter the formula: R13C2 + VINCREASE	RC[− 1] + VINCREASE
Execute the command	Enter

Copying the Formulas in Groups

Now copy Formula 2 and Formula 4 to the right so that they can calculate the incremental price decreases and incremental volume increases in Tests 3 through 5.

Leave the cursor on R13C3:	Type or press:
Start the Copy command	C
Select the Right option	R
Specify the number of cells to copy into	3
Move the highlight to *starting at*	Tab
(Multiplan displays *starting at: R13C3*)	

| Specify the last cell to copy from | :R12C3 |
| Execute the command | Enter |

FORMULA 5: Fixed Costs per Unit

FIXED/R[– 1]C

Formula 5 divides the total fixed costs (R7C3, FIXED) by the volume in units in R13C2 and enters the fixed costs per unit in R14C2.

Place the cursor on R14C2:	Type or move the cursor:
Start the Value command	V
Enter the formula: FIXED/R13C2	FIXED/R[– 1]C
Execute the command	Enter

Formula 5 has no numbers to divide yet, so the message *#DIV/0!* appears. *#DIV/0!* will remain until you enter the practice numbers later on.

FORMULA 6: Total Fixed Costs

FIXED

Formula 6 copies the total fixed costs (R7C3, FIXED) to R15C2 so that you can easily compare that amount with the total variable costs in the cell immediately below (R16C2). Type the one-word formula.

Place the cursor on R15C2:	Type or press:
Start the Value command	V
Enter the formula: FIXED	FIXED
Execute the command	Enter

FORMULA 7: Total Variable Costs

VARIABLE * R[– 3]C

Formula 7 multiplies the variable costs per unit (R8C3, VARIABLE) by the volume in units in R13C2 and enters the total variable costs in R16C2.

Place the cursor on R16C2:	Type or move the cursor:
Start the Value command	V
Enter the formula: VARIABLE * R13C2	VARIABLE * R[– 3]C
Execute the command	Enter

FORMULA 8: Sales Income

$R[-6]C * R[-5]C$

Formula 8 multiplies the unit selling price in R12C2 by the projected volume in R13C2 and enters the sales income in R18C2.

Place the cursor on R18C2:	**Type or move the cursor:**
Start the Value command	V
Enter the formula: R12C2 * R13C2	$R[-6]C * R[-5]C$
Execute the command	Enter

FORMULA 9: Cost of Goods Sold

$R[-4]C + R[-3]C$

Formula 9 adds the total fixed costs (R15C2) and the total variable costs (R16C2) to produce the cost of goods sold in R19C2.

Place the cursor on R19C2:	**Type or move the cursor:**
Start the Value command	V
Enter the formula: R15C2 + R16C2	$R[-4]C + R[-3]C$
Execute the command	Enter

FORMULA 10: Total Profit

$R[-3]C - R[-2]C$

Formula 10 subtracts the cost of goods sold (R19C2) from the sales income (R18C2) to produce the total profit in R21C2.

Place the cursor on R21C2:	**Type or move the cursor:**
Start the Value command	V
Enter the formula: R18C2 - R19C2	$R[-3]C - R[-2]C$
Execute the command	Enter

FORMULA 11: Profit per Unit

$R[-1]C / R[-9]C$

Formula 11 divides the total profit (R21C2) by the volume in units (R13C2) and enters the profit per unit in R22C2.

Place the cursor on R22C2:	**Type or move the cursor:**
Start the Value command	V

| Enter the formula: R21C2/R13C2 | R[− 1]C/R[− 9]C |
| Execute the command | Enter |

Copying Another Group of Formulas

Now copy Formulas 5 through 11 (and the line in R20C2) to the right. (We can copy these formulas and they will produce accurate results in their new locations because they contain relative references only.) This will give you the changes in cost, income, and profit in Tests 2 through 5.

Leave the cursor on R22C2:	**Type or press:**
Start the Copy command	C
Select the Right option	R
Specify the number of cells to copy into	4
Move the highlight to *starting at*	Tab
(Multiplan displays *starting at: R22C2*)	
Specify the last cell to copy from	:R14C2
Execute the command	Enter

FORMULA 12: Spreadsheet Filename

NAME()

Formula 12 enters the spreadsheet filename on the spreadsheet. Type the function name and parentheses.

Place the cursor on R1C6:	**Type or press:**
Start the Value command	V
Enter the formula: NAME()	NAME()
Execute the command	Enter

Locking the Formulas

To avoid accidental alteration, lock the formulas and titles.

Leave the cursor where it is:	**Type:**
Start the Lock command	L
Select the Formulas option	F
(Multiplan displays *Enter Y to confirm*)	
Execute the command	Y

Saving the Formulas

Now store all the formulas on disk. Because you saved the spreadsheet before, Multiplan asks you to confirm overwriting the earlier version.

Leave the cursor where it is:	Type or press:
Start the Transfer command	T
Select the Save option	S
(Multiplan displays *PRICE*—there's no need to retype)	
Execute the command	Enter
(Multiplan displays *Enter Y to overwrite file*)	
Confirm the overwrite	Y

USING YOUR SPREADSHEET

Figure 4-4 shows sample numbers in rows 3 through 8. You can type a number any time you see the command menu on the screen or *ALPHA/VALUE* on the command line. You don't enter the dollar signs, decimal places, and commas. Because of the formatting you did earlier, Multiplan will produce them for you.

```
              1                2            3          4         5         6
 1                                  PRICE-VOLUME ANALYSIS                    PRICE
 2 =================================================================================
 3 Selling Price per Unit                   10
 4 Projected Price Decrease                  1
 5 Sales Volume in Units                  10000
 6 Projected Volume Increase               2000
 7 Total Fixed Costs                      10000
 8 Variable Costs per Unit                   3
 9 =================================================================================
10 PRICE-VOLUME RESULTS          TEST 1      TEST 2     TEST 3    TEST 4    TEST 5
11 ---------------------------------------------------------------------------------
12 Selling Price per Unit
13 Volume in Units
14 Fixed Costs per Unit
15 Total Fixed Costs
16 Total Variable Costs
17
18 Sales Income
19 Cost of Goods Sold
20          ----------  ----------  ----------  ----------  ----------
21 Total Profit
22 Profit per Unit
23 =================================================================================
```

FIGURE 4-4.
Price-volume analysis with sample numbers

To enter the numbers shown in Figure 4-4, place the cursor on R3C3 and type *10*. Now move the cursor to R4C3 and type *1*. Continue moving the cursor and typing until you type the last number in R8C3. Now press Enter.

Now press the F4 (recalculate) key. In a fraction of a second, your spreadsheet should look like the one in Figure 4-1. You can now see the relationship of price and volume to profit. We tested five selling prices, reducing the price in $1 increments for each test, and projected a sales increase of 2,000 units for each reduction. The prices at the low end of the range, $7 and $6, will sell the most units. The prices in the middle, $8 and $7, will bring in the most sales dollars. But the best price is the one that maximizes the profits. In this case, that price is $9. To save the spreadsheet, type *TS*, and press Enter. Type *Y*.

PRINTING YOUR SPREADSHEET

This spreadsheet is 90 characters wide, including the five characters Multiplan needs for row numbers and a space. It is printed in 12-pitch type on one sheet of 8½-by-11-inch paper.

Setting the Print Margins

Before you print the spreadsheet, you must set the margins.

Leave the cursor where it is:	**Type:**
Start the Print command	P
Select the Margins option	M

Type the following numbers in the margins fields. Tab past those that are already at the proper setting. If you overshoot a field, press Shift-Tab to move the highlight back one field. The highlight is now in the *left* field.

To do this:	**Type or press:**
Specify the number of characters	2
Move the highlight to *top*	Tab
Specify the number of lines	6
Move the highlight to *print width*	Tab
Specify the number of characters	102
Move the highlight to *print length*	Tab
Specify the number of lines	60
Move the highlight to *page length*	Tab
Specify the number of lines	66
Execute the command	Enter

Setting the Print Options

You are still in the Print command. The next step is to set the print options. The options settings are the same for all spreadsheets in this book: Print the entire spreadsheet, print in 12-pitch type, and print row and column numbers. You can find the printer code for 12-pitch type in your printer manual.

Type O to select the Options option. Type in the following responses. (Tab past any fields that already have the proper settings.) The highlight is now in the *area* field.

To do this:	Type or press:
Define the print area	R1:4095
Move the highlight to *setup*	Tab
Enter your printer code for 12-pitch type	(your code)
Move the highlight to *formulas*	Tab Tab
Select *No*	N
Move the highlight to *row-col numbers*	Tab
Select *Yes*	Y
Execute the command	Enter

Now, before you print, store the spreadsheet with these print settings: Press the Escape key to exit the Print command. Leave the cursor where it is. Type *TS*, press Enter, and type *Y*.

Printing the Spreadsheet

Now, turn on your printer and print your spreadsheet.

Leave the cursor where it is:	Type:
Start the Print command	P
Select the Printer option	P

And there's a copy of your spreadsheet.

SPREADSHEET SUMMARY

General: The completed spreadsheet is shown in Figure 4-1. Use Value to enter REPT(" = ",25) and REPT(" − ",25) for long lines. Use Lock Formulas to lock formulas.

Column Width: Use Format Width as follows: Set column 1 to 25 characters wide. Set columns 2 through 6 to 12 characters wide.

Format: Use Format Default Cells to give every cell the dollar code with 0 decimal places, then use Format Cells as follows: Dollar code with 2 decimal places R3C3, R4C3, R8C3, R12C2:6, R14C2:6, R22C2:6. Integer code R5:6C3 and R13C2:6. Continue R1C3:4. Right-justify R1C6 and R10C2:6. Use Format Options to insert commas.

Name: Use Name as follows: R3C3 is PRICE. R4C3 is PDECREASE. R5C3 is VOLUME. R6C3 is VINCREASE. R7C3 is FIXED. R8C3 is VARIABLE.

Print: Price-Volume Analysis is 90 characters wide, including Multiplan row numbers, and is printed in 12-pitch type on 8½-by-11-inch paper. Use Print Margins to set the following margins: *left* 2, *top* 6, *print width* 102, *print length* 60, and *page length* 66.

Formulas: Formulas use relative and named cell references.

1	R12C2	Starting Selling Price PRICE
2	R12C3	Decrease in Selling Price RC[− 1] − PDECREASE
3	R13C2	Starting Volume VOLUME
4	R13C3	Increase in Volume RC[− 1] + VINCREASE
5	R14C2	Fixed Costs per Unit FIXED/R[− 1]C
6	R15C2	Total Fixed Costs FIXED
7	R16C2	Total Variable Costs VARIABLE * R[− 3]C
8	R18C2	Sales Income R[− 6]C * R[− 5]C
9	R19C2	Cost of Goods Sold R[− 4]C + R[− 3]C
10	R21C2	Total Profit R[− 3]C − R[− 2]C
11	R22C2	Profit per Unit R[− 1]C/R[− 9]C
12	R1C6	Spreadsheet Filename NAME()

5

Loan Amortization Analysis

Before you commit yourself or your company to long-term debt, whether it's for day-to-day operations, business expansion, or investment opportunities such as real estate, you need to answer three basic questions: How much money do you need to borrow? How long will you need it? How can you repay it?

Most term loans obtained from commercial lenders are amortized. Loan amortization is the gradual reduction of a debt by a series of equal periodic payments, usually monthly, that are sufficient to meet the interest requirements and liquidate the debt at maturity. Simply put, amortization lets you repay the loan gradually over its life instead of having it fall due all at once.

Figure 5-1 shows a loan amortization spreadsheet that lets you quickly and easily see the effects of a loan so that you can compare the terms offered by different lenders. You make only three entries: The amount you plan to borrow, the interest rate you expect to pay, and the number of years in the loan period. Everything else—monthly repayment, annual repayment, total repayment, interest and principal paid, and principal remaining in each month of the term— is calculated for you. You'll see the mix of principal and interest change from heavy interest payments in the early months of the term to heavy principal payments in the later months and, in the last month of the term, a liquidated loan.

Initially, you'll be creating a spreadsheet that can handle terms of up to 36 months. In the real world, however, mortgage and many other kinds of loans

```
              1                    2                   3              4
1                         LOAN AMORTIZATION ANALYSIS                     AMOR
2    ===========================================================================
3    Amount Financed         $90,000.00
4    Annual Interest (%)         15.00
5    Term in Years                   2
6    Monthly Loan Payment     $4,363.80
7    Annual Loan Payment     $52,365.58
8    Total Loan Payment     $104,731.16
9    ===========================================================================
10          End of              Interest         Principal       Principal
11          Month                 Paid             Paid          Remaining
12   ----------------------------------------------------------------------------
13            1                 1,125.00          3,238.80        86,761.20
14            2                 1,084.52          3,279.28        83,481.92
15            3                 1,043.52          3,320.27        80,161.64
16            4                 1,002.02          3,361.78        76,799.87
17            5                   960.00          3,403.80        73,396.07
18            6                   917.45          3,446.35        69,949.72
19            7                   874.37          3,489.43        66,460.29
20            8                   830.75          3,533.04        62,927.25
21            9                   786.59          3,577.21        59,350.04
22           10                   741.88          3,621.92        55,728.12
23           11                   696.60          3,667.20        52,060.92
24           12                   650.76          3,713.04        48,347.88
25           13                   604.35          3,759.45        44,588.43
26           14                   557.36          3,806.44        40,781.99
27           15                   509.77          3,854.02        36,927.97
28           16                   461.60          3,902.20        33,025.77
29           17                   412.82          3,950.98        29,074.79
30           18                   363.43          4,000.36        25,074.43
31           19                   313.43          4,050.37        21,024.06
32           20                   262.80          4,101.00        16,923.06
33           21                   211.54          4,152.26        12,770.80
34           22                   159.64          4,204.16         8,566.64
35           23                   107.08          4,256.72         4,309.92
36           24                    53.87          4,309.92             0.00
37           25
38           26
39           27
40           28
41           29
42           30
43           31
44           32
45           33
46           34
47           35
48           36
```

FIGURE 5-1.

The completed loan amortization spreadsheet

extend far beyond 36 months. So later in the chapter, you'll expand the spreadsheet to calculate a term of 360 months (30 years).

Because loan amortization plays an essential role in business, this topic shows up elsewhere in this book. The business start-up spreadsheet in Chapter 3 includes a loan repayment amount, which was calculated by using the spreadsheet in this chapter. The cash flow spreadsheet in Chapter 14 shows how to integrate loan amortization formulas into another, very different type of spreadsheet.

The loan amortization spreadsheet contains several IF formulas that test whether a given condition is true or false. You can learn a great deal more about IF formulas in Chapter 16.

If you're familiar with Multiplan and prefer to create this spreadsheet without following the step-by-step instructions, refer to the summary at the end of this chapter.

SETTING UP YOUR SPREADSHEET

Bring up the Multiplan screen. If you turned off automatic recalculation on your last spreadsheet, you can skip the following instructions and go on to "Adjusting the Column Widths." Otherwise, to make data entry faster, leave the cursor on R1C1. Type *O* to start the Options command, type *N* for no recalculation, and press Enter. Now let's make your spreadsheet look like the one in Figure 5-2.

Adjusting the Column Widths

This spreadsheet contains only four columns of information. Therefore, we can increase the width of each column to give the entries ample room and still keep all four columns on the screen. Let's begin by increasing the width of column 1 to 20 characters.

```
                    1                  2                3                 4
 1                            LOAN AMORTIZATION ANALYSIS
 2  ==========================================================================
 3  Amount Financed
 4  Annual Interest (%)
 5  Term in Years
 6  Monthly Loan Payment
 7  Annual Loan Payment
 8  Total Loan Payment
 9  ==========================================================================
10      End of                  Interest          Principal          Principal
11      Month                     Paid              Paid              Remaining
12  --------------------------------------------------------------------------
```

FIGURE 5-2.

The titles and lines on the loan amortization spreadsheet

Leave the cursor on R1C1:	Type or press:
Start the Format command	F
Select the Width option	W
Specify the number of characters in the column	20
Execute the command	Enter

Now increase the widths of columns 2 through 4 to 18 characters each.

Place the cursor on R1C2:	Type or press:
Start the Format command	F
Select the Width option	W
Specify the number of characters in each column	18
Move the highlight to *through*	Tab Tab
Select column 2 through 4	4
Execute the command	Enter

Entering the Titles

The next step is to type the titles (but not the lines) shown in Figure 5-2. The titles in rows 10 and 11 appear to be indented, but they're not: they are right-aligned. Type them as you would any title, and we'll align them later. If you mistype, press the Backspace key (not a direction key) to back up the cursor and erase one character at a time. Now start entering the titles.

Leave the cursor on R1C2:	Type:
Start the Alpha command	A
Type the first title	LOAN AMORTIZATION ANALYSIS

LOAN AMORTIZATION ANALYSIS appears on the command line, where Multiplan displays what you type. You don't have to press Enter to place it in its cell. Simply move the cursor to R3C1, the next cell that will contain a title. When you do so, the words *LOAN AMORTIZATION* appear in cell R1C1. You will see the complete title when you format the cells.

You now see *ALPHA/VALUE* on the command line, which means you can type another title without starting the Alpha command again. Type *Amount Financed* and move your cursor to R4C1. Type *Annual Interest (%)* and move the cursor to the next cell (R5C1). Continue typing titles and moving the cursor. After you type the last title, press Enter.

Entering the Long Lines

Next let's use the REPT function and an equal sign to enter a double line across row 2. We need to put quotation marks around the equal sign to tell Multiplan that the equal sign is text, not a mathematical symbol. Column 1 is 20 characters wide, so we'll create a formula in R2C1 that repeats the equal sign 20 times.

Place the cursor on R2C1:	**Type or press:**
Start the Value command	V
Repeat an equal sign 20 times	REPT(" = ",20)
Execute the command	Enter

Now copy the REPT formula into the columns to the right.

Leave the cursor on R2C1:	**Type or press:**
Start the Copy command	C
Select the Right option	R
Specify the number of cells to copy into	3
Execute the command	Enter

The double line now extends through column 4. The next step is to copy the line from row 2 to row 9. When you see a colon (Multiplan's range operator) in the column on the right side of the following instructions, you can press the F6 key to produce it. It's easier than pressing the Shift and Colon keys.

Leave the cursor on R2C1:	**Type or press:**
Start the Copy command	C
Select the From option	F
(Multiplan displays *COPY FROM cells: R2C1*,the first cell to copy from)	
Specify the last cell to copy from	:4
Move the highlight to *to cells*	Tab
Specify the first cell to copy into	R9C1
Execute the command	Enter

Now use this same technique to enter a single line (minus signs) across row 12: Place the cursor on R12C1 and type *V* (Value). Type *REPT(" – ",20)* and press Enter. Leave the cursor on R12C1 and type *CR* (Copy Right). Multiplan proposes that you copy into 3 cells, a repeat of your last copy instruction. Since 3 is correct, all you do is press Enter.

Formatting the Title and Number Cells

Let's extend the title *LOAN AMORTIZATION ANALYSIS* into the next cell to the right.

Place the cursor on R1C2:	Type or press:
Start the Format command	F
Select the Cells option	C
(Multiplan displays *FORMAT cells: R1C2*, the first cell to be continuous)	
Specify the last cell to format	:3
Move the highlight to *format code*	Tab Tab
Select *Cont* (continuous)	C
Execute the command	Enter

Now center the title *End of Month* (R10C1 and R11C1), and apply the centered format to the first cell (R13C1) that will contain a month number. Later, we'll copy the formula you enter in R13C1 down the column. This process will copy the centering, too.

Place the cursor on R10C1:	Type or press:
Start the Format command	F
Select the Cells option	C
(Multiplan displays *FORMAT cells: R10C1*, the first cell to format)	
Specify the last cell to format	:R13C1
Move the highlight to *alignment*	Tab
Select *Ctr* (center)	C
Execute the command	Enter

Next, right-justify the titles in rows 10 and 11 (columns 2 through 4) and R1C4, the cell that will contain the spreadsheet filename.

Place the cursor on R10C2:	**Type or press:**
Start the Format command	F
Select the Cells option	C
(Multiplan displays *FORMAT cells: R10C2,* the first cell to format)	
Specify the other cells to format	:R11C4,R1C4
Move the highlight to *alignment*	Tab
Select *Right*	R
Execute the command	Enter

Now let's have Multiplan show the amount financed (R3C2), monthly loan payment (R6C2), annual loan payment (R7C2), and total loan payment (R8C2) in dollars and cents.

Place the cursor on R3C2:	**Type or press:**
Start the Format command	F
Select the Cells option	C
(Multiplan displays *FORMAT cells: R3C2,* the first cell to format)	
Specify the other cells to format	,R6:8C2
Move the highlight to *format code*	Tab Tab
Select *$*	$
Execute the command	Enter

Now let's give the fixed format with two decimal places to the cell that will contain the annual interest rate (R4C2) and to the first two rows (13 and 14) in the columns that will hold the interest paid, principal paid, and principal remaining. Later, we'll copy the formulas you enter in these two rows down the columns. Doing so will carry the fixed format into the other cells.

Place the cursor on R4C2:	**Type or press:**
Start the Format command	F
Select the Cells option	C
(Multiplan displays *FORMAT cells: R4C2,* the first cell to format)	

Specify the other cells to format	,R13:14C2:4
Move the highlight to *format code*	Tab Tab
Select *Fix*	F
Move the highlight to *# of decimals*	Tab
Specify the number of decimals	2
Execute the command	Enter

Inserting Commas in the Large Numbers

To make the large numbers easy to read, tell Multiplan to insert commas in them.

Leave the cursor where it is:	Type or press:
Start the Format command	F
Select the Options option	O
(The highlight is on *No* in the *commas* field)	
Select *Yes*	Y
Execute the command	Enter

NAMING THE CELLS

You can give cells plain English names, then use these names in formulas to make your formulas easy to create and understand. The unshaded areas in Figure 5-3 show the locations of named cells. Let's start by naming R3C2 (the amount financed) LOAN.

Place the cursor on R3C2:	Type or press:
Start the Name command	N
Name the cell	LOAN

In the *to refer to* field at the right of your screen, you can see cell location R3C2. Since this is correct, all you do is press Enter.

Follow this procedure to name the other cells, and be sure to press Enter after typing each name.

Place the cursor on:	Name the cell:
R4C2	RATE
R5C2	TERM
R6C2	PAY

```
                    1                   2              3                4
 1                        LOAN AMORTIZATION ANALYSIS                      ⑩AMOR
 2   ============================================================================
 3   Amount Financed                          LOAN
 4   Annual Interest (%)           15.00       RATE
 5   Term in Years                    2        TERM
 6   Monthly Loan Payment         $0.00 ❶     PAY
 7   Annual Loan Payment          $0.00 ❷
 8   Total Loan Payment           $0.00 ❸
 9   ============================================================================
10          End of              Interest       Principal        Principal
11          Month                 Paid           Paid          Remaining
12   ----------------------------------------------------------------------------
13           1 ❹                 0.00 ❺         0.00 ❼        ❽0.00
14           2                    0.00 ❻         0.00          ❾0.00
15           3                    0.00           0.00           0.00
16           4                    0.00           0.00           0.00
17           5                    0.00           0.00           0.00
18           6                    0.00           0.00           0.00
19           7                    0.00           0.00           0.00
20           8                    0.00           0.00           0.00
21           9                    0.00           0.00           0.00
22          10                    0.00           0.00           0.00
23          11                    0.00           0.00           0.00
24          12                    0.00           0.00           0.00
25          13                    0.00           0.00           0.00
26          14                    0.00           0.00           0.00
27          15                    0.00           0.00           0.00
28          16                    0.00           0.00           0.00
29          17                    0.00           0.00           0.00
30          18                    0.00           0.00           0.00
31          19                    0.00           0.00           0.00
32          20                    0.00           0.00           0.00
33          21                    0.00           0.00           0.00
34          22                    0.00           0.00           0.00
35          23                    0.00           0.00           0.00
36          24                    0.00           0.00           0.00
37          25
38          26
39          27
40          28
41          29
42          30
43          31
44          32
45          33
46          34
47          35
48          36
```

FIGURE 5-3.

Loan amortization analysis sample numbers, named cells, and formula locations

Saving and Naming the Spreadsheet

Now store your spreadsheet on disk with the titles, lines, formats, and cell names, and give the spreadsheet its own filename. If you need to tell Multiplan which drive contains your data disk, type the drive letter or pathname and press F6 (to produce a colon) *before* you type *AMOR*, the filename.

Leave the cursor where it is:	Type or press:
Start the Transfer command	T
Select the Save option	S
Name the spreadsheet	AMOR
Execute the command	Enter

ENTERING THE SAMPLE NUMBERS

To prevent error messages from appearing when you enter the formulas, type in the following numbers:

1. Place the cursor on R4C2 (the cell for the annual interest rate). Type *15* without decimal places. (The formatting you did earlier enters the decimal places for you.)

2. Move the cursor to R5C2 (the cell for the term in years). Type *2* and press Enter.

ENTERING THE FORMULAS

Figure 5-3 shows the locations of the formulas that perform your calculations. They use relative and named cell references. The left column in the following instructions shows the cell locations, cell names, and other elements that the formula works with. The column on the right and the line immediately below the formula heading show the finished formula.

To build a formula, you move the cursor to each cell location shown in the left column (Multiplan will produce the relative notation) and type everything else—operators, symbols, function names, and cell names. When you type a character, the cursor returns to the formula cell so that you can type another character, move the cursor to another cell, or enter the formula.

When your formula agrees with the one in the following instructions, press Enter. If Multiplan then displays *Not a valid formula*, check each character.

Use the F7 through F10 keys to move the highlight, and correct the problem by typing missing characters or pressing the Delete key to delete unwanted characters. Or, you can start the formula from scratch by simply pressing the Escape key and beginning again.

FORMULA 1: Monthly Loan Payment

ABS(PMT(RATE%/12,TERM * 12,LOAN))

Formula 1 amortizes the loan as a series of equal monthly payments including principal and interest and enters the result in R6C2. The PMT (payment) function calculates the amount of each payment based on the monthly interest rate, the number of payments, and the amount of the loan (R3C2, LOAN).

To get the monthly interest rate, the formula divides the annual interest rate (R4C2, RATE) by 12. To get the number of payments, it multiplies the term in years (R5C2, TERM) by 12. Because a payment is an outflow of funds, the result of the PMT function is negative. The ABS (absolute) function converts the negative result to a positive result. All the cell locations are named, so type the entire formula.

	Type or press:
Place the cursor on R6C2:	
Start the Value command	V
Enter the formula: ABS(PMT (RATE%/12,TERM * 12,LOAN))	ABS(PMT(RATE%/12, TERM * 12,LOAN))
Execute the command	Enter

FORMULA 2: Annual Loan Payment

PAY * 12

Formula 2 multiplies the monthly loan payment (R6C2, PAY) by 12 and enters the annual loan payment in R7C2. Type the entire formula.

	Type or press:
Place the cursor on R7C2:	
Start the Value command	V
Enter the formula: PAY * 12	PAY * 12
Execute the command	Enter

FORMULA 3: Total Loan Payment

PAY * TERM * 12

Formula 3 multiplies the monthly loan payment (R6C2, PAY) by the term in months (the years in R5C2, TERM, multiplied by 12) and enters the total loan payment during the life of the loan in R8C2. Type the entire formula.

Place the cursor on R8C2:	**Type or press:**
Start the Value command	V
Enter the formula: PAY * TERM * 12	PAY * TERM * 12
Execute the command	Enter

FORMULA 4: Month Numbers

ROW() − 12

Formula 4 uses the ROW function to show consecutive month numbers in column 1. If we entered *ROW()*, Multiplan would display the row number of the cell the formula is in. Since we want month number 1 on Multiplan's row 13, we'll have the formula subtract 12 from the row number. Type the entire formula.

Place the cursor on R13C1:	**Type or press:**
Start the Value command	V
Enter the formula: ROW() − 12	ROW() − 12
Execute the command	Enter

Month 1 appears. To show a total of 36 month numbers, copy Formula 4 down column 1.

Leave the cursor on R13C1:	**Type or press:**
Start the Copy command	C
Select the Down option	D
Specify the number of cells to copy into	35
Execute the command	Enter

Press the F4 (recalculate) key to show the month numbers.

FORMULA 5: Interest Paid—Month 1

LOAN * RATE%/12

Formula 5 multiplies the amount financed (R3C2, LOAN) by the annual interest rate (R4C2, RATE) converted into a monthly interest rate and enters the interest paid in the first month in R13C2. Again, type the entire formula.

Place the cursor on R13C2:	Type or press:
Start the Value command	V
Enter the formula: LOAN * RATE%/12	LOAN * RATE%/12
Execute the command	Enter

FORMULA 6: Interest Paid—Month 2

IF(RC[− 1]< = TERM * 12,R[− 1]C[+ 2] * RATE%/12,"")

Formula 6 calculates the interest paid in the second month. The result is based on the three parts of the IF function: the Test statement, the Then statement, and the Else statement. The Test statement compares the term in months (R5C2, TERM, converted into months) with the month number in column 1. If the month number is less than or equal to the term in months, the Then statement multiplies the principal remaining at the end of the first month (R13C4) by the monthly interest rate (R4C2, RATE, converted into months) and enters the result in R14C2. If the month number is greater than the term in months, the Else statement ("") makes the cell appear blank. This "invisible" answer prevents a string of zeros from appearing down the column after the month the loan is liquidated.

Place the cursor on R14C2:	Type or move the cursor:
Start the Value command	V
Enter the formula: IF(R14C1 < = TERM * 12,R13C4 * RATE%/12,"")	IF(RC[− 1]< = TERM * 12, R[− 1]C[+ 2] * RATE%/12,"")
Translation: IF(month is less than or equal to the term in months, then enter principal remaining times interest rate, else display nothing)	
Execute the command	Enter

To calculate the interest paid during each successive month of the term, copy Formula 6 down column 2: Leave the cursor on R14C2 and type *CD* (Copy Down). Type *34* (the number of cells to copy into) and press Enter. We now have 36 cells in column 2 for interest paid, the same as the number of month cells in column 1.

FORMULA 7: Principal Paid

IF(RC[− 2]< = TERM * 12,PAY − RC[− 1],"")

Formula 7 calculates the principal paid at the end of the first month (R13C3) by deducting the interest paid (R13C2) from the monthly loan payment (R6C2, PAY). As in Formula 6, the Else statement prevents zeros from appearing when the month number is greater than the term you select.

Place the cursor on R13C3:	Type or move the cursor:
Start the Value command	V
Enter the formula: IF(R13C1 < = TERM * 12,PAY − R13C2,"")	IF(RC[− 2]< = TERM * 12, PAY − RC[− 1],"")
Translation: IF(month is less than or equal to the term in months, then enter monthly loan payment minus interest paid, else display nothing)	
Execute the command	Enter

To calculate the principal paid during each successive month of the term, copy Formula 7 down column 3: Leave the cursor on R13C3 and type *CD* (Copy Down). Type *35* (the number of cells to copy into) and press Enter. We now have 36 principal paid cells in column 3, the same as the number of months cells in column 1.

FORMULA 8: Principal Remaining — Month 1

LOAN − RC[− 1]

Formula 8 deducts the principal paid (R13C3) from the amount of the loan (R3C2, LOAN) and enters the principal remaining at the end of the first month in R13C4.

Place the cursor on R13C4:	Type or move the cursor:
Start the Value command	V

Enter the formula: LOAN – R13C3	LOAN – RC[– 1]
Execute the command	Enter

FORMULA 9: Principal Remaining—Month 2

$$IF(RC[-3] < = TERM * 12, R[-1]C - RC[-1], "")$$

Formula 9 subtracts the principal paid in the second month (R14C3) from the principal remaining in the first month (R13C4) and enters the principal remaining in the second month in R14C4. The double quotes prevent zeros from appearing in column 4 after the loan is liquidated.

Place the cursor on R14C4:	**Type or move the cursor:**
Start the Value command	V
Enter the formula: IF(R14C1 $< = TERM * 12, R13C4$ $- R14C3, "")$	$IF(RC[-3] < = TERM * 12,$ $R[-1]C - RC[-1], "")$
Translation: IF(month is less than or equal to the term in months, then enter month 1 principal remaining minus month 2 principal paid, else display nothing)	
Execute the command	Enter

To calculate the principal remaining during each successive month of the term, copy Formula 9 down column 4: Leave the cursor on R14C4 and type *CD* (Copy Down). Type *34* and press Enter. We now have 36 principal remaining cells in column 4, the same as the number of months cells in column 1.

FORMULA 10: Spreadsheet Filename

NAME()

As a final touch, have Multiplan generate the spreadsheet filename in R1C4. Type the function name and parentheses.

Place the cursor on R1C4:	**Type or press:**
Start the Value command	V
Enter the formula: NAME()	NAME()
Execute the command	Enter

This completes the formulas.

CALCULATING LOAN AMORTIZATION

This is the moment when all your work pays off. To give the formulas something to work with, place the cursor on R3C2 (the cell for the amount financed). Type *90000* and press Enter. Now press the F4 (recalculate) key. Your spreadsheet should look like the one in Figure 5-1. The principal remaining at the end of month 24 (row 36) is zero. The debt has been liquidated on schedule, and the IF formulas have worked their magic—there are no visible entries below row 36 except for the month numbers in column 1.

LOCKING AND SAVING THE FORMULAS

To prevent accidental alteration, lock the formulas and titles.

Leave the cursor where it is:	**Type:**
Start the Lock command	L
Select the Formulas option	F
(Multiplan displays *Enter Y to confirm*)	
Execute the command	Y

Now store all the formulas on disk. Because you saved the spreadsheet before, Multiplan asks you to confirm your intention to overwrite the earlier version.

Leave the cursor where it is:	**Type or press:**
Start the Transfer command	T
Select the Save option	S
(Multiplan displays *AMOR*, so there's no need to retype)	
Execute the command	Enter
(Multiplan displays *Enter Y to overwrite file*)	
Confirm the overwrite	Y

PRINTING YOUR SPREADSHEET

This spreadsheet is 79 characters wide including Multiplan row numbers and is printed in 12-pitch type on one sheet of 8½-by-11-inch paper.

Setting the Print Margins

The first step before printing is to set the margins.

Leave the cursor where it is:	Type or press:
Start the Print command	P
Select the Margins option	M

Type the following numbers in the margins fields. Tab past those that are already at the proper settings. If you overshoot a field, press Shift-Tab to move back one field or press Tab a few times to move full circle through the fields. The highlight is in the *left* field.

To do this:	Type or press:
Specify the number of characters	8
Move the highlight to *top*	Tab
Specify the number of lines	6
Move the highlight to *print width*	Tab
Specify the number of characters	102
Move the highlight to *print length*	Tab
Specify the number of lines	60
Move the highlight to *page length*	Tab
Specify the number of lines	66
Execute the command	Enter

Setting the Print Options

You are still in the Print command. The next step is to set the print options. The options settings (the same for all the spreadsheets in this book) print the entire spreadsheet in 12-pitch type with row and column numbers. You can find the printer code for 12-pitch type in your printer manual. Now type O to select the Options option. Type in the following responses. Tab past any field that already has the proper setting. The highlight is in the *area* field.

To do this:	Type or press:
Define the print area	R1:4095
Move the highlight to *setup*	Tab
Enter your printer code for 12-pitch type	(your code)

Move the highlight to *formulas*	Tab Tab
Select *No*	N
Move the highlight to *row-col numbers*	Tab
Select *Yes*	Y
Execute the command	Enter

Now before you print, store the spreadsheet with the print settings: Exit the Print command by pressing the Escape key. Leave the cursor where it is. Type *TS* (Transfer Save) and press Enter. Type *Y* to confirm the overwrite.

Printing Your Spreadsheet

Now turn on your printer and print of your spreadsheet.

Leave the cursor where it is:	**Type:**
Start the Print command	P
Select the Printer option	P

And there's a copy of your spreadsheet.

CALCULATING A LONG-TERM LOAN

To see how your formulas work, let's increase the length of term to 30 years. Place the cursor on R5C2. Type *30* and press Enter. Now press F4 to make your spreadsheet look like the one in Figure 5-4.

It's easy to modify your spreadsheet to calculate the interest paid, principal paid, and principal remaining for all 360 months of a 30-year loan. First, store the spreadsheet under the filename AMOR1 so that you have two versions— the short-term AMOR and the long-term AMOR1: Leave the cursor where it is and type *TS* (Transfer Save). Press the F8 key to jump the highlight to the end of the filename. Type *1* and press Enter.

Now copy the formulas into the new rows: Press the End key to jump the cursor to row 48. Place the cursor on R48C1 and type *CF* (Copy From). Type *:4* and press the Tab key to move the highlight to *to cells*. Type *R49:372C1* and press Enter. Press the F4 key to recalculate the spreadsheet. To jump to the end of the spreadsheet, press the End key. At the 360th month (row 372), the interest paid is *14.05,* the principal paid is *1,123.95,* and the principal remaining is *0.00.* Not bad for 30 years.

```
             1                    2                 3              4
 1                       LOAN AMORTIZATION ANALYSIS                        AMOR1
 2  =================================================================================
 3  Amount Financed          $90,000.00
 4  Annual Interest (%)           15.00
 5  Term in Years                    30
 6  Monthly Loan Payment      $1,138.00
 7  Annual Loan Payment      $13,656.00
 8  Total Loan Payment      $409,679.86
 9  =================================================================================
10      End of               Interest          Principal        Principal
11       Month                  Paid              Paid           Remaining
12  ---------------------------------------------------------------------------------
13         1                 1,125.00             13.00          89,987.00
14         2                 1,124.84             13.16          89,973.84
15         3                 1,124.67             13.33          89,960.51
16         4                 1,124.51             13.49          89,947.02
17         5                 1,124.34             13.66          89,933.36
18         6                 1,124.17             13.83          89,919.52
19         7                 1,123.99             14.01          89,905.52
20         8                 1,123.82             14.18          89,891.34
21         9                 1,123.64             14.36          89,876.98
22        10                 1,123.46             14.54          89,862.44
23        11                 1,123.28             14.72          89,847.72
24        12                 1,123.10             14.90          89,832.82
25        13                 1,122.91             15.09          89,817.73
26        14                 1,122.72             15.28          89,802.45
27        15                 1,122.53             15.47          89,786.98
28        16                 1,122.34             15.66          89,771.32
29        17                 1,122.14             15.86          89,755.46
30        18                 1,121.94             16.06          89,739.41
31        19                 1,121.74             16.26          89,723.15
32        20                 1,121.54             16.46          89,706.69
33        21                 1,121.33             16.67          89,690.02
34        22                 1,121.13             16.87          89,673.15
35        23                 1,120.91             17.09          89,656.06
36        24                 1,120.70             17.30          89,638.77
37        25                 1,120.48             17.52          89,621.25
38        26                 1,120.27             17.73          89,603.52
39        27                 1,120.04             17.96          89,585.56
40        28                 1,119.82             18.18          89,567.38
41        29                 1,119.59             18.41          89,548.97
42        30                 1,119.36             18.64          89,530.34
43        31                 1,119.13             18.87          89,511.47
44        32                 1,118.89             19.11          89,492.36
45        33                 1,118.65             19.35          89,473.01
46        34                 1,118.41             19.59          89,453.43
47        35                 1,118.17             19.83          89,433.60
48        36                 1,117.92             20.08          89,413.52
49        37                 1,117.67             20.33          89,393.18
50        38                 1,117.41             20.58          89,372.60
51        39                 1,117.16             20.84          89,351.76
52        40                 1,116.90             21.10          89,330.66
53        41                 1,116.63             21.37          89,309.29
54        42                 1,116.37             21.63          89,287.66
```

FIGURE 5-4.

Amortization spreadsheet for a loan with a 30-year term, first page

Printing Page Numbers

This spreadsheet prints on several pages, so it makes sense to number the pages. We'll put the page numbers at the bottoms of the pages as footers. The first step is to enter the code—an ampersand and the letter P—that tells Multiplan to print page numbers. The style we'll use prints a dash before and after the page number. Press the Home key to jump the cursor to R1C1.

Place the cursor on R3C5:	Type or press:
Start the Alpha command	A
Identify the page number code and style (hyphen space &P space hyphen)	- &P -
Execute the command	Enter

Next, identify the page number code as a footer and tell Multiplan its location. We can leave two blank lines between the last row printed on each page and the page number by including the two empty cells above the page-number code in the footer location.

Leave the cursor where it is:	Type or press:
Start the Print command	P
Select the Heading option	H
Move the highlight to *footer*	Tab
Specify the cell location	R1:3C5
Execute the command	Enter

Changing the Print Settings

You are still in the Print command. The next step is to modify the print settings to allow for more rows per page by reducing the top margin from 6 to 4 lines: Type *M* to select the Margins option. Press Tab to move to the *top* field and type *4*.

Now we want to set a print width that will center the page number on the page: Press Tab to move to the *print width* field and type *86*.

Next, we need to reduce the print length by two lines to allow for the page number at the bottom of each page: Press the Tab key again to move the highlight to the *print length* field. Type *58* and press Enter.

Now change the print area to keep the footer input from printing: You're still in the Print command, so type *O* to select the Options option. The highlight is in the *area* field. Type *R1:372C1:4* and press Enter. Press Escape to exit the Print command, so you can store the spreadsheet on disk: Leave the cursor where it is. Type *TS* (Transfer Save) and press Enter. Type *Y* to overwrite.

You're all set to print. Be sure your printer is turned on. Type *PP* (Print Printer). Now settle back and relax while Multiplan presents a page-numbered spreadsheet for a 30-year loan.

SPREADSHEET SUMMARY

General: The completed spreadsheet is shown in Figure 5-1. Use Options to set automatic recalculation to *No*. Use Value to enter REPT(" = ",20) and REPT(" − ",20) for long lines. Use Lock Formulas to lock the formulas.

Column Width: Use Format Width as follows: Set column 1 to 20 characters wide. Set columns 2 through 4 to 18 characters wide.

Format: Use Format Cells as follows: Continue R1C2:3. Center R10:48C1. Right-justify R10C2:R11C4 and R1C4. Dollar code R3C2 and R6:8C2. Fix code with 2 decimal places R4C2 and R13C2:R48C4. Use Format Options to insert commas.

Name: Use Name as follows: R3C2 is LOAN. R4C2 is RATE. R5C2 is TERM. R6C2 is PAY.

Print: Loan Amortization Analysis is 79 characters wide, including Multiplan row numbers, and is printed in 12-pitch type on 8½-by-11-inch paper. Use Print Margins to set the following margins: *left* 8, *top* 6, *print width* 102, *print length* 60, and *page length* 66. For the long-term version, change the *top* setting to 4, the *print width* setting to 86, and the *print length* setting to 58 to squeeze more lines on the page and to allow for the page number footer. Use Print Heading to locate the footer in R1:3C5.

Formulas: Formulas use relative and named cell references.

1	R6C2	Monthly Loan Payment ABS(PMT(RATE%/12,TERM * 12,LOAN))
2	R7C2	Annual Loan Payment PAY * 12
3	R8C2	Total Loan Payment PAY * TERM * 12
4	R13C1	Month Numbers ROW() − 12

5	R13C2	Interest Paid—Month 1
		LOAN * RATE%/12
6	R14C2	Interest Paid—Month 2
		IF(RC[– 1]< = TERM * 12,
		R[– 1]C[+ 2] * RATE%/12,"")
7	R13C3	Principal Paid
		IF(RC[– 2]< = TERM * 12,
		PAY – RC[– 1],"")
8	R13C4	Principal Remaining—Month 1
		LOAN – RC[– 1]
9	R14C4	Principal Remaining—Month 2
		IF(R[– 3]< = TERM * 12,
		R[– 1]C – RC[– 1],"")
10	R1C4	Spreadsheet Filename
		NAME()

6

Economic Order Quantity (EOQ) Analysis

Effective inventory management means keeping inventory at optimum levels and converting it to cash at a profit. If you carry too much inventory, your operating expenses will balloon because of greater handling and storage costs, deterioration and obsolescence, increased taxes and insurance, and excessive working capital tied up in stock. However, if you carry too little inventory, you face lost sales, costly production delays, expensive rush orders, and ordering in uneconomical quantities.

Choosing the best quantity to order is a matter of balancing ordering costs and inventory costs. Placing many small orders produces high ordering costs. Placing a few large orders produces high inventory costs. Do the savings on less frequent ordering outweigh the costs of carrying inventory?

In this chapter, we'll develop a spreadsheet that shows the economic order quantity, or EOQ—that point at which the total ordering cost plus the total carrying cost is at a minimum. When you enter the amount of an item you need and its acquisition and possession costs, the formulas automatically calculate the EOQ. Other formulas calculate the costs when a quantity discount is available, letting you compare the EOQ with the discount cost to determine if it is advantageous to order more than the EOQ of goods. Figure 6-1 shows the completed spreadsheet.

```
        1        2        3        4        5        6        7
                            ECONOMIC ORDER QUANTITY ANALYSIS          EOQ
1
2   =====================================================================
3   Purchased Item                            Oak Cabinet
4   Item Number                                A-6230-3
5   -----------------------------------------------------------------
6   Annual Requirement in Units                1,000
7   Regular Price per Unit                     $100
8   Acquisition Cost per Order                 $50
9   Annual Possession (%)                      40.0
10  Annual Possession Cost per Unit            $40
11  Economic Order Level in Units              50
12  -----------------------------------------------------------------
13  Discount Order Level in Units              100
14  Quantity Discount (%)                      5.0
15  Discount Price per Unit                    $95
16  Discount Annual Possess Cost per Unit      $38
17  -----------------------------------------------------------------
18  Economic Order Cost per Year               $102,000
19  Discount Order Cost per Year               $97,400
20  Discount Savings (Loss) per Year           $4,600
21  =====================================================================
```

Order Size in Units	EOQ	Orders per Year	Acquisition Cost per Year	Possession Cost per Year	Acq & Poss Cost per Year	Discount Poss Cost per Year
20		50	$2,500	$400	$2,900	$380
30		33	$1,667	$600	$2,267	$570
40		25	$1,250	$800	$2,050	$760
50	<<<<<<	20	$1,000	$1,000	$2,000	$950
60		17	$833	$1,200	$2,033	$1,140
70		14	$714	$1,400	$2,114	$1,330
80		13	$625	$1,600	$2,225	$1,520
90		11	$556	$1,800	$2,356	$1,710
100		10	$500	$2,000	$2,500	$1,900
110		9	$455	$2,200	$2,655	$2,090
120		8	$417	$2,400	$2,817	$2,280
130		8	$385	$2,600	$2,985	$2,470
140		7	$357	$2,800	$3,157	$2,660
150		7	$333	$3,000	$3,333	$2,850
160		6	$313	$3,200	$3,513	$3,040
170		6	$294	$3,400	$3,694	$3,230
180		6	$278	$3,600	$3,878	$3,420
190		5	$263	$3,800	$4,063	$3,610
200		5	$250	$4,000	$4,250	$3,800

FIGURE 6-1.
The completed EOQ spreadsheet

One of the interesting features of this spreadsheet is its use of three tables designed for use with the LOOKUP function. These tables consist entirely of existing cells, some of which have three different names. The formulas use these tables to extract the economic order cost and discount order cost for the year. Chapter 17 provides a detailed explanation of lookup tables. The formulas in our EOQ spreadsheet also use the IF function. You can find details about IF in Chapter 16.

If you're familiar with Multiplan and prefer to create this spreadsheet without following the step-by-step instructions, refer to the summary at the end of this chapter.

SETTING UP YOUR SPREADSHEET

Bring up the Multiplan screen. If you turned off automatic recalculation on your last spreadsheet, you can skip the following step and go directly to the next step, "Adjusting the Column Widths." Otherwise, to make data entry faster, leave the cursor on R1C1. Type O to start the Options command, type N for no recalculation, and press Enter. Now let's make your spreadsheet look like the one in Figure 6-2.

```
            1        2       3        4           5          6          7
 1                              ECONOMIC ORDER QUANTITY ANALYSIS
 2 ========================================================================
 3 Purchased Item
 4 Item Number
 5 -----------------------------------------------------------------------
 6 Annual Requirement in Units
 7 Regular Price per Unit
 8 Acquisition Cost per Order
 9 Annual Possession (%)
10 Annual Possession Cost per Unit
11 Economic Order Level in Units
12 -----------------------------------------------------------------------
13 Discount Order Level in Units
14 Quantity Discount (%)
15 Discount Price per Unit
16 Discount Annual Possess Cost per Unit
17 -----------------------------------------------------------------------
18 Economic Order Cost per Year
19 Discount Order Cost per Year
20 Discount Savings (Loss) per Year
21 ========================================================================
22  Order           Orders  Acquisition  Possession  Acq & Poss   Discount
23  Size             per       Cost         Cost        Cost      Poss Cost
24 in Units   EOQ    Year    per Year     per Year    per Year    per Year
25 -----------------------------------------------------------------------
```

FIGURE 6-2.

The titles and lines on the EOQ analysis spreadsheet

Adjusting the Column Widths

To give the entries the space they need and to allow for all seven columns of information on the screen at one time, let's adjust the column widths. Start by reducing the width of column 1 from 10 characters to 9 characters.

Leave the cursor on R1C1:	Type or press:
Start the Format command	F
Select the Width option	W
Specify the number of characters in the column	9
Execute the command	Enter

Reduce the width of column 2 in the same way: Place the cursor on R1C2 and type *FW* (Format Width). Type *8* and press Enter. Now increase the width of columns 4 through 7 to 12 characters. (We'll leave column 3 at the default column width of 10 characters.)

Place the cursor on R1C4:	Type or press:
Start the Format command	F
Select the Width option	W
Specify the number of characters in each column	12
Move the highlight to *through*	Tab Tab
Select column 4 through 7	7
Execute the command	Enter

Entering the Titles

The next step is to type the titles shown in Figure 6-2. Only a portion of the long titles (ECONOMIC ORDER QUANTITY ANALYSIS in row 1 and most of the titles in rows 3 through 20 of column 1) will appear in their cells when you enter them. We'll take care of that shortly when we format the titles.

First, put Multiplan in the alpha/value mode to make entering the titles quick and easy.

Leave the cursor where it is:	Type or press:
Start the Options command	O
Move the highlight to *alpha/value*	Tab (four times)
Select *Yes*	Y
Execute the command	Enter

ALPHA/VALUE now replaces the command menu and will remain active until you cancel it after you enter all the titles. If you mistype a title, you can:

■ Press Backspace (not a direction key) to erase one character at a time.

■ Use the F7 through F10 keys to move the highlight through the title without erasing. You can then type missing characters or press the Delete key to delete unwanted characters.

Now type *ECONOMIC ORDER QUANTITY ANALYSIS* and move the cursor to R3C1, the next cell that contains a title. As you can see, you don't have to press Enter to enter a title into its cell. Moving the cursor serves the same purpose. Now type *Purchased Item* and move the cursor to R4C1. Type *Item Number* and move the cursor to the next cell. Continue in this way, typing a title and moving the cursor, until you type all the titles. When you finish the last title, press Enter.

Press Escape to return the command menu to the screen. Now turn off the alpha/value mode: Leave the cursor where it is and type O (Options). Press the Tab key four times to move the highlight to *alpha/value*. Type *N* to select *No* and press Enter.

Entering the Long Lines

Lines separate the entries into easy-to-read categories. Reading from the top down, the first category contains the item and item number, the second shows the item with no discount, the third shows the item with a discount, and the fourth shows a comparison of costs with and without a discount. The final category, in the lower half of the spreadsheet, contains the calculations related to the item you want to analyze.

Let's use the REPT function and an equal sign to enter a double line in R2C1. To avoid gaps in the line when it's copied across row 2, we'll repeat the sign enough times to fill any cell, even the widest in columns 4 through 7.

Place the cursor on R2C1:	Type or press:
Start the Value command	V
Repeat an equal sign 12 times	REPT(" = ",12)
Execute the command	Enter

Now copy the REPT formula into the columns to the right.

Leave the cursor on R2C1:	Type or press:
Start the Copy command	C
Select the Right option	R

| Specify the number of cells to copy into | 6 |
| Execute the command | Enter |

Next, copy the entire row of formulas to row 21. (Remember, you can produce a colon by pressing the F6 key.)

Leave the cursor on R2C1:	**Type or press:**
Start the Copy command	C
Select the From option	F
(Multiplan displays *COPY FROM cells: R2C1,* the first cell to copy from)	
Specify the last cell to copy from	:7
Move the highlight to *to cells*	Tab
Specify the first cell to copy into	R21C1
Execute the command	Enter

Now use the REPT function and a minus sign to enter a single line in R5C1.

Place the cursor on R5C1:	**Type or press:**
Start the Value command	V
Repeat a minus sign 12 times	REPT(" − ",12)
Execute the command	Enter

Copy the REPT formula into the columns to the right: Leave the cursor on R5C1 and type *CR* (Copy Right). Multiplan "remembered" your last Copy command and proposes 6 as the number of cells to copy into. Since this is correct, all you need to do is press Enter.

Other rows also need single lines, so copy the REPT formulas from row 5 to rows 12, 17, and 25.

Leave the cursor on R5C1:	**Type or press:**
Start the Copy command	C
Select the From option	F
(Multiplan displays *COPY FROM cells: R5C1,* the first cell to copy from)	
Specify the last column to copy from	:7
Move the highlight to *to cells*	Tab
Specify the first cell in each row to copy into	R12C1,R17C1,R25C1
Execute the command	Enter

Formatting the Title Cells

Next, let's display the long titles completely by continuing them into the cells to their right. These are ECONOMIC ORDER QUANTITY ANALYSIS in row 1 and the titles in rows 3 through 20 of column 1.

Place the cursor on R1C4:	**Type or press:**
Start the Format command	F
Select the Cells option	C
(Multiplan displays *FORMAT cells: R1C4,* the first cell to be continuous)	
Specify the other cells to be continuous	:6,R3:20C1:4
Move the highlight to *format code*	Tab Tab
Select *Cont* (continuous)	C
Execute the command	Enter

Next, right-justify the cells that will contain the spreadsheet filename (R1C7), the item (R3C5), and the item number (R4C5).

Place the cursor on R1C7:	**Type or press:**
Start the Format command	F
Select the Cells option	C
(Multiplan displays *FORMAT cells: R1C7,* the cell to format)	
Specify the other cells to format	,R3:4C5
Move the highlight to *alignment*	Tab
Select *Right*	R
Execute the command	Enter

Now center the titles in rows 22 through 24 of columns 1 through 7.

Place the cursor on R22C1:	**Type or press:**
Start the Format command	F
Select the Cells option	C
(Multiplan displays *FORMAT cells: R22C1,* the first cell to format)	
Specify the last cell to format	:R24C7
Move the highlight to *alignment*	Tab
Select *Ctr* (center)	C
Execute the command	Enter

Formatting the Number Cells

Most of the numbers are dollar amounts, so let's make the dollar format with no decimal places the standard format on this spreadsheet. (We'll reformat the cells that take other formats.)

Leave the cursor on R22C1:	**Type or press:**
Start the Format command	F
Select the Default option	D
Select the Cells option	C
Move the highlight to *format code*	Tab
Select *$*	$
Move the highlight to *# of decimals*	Tab
Specify the number of decimal places	0
Execute the command	Enter

Now override the dollar format in the cells that contain the annual requirements (R6C5), economic order level (R11C5), and discount order level (R13C5). Give these cells an integer format.

Place the cursor on R6C5:	**Type or press:**
Start the Format command	F
Select the Cells option	C
(Multiplan displays *FORMAT cells: R6C5,* the first cell to format)	
Specify the other cells to format	,R11C5,R13C5
Move the highlight to *format code*	Tab Tab
Select *Int* (integer)	I
Execute the command	Enter

Now format the cells that will contain percentages—the annual possession amount (R9C5) and quantity discount amount (R14C5)—to a fixed format with one decimal place.

Place the cursor on R9C5:	**Type or press:**
Start the Format command	F
Select the Cells option	C
(Multiplan displays *FORMAT cells: R9C5,* the first cell to format)	

Specify the other cell to format	,R14C5
Move the highlight to *format code*	Tab Tab
Select *Fix*	F
Move the highlight to *# of decimals*	Tab
Specify the number of decimals	1
Execute the command	Enter

Next, center only the cells in rows 26 and 27 of columns 1 through 3, and format them to an integer code at the same time. When you copy the formulas you'll enter in rows 26 and 27 down the columns, they'll carry the centered integer format into the other cells at the same time.

Place the cursor on R26C1:	**Type or press:**
Start the Format command	F
Select the Cells option	C
(Multiplan displays *FORMAT cells: R26C1*, the first cell to format)	
Specify the last cell to format	:R27C3
Move the highlight to *alignment*	Tab
Select *Ctr*	C
Move the highlight to *format code*	Tab
Select *Int* (integer)	I
Execute the command	Enter

Inserting Commas in the Large Numbers

To make the numbers easier to read, let's tell Multiplan to insert commas in large numbers.

Leave the cursor on R26C1:	**Type or press:**
Start the Format command	F
Select the Options option	O
(The highlight is on *No* in the *commas* field)	
Select *Yes*	Y
Execute the command	Enter

This completes the formatting.

NAMING THE CELLS

Most of the formulas on this spreadsheet use named cell references, which makes them easier to enter and understand. The unshaded areas in Figure 6-3 show the locations of the named cells. Let's start the naming process with the cell that contains the annual requirements.

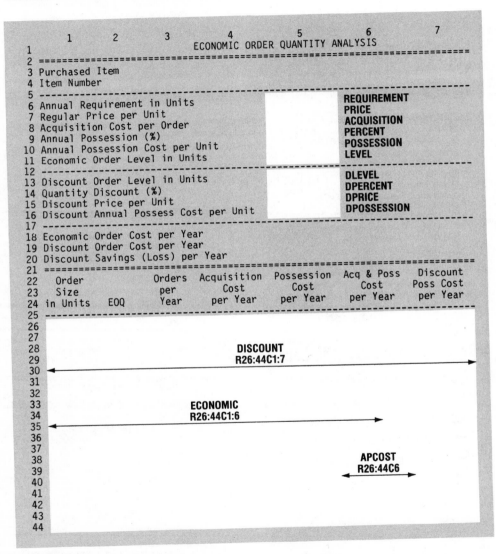

```
        1       2       3       4       5       6       7
                            ECONOMIC ORDER QUANTITY ANALYSIS
 1
 2 ===============================================================
 3 Purchased Item
 4 Item Number
 5 ---------------------------------------------------------------
 6 Annual Requirement in Units                    REQUIREMENT
 7 Regular Price per Unit                         PRICE
 8 Acquisition Cost per Order                     ACQUISITION
 9 Annual Possession (%)                          PERCENT
10 Annual Possession Cost per Unit                POSSESSION
11 Economic Order Level in Units                  LEVEL
12 ---------------------------------------------------------------
13 Discount Order Level in Units                  DLEVEL
14 Quantity Discount (%)                          DPERCENT
15 Discount Price per Unit                        DPRICE
16 Discount Annual Possess Cost per Unit          DPOSSESSION
17 ---------------------------------------------------------------
18 Economic Order Cost per Year
19 Discount Order Cost per Year
20 Discount Savings (Loss) per Year
21 ===============================================================
22   Order              Orders  Acquisition  Possession  Acq & Poss  Discount
23   Size                per       Cost         Cost        Cost     Poss Cost
24 in Units     EOQ      Year    per Year     per Year    per Year   per Year
25 ---------------------------------------------------------------
26
27
28                            DISCOUNT
29                            R26:44C1:7
30
31
32
33                            ECONOMIC
34                            R26:44C1:6
35
36
37
38                                              APCOST
39                                              R26:44C6
40
41
42
43
44
```

FIGURE 6-3.
EOQ analysis named cells

Place the cursor on R6C5:	**Type:**
Start the Name command	N
Name the cell	REQUIREMENT

Now look at the next field to the right. In the *to refer to* field, you see *R6C5*. Since this cell location is correct, all you do is press Enter.

Use this same procedure to name the following cells, and be sure to press Enter after typing each name. The D in DLEVEL, DPERCENT, DPRICE, and DPOSSESSION stands for Discount.

Place the cursor on:	**Name the cell:**
R7C5	PRICE
R8C5	ACQUISITION
R9C5	PERCENT
R10C5	POSSESSION
R11C5	LEVEL
R13C5	DLEVEL
R14C5	DPERCENT
R15C5	DPRICE
R16C5	DPOSSESSION

Now name the cells in column 6 that will hold the annual acquisition and possession costs. Formula 8 will scan the information in these cells to show you the economic order quantity. Let's name these cells APCOST.

Place the cursor on R26C6:	**Type or press:**
Start the Name command	N
Name the cells	APCOST
Move the highlight to *to refer to*	Tab
(Multiplan displays *to refer to: R26C6*, the first cell to name)	
Specify the last cell to name	:R44C6
Execute the command	Enter

The next group we want to name is in rows 26 through 44 of columns 1 through 6 and includes the cells you just named APCOST. There's no problem with this because a cell can have more than one name. The cells we're about to name form a lookup table that Formula 4 uses to calculate the economic order cost per year.

Let's name them ECONOMIC.

Place the cursor on R26C1:	**Type:**
Start the Name command	N
Name the cells	.ECONOMIC

In the *to refer to* field, Multiplan proposes *R26:44C1*, the same rows (but not the same column) you just named APCOST. The rows are correct, but we need to include columns 2 through 6.

With the cursor in the *define name* field:	**Type or press:**
Move the highlight to *to refer to*	Tab
Specify the last cell to name	:6
Execute the command	Enter

The last group of named cells is in rows 26 through 44 of columns 1 through 7. This group forms a lookup table that Formula 5 uses and includes the cells named ECONOMIC and APCOST. Let's name these cells DISCOUNT.

Leave the cursor on R26C1:	**Type or press:**
Start the Name command	N
Name the cells	DISCOUNT
Move the highlight to *to refer to*	Tab
(Multiplan displays *to refer to: R26C1*, the first cell to name)	
Specify the last cell to name	:R44C7
Execute the command	Enter

You now have three groups of named cells in rows 26 through 44. These groups are APCOST in column 6, ECONOMIC in columns 1 through 6 (which also contains APCOST), and DISCOUNT in columns 1 through 7 (which contains both APCOST and ECONOMIC). The ECONOMIC and DISCOUNT tables are interesting because they consist of working cells that contain formulas instead of data used by other formulas, as is typically the case with a lookup table.

Saving and Naming the Spreadsheet

Now store the spreadsheet titles, lines, formats, and cell names on disk and give the spreadsheet its own filename. If you need to specify which drive contains your data disk or which directory you want to store the file in, type the drive letter and press F6 (to produce a colon) or type the pathname before you type *EOQ*, the filename.

Leave the cursor where it is:	Type or press:
Start the Transfer command	T
Select the Save option	S
Name the spreadsheet	EOQ
Execute the command	Enter

ENTERING THE FORMULAS

The circled numbers in Figure 6-4 show the locations of the formulas that perform your calculations. The formulas use relative and named cell references. The left column in the following instructions contains the locations of the relative references, names of named cells, and other elements in the formula. The column on the right and the line immediately below the formula heading show the finished formula.

To build a formula, move the cursor to each cell shown in the left column (Multiplan will produce the relative notation) and type everything else—operators, symbols, function names, and cell names. When you type a character, the cursor returns to the formula cell so that you can type another character, move the cursor to another cell, or enter the formula. Many formulas use only named cells and are, therefore, typed entirely. The instructions will alert you to this.

When your formula matches the one in the instructions, press Enter. If Multiplan then displays *Not a valid formula*, check each character. If you need to correct a mistake, use the F7 through F10 keys to move the highlight, then type the missing characters or press the Delete key to delete the unwanted characters. If you prefer to start the formula from scratch, simply press the Escape key and begin again.

FORMULA 1: Annual Possession Cost per Unit

PRICE * PERCENT%

Formula 1 multiplies the regular unit price of the item (R7C5, PRICE) by the annual possession percent (R9C5, PERCENT) and enters the annual possession cost per unit in R10C5. Formula 1 uses named cell references only, so type the entire formula.

Place the cursor on R10C5:	Type or press:
Start the Value command	V
Enter the formula: PRICE * PERCENT%	PRICE * PERCENT%
Execute the command	Enter

```
          1        2        3        4        5        6        7
                              ECONOMIC ORDER QUANTITY ANALYSIS      ⑭EOQ
 1
 2 ================================================================
 3 Purchased Item
 4 Item Number
 5 ----------------------------------------------------------------
 6 Annual Requirement in Units
 7 Regular Price per Unit
 8 Acquisition Cost per Order
 9 Annual Possession (%)
10 Annual Possession Cost per Unit                  $0 ❶
11 Economic Order Level in Units
12 ----------------------------------------------------------------
13 Discount Order Level in Units
14 Quantity Discount (%)
15 Discount Price per Unit                          $0 ❷
16 Discount Annual Possess Cost per Unit            $0 ❸
17 ----------------------------------------------------------------
18 Economic Order Cost per Year                   #N/A ❹
19 Discount Order Cost per Year                   #N/A ❺
20 Discount Savings (Loss) per Year                 $0 ❻
21 ================================================================
22    Order              Orders  Acquisition Possession Acq & Poss   Discount
23    Size                 per      Cost        Cost       Cost     Poss Cost
24  in Units     EOQ      Year    per Year    per Year   per Year   per Year
25 ----------------------------------------------------------------
26     20    <<<<<< ❽    0 ❾      $0 ❿        $0 ⓫       $0 ⓬       $0 ⓭
27     30 ❼  <<<<<<      0        $0          $0          $0          $0
28     40    <<<<<<      0        $0          $0          $0          $0
29     50    <<<<<<      0        $0          $0          $0          $0
30     60    <<<<<<      0        $0          $0          $0          $0
31     70    <<<<<<      0        $0          $0          $0          $0
32     80    <<<<<<      0        $0          $0          $0          $0
33     90    <<<<<<      0        $0          $0          $0          $0
34    100    <<<<<<      0        $0          $0          $0          $0
35    110    <<<<<<      0        $0          $0          $0          $0
36    120    <<<<<<      0        $0          $0          $0          $0
37    130    <<<<<<      0        $0          $0          $0          $0
38    140    <<<<<<      0        $0          $0          $0          $0
39    150    <<<<<<      0        $0          $0          $0          $0
40    160    <<<<<<      0        $0          $0          $0          $0
41    170    <<<<<<      0        $0          $0          $0          $0
42    180    <<<<<<      0        $0          $0          $0          $0
43    190    <<<<<<      0        $0          $0          $0          $0
44    200    <<<<<<      0        $0          $0          $0          $0
```

FIGURE 6-4.
EOQ analysis formula locations

FORMULA 2: Discount Price per Unit

IF(DPERCENT>0,PRICE * (100 − DPERCENT)%,0)

Formula 2 calculates the discount price per unit. The result is based on the three parts of the IF function: the Test statement, the Then statement, and the Else statement. The Test statement looks at the quantity discount (R14C5, DPERCENT). If R14C5 contains a number greater than zero (meaning the item is available at a discount), the Then statement multiplies the regular unit price (R7C5, PRICE) by the quantity discount percentage (R14C5, DPERCENT) and enters the result in R15C5. If R14C5 contains a zero or is empty (meaning this item cannot be purchased at a discount), the Else statement enters a zero. Again, type the entire formula.

Place the cursor on R15C5:	**Type or press:**
Start the Value command	V
Enter the formula: IF(DPERCENT >0,PRICE * (100 − DPERCENT)%,0)	IF(DPERCENT>0,PRICE * (100 − DPERCENT)%,0)
Translation: IF(discount percent is greater than zero, then multiply regular unit price by (100 minus discount) percent, else enter zero)	
Execute the command	Enter

FORMULA 3: Discount Annual Possession Cost per Unit

IF(DPERCENT>0,POSSESSION * (100 − DPERCENT)%,0)

Formula 3 calculates the discount annual possession cost per unit. The Test statement looks at the quantity discount (R14C5, DPERCENT). If R14C5 contains a number greater than zero (meaning a discount is available), the Then statement reduces the annual possession cost per unit (R10C5, POSSESSION) by the amount of the quantity discount (R14C5, DPERCENT) and enters the result in R16C5. If the cell contains a zero or is empty, the Else statement enters a zero. Again, type the entire formula.

Place the cursor on R16C5:	**Type or press:**
Start the Value command	V
Enter the formula: IF(DPERCENT >0,POSSESSION * (100 − DPERCENT)%,0)	IF(DPERCENT>0,POSSESSION * (100 − DPERCENT)%,0)

Translation: IF(discount percent is
greater than zero, then multiply
annual possession cost per unit by
(100 minus discount) percent, else
enter zero)

Execute the command   Enter

FORMULA 4: Economic Order Cost per Year

REQUIREMENT * PRICE + LOOKUP(LEVEL;ECONOMIC)

Formula 4 uses Multiplan's LOOKUP function and the table named ECO-
NOMIC (rows 26 through 44 of columns 1 through 6) to calculate the total annual cost of an item regularly purchased in the economic order quantity; it then
enters the result in R18C5. The total annual cost consists of the acquisition and
possession cost (column 6) and the unit price without a discount (R7C5),
based on your annual requirements (R6C5).

The LOOKUP function allows you to search a table of information for a
specific piece of data. A table is simply a set of rows and columns; for example,
this spreadsheet contains three tables named DISCOUNT, ECONOMIC, and
APCOST. The LOOKUP function takes two elements: the value to look for and
the place to look (the name or cell locations of the table). For more information
about the LOOKUP function, see Chapter 17.

Formula 4 first multiplies the annual requirement (R6C5, REQUIRE-
MENT) by the regular unit price (R7C5, PRICE). Then it uses LOOKUP to
work with the ECONOMIC table. This table consists of six columns of information, but only columns 1 and 6 are relevant to Formula 4. The formula looks
at the economic order level you enter in R11C5 (LEVEL) and then scans the
order sizes in column 1 for the matching number. When it finds a match, it adds
the corresponding annual acquisition and possession cost in column 6 to its
prior calculation. Because ECONOMIC has more rows than columns, the formula takes the corresponding amount from the rightmost column in the table.
Type the entire formula.

Place the cursor on R18C5:	Type or press:
Start the Value command	V
Enter the formula: REQUIREMENT * PRICE + LOOKUP(LEVEL, ECONOMIC)	REQUIREMENT * PRICE + LOOKUP(LEVEL, ECONOMIC)
Execute the command	Enter

The message *#N/A* (not available) appears in R18C5 and remains until you enter the numbers for the formula to calculate.

FORMULA 5: Discount Order Cost per Year

REQUIREMENT * DPRICE + LOOKUP(DLEVEL,C1:4)
+ LOOKUP(DLEVEL,DISCOUNT)

Formula 5 calculates the total annual cost of an item regularly purchased at a quantity discount and enters the result in R19C5. The total annual cost consists of the acquisition cost (column 4), the discount possession cost (column 7), and the discount unit price (R15C5, DPRICE), based on your annual requirements (R6C5, REQUIREMENT).

The formula first multiplies the annual requirement (R6C5, REQUIRE-MENT) by the discount unit price (R15C5, DPRICE) to produce the annual cost of the item at a discount. Then it uses the LOOKUP function in two ways:

■ The first LOOKUP looks at the discount order level (R13C5, DLEVEL), scans the cells in column 1 (the order sizes) for a matching number, and then retrieves the corresponding amount from column 4 (the rightmost column in the table, which contains the acquisition cost per year). Multiplan handles the C1:C4 reference by scanning every row in column 1 until it finds the number and then adds the corresponding amount to the annual discount cost.

■ The second LOOKUP also looks at the discount order level (R13C5, DLEVEL) and then scans the cells in column 1 in the table named DISCOUNT (rows 26 through 44 of columns 1 through 7). When it finds a match, it adds the corresponding amount in column 7 (the discount possession cost per year, the rightmost column in the table) to the annual discount cost. Type the entire formula.

Place the cursor on R19C5:	Type or press:
Start the Value command	V
Enter the formula: REQUIREMENT * DPRICE + LOOKUP(DLEVEL, C1:C4) + LOOKUP(DLEVEL, DISCOUNT)	REQUIREMENT * DPRICE + LOOKUP(DLEVEL,C1:4) + LOOKUP(DLEVEL, DISCOUNT)
Execute the command	Enter

Once again, you see *#N/A* (not available) in the formula cell.

FORMULA 6: Discount Savings (Loss) per Year

IF(ISNA(R[−1]C),0,R[−2]C−R[−1]C)

Formula 6 uses the IF and ISNA (IS Not Available) functions to produce your answer. If the item is not offered at a discount, Formula 5 enters *#N/A* (not available) in R19C5. Formula 6 looks at R19C5 and, in response to #N/A, enters a zero in R20C5. If the item is offered at a discount and R19C5 contains a number, Formula 6 subtracts that amount from the cost of a typical order (R18C5) to produce the potential savings or loss if you purchase in quantity at the discount price.

Place the cursor on R20C5:	**Type or move the cursor:**
Start the Value command	V
Enter the formula: IF(ISNA(R19C5), 0,R18C5 − R19C5)	IF(ISNA(R[− 1]C), 0,R[− 2]C − R[− 1]C)
Translation: IF(discount order cost per year IS Not Available, then enter zero, else subtract discount order cost per year from economic order cost per year)	
Execute the command	Enter

FORMULA 7: Order Size

$$10 + R[− 1]C$$

Formula 7 calculates in units of ten the number of items ordered at one time. It does this by adding 10 to any number you enter in R26C1. You can later change both the initial and incremental numbers to suit your operation. Before you enter the formula, type the number *20* in R26C1 to prevent error messages when you enter the other formulas. Formula 7 starts with a number, so you don't have to type *V* first.

Place the cursor on R27C1:	**Type or move the cursor:**
Enter the formula: 10 + R26C1	10 + R[− 1]C
Execute the command	Enter

To produce the series of numbers in column 1, copy Formula 7 down the column.

Leave the cursor on R27C1:	**Type or press:**
Start the Copy command	C
Select the Down option	D
Specify the number of cells to copy into	17
Execute the command	Enter

Press the F4 key to recalculate the numbers in column 1.

FORMULA 8: EOQ

IF(RC[+4] = MIN(APCOST),"<<<<<<","")

The economic order quantity (EOQ) is the point at which the total cost of acquiring and possessing the item (column 6) is at a minimum. For this example, let's assume that stock usage is fairly constant and that the stock level is replenished in full when the inventory is close to, or reaches, zero. Formula 8 uses the MIN (minimum) function to find the smallest number in column 6, the cells you named APCOST. When it finds this number, the Then statement ("<<<<<<") points to the economic order quantity in column 1. All the other cells in column 2 receive the Else statement ("") and appear blank.

Place the cursor on R26C2:	Type or move the cursor:
Start the Value comand	V
Enter the formula: IF(R26C6 = MIN(APCOST), "<<<<<<","")	IF(RC[+4] = MIN(APCOST), "<<<<<<","")
Translation: IF(acquisition and possession costs per year equal the minimum of APCOST, then enter <<<<<<, else display nothing)	
Execute the command	Enter

Formulas 8 through 13 belong in every row from 26 through 44. You'll copy them as a group after you enter Formula 13.

FORMULA 9: Orders per Year

REQUIREMENT/RC[−2]

Formula 9 divides your annual requirements (R6C5, REQUIREMENT) by the order size (R26C1) and enters the anual orders in R26C3. The cells containing the annual orders are formatted to show integers (because you can't order 33.3 times per year, for example). Keep in mind when you order that the order size multiplied by the number of orders may not equal your exact annual requirement. For example, 30 units ordered 33 times a year is 990, which is 10 units short of the annual requirement of 1000 shown on the spreadsheet.

Place the cursor on R26C3:	Type or move the cursor:
Start the Value command	V
Enter the formula: REQUIREMENT /R26C1	REQUIREMENT/RC[−2]
Execute the command	Enter

FORMULA 10: Acquisition Cost per Year

RC[− 1] * ACQUISITION

Formula 10 multiplies the number of orders written each year (R26C3) by the acquisition cost per order (R8C5, ACQUISITION) and enters the annual acquisition cost in R26C4. The acquisition cost of each order isn't calculated on this spreadsheet. To determine the amount to enter in R8C5, divide the total operating expenses of the purchasing function during a representative period of time by the number of purchase orders written during the period. The purchasing function usually includes evaluating suppliers, maintaining records of materials, and preparing requisitions and purchase orders.

Place the cursor on R26C4:	Type or move the cursor:
Start the Value command	V
Enter the formula: R26C3 * ACQUISITION	RC[− 1] * ACQUISITION
Execute the command	Enter

FORMULA 11: Possession Cost per Year

POSSESSION * RC[− 4]/2

Formula 11 multiplies the annual possession cost per unit (R10C5, POSSESSION) by the order size (R26C1) and divides the result by 2 to calculate the average total annual possession cost in R26C5. Possession cost, which is not calculated on this spreadsheet, usually includes warehouse expenses, depreciation, clerical work, labor, and insurance.

Place the cursor on R26C5:	Type or move the cursor:
Start the Value command	V
Enter the formula: POSSESSION * R26C1/2	POSSESSION * RC[− 4]/2
Execute the command	Enter

FORMULA 12: Acquisition and Possession Cost per Year

RC[− 2] + RC[− 1]

Formula 12 adds the annual acquisition cost (R26C4) to the annual possession cost (R26C5) and enters the total in R26C6.

Place the cursor on R26C6:	Type or move the cursor:
Start the Value command	V

Enter the formula: R26C4 + R26C5	RC[− 2] + RC[− 1]
Execute the command	Enter

FORMULA 13: Discount Possession Cost per Year

DPOSSESSION ∗ RC[− 6]/2

Formula 13 multiplies the discount possession cost per unit (R16C5, DPOSSESSION) by the order size (R26C1) and divides the result by 2 to calculate the average annual discount possession cost in R26C7.

Place the cursor on R26C7:	**Type or move the cursor:**
Start the Value command	V
Enter the formula: DPOSSESSION ∗ R26C1/2	DPOSSESSION ∗ RC[− 6]/2
Execute the command	Enter

Copying the Formulas as a Group

Now copy Formulas 8 through 13 down their respective columns.

Place the cursor on R26C2:	**Type or press:**
Start the Copy command	C
Select the Down option	D
Specify the number of cells to copy into	18
Move the highlight to *starting at*	Tab
Specify the last column to copy from	:7
Execute the command	Enter

FORMULA 14: Spreadsheet Filename

NAME()

Formula 14 enters the spreadsheet filename in R1C7. Type the function name and parentheses.

Place the cursor on R1C7:	**Type or press:**
Start the Value command	V
Enter the formula: NAME()	NAME()
Execute the command	Enter

Locking the Formulas

To prevent accidental alteration, lock all your formulas.

Leave the cursor where it is:	Type:
Start the Lock command	L
Select the Formulas option	F
(Multiplan displays *Enter Y to confirm*)	
Confirm the lock	Y

Saving the Formulas

Now store all the formulas on disk. Because you saved the spreadsheet before, Multiplan asks you to confirm overwriting the earlier version.

Leave the cursor where it is:	Type or press:
Start the Transfer command	T
Select the Save option	S
(Multiplan displays *EOQ*—no need to retype)	
Execute the command	Enter
(Multiplan recalculates, then displays *Enter Y to overwrite file*)	
Confirm the overwrite	Y

Your spreadsheet should now look like the one in Figure 6-4.

ENTERING THE TRANSIENT TEXT AND NUMBERS

Figure 6-5 shows practice entries for the oak cabinets purchased by our sample company. Here's how to make these entries:

1. Place the cursor on R3C5 and type *A* to start the Alpha command. Type the title *Oak Cabinet* and move the cursor to R4C5. Type the item number *A-6230-3* and move the cursor to R6C5.

2. Type each number in column 5. Because of the formatting you did earlier, Multiplan will produce the dollar signs, commas, and decimal places for you. Don't bother to press Enter after each entry—simply type a number and move the cursor to the next cell that contains a number. After you type the last number in R14C5, press Enter.

```
          1       2       3       4       5       6       7
 1                              ECONOMIC ORDER QUANTITY ANALYSIS      EOQ
 2  ====================================================================
 3  Purchased Item                         Oak Cabinet
 4  Item Number                            A-6230-3
 5  --------------------------------------------------------------------
 6  Annual Requirement in Units                  1000
 7  Regular Price per Unit                        100
 8  Acquisition Cost per Order                     50
 9  Annual Possession (%)                          40
10  Annual Possession Cost per Unit
11  Economic Order Level in Units                  50
12  --------------------------------------------------------------------
13  Discount Order Level in Units                 100
14  Quantity Discount (%)                           5
15  Discount Price per Unit
16  Discount Annual Possess Cost per Unit
17  --------------------------------------------------------------------
18  Economic Order Cost per Year
19  Discount Order Cost per Year
20  Discount Savings (Loss) per Year
21  ====================================================================
22   Order          Orders  Acquisition Possession  Acq & Poss  Discount
23   Size            per      Cost        Cost         Cost     Poss Cost
24  in Units  EOQ    Year   per Year    per Year     per Year   per Year
25  --------------------------------------------------------------------
```

FIGURE 6-5.
EOQ analysis transient text and numbers

Now press the F4 (recalculate) key. Your spreadsheet should look like the completed one in Figure 6-1 at the beginning of this chapter. Store it on disk by typing *TS* (Transfer Save) and pressing Enter. Type *Y* to overwrite.

PRINTING YOUR SPREADSHEET

This spreadsheet is 80 characters wide, including the five characters Multiplan sets aside for row numbers. It is printed in 12-pitch type on one sheet of 8½-by-11-inch paper.

Setting the Print Margins

The first step before printing your spreadsheet is to set the margins.

Leave the cursor where it is:	Type or press:
Start the Print command	P
Select the Margins option	M

Type the following numbers in the margins fields, and simply tab past those that are already at the proper setting. If you overshoot a field, press Shift-Tab to move the highlight back a field or press Tab a few times to move full circle through the fields. The highlight is in the *left* field.

To do this:	Type or press:
Specify the number of characters	6
Move the highlight to *top*	Tab
Specify the number of lines	6
Move the highlight to *print width*	Tab
Specify the number of characters	102
Move the highlight to *print length*	Tab
Specify the number of lines	60
Move the highlight to *page length*	Tab
Specify the number of lines	66
Execute the command	Enter

Setting the Print Options

You are still in the Print command. The next step is to set the printing options. The options settings (the same for all the spreadsheets in this book) print the entire spreadsheet in 12-pitch type with row and column numbers (which help you compare your results with the illustrations). You can find the printer code for 12-pitch type in your printer manual.

Now type O to select the Options option. Type in the following responses. (Tab past any field that already has the proper setting.) The highlight is in the *area* field.

To do this:	Type or press:
Define the print area	R1:4095
Move the highlight to *setup*	Tab
Enter your printer code for 12-pitch type	(your code)
Move the highlight to *formulas*	Tab Tab
Select *No*	N
Move the highlight to *row-col numbers*	Tab
Select *Yes*	Y
Execute the command	Enter

Before you print, store the spreadsheet with the printing settings: Press the Escape key to leave the Print command. Type *TS* (Transfer Save) and press Enter. Type *Y* to overwrite.

Printing Your Spreadsheet

Now turn on your printer and print a copy of your spreadsheet, as follows:

Leave the cursor where it is:	**Type:**
Start the Print command	P
Select the Printer option	P

And there's your spreadsheet.

AUDITING YOUR SPREADSHEET

Sometimes, when you're working on a spreadsheet of your own design, things won't work out with quite the same degree of precision and accuracy as they have with this spreadsheet. You may end up with wrong answers or error messages in the cells. That's when Multiplan's audit feature comes in handy. To see how this works, let's closely examine the formula in R20C5.

Place the cursor on R20C5:	**Type or press:**
Start the Run command	R
Select the Audit option	A
Select the Formulas option	F
Confirm the command	Enter

Instantly, Multiplan splits the screen into two windows, as shown in Figure 6-6. The top window shows the exact contents of R20C5, including the stored value, the displayed value, the format (alignment and format code), the cell reference, and the formula *IF(ISNA(R[− 1]C),0,R[− 2]C − R[− 1]C)* (which is our Formula 6). The bottom window shows information about the relative reference *R[− 1]C* highlighted in the formula in the upper window. Press the Right Arrow key to step through the other cell references in the formula, and you can see the contents of each in turn in the bottom window.

When you have problems, Run Audit lets you explore the contents of a cell from several angles, so that you can troubleshoot your way to an error-free spreadsheet. Now press the Escape key to return to the spreadsheet.

```
Formula/Value in R20C5:
IF(ISNA(R[-1]C),0,R[-2]C-R[-1]C)



Value: 4600                          Displayed Value: $4,600
Format: Def, Def(0)
Cells in R[-1]C: R19C5


Formula/Value in R19C5:
REQUIREMENT*DPRICE+LOOKUP(DLEVEL,C1:C4)+LOOKUP(DLEVEL,DISCOUNT)



Value: 97400                         Displayed Value: $97,400
Format: Def, Def(0)

RUN AUDIT FORMULAS cell: R20C5

Press arrow keys or Cancel to return to main menu
R20C5      IF(ISNA(R[-1]C),0,R[-2]C-R[ ?  98% Free    Multiplan: EOQ
```

FIGURE 6-6.
The result of a Run Audit Formulas operation

USING YOUR SPREADSHEET

Using EOQ Analysis for your own business is as easy as this:

1. Type your item descriptions in R3C5 and R4C5 and your numbers in R6C5 through R9C5, R11C5, R13C5, and R14C5. Press the F4 (recalculate) key and let Multiplan go to work.

2. The EOQ <<<<<< pointer in column 2 now shows you the economic order size. Enter this number in R11C5 and press F4 again. The formulas now calculate the economic order cost per year in R18C5. If you haven't yet entered any discount information, the annual discount order cost in R19C5 will show #N/A.

That's all there is to it. You'll find EOQ analysis a valuable tool that can save your business many dollars.

SPREADSHEET SUMMARY

General: The completed spreadsheet is shown in Figure 6-1. Use Options to set automatic recalculation to *No*. Use Value to enter REPT(" = ",12) and REPT(" − ",12) for long lines. Use Lock Formulas to lock formulas.

Column Width: Use Format Width to set column 1 to 9 characters, column 2 to 8 characters, and columns 4 through 7 to 12 characters.

Format: Use Format Default Cells to set dollars with no decimal places as the standard. Use Format Cells as follows: Continue R1C4:6 and R3:20C1:4. Right-justify R1C7 and R3:4C5. Center R22C1:R24C7. Integer code R6C5, R11C5, and R13C5. Fix code with 1 decimal place R9C5 and R14C5. Center and integer code R26C1:R27C3 (you will copy this format down the columns when you copy the formulas). Use Format Options to insert automatic commas.

Name: Use Name as follows: R6C5 is REQUIREMENT. R7C5 is PRICE. R8C5 is ACQUISITION. R9C5 is PERCENT. R10C5 is POSSESSION. R11C5 is LEVEL. R13C5 is DLEVEL. R14C5 is DPERCENT. R15C5 is DPRICE. R16C5 is DPOSSESSION. R26C6:R44C6 is APCOST. R26:44C1:6 is ECONOMIC. R26C1:R44C7 is DISCOUNT.

Print: Economic Order Quantity Analysis is 80 characters wide, including Multiplan row numbers, and is printed in 12-pitch type. Set print margins for 8½-by-11-inch paper as follows: *left* 6, *top* 6, *print width* 102, *print length* 60, and *page length* 66.

Formulas: Formulas use relative and named cell references.

1	R10C5	Annual Possession Cost per Unit PRICE * PERCENT%
2	R15C5	Discount Price per Unit IF(DPERCENT>0,PRICE * (100 − DPERCENT)%,0)
3	R16C5	Discount Annual Possession Cost per Unit IF(DPERCENT>0,POSSESSION * (100 − DPERCENT)%,0)
4	R18C5	Economic Order Cost per Year REQUIREMENT * PRICE + LOOKUP(LEVEL,ECONOMIC)

5   R19C5   Discount Order Cost per Year
REQUIREMENT * DPRICE
+ LOOKUP(DLEVEL,C1:4)
+ LOOKUP(DLEVEL,DISCOUNT)

6   R20C5   Discount Savings (Loss) per Year
IF(ISNA(R[−1]C),0,R[−2]C−R[−1]C)

7   R27C1   Order Size
10 + R[−1]C

8   R26C2   EOQ
IF(RC[+4] = MIN(APCOST),"<<<<<<","")

9   R26C3   Orders per Year
REQUIREMENT/RC[−2]

10   R26C4   Acquisition Cost per Year
RC[−1] * ACQUISITION

11   R26C5   Possession Cost per Year
POSSESSION * RC[−4]/2

12   R26C6   Acquisition and Possession Cost per Year
RC[−2] + RC[−1]

13   R26C7   Discount Possession Cost per Year
DPOSSESSION * RC[−6]/2

14   R1C7   Spreadsheet Filename
NAME()

7

Project Cost Estimate

One of the most difficult aspects of business management is estimating the cost of manufacturing or selling a product or delivering a service. To stay competitive and profitable, a company must identify each cost involved in a project—direct labor, indirect labor, expenses, materials, and overhead—and allocate each one properly. If an estimate is too high, the company can lose sales or lose the bid. If the estimate is too low, the company can lose its shirt.

Though the overall procedures for estimating costs in manufacturing, sales, and service are similar, there are significant differences. A manufacturer, for instance, is likely to have higher costs for materials and capital equipment than a service firm, whose major cost is payroll, or a sales organization, whose major cost is the price of the products purchased for resale.

In this chapter, we'll explore cost estimating procedures that might be used by a small engineering and design firm—a service business whose charges are based on the number of hours spent on a project. Figure 7-1 shows their project cost spreadsheet.

Prospective clients usually require a bid that includes either a fixed fee or a not-to-exceed figure. In preparing a proposal, management must look carefully at the resources of the firm, calculate the payroll cost of the people working directly on the project, and allocate support and overhead costs properly.

	1	2	3	4	5	6	7
1							PROJECT CO
2	==
3	Client:	Fast Foods, Inc.			Total Project Cost		
4	Project:	TV Surveillance System			Profit Margin (%)		40.0
5	Location:	Albany, Oregon			Estimate to Client		
6	Prepared:	June 21, 1987					
7	By:	R J Nilssen					
8	==

Employee Number	Name	************ Estimated Project Hours *************				
		Analysis	Report	Design	Suprvsion	Checkout
1	Nilssen, Bob	15.0	10.0	15.0	16.0	10.0
13	Spolberg, Karen			36.0	8.5	
6	Aven, Michael	7.5	5.0	6.0		
16	Byrd, Burtie	5.0				7.5
15	Wennerstrom, Jeff			12.0		
20	YOUR NAME			7.5		
5	Yamaguchi, Taeko			16.0	5.0	
	Totals	27.5	15.0	92.5	29.5	17.5

BILLABLE-TIME LOOKUP TABLE

Number	Name	Rate/Hr	Benefit/Hr	Total
1	Nilssen, Bob	$24.52	$8.58	$33.10
2	Freeman, Gil	$19.23	$6.73	$25.96
3	Corallo, Mike	$8.65	$3.03	$11.68
4	Clark, David	$16.23	$5.68	$21.91
5	Yamaguchi, Taeko	$12.20	$4.27	$16.47
6	Aven, Michael	$13.46	$4.71	$18.17
7	Tate, Tony	$19.23	$6.73	$25.96
8	Norick, Paul	$8.00	$2.80	$10.80
9	Cabral, Glenn	$11.00	$3.85	$14.85
10	Weissman, Evelyn	$16.23	$5.68	$21.91
11	Chu, Lin	$8.00	$2.80	$10.80
12	Maiwald, Lois	$12.46	$4.36	$16.82
13	Spolberg, Karen	$19.23	$6.73	$25.96
14	Hill, Howard	$6.25	$2.19	$8.44
15	Wennerstrom, Jeff	$19.71	$6.90	$26.61
16	Byrd, Burtie	$9.50	$3.33	$12.83
17	LeMay, Yves	$6.00	$2.10	$8.10
18	Greene, Nat	$12.00	$4.20	$16.20
19	Smith, Clinton	$14.50	$5.08	$19.58
20	YOUR NAME	$19.90	$6.96	$26.87

FIGURE 7-1.
The completed project cost estimate spreadsheet

```
     8                  9            10            11             12            13
ST ESTIMATE                                                                 PROJECT
=============================================================================
   $8285.54                            Project Deadline Date              3/25/88
   $5523.69                            Today's Date                      11/19/87
  $13809.23                            Calendar Days Remaining                128
                                       Weekdays Remaining                      92
=============================================================================
```

Billable Hours	Billable Rate/Hour	Total Billable	Allocated Overhead	Allocated Mktng & Admin	Total Costs
66.0	$33.10	$2184.73	$554.01	$745.11	$3483.85
44.5	$25.96	$1155.24	$373.54	$502.38	$2031.17
18.5	$18.17	$336.16	$155.29	$208.86	$700.31
12.5	$12.83	$160.31	$104.93	$141.12	$406.36
12.0	$26.61	$319.30	$100.73	$135.47	$555.51
7.5	$26.87	$201.49	$62.96	$84.67	$349.12
21.0	$16.47	$345.87	$176.28	$237.08	$759.23
0.0	$0.00	$0.00	$0.00	$0.00	$0.00
0.0	$0.00	$0.00	$0.00	$0.00	$0.00
0.0	$0.00	$0.00	$0.00	$0.00	$0.00
0.0	$0.00	$0.00	$0.00	$0.00	$0.00
182.0	$160.00	$4703.11	$1527.74	$2054.69	$8285.54

```
=============================================================
Annual Hours per Employee                            1950
Benefits Rate per Hour (%)                           35.0
=============================================================
GENERAL OVERHEAD
-------------------------------------------------------------
Overhead Expense per Year                      $540164.00
All Employees                                          33
All Employee Hours per Year                         64350
Overhead Rate per Hour                              $8.39
=============================================================
MARKETING AND ADMINISTRATION
-------------------------------------------------------------
Salaries                                       $211992.00
Benefits                                        $74197.20
                                              ------------
Total Salaries & Benefits                      $286189.20
Mktng & Admin Employees                                13
Employee Hours per Year                             25350
Mktng & Admin Rate per Hour                        $11.29
=============================================================
```

Projects typically involve five phases of activity:

■ *Analysis*. This involves determining the client's requirements, preparing feasibility studies, and deciding on design approaches.

■ *Reporting*. This involves writing reports of recommendations, planning budgets, and preparing other reports as needed.

■ *Design*. This involves the technical design of the facility, including the preparation of design drawings, specifications, and equipment lists.

■ *Supervision*. This involves overseeing the work of the contractor and reviewing shop drawings during implementation of the project.

■ *Checkout*. This involves on-site inspections to check the quality of the work and verify that the completed phase or project meets all specifications.

The spreadsheet contains a lookup table of engineers, designers, and drafters whose time is directly billable to the project. From this technical resource pool, the project leader selects employees to work on the project.

The formulas retrieve the hourly rates and the cost of salary-related benefits of the selected employees from the table and calculate the cost of their billable hours. The costs of overhead, marketing, administration, accounting, and clerical support are then allocated based on the hours spent by a billable employee on the project. The result is the estimated project cost. We can then use Multiplan's iteration capability to calculate a bid based on the company's required profit margin. When the company receives the contract, we use Multiplan's date functions to compute how many workdays there are before the project deadline.

The techniques used to prepare the cost estimate for our engineering and design company are easily adaptable to any service firm (accounting, legal, architectural, and others) whose charges are based on time. If you have many job classifications, you can use job titles and average rates instead of specific employee names and rates in the billable-time lookup table.

Lookup tables use Multiplan's LOOKUP function. You'll find explanations of lookup tables in this chapter and in Chapter 17. If you're familiar with Multiplan and prefer to create this spreadsheet without following the step-by-step instructions, refer to the summary at the end of this chapter.

SETTING UP YOUR SPREADSHEET

Bring up the Multiplan screen. If you turned off automatic recalculation on your last spreadsheet, you can skip the following step and go directly to the next step, "Adjusting the Column Widths." Otherwise, to make data entry faster, leave the cursor where it is. Type *O* to start the Options command, type *N* for no recalculation, and press Enter. Now we're ready to make your spreadsheet look like the one in Figure 7-2.

Adjusting the Column Widths

Let's start by increasing the widths of some of the columns to give our entries the room they need and produce a well-spaced spreadsheet. Increase the width of column 1 from Multiplan's standard 10 characters to 12 characters.

Leave the cursor on R1C1:	**Type or press:**
Start the Format command	F
Select the Width option	W
Specify the number of characters in the column	12
Execute the command	Enter

Next, increase the width of column 2 to 18 characters: Place the cursor on R1C2 and type *FW* (Format Width). Type *18* and press Enter. Now increase the width of column 8 to 12 characters: Place the cursor on R1C8 and type *FW*. Type *12* and press Enter.

You can increase the width of columns 9 through 13 in one step.

Place the cursor on R1C9:	**Type or press:**
Start the Format command	F
Select the Width option	W
Specify the number of characters in each column	13
Move the highlight to *through*	Tab Tab
Specify column 9 through 13	13
Execute the command	Enter

Entering the Titles

You are about to type the titles (but not the lines) you see in Figure 7-2. Several titles are longer than can fit in their cells at this time, so don't be concerned if you see only part of a title. We'll take care of that shortly when we format the titles.

Here's some additional information to help you enter the titles:

■ When you get to R9C3, type 12 asterisks and press the Spacebar once. Then type *Estimated Project Hours* and press the Spacebar again. Finish the title by typing 13 asterisks. You'll see only the first 10 asterisks in the cell after you enter the title.

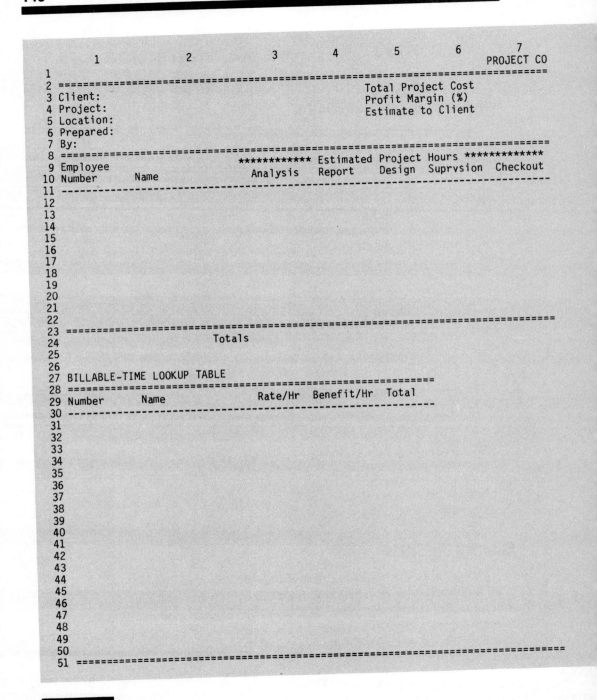

FIGURE 7-2.
The titles and lines on the project cost estimate spreadsheet

```
        8           9          10          11          12          13
ST ESTIMATE
===================================================================
                              Project Deadline Date
                              Today's Date
                              Calendar Days Remaining
                              Weekdays Remaining
===================================================================
Billable    Billable     Total    Allocated   Allocated    Total
  Hours     Rate/Hour   Billable   Overhead   Mktng & Admin  Costs
-------------------------------------------------------------------



=====================================================================


            ================================================
            Annual Hours per Employee
            Benefits Rate per Hour (%)

            ================================================
            GENERAL OVERHEAD
            ------------------------------------------------
            Overhead Expense per Year
            All Employees
            All Employee Hours per Year
            Overhead Rate per Hour

            ================================================
            MARKETING AND ADMINISTRATION
            ------------------------------------------------
            Salaries
            Benefits
                                        ------------
            Total Salaries & Benefits
            Mktng & Admin Employees
            Employee Hours per Year
            Mktng & Admin Rate per Hour

=====================================================================
```

■ Type the title *Totals* in R24C2. You'll right-justify it later so that it looks like the one in Figure 7-2.

With so many titles, it's worthwhile to put Multiplan in the alpha/value mode before you start typing.

Leave the cursor where it is:	Type or press:
Start the Options command	O
Move the highlight to *alpha/value*	Tab (four times)
Select *Yes*	Y
Execute the command	Enter

ALPHA/VALUE now replaces the command menu and will remain until you turn off the alpha/value mode after typing all the titles. If you mistype, press the Backspace key (not a direction key) to erase the character, or use the F7 through F10 keys to move the highlight through the title without erasing, then type any missing characters or press the Delete key to erase unwanted characters.

Now place the cursor on R1C7. Type *PROJECT COST ESTIMATE* and move the cursor to R3C1, the next cell that will contain a title. It's not necessary to press Enter to enter the title in its cell. Moving the cursor serves the same purpose. If cell R1C7 were still in view, you'd see only the first part of the title you just typed because the cell isn't wide enough to display it completely. There's no need for concern—we'll extend the title across adjacent cells later when we format the cells.

Type *Client:* and move the cursor to R4C1. Type *Project:* and move the cursor to the next cell that contains a title. Continue in this way, typing a title and moving the cursor, until you've typed all the titles shown in Figure 7-2. Then press Enter.

Now press Escape to return the command menu to the screen. Turn off the alpha/value mode: Leave the cursor where it is and type O (Options). Press the tab key four times to move the highlight to *alpha/value*. Type N to select *No* and press Enter. Things are now back to normal.

Entering the Lines

Next, let's use the REPT (repeat) function and an equal sign to enter a double line in R2C1. We'll tell Multiplan to repeat an equal sign 18 times—enough to fill even the widest cell in row 2. That way, when we copy the formula across row 2, there won't be any gaps in the line.

Place the cursor on R2C1:	**Type or press:**
Start the Value command	V
Repeat an equal sign 18 times	REPT(" = ",18)
Execute the command	Enter

Now copy the REPT formula into the columns to the right.

Leave the cursor on R2C1:	**Type or press:**
Start the Copy command	C
Select the Right option	R
Specify the number of cells to copy into	12
Execute the command	Enter

The line now extends from column 1 through column 13. Rows 8, 23, and 51 need the same kind of line, so copy the formula from row 2. To produce the colon before the 13, press the F6 key.

Leave the cursor on R2C1:	**Type or press:**
Start the Copy command	C
Select the From option	F
(Multiplan displays *COPY FROM cells: R2C1*, the first cell to copy from)	
Specify the last cell to copy from	:13
Move the highlight to *to cells*	Tab
Specify the first cell in each row to copy into	R8C1,R23C1,R51C1
Execute the command	Enter

The same process can put a single line across row 11. First, enter a REPT formula containing a minus sign in R11C1.

Place the cursor on R11C1:	**Type or press:**
Start the Value command	V
Repeat a minus sign 18 times	REPT(" – ",18)
Execute the command	Enter

Copy the REPT formula into the columns to the right: Leave the cursor on R11C1 and type *CR* (Copy Right). Multiplan "remembers" the copying you did for the double line and proposes 12 as the number of cells to copy into. Since 12 is correct, all you do is press Enter. The line now extends through column 13.

This spreadsheet needs single and double lines that are only five columns wide. Instead of creating them from scratch, first copy a five-column piece of the single line from row 11 to row 30.

Leave the cursor on R11C1:	**Type or press:**
Start the Copy command	C
Select the From option	F
(Multiplan displays COPY FROM cells: R11C1, the first cell to copy from)	
Specify the last cell to copy from	:5
Move the highlight to to cells	Tab
Specify the first cell to copy into	R30C1
Execute the command	Enter

Now copy a 5-column piece of the double line from row 23 to row 28 in the same way: Place the cursor on R23C1 and type *CF* (Copy From). Type :5 as the last cell to copy from. Press the Tab key to move the highlight to *to cells*. Type *R28C1* and press Enter.

The right side of the spreadsheet needs single and double lines that are only four columns wide. So, copy a 4-column piece of a double line in row 23: Leave the cursor on R23C1 and type *CF*. Type :4 and press the Tab key. Now type *R28C9,R32C9,R40C9* and press Enter. And finally, copy a 4-column piece of the single line to rows 34 and 42: Place the cursor on R30C1 and type *CF*. Type :4 and press the Tab key. Type *R34C9,R42C9* and press Enter.

The last line is in R45C12: Place the cursor on R45C12 and type *V* (Value). Type *REPT(" — ",12)* and press Enter. Your lines are now all in place.

Formatting the Titles

There are many long titles on this spreadsheet. Let's tell Multiplan to put them into a continuous format so that they extend into the cells to the right and are displayed completely.

Place the cursor on R1C2:	**Type or press:**
Start the Format command	F
Select the Cells option	C
(Multiplan displays FORMAT cells: R1C2, the first cell to be continuous)	

Specify the other cells to be continuous	:R7C13,R9C3:7, R27C1:2, R29:49C9:11
Move the highlight to *format code*	Tab Tab
Select *Cont* (continuous)	C
Execute the command	Enter

Next, center the titles in row 9 (columns 8 through 13), row 10 (columns 3 through 13), and row 29 (columns 3 through 5).

Place the cursor on R9C8:	**Type or press:**
Start the Format command	F
Select the Cells option	C
(Multiplan displays *FORMAT cells: R9C8*, the first cell to format)	
Specify the other cells to format	:13,R10C3:13, R29C3:5
Move the highlight to *alignment*	Tab
Select *Ctr* (center)	C
Execute the command	Enter

The next step is to right-justify R1C13, which will contain the filename, and the title *Totals* in R24C2.

Place the cursor on R1C13:	**Type or press:**
Start the Format command	F
Select the Cells option	C
(Multiplan displays *R1C13*, the first cell to format)	
Specify the other cell to format	,R24C2
Move the highlight to *alignment*	Tab
Select *Right*	R
Execute the command	Enter

That takes care of the title cells. Let's move on to the number cells.

Formatting the Number Cells

First, let's center the cells in column 1 (rows 12 through 22 and rows 31 through 50) that will contain the employee numbers.

Place the cursor on R12C1:	Type or press:
Start the Format command	F
Select the Cells option	C
(Multiplan displays *FORMAT cells: R12C1*, the first cell to format)	
Specify the other cells to format	:R22C1,R31:50C1
Move the highlight to *alignment*	Tab
Select *Ctr* (center)	C
Execute the command	Enter

Now center R4C7 (the cell that will contain the profit margin) and the cells in rows 12 through 24 (columns 3 through 8) and format them for a fixed code with one decimal place.

Place the cursor on R4C7:	Type or press:
Start the Format command	F
Select the Cells option	C
(Multiplan displays *FORMAT cells: R4C7*, the first cell to format)	
Specify the other cells to format	,R12:24C3:8
Move the highlight to *alignment*	Tab
Select *Ctr* (center)	C
Move the highlight to *format code*	Tab
Select *Fix*	F
Move the highlight to *# of decimals*	Tab
Specify the number of decimals	1
Execute the command	Enter

Now format the cell that will hold the hourly benefits rate (R30C12) to a fixed code with one decimal place: Place the cursor on R30C12. Type *FC* (Format Cells) and press the Tab key twice to move the highlight to *format code*. Type *F* to select *Fix* and press the Tab key again to move the highlight to *# of decimals*. Type *1* and press Enter.

We have large groups of cells and scattered single cells that show dollar amounts. Let's format them for dollars and cents. (We'll wait until later to format R24C9:R24C13.)

Place the cursor on R3C8:	Type or press:
Start the Format command	F
Select the Cells option	C
(Multiplan displays *FORMAT cells: R3C8,* the cell to format)	
Specify the other cells to format	,R4:5C8,R12:22C9:13, R31:50C3:5,R35C12, R38C12,R43:44C12, R46C12,R49C12
Move the highlight to *format code*	Tab Tab
Select *$*	$
Execute the command	Enter

And finally, format the cell that will contain the remaining calendar days (R5C13) to show its contents as an integer: Place the cursor on R5C13 and type *FC* (Format Cells). Press the Tab key twice to move the highlight to *format code.* Type *I* to select *Int* and press Enter. This completes the formatting for now. We'll do a bit more after you enter and copy the formulas.

NAMING THE CELLS

The next step is to name the cells. This way, the formulas can refer to cells in everyday English words. The unshaded areas in Figure 7-3 show the locations of the named cells. Let's start with R4C7.

Place the cursor on R4C7:	Type:
Start the Name command	N
Name the cell	MARGIN

Look at the next field to the right. In the *to refer to* field, you see R4C7. This is the correct cell location, so all you do is press Enter.

Use the same procedure to name the following cells. Be sure to press Enter after you type each name.

Place the cursor on:	Name the cell:
R4C8	PROFIT
R5C8	ESTIMATE
R3C13	END
R4C13	TODAY
R5C13	CDAYS

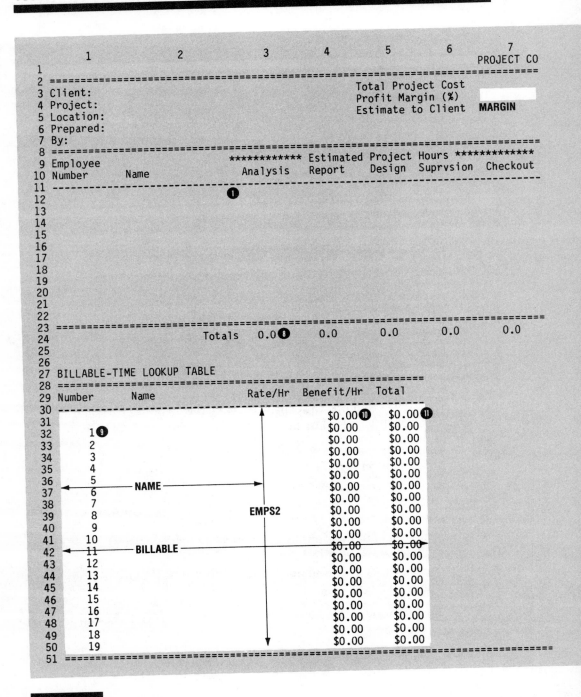

FIGURE 7-3.
Project cost estimate named cells and formula locations

	8	9	10	11	12	13
ST ESTIMATE						PROJECT ⓴

```
========================================================================
#DIV/0! ⓳
              PROFIT          Project Deadline Date           END
              ESTIMATE        Today's Date                    TODAY
                              Calendar Days Remaining         CDAYS
                              Weekdays Remaining
========================================================================
```

Billable Hours	Billable Rate/Hour	Total Billable	Allocated Overhead	Allocated Mktng & Admin	Total Costs
0.0 ❷	$0.00 ❸	$0.00 ❹	#DIV/0! ❺	#DIV/0! ❻	#DIV/0! ❼
0.0	$0.00	$0.00	#DIV/0!	#DIV/0!	#DIV/0!
0.0	$0.00	$0.00	#DIV/0!	#DIV/0!	#DIV/0!
0.0	$0.00	$0.00	#DIV/0!	#DIV/0!	#DIV/0!
0.0	$0.00	$0.00	#DIV/0!	#DIV/0!	#DIV/0!
0.0	$0.00	$0.00	#DIV/0!	#DIV/0!	#DIV/0!
0.0	$0.00	$0.00	#DIV/0!	#DIV/0!	#DIV/0!
0.0	$0.00	$0.00	#DIV/0!	#DIV/0!	#DIV/0!
0.0	$0.00	$0.00	#DIV/0!	#DIV/0!	#DIV/0!
0.0	$0.00	$0.00	#DIV/0!	#DIV/0!	#DIV/0!
0.0	$0.00	$0.00	#DIV/0!	#DIV/0!	#DIV/0!

| 0.0 | $0.00 | $0.00 | #DIV/0! | #DIV/0! | #DIV/0! TOTAL |

```
========================================================================
Annual Hours per Employee                                    HOURS
Benefits Rate per Hour (%)                                   BENEFITS

========================================================================
GENERAL OVERHEAD
------------------------------------------------------------------------
Overhead Expense per Year
All Employees
All Employee Hours per Year                          0 ⓬
Overhead Rate per Hour                  0 ⓭
                                        #DIV/0! ⓮      OVERHEAD

========================================================================
MARKETING AND ADMINISTRATION
------------------------------------------------------------------------
Salaries
Benefits                                $0.00 ⓯
                                        ------------
Total Salaries & Benefits               $0.00 ⓰
Mktng & Admin Employees                                      EMPS1
Employee Hours per Year
Mktng & Admin Rate per Hour             0 ⓱
                                        #DIV/0! ⓲      MADMIN

========================================================================
```

R24C13	TOTAL
R29C12	HOURS
R30C12	BENEFITS
R38C12	OVERHEAD
R47C12	EMPS1
R49C12	MADMIN

Formula 12 will count the number of employee rates in the billable-time lookup table, so give R31C3 through R50C3 the name EMPS2 (EMPloyeeS2).

Place the cursor on R31C3:	**Type or press:**
Start the Name command	N
Name the cells	EMPS2
Move the highlight to *to refer to*	Tab
(Multiplan displays *to refer to:* R31C3, the first cell to name)	
Specify the last cell to name	:R50C3
Execute the command	Enter

The billable-time lookup table actually contains two lookup tables—one in columns 1 and 2 and the other in columns 1 through 5. It doesn't matter that the cells in columns 1 and 2 are in both lookup tables and can answer to either name. The first table contains the employee numbers and names. Formula 1 will look up the employee number, retrieve the employee name, and enter it in the project section, so let's name this table NAME.

Place the cursor on R31C1:	**Type or press:**
Start the Name command	N
Name the cells	NAME
Move the highlight to *to refer to*	Tab
(Multiplan displays *to refer to:* R31:50C1, the first cell to name)	
Specify the last cell to name	:2
Execute the command	Enter

The second table contains the employee numbers, names, rates, benefits, and totals. Formula 3 will look up the employee's number, retrieve the hourly rate plus benefits, and enter it in the project section of the spreadsheet. Let's name this table BILLABLE.

Leave the cursor on R31C1:	Type or press:
Start the Name command	N
Name the cells	BILLABLE
Move the highlight to *to refer to*	Tab
(Multiplan displays *to refer to: R31C1*, the first cell to name)	
Specify the last cell to name	:R50C5
Execute the command	Enter

Saving and Naming the Spreadsheet

Now store the spreadsheet on disk with the titles, lines, formats, and cell names, and give the spreadsheet its own filename. If you need to tell Multiplan which drive contains your data disk or which directory you want to store the file in, type the drive letter and press F6 (to produce a colon) or type the pathname before you type *PROJECT*, the filename.

Leave the cursor where it is:	Type or press:
Start the Transfer command	T
Select the Save option	S
Name the spreadsheet	PROJECT
Execute the command	Enter

ENTERING THE FORMULAS

The circled numbers in Figure 7-3 show the locations of the formulas. The formulas require both relative and named cell references. The left column in the instructions shows the locations of the relative references, names of named cells, and other elements in the formula. The column on the right and the line immediately below the formula heading show the finished formula.

To build a formula, move the cursor to each cell location shown in the left column (Multiplan will produce the relative notation) and type everything else—operators, symbols, and function names. When you type a character, the cursor returns to the formula cell so that you can type another character, move the cursor to another cell, or enter the formula.

When your formula agrees with the instructions, press Enter. If Multiplan then displays *Not a valid formula*, check each character. When you find the problem, use the F7 through F10 keys to move the highlight, then type missing characters or press the Delete key to delete unwanted characters. If you prefer to start the formula from scratch, simply press the Escape key and begin again.

FORMULA 1: Employee Name

IF(RC[– 1]>0,LOOKUP(RC[– 1],NAME),"")

Formula 1 enters the name of an employee assigned to the project, which saves you the task of typing names and lets you make rapid changes in project assignments simply by typing a different employee number. The formula uses the IF function, which has three required parts: the Test statement, the Then statement, and the Else statement.

The Test statement looks at R12C1. If R12C1 contains a number greater than zero, the Then statement uses the LOOKUP function to look it up in the first column of the NAME table (R31C1 to R50C2, NAME). It then plucks the corresponding name from column 2 of the table, and enters that name in R12C2. If R12C1 is empty, the Else statement ("") makes R12C2 appear empty.

Place the cursor on R12C2:	**Type or move the cursor:**
Start the Value command	V
Enter the formula: IF(R12C1>0, LOOKUP(R12C1,NAME),"")	IF(RC[– 1]>0,LOOKUP (RC[– 1],NAME),"")
Translation: IF(employee number is greater than zero, then look up employee number in the NAME table and enter the corresponding name, else display nothing)	
Execute the command	Enter

Even though the cell is blank, Formula 1 is doing exactly what you told it to do: If there is no employee number, display nothing. On the status line at the bottom of your screen, you can see that the formula is entered. We'll copy Formulas 1 through 7 down their respective columns after you enter all of them.

FORMULA 2: Billable Hours

SUM(RC[– 5]:RC[– 1])

Formula 2 adds the project hours in row 2 of columns 3 through 7 and enters the number of billable hours for this employee in R12C8.

Place the cursor on R12C8:	**Type or move the cursor:**
Start the Value command	V
Enter the formula: SUM(R12C3: R12C7)	SUM(RC[– 5]:RC[– 1])
Execute the command	Enter

FORMULA 3: Billable Rate per Hour

IF(RC[− 1]>0,LOOKUP(RC[− 8],BILLABLE),0)

Formula 3 calculates the employee's billable rate per hour. The Test statement looks at the number of hours in R12C8. If the number of hours is greater than zero, the Then statement looks up the employee number in column 1 of the billable-time lookup table (R31C1 to R50C5, BILLABLE), retrieves the employee rate plus benefits (total income per hour) from the corresponding cell in column 5, and enters this amount in R12C9. If R12C8 contains a zero, the Else statement enters a zero in R12C9.

Place the cursor on R12C9:	**Type or move the cursor:**
Start the Value command	V
Enter the formula: IF(R12C8>0, LOOKUP(R12C1,BILLABLE),0)	IF(RC[− 1]>0,LOOKUP (RC[− 8],BILLABLE),0)
Translation: IF(billable hours are greater than zero, then look up employee number in BILLABLE table and enter total, else enter zero)	
Execute the command	Enter

FORMULA 4: Total Billable

RC[− 2] * RC[− 1]

Formula 4 multiplies the employee's billable hours (R12C8) by the billable rate per hour (R12C9) and enters the total billable amount in R12C10 for an employee assigned to this project.

Place the cursor on R12C10:	**Type or move the cursor:**
Start the Value command	V
Enter the formula: R12C8 * R12C9	RC[− 2] * RC[− 1]
Execute the command	Enter

FORMULA 5: Allocated Overhead

OVERHEAD * RC[− 3]

Formula 5 multiplies the employee's billable hours (R12C8) by the overhead rate per hour (R38C12, OVERHEAD) and enters in R12C11 the overhead allocated to the time this employee spends on the project.

Place the cursor on R12C11:	Type or move the cursor:
Start the Value command	V
Enter the formula: OVERHEAD * R12C8	OVERHEAD * RC[− 3]
Execute the command	Enter

At this point, Formula 5 produces $0.00, not the error message #DIV/0! shown in Figure 7-3.

FORMULA 6: Allocated Marketing and Administration

MADMIN * RC[− 4]

Formula 6 multiplies the employee's billable hours (R12C8) by the marketing and administration rate per hour (R49C12, MADMIN) and enters in R12C12 the dollar amount of support services allocated to the time the employee spends on this project.

Place the cursor on R12C12:	Type or move the cursor:
Start the Value command	V
Enter the formula: MADMIN * R12C8	MADMIN * RC[− 4]
Execute the command	Enter

Formula 6 also produces $0.00, not the error message #DIV/0!.

FORMULA 7: Total Costs

SUM(RC[− 3]:RC[− 1])

Formula 7 adds the total billable costs (R12C10), allocated overhead costs (R12C11), and allocated marketing and administration costs (R12C12) and enters in R12C13 the total cost for an employee assigned to this project.

Place the cursor on R12C13:	Type or move the cursor:
Start the Value command	V
Enter the formula: SUM(R12C10: R12C12)	SUM(RC[− 3]:RC[− 1])
Execute the command	Enter

Formula 7 also produces $0.00, not the error message #DIV/0!. Now copy Formulas 1 through 7 down their respective columns.

Place the cursor on R12C2:	**Type or press:**
Start the Copy command	C
Select the Down option	D
Specify the number of cells to copy into	10
Move the highlight to *starting at*	Tab
Specify the last cell to copy from	:13
Execute the command	Enter

FORMULA 8: Totals

SUM(R[−13]C:R[−1]C)

Formula 8 adds the hours in column 3 (rows 12 through 22) that are spent in the analysis phase of this project and enters the result in R24C3. We'll include the lines in rows 11 and 23 in the formula. Then, if you later add rows in this area, Multiplan will adjust the formula to add the new entries along with the old ones.

Place the cursor on R24C3:	**Type or move the cursor:**
Start the Value command	V
Enter the formula: SUM(R11C3:R23C3)	SUM(R[−13]C:R[−1]C)
Execute the command	Enter

Formula 8 can add the hours in the report, design, supervision, and checkout phases of the project to produce the total billable hours, rates per hour, allocated costs, and total costs (row 24 of columns 4 through 13). So copy it to the right: Leave the cursor on R24C3 and type CR (Copy Right). Multiplan proposes 10 as the number of cells to copy into, which is the number you entered when you copied Formulas 1 through 7 down their columns. This number is correct, so press Enter.

In copying Formula 8 to the right, you copied its center alignment and fixed code with one decimal place. The totals in columns 9 through 13 are dollar amounts, so let's reformat those cells.

Place the cursor on R24C9:	**Type or press:**
Start the Format command	F
Select the Cells option	C
(Multiplan displays *FORMAT cells: R24C9,* the first cell to format)	
Specify the last cell to format	:13
Move the highlight to *alignment*	Tab

Select *Def* (default)	D
Move the highlight to *format code*	Tab
Select *$*	$
Execute the command	Enter

FORMULA 9: Employee Numbers

1 + R[− 1]C

Formula 9 adds 1 to the number in the cell above (R31C1) to produce a series of sequential numbers in column 1 of the billable-time table. Formula 9 starts with a number, so you don't have to type V first.

Place the cursor on R32C1:	**Type or move the cursor:**
Enter the formula: 1 + R31C1	1 + R[− 1]C
Execute the command	Enter

Now copy Formula 9 down the column.

Leave the cursor on R32C1:	**Type or press:**
Start the Copy command	C
Select the Down option	D
Specify the number of cells to copy into	18
Execute the command	Enter

Now press the F4 (recalculate) key, and the sequential numbers appear.

FORMULA 10: Benefits per Hour

RC[− 1] ∗ BENEFITS%

Formula 10 multiplies the employee's hourly rate (R31C3) by the benefits rate per hour (R30C12, BENEFITS) and enters the result in R31C4. Currently, an employer pays about 35% over and above each salary dollar for a typical package of employee benefits (paid time off, insurance, social security, disability, and so on). You'll enter the benefits figure in R30C12 later. Be sure to type the percent sign at the end of the formula.

Place the cursor on R31C4:	**Type or move the cursor:**
Start the Value command	V
Enter the formula: R31C3 ∗ BENEFITS%	RC[− 1] ∗ BENEFITS%
Execute the command	Enter

FORMULA 11: Total

$$RC[-2] + RC[-1]$$

Formula 11 adds the rate per hour (R31C3) and the benefits per hour (R31C4) to produce the total billable rate per hour in R31C5. This is the amount that Formula 3 looks up and enters in the project hours section.

Place the cursor on R31C5:	Type or move the cursor:
Start the Value command	V
Enter the formula: R31C3 + R31C4	$RC[-2] + RC[-1]$
Execute the command	Enter

Now use Copy Down to copy Formulas 10 and 11 down their corresponding columns.

Leave the cursor on R31C5:	Type or press:
Start the Copy command	C
Select the Down option	D
Specify the number of cells to copy	19
Move the highlight to *starting at*	Tab
Specify the first cell to copy from	:4
Execute the command	Enter

FORMULA 12: General Overhead—All Employees

$$EMPS1 + COUNT(EMPS2)$$

Formula 12 calculates the total number of employees, which is used in calculating the general overhead rate in R38C12. The formula adds the number of marketing and administration employees (R47C12, EMPS1) to a count of the employees in the billable-time table (R31C3 through R50C3, EMPS2) and enters the result in R36C12. The COUNT function counts numeric cells, including cells containing zeros. This formula will count the rates in column 3 of the table because this is the only numeric column that will be empty (that is, will not contain zeros) if no employee name is listed. Type the entire formula.

Place the cursor on R36C12:	Type or press:
Start the Value command	V
Enter the formula: EMPS1 + COUNT(EMPS2)	EMPS1 + COUNT (EMPS2)
Execute the command	Enter

FORMULA 13: General Overhead—All Employee Hours per Year

R[−1]C∗HOURS

Formula 13 multiplies the number of employees (R36C12) by the annual hours per employee (R29C12, HOURS) and enters the total annual hours per year in R37C12. This number is needed to calculate the general overhead rate in R38C12. The employees in our fictional engineering and design company work 7½ hours per day and 5 days per week, a total of 1950 hours per year. (You will soon enter 1950 in the HOURS cell.) If your employees work a different schedule, change the number in the HOURS cell later. For an 8-hour day, 5 days per week, the number of annual hours is 2080. For a 7-hour day, 5 days per week, the number is 1820.

Place the cursor on R37C12:	**Type or move the cursor:**
Start the Value command	V
Enter the formula: R36C12∗HOURS	R[−1]C∗HOURS
Execute the command	Enter

FORMULA 14: Overhead Rate per Hour

R[−3]C/R[−1]C

Formula 14 divides the overhead expense per year (R35C12) by the total annual hours of all employees (R37C12) and enters the general overhead rate per hour in R38C12.

Place the cursor on R38C12:	**Type or move the cursor:**
Start the Value command	V
Enter the formula: R35C12/R37C12	R[−3]C/R[−1]C
Execute the command	Enter

The #DIV/0! message now appears in R38C12. Press the F4 key. The cells in columns 11 and 13 also show *#DIV/0!*, because Formula 5 (column 11) references Formula 14, and Formula 7 (column 13) references Formula 5.

FORMULA 15: Support Staff Benefits

R[−1]C∗BENEFITS%

Formula 15 multiplies the marketing and administration salaries (R43C12) by the benefits rate (R30C12, BENEFITS) and enters the amount of the support staff benefits in R44C12. Be sure that you type the percent sign at the end of the formula.

Place the cursor on R44C12:	Type or move the cursor:
Start the Value command	V
Enter the formula: R43C12 * BENEFITS%	R[− 1]C * BENEFITS%
Execute the command	Enter

FORMULA 16: Support Staff—Total Salaries and Benefits

R[− 3]C + R[− 2]C

Formula 16 adds the marketing and administration salaries (R43C12) to benefits (R44C12) and enters the result in R46C12. This amount is used to calculate the marketing and administration rate per hour in R49C12.

Place the cursor on R46C12:	Type or move the cursor:
Start the Value command	V
Enter the formula: R43C12 + R44C12	R[− 3]C + R[− 2]C
Execute the command	Enter

FORMULA 17: Support Staff—Employee Hours per Year

EMPS1 * HOURS

Formula 17 multiplies the number of marketing and administration employees (R47C12, EMPS1) by the annual hours per employee (R29C12, HOURS) and enters the total annual marketing and administration hours in R48C12. Type the entire formula.

Place the cursor on R48C12:	Type or press:
Start the Value command	V
Enter the formula: EMPS1 * HOURS	EMPS1 * HOURS
Execute the command	Enter

FORMULA 18: Support Staff—Rate Per Hour

R[− 3]C/R[− 1]C

Formula 18 divides the marketing and administration salaries and benefits (R46C12) by the hours per year for marketing and administration employees (R48C12) and enters the marketing and administration rate per hour in cell R49C12.

Place the cursor on R49C12:	Type or move the cursor:
Start the Value command	V
Enter the formula: R46C12/R48C12	R[−3]C/R[−1]C
Execute the command	Enter

You now see *#DIV/0!* in R49C12. Press the F4 key, and *#DIV/0!* also appears in column 12, rows 12 through 22 and row 24, because Formula 6 references Formula 18.

FORMULA 19: Estimate—Total Project Cost

TOTAL

Formula 19 copies the amount from the total costs cell (R24C13, TOTAL) to the total project cost cell (R3C8). This number forms the basis for the estimate to the client. Type the one-word formula.

Place the cursor on R3C8:	Type or press:
Start the Value command	V
Enter the formula: TOTAL	TOTAL
Execute the command	Enter

FORMULA 20: Spreadsheet Filename

NAME()

Formula 20 generates the spreadsheet filename in R1C13. Type the function name and parentheses.

Place the cursor on R1C13:	Type or press:
Start the Value command	V
Enter the formula: NAME()	NAME()
Execute the command	Enter

Saving the Formulas

Now store all the formulas on disk. Because you saved the spreadsheet before, Multiplan asks you to confirm overwriting the earlier version.

Leave the cursor where it is:	Type or press:
Start the Transfer command	T
Select the Save option	S
(Multiplan displays *PROJECT*— there's no need to retype)	
Execute the command	Enter
(Multiplan recalculates, then displays *Enter Y to overwrite file*)	
Confirm the overwrite	Y

ENTERING THE PRACTICE NUMBERS

Figure 7-4 shows sample numbers and two more formula locations. Let's tackle the numbers first. You can type a number whenever you see the command menu or *ALPHA/VALUE* on the command line. Simply type the number and use the direction keys to move the cursor to the next cell that contains a number. Because of the formatting you did earlier, Multiplan will enter the dollar signs and decimal places for you. Here's the most efficient way to enter the numbers:

1. Place the cursor on R4C7 (the cell for the profit margin). Type *40* and move the cursor to R12C1.

2. Type the employee numbers shown in Figure 7-4 in rows 12 through 18 of column 1. Move the cursor to R12C3.

3. Type the estimated project hours shown in Figure 7-4 in rows 12 through 18 of columns 3 through 7. Move the cursor to R31C1.

4. Type the number *1* in R31C1, and move the cursor to R31C3.

5. Type the hourly rates shown in Figure 7-4 in column 3 in the billable-time table. Move the cursor to R29C12.

6. Type the numbers shown in Figure 7-4 in column 12. Don't type decimal points or zeros—your formatting will add them. Press Enter.

Now store your work on disk: Type *TS* (Transfer Save) and press Enter. Type *Y* to overwrite. When Multiplan saves your spreadsheet, it also recalculates, so your numbers should agree with those in Figure 7-1. Check them carefully to be sure everything is correct before you go on to the next step.

	1	2	3	4	5	6	7
1							PROJECT CO
2	==
3	Client:				Total Project Cost		
4	Project:				Profit Margin (%)		40.0
5	Location:				Estimate to Client		
6	Prepared:						
7	By:						
8	==
9	Employee		************ Estimated Project Hours ************
10	Number	Name	Analysis	Report	Design	Suprvsion	Checkout
11	--
12	1		15	10	15	16	10
13	13				36	8.5	
14	6		7.5	5	6		
15	16		5				7.5
16	15				12		
17	20				7.5		
18	5				16	5	
19							
20							
21							
22							
23	==
24			Totals				
25							
26							
27	BILLABLE-TIME LOOKUP TABLE
28	==
29	Number	Name		Rate/Hr	Benefit/Hr	Total	
30	--
31	1		24.52				
32			19.23				
33			8.65				
34			16.23				
35			12.2				
36			13.46				
37			19.23				
38			8				
39			11				
40			16.23				
41			8				
42			12.46				
43			19.23				
44			6.25				
45			19.71				
46			9.5				
47			6				
48			12				
49			14.5				
50			19.9				
51	==

FIGURE 7-4.
Project cost estimate sample numbers and Formulas 21 and 22

8	9	10	11	12	13
ST ESTIMATE					PROJECT

$0.00 ㉑			Project Deadline Date		
$0.00 ㉒			Today's Date		
			Calendar Days Remaining		
			Weekdays Remaining		

Billable Hours	Billable Rate/Hour	Total Billable	Allocated Overhead	Allocated Mktng & Admin	Total Costs

Annual Hours per Employee	1950
Benefits Rate per Hour (%)	35.0

GENERAL OVERHEAD

Overhead Expense per Year	540164
All Employees	
All Employee Hours per Year	
Overhead Rate per Hour	

MARKETING AND ADMINISTRATION

Salaries	211992
Benefits	
Total Salaries & Benefits	
Mktng & Admin Employees	13
Employee Hours per Year	
Mktng & Admin Rate per Hour	

SOLVING PROBLEMS WITH ITERATION

Multiplan has calculated a total project cost of $8285.54, as shown in R3C8. Our final requirements—profit margin and estimate to the client—present a challenge. We want Formula 21 (R4C8) to calculate a profit of 40 percent of the estimate, but we don't know the estimate amount. We want Formula 22 (R5C8) to calculate an estimate that includes 40 percent profit, but we don't know the profit amount. It's a case of the chicken and the egg—the estimate depends on the profit, the profit depends on the estimate. We can solve this problem with iteration. Iteration repeats the calculations of a formula by using the result of the previous calculation in the next calculation.

Before we set up the iteration for our project cost estimate spreadsheet, let's enter Formulas 21 and 22.

FORMULA 21: Profit Margin

ESTIMATE * MARGIN%

Formula 21 multiplies the estimate (R5C8, ESTIMATE) by the amount you enter in the profit margin cell (R4C7, MARGIN) and enters the profit in R4C8. Type the entire formula, including the percent sign at the end.

Place the cursor on R4C8:	Type or press:
Start the Value command	V
Enter the formula: ESTIMATE * MARGIN%	ESTIMATE * MARGIN%
Execute the command	Enter

Zeros now appear in R4C8.

FORMULA 22: Estimate to Client

TOTAL + PROFIT

Formula 22 adds the project cost (R24C13, TOTAL) to the profit (R4C8, PROFIT) and enters the estimate in R5C8. Type the entire formula.

Place the cursor on R5C8:	Type or press:
Start the Value command	V
Enter the formula: TOTAL + PROFIT	TOTAL + PROFIT
Execute the command	Enter

Keep a watchful eye on the message line and press the F4 key. While Multiplan recalculates, the message *Circular references unresolved* appears briefly. Calculation did take place, but look at the result: The amount in R4C8 is $3314.22 and the amount in R5C8 is $8285.54, the same as in R3C8. Multiplan calculated Formulas 21 and 22, found that they referred to each other and then stopped. Now let's turn on iteration.

Leave the cursor where it is:	Type or press:
Start the Options command	O
Move the highlight to *iteration*	Tab Tab
Select *Yes*	Y
Execute the command	Enter

Now press the F4 key again and watch Formulas 21 and 22 wend their way through successive calculations. Each calculation of one formula works on the result of the previous calculation of the other formula until the profit becomes $5523.69 (based on a 40% profit margin) and the estimate becomes $13809.23. Ah—sweet success.

Locking the Formulas

To prevent accidental alteration, lock the formulas on the spreadsheet.

Leave the cursor where it is:	Type:
Start the Lock command	L
Select the Formulas option	F
(Multiplan displays *Enter Y to confirm*)	
Confirm the lock	Y

ENTERING THE TRANSIENT TEXT

Figure 7-5 shows client information in the top left corner of the page, employee names in the billable-time table, and three more formulas. These formulas calculate the current date and the weekdays remaining before the project deadline.

First, enter the text: Place the cursor on R3C2, type *A* to start the Alpha command, and type the client information shown in rows 3 through 7 of column 2. Move the cursor to R31C2 and type the employee names shown in rows

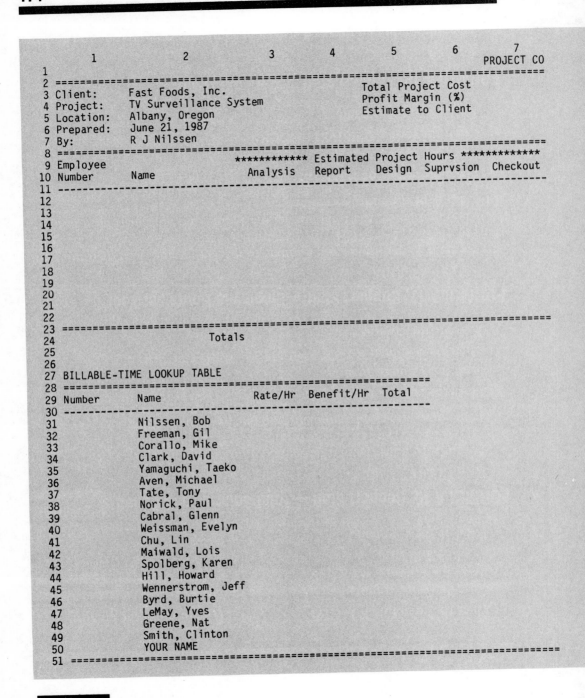

```
                 1              2           3        4       5        6       7
                                                                        PROJECT CO
 1
 2  ==================================================================================
 3  Client:     Fast Foods, Inc.                       Total Project Cost
 4  Project:    TV Surveillance System                 Profit Margin (%)
 5  Location:   Albany, Oregon                          Estimate to Client
 6  Prepared:   June 21, 1987
 7  By:         R J Nilssen
 8  ==================================================================================
 9  Employee                      ************ Estimated Project Hours ************
10  Number      Name                  Analysis  Report   Design  Suprvsion Checkout
11  ----------------------------------------------------------------------------------
12
13
14
15
16
17
18
19
20
21
22                                                                                 ===
23  ==================================================================================
24                          Totals
25
26
27  BILLABLE-TIME LOOKUP TABLE
28  ==========================================================================
29  Number      Name                  Rate/Hr  Benefit/Hr  Total
30  ----------------------------------------------------------------------------------
31              Nilssen, Bob
32              Freeman, Gil
33              Corallo, Mike
34              Clark, David
35              Yamaguchi, Taeko
36              Aven, Michael
37              Tate, Tony
38              Norick, Paul
39              Cabral, Glenn
40              Weissman, Evelyn
41              Chu, Lin
42              Maiwald, Lois
43              Spolberg, Karen
44              Hill, Howard
45              Wennerstrom, Jeff
46              Byrd, Burtie
47              LeMay, Yves
48              Greene, Nat
49              Smith, Clinton
50              YOUR NAME
51  ==================================================================================
```

FIGURE 7-5.
The client and employee entries on the project cost estimate spreadsheet, and Formulas
23, 24, and 25

```
      8              9            10             11             12            13
ST ESTIMATE                                                              PROJECT
================================================================================
                                          Project Deadline Date        3/25/88
                                          Today's Date                11/19/87 ㉓
                                          Calendar Days Remaining          128 ㉔
                                          Weekdays Remaining                92 ㉕

================================================================================
Billable      Billable       Total      Allocated     Allocated       Total
  Hours      Rate/Hour     Billable     Overhead     Mktng & Admin     Costs
--------------------------------------------------------------------------------




================================================================================




         ================================================
         Annual Hours per Employee
         Benefits Rate per Hour (%)

         ================================================
         GENERAL OVERHEAD
         ------------------------------------------------
         Overhead Expense per Year
         All Employees
         All Employee Hours per Year
         Overhead Rate per Hour

         ================================================
         MARKETING AND ADMINISTRATION
         ------------------------------------------------
         Salaries
         Benefits
                                      ------------
         Total Salaries & Benefits
         Mktng & Admin Employees
         Employee Hours per Year
         Mktng & Admin Rate per Hour

================================================================================
```

31 through 49 of column 2. Cell R50C2 is reserved for your name. If you want to have some fun, replace some of the other names with the names of your friends and relatives. But don't change any pay rates. After you type the last name, press Enter.

Now press the Home key to jump the cursor to R1C1, where you'll have a bird's-eye view of the action. Press the F4 (recalculate) key. As your LOOKUP formula goes to work, names appear in column 2.

Except for the empty cells in the top right corner, your spreadsheet should now look like the one in Figure 7-1. Store it on disk by typing *TS* (Transfer Save) and pressing Enter. Type *Y* to overwrite.

WORKING WITH DATES

Let's skip ahead in time. Your proposal was well-received and your company won the contract. Now you want to monitor the progress of the project day-by-day to make sure it is completed on schedule. Every time you review or modify your initial input, you want Multiplan to enter today's date and show how many days remain until the deadline date. Therefore, you are working with two dates—the project deadline in R3C13 and today's date in R4C13.

Multiplan stores dates as serial numbers. The serial number for a date is a number from 1 to 65380 (1 is the number for January 1, 1900, and 65380 is the number for December 31, 2078). The cell format determines what the serial number looks like on the spreadsheet. Let's format both cells to show a month, a day, and a year.

Place the cursor on R3C13:	Type or press:
Start the Format command	F
Select the Time-Date option	T
Select the Cells option	C
(Multiplan displays *FORMAT TIME-DATE cells: R3C13*, the first cell to format)	
Specify the last cell to format	:R4C13
Move the highlight to *Format*	Tab
Bring up the *Time-Date* format screen	Right Arrow
Select *m/d/yy*	Down Arrow (eight times)
Execute the command	Enter

Next, enter the project deadline date: Leave the cursor on R3C13 and type *A* (Alpha). Type *3/25/88* and press Enter. The date appears in its cell, and you can now see *32227*, its serial number, on the status line at the bottom of the screen. Now enter the formulas that will help you keep close tabs on this project.

FORMULA 23: Today's Date

NOW()

Formula 23 takes the date you entered with the MS-DOS command Date or the date kept by your computer's battery-operated clock and enters it in R4C13. Type the function name and parentheses.

Place the cursor on R4C13:	Type or press:
Start the Value command	V
Enter the formula: NOW()	NOW()
Execute the command	Enter

Your date probably doesn't match the one in Figure 7-5, so temporarily return to MS-DOS with the Run Dos command and change it.

Leave the cursor where it is:	Type or press:
Start the Run command	R
Select the Dos option	D
Specify the DOS Date command	DATE
Execute the command	Enter

MS-DOS now displays the current date and asks you to enter a new date. Type *11-19-87* and press Enter twice to return to Multiplan. Now press F4 to recalculate the spreadsheet. After you do, you see *11/19/87* in R4C13.

FORMULA 24: Calendar Days Remaining

END − TODAY + 1

Formula 24 subtracts the serial number of today's date (R4C13, TODAY) from the serial number of the project deadline date (R3C13, END), adds one day to start the calculation with tomorrow's date, and enters the number of calendar days remaining in R5C13. Type the entire formula.

Place the cursor on R5C13:	Type or move the cursor:
Start the Value command	V
Enter the formula: END − TODAY + 1	END − TODAY + 1
Execute the command	Enter

FORMULA 25: Weekdays Remaining

$$\text{IF(WEEKDAY(TODAY)} > 1, 7 - \text{WEEKDAY(TODAY)}, 0)$$
$$+ \text{ROUND((CDAYS} - (\text{IF(WEEKDAY(TODAY)} > 1,$$
$$7 - \text{WEEKDAY(TODAY)}, 0) + \text{IF(WEEKDAY(END)} < 7,$$
$$\text{WEEKDAY(END)}, 0)))/7, 0) * 5 + \text{IF(WEEKDAY(END)} < 7,$$
$$\text{WEEKDAY(END)} - 1, 0)$$

Formula 25 produces the number of weekdays between today's date (R4C13, TODAY) and the deadline date (R3C13, END). To do this, it must be able to distinguish weekdays from weekends—a formidable task. It doesn't take company holidays into consideration. The formula works with three variables:

■ The day of the week that today is, which can be any number from 1 to 7, representing Sunday through Saturday.

■ The number of full weeks between the current week and the ending week of the project.

■ The day of the week that the deadline date falls on, which again can be any number from 1 to 7.

Splitting the explanation of Formula 25 into three parts will make it more understandable. Let's start with the first part, which works with the current week:

PART 1

$$\text{IF(WEEKDAY(TODAY)} > 1, 7 - \text{WEEKDAY(TODAY)}, 0)$$

The Test statement generates today's number (R4C13, TODAY) and compares it with 1, which represents Sunday. If today's number is greater than 1, it is either a weekday or a Saturday. The Then statement then subtracts today's number from 7 to produce the remaining number of weekdays in the current week, including today. For example, if today's number is 3, today is a Tuesday. Subtracting 3 from 7 leaves 4 days in the current week—Tuesday, Wednesday, Thursday, and Friday. If today's number is 1, today is Sunday, and the Else statement enters a zero. This produces the number of weekdays in the current week.

PART 2

$$+ \text{ROUND((CDAYS} - (\text{IF(WEEKDAY(TODAY)} > 1,$$
$$7 - \text{WEEKDAY(TODAY)}, 0) + \text{IF(WEEKDAY(END)} < 7,$$
$$\text{WEEKDAY(END)}, 0)))/7, 0) * 5$$

The second part of the formula works with the weeks between the current week and the week of the deadline (R3C13, END). The formula subtracts the number of weekdays in the current and ending weeks from the number of calendar days (R5C13, CDAYS), divides the result by 7 to get the number of weeks, then multiplies by 5 to get the number of weekdays. The ROUND function with zero digits rounds the result to the next higher integer. This produces the number of weekdays in the intervening weeks.

PART 3

+ IF(WEEKDAY(END)<7,WEEKDAY(END) – 1,0)

The third part works with the ending week. The Test statement generates the end day's number and compares it with 7 (representing Saturday). If it is less than 7, the end day is either a weekday or a Sunday. The Then statement then subtracts 1 from the end day's number to produce the remaining number of weekdays in the ending week. For example, if the end day's number is 4, it is a Wednesday. Subtracting 1 from 4 leaves 3 days in the ending week — Monday, Tuesday, and Wednesday. If the end day's number is 7, it is a Saturday, and the Else statement enters a zero. The Else statement thus produces the number of weekdays in the ending week.

The formula adds the result of these three calculations and enters the total number of weekdays in R6C13. Now type the entire formula slowly and carefully.

Place the cursor on R6C13:	Type or press:
Start the Value command	V
Enter the formula: IF(WEEKDAY(TODAY)>1, 7 – WEEKDAY(TODAY),0) + ROUND((CDAYS – (IF(WEEKDAY(TODAY)>1, 7 – WEEKDAY(TODAY),0) + IF(WEEKDAY(END)<7, WEEKDAY(END),0)))/7,0) * 5 + IF(WEEKDAY(END)<7, WEEKDAY(END) – 1,0)	IF(WEEKDAY(TODAY)>1, 7 – WEEKDAY(TODAY),0) + ROUND((CDAYS – (IF(WEEKDAY(TODAY)>1, 7 – WEEKDAY(TODAY),0) + IF(WEEKDAY(END)<7, WEEKDAY(END),0)))/7,0) * 5 + IF(WEEKDAY(END)<7, WEEKDAY(END) – 1,0)
Execute the command	Enter

Now lock the cells containing the date formulas: Leave the cursor on R6C13 and type *LC* (Lock Cells). Type *:R4C13* and press the Tab key to move the highlight to *status*. Type *L* to select Locked and press Enter.

PRINTING YOUR SPREADSHEET

This spreadsheet is 162 characters wide, including one set of Multiplan row numbers. It prints in 12-pitch type on two sheets of 8½-by-11-inch paper or, with a wide-carriage printer, on one sheet of 15-by-11-inch paper.

Setting the Print Margins

The first step before printing is to set the margins.

Leave the cursor where it is:	Type or press:
Start the Print command	P
Select the Margins option	M

Type the following numbers in the margins fields (tabbing past any fields that are already at the proper setting). If you overshoot a field, press Tab to move full circle through the fields or press Shift-Tab to move backward one field. The highlight is in the *left* field.

Leave the cursor where it is:	Type or press:
Specify the number of characters	
For 8½-by-11-inch paper	5
For 15-by-11-inch paper	0
Move the highlight to *top*	Tab
Specify the number of lines	6
Move the highlight to *print width*	Tab
Specify the number of characters:	
For 8½-by-11-inch paper	96
For 15-by-11-inch paper	162
Move the highlight to *print length*	Tab
Specify the number of lines	60
Move the highlight to *page length*	Tab
Specify the number of lines	66
Execute the command	Enter

Setting the Print Options

You are still in the Print command. The next step is to set the print options. The options settings are the same for all the spreadsheets in this book: Print the entire spreadsheet in 12-pitch type with row and column numbers, which help you compare your results with the illustrations. You can find the printer code for 12-pitch type in your printer manual.

Type O to select the Options option. Type in the following responses. Tab past any fields that already have the proper settings. The highlight is now in the *area* field.

Leave the cursor where it is:	Type or press:
Define the print area	R1:4095
Move the highlight to *setup*	Tab
Enter your printer code for 12-pitch type	(your code)
Move the highlight to *formulas*	Tab Tab
Select *No*	N
Move the highlight to *row-col numbers*	Tab
Select *Yes*	Y
Execute the command	Enter

Now, before you print, store the spreadsheet with the print settings: Press the Escape key to leave the Print command. Leave the cursor where it is. Type *TS* (Transfer Save) and press Enter. Type *Y* to overwrite.

Now turn on your printer and print your spreadsheet.

Leave the cursor where it is:	Type:
Start the Print command	P
Select the Printer option	P

And there's a copy of your spreadsheet.

USING YOUR SPREADSHEET

When you use this spreadsheet for your own entries, you may want more rows in the project hours section. To add 4 rows, for example, place the cursor on row 23 and type *IR* (Insert Row). Type *4* and press Enter. Then copy the formulas in column 2 and in columns 8 through 13 down their columns. Type *TR* (Transfer Save) to save your changes. Multiplan will adjust the other formulas and named cells to include the 4 new rows. You can do the same thing to insert rows in the billable-time lookup table.

SPREADSHEET SUMMARY

General: The completed spreadsheet is shown in Figure 7-1. Use Options to set automatic recalculation to *No* and iteration to *Yes*. Use Value to enter REPT(" = ",18) and REPT(" – ",18) for the long lines, and REPT(" – ",12) for the line in R45C12. Use Lock Formulas to lock the formulas.

Column Width: Use Format Width as follows: Set column 1 to 12 characters, column 2 to 18 characters, column 8 to 12 characters, and columns 9 through 13 to 13 characters.

Format: Use Format Cells as follows: Continue R1C2:R7C13, R9C3:7, R27C1:2, and R29:49C9:11. Center R9C8:13, R10C3:13, R29C3:5, R12:22C1, and R31:50C1. Right-justify R1C13 and R24C2. Center and fix code with 1 decimal place R4C7 and R12:24C3:8. Fix code with 1 decimal place R30C12. Dollar code R3:5C8, R12:22C9:13, R31:50C3:5, R35C12, R38C12, R43:44C12, R46C12, and R49C12. Integer code R5C13. After copying Formula 8 to the right, dollar code R24C9:13. Use Format Time-Date Cells to give R3C13 and R4C13 the *m/d/yy* format.

Name: Use Name as follows: R4C7 is MARGIN. R4C8 is PROFIT. R5C8 is ESTIMATE. R3C13 is END. R4C13 is TODAY. R5C13 is CDAYS. R24C13 is TOTAL. R29C12 is HOURS. R30C12 is BENEFITS. R38C12 is OVERHEAD. R47C12 is EMPS1. R49C12 is MADMIN. R31C3:R50C3 is EMPS2. R31:50C1:2 is NAME. R31:50C1:5 is BILLABLE.

Print: Project Cost Estimate is 162 characters wide, including Multiplan row numbers, and is printed in 12-pitch type. Set the margins for 8½-by-11-inch paper as follows: *left 5, top 6, print width 96, print length 60,* and *page length 66.* Use the same settings for 15-by-11-inch paper, but change *left* to 0 and *print width* to 162.

Formulas: Formulas use relative and named cell references.

1	R12C2	Employee Name IF(RC[– 1]>0,LOOKUP(RC[– 1],NAME),"")
2	R12C8	Billable Hours SUM(RC[– 5]:RC[– 1])
3	R12C9	Billable Rate Per Hour IF(RC[– 1]>0,LOOKUP(RC[– 8],BILLABLE),0)
4	R12C10	Total Billable RC[– 2] * RC[– 1]

5	R12C11	Allocated Overhead OVERHEAD * RC[-3]
6	R12C12	Allocated Marketing and Administration MADMIN * RC[-4]
7	R12C13	Total Costs SUM(RC[-3]:RC[-1])
8	R24C3	Totals SUM(R[-13]C:R[-1]C)
9	R32C1	Employee Numbers 1+R[-1]C
10	R31C4	Benefits Per Hour RC[-1] * BENEFITS%
11	R31C5	Total RC[-2]+RC[-1]
12	R36C12	General Overhead—All Employees EMPS1+COUNT(EMPS2)
13	R37C12	General Overhead—All Employee Hours Per Year R[-1]C * HOURS
14	R38C12	Overhead Rate Per Hour R[-3]C/R[-1]C
15	R44C12	Support Staff Benefits R[-1]C * BENEFITS%
16	R46C12	Support Staff—Total Salaries and Benefits R[-3]C+R[-2]C
17	R48C12	Support Staff—Employee Hours Per Year EMPS1 * HOURS
18	R49C12	Support Staff—Rate Per Hour R[-3]C/R[-1]C
19	R3C8	Estimate—Total Project Cost TOTAL
20	R1C13	Spreadsheet Filename NAME()

21   R4C8   Profit Margin
ESTIMATE * MARGIN%

22   R5C8   Estimate To Client
TOTAL + PROFIT

23   R4C13   Today's Date
NOW()

24   R5C13   Calendar Days Remaining
END – TODAY + 1

25   R6C13   Weekdays Remaining
IF(WEEKDAY(TODAY)>1,
  7 – WEEKDAY(TODAY),0) + ROUND((CDAYS
  – (IF(WEEKDAY(TODAY)>1,
  7 – WEEKDAY(TODAY),0)
  + IF(WEEKDAY(END)<7,
  WEEKDAY(END),0)))/7,0) * 5
  + IF(WEEKDAY(END)<7,
  WEEKDAY(END) – 1,0)

8

Financial Analysis: Balance Sheet

Financial statements—particularly the balance sheet and the income statement—provide important information about the way a company operates. Like a fingerprint, the information in these reports is unique for every company. Although financial statements sometimes appear complicated, there's nothing mysterious about them. They are simply a summary of a company's daily accounting records.

Analyzing and understanding your balance sheet and income statement can help you run your business more efficiently and profitably. For instance, these reports can answer such essential questions as: Are assets being used to generate the highest possible return on money invested? Can the business service its obligations as they come due? Are operating costs in line with revenues? Are credit and collections under control? Are inventories excessive?

As a company report card, financial statement analysis can:

- Report on the effectiveness of management.

- Provide management with a means of self-evaluation.

- Reveal shortcomings that should be corrected.

- Provide a basis for planning, budgeting, and control.

```
                1                2    3     4     5        6
                                                      AVEN CO
 1
 2  ================================================================
                                                   COMPARATIVE
 3
 4  ----------------------------------------------------------------
 5
 6  Assets                      June 30, 1987  June 30, 1986
 7  ----------------------------------------------------------------
 8  Current assets:
 9   Cash                         $  185,890    $  182,506
10   Marketable securities            36,503        30,090
11   Accounts receivable             771,080       807,289
12   Inventories                   1,234,567     1,115,876
13   Prepaid expenses                 19,880        16,540
14                                ---------     ---------
15     Total current assets       $2,247,920    $2,152,301
16                                ---------     ---------
17  Fixed assets:
18   Plant, property, and equipment 1,579,150     1,494,235
19   Less: Accumulated depreciation   876,820       766,031
20                                ---------     ---------
21     Total fixed assets         $  702,330    $  728,204
22                                ---------     ---------
23  Other assets:
24   Investments                      63,589             0
25   Goodwill                        200,000       200,000
26                                ---------     ---------
27     Total other assets         $  263,589    $  200,000
28                                ---------     ---------
29     Total assets               $3,213,839    $3,080,505
30                                =========     =========
```

FIGURE 8-1.
The completed balance sheet

The next three chapters explain how to develop a powerful spreadsheet that combines the balance sheet, income statement, and financial ratios for the fictional Aven Corporation, a publicly-held manufacturer of pet products. We'll develop the spreadsheet in three easy stages.

In this chapter, we will create a comparative balance sheet that lists Aven's assets, liabilities, and owners' equity for the fiscal years ending June 30, 1987 and June 30, 1986. (Financial statements present the figures for the current year first.) Figure 8-1 shows the completed balance sheet.

In Chapter 9, we will add a comparative income statement for the same two-year period. The income statement, also called a profit-and-loss statement,

```
                        7              8    9    10    11
RPORATION                                              FINANCE
=================================================================
BALANCE SHEET
-----------------------------------------------------------------
   Liabilities and
   Stockholders' Equity      June 30, 1987  June 30, 1986
-----------------------------------------------------------------
   Current liabilities:
   Notes payable (current portion)   $  447,500   $  355,670
   Accounts payable                     152,897      140,800
   Accrued taxes                         41,234      110,560
   Other accrued liabilities            185,670      159,323
                                     ----------   ----------
   Total current liabilities        $  827,301   $  766,353
                                     ----------   ----------
   Long-term liabilities:
   Notes payable (long-term)            626,017      829,371
                                     ----------   ----------
   Total liabilities                $1,453,318   $1,595,724
                                     ----------   ----------
   Stockholders' equity
   Common stock ($10 par value,
     40,000 shares outstanding)         400,000      400,000
   Paid-in capital                      344,550      344,550
   Retained earnings                  1,015,971      740,231
                                     ----------   ----------
   Total stockholders' equity       $1,760,521   $1,484,781
                                     ----------   ----------
      Total liabilities and         $3,213,839   $3,080,505
      stockholders' equity          ========     ========
```

lists Aven's income and expenses. Figure 9-1 shows the combined balance sheet and income statement.

In Chapter 10, we will add a group of commonly used financial ratios. These ratios express the relationship between the balance sheet and income statement. They are useful in evaluating the financial condition and managerial performance of a business. Figure 10-1 shows the final version of the balance sheet, income statement, and ratios spreadsheet.

You can use this spreadsheet to analyze the performance of a company that interests you as an investment. Simply plug in the numbers gleaned from recent annual reports, and let the financial ratios tell you how the company is doing.

If you're familiar with Multiplan and prefer to create these spreadsheets without following the step-by-step instructions, refer to the summary at the end of each chapter.

THE BALANCE SHEET

The balance sheet summarizes the business activities of the Aven Corporation at a specific point in time. It lists what Aven owns (assets), what it owes to creditors (liabilities), and how much investors' money is in the business (stockholders' equity), presenting this information as Assets = Liabilities + Equity.

■ Current assets are cash and assets that can be converted into cash during the normal operating cycle of the business, usually no longer than a year. Assets are listed on the balance sheet in order of liquidity: Cash, marketable securities, inventories, and prepaid expenses, such as insurance and rent, appear first; fixed assets and long-term (other) assets are the least liquid, so they appear last. Goodwill is an intangible asset that reflects the value of Aven's name and reputation in the pet products marketplace.

■ Current liabilities are debts due for repayment within one year. Payments for these obligations are usually taken from current assets. Long-term liabilities are debts that are not due in the current year.

■ Stockholders' equity shows the components of the owners' share in the business: Common stock outstanding, paid-in capital, and retained earnings.

Now let's create the balance sheet shown in Figure 8-1.

SETTING UP YOUR SPREADSHEET

Bring up the Multiplan screen. If you turned off automatic recalculation on your last spreadsheet, you can skip the following step and go directly to "Adjusting the Column Widths." Otherwise, to make data entry faster, leave the cursor on R1C1. Type *O* to start the Options command, type *N* for no recalculation, and press Enter. Now we're ready to make your spreadsheet look like the one in Figure 8-2.

Adjusting the Column Widths

When you start a new spreadsheet, each of Multiplan's columns is 10 characters wide. To give the assets titles the room they need, let's increase column 1 to 32 characters.

Leave the cursor on R1C1:	Type or press:
Start the Format command	F
Select the Width option	W
Specify the number of characters in the column	32
Execute the command	Enter

Give the liabilities and stockholders' equity titles an equal amount of room: Place the cursor on R1C7 and type *FW* (Format Width). Then type *32* and press Enter.

Now let's reduce the widths of columns 2, 4, 8, and 10 to 5 characters each. These narrow columns are used in an interesting way—to display a dollar sign to the left of the top number in each column and to the left of each total. Although each dollar sign is in its own cell, it will seem to be integrated with the number beside it. With this technique the dollar signs will line up in a column, unlike the staggered dollar signs you end up with when you format for dollars. Start with column 2.

Place the cursor on R1C2:	Type or press:
Start the Format command	F
Select the Width option	W
Specify the number of characters in the column	5
Execute the command	Enter

Reduce the widths of columns 4, 8, and 10 to 5 characters in the same way.

Entering Balance Sheet Titles

You are now ready to type the titles shown in Figure 8-2. But first, a few instructions:

■ The titles are indented in a stair-step fashion, which is the standard accounting practice, so that you can easily examine the numbers they relate to. Indent one space before typing general heading titles, such as *Cash* (R9C1). Indent two spaces before typing titles that identify totals, such as *Total current assets* (R15C1). Indent four spaces before typing titles identifying final totals, such as *Total assets* (R29C1). To indent, press the Spacebar the proper number of times before typing the title.

■ Type *June 30, 1987* in R6C2 and again in R6C8. Type *June 30, 1986* in R6C4 and again in R6C10. Only part of these titles will appear in their cells when you enter them. We'll take care of that shortly when we format the titles.

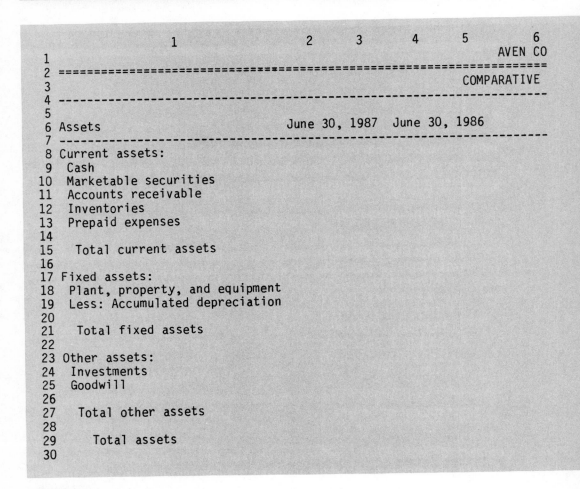

```
                   1                  2      3      4      5           6
                                                              AVEN CO
 1
 2  =========================================================================
 3                                                            COMPARATIVE
 4  -------------------------------------------------------------------------
 5
 6  Assets                             June 30, 1987  June 30, 1986
 7  -------------------------------------------------------------------------
 8  Current assets:
 9   Cash
10   Marketable securities
11   Accounts receivable
12   Inventories
13   Prepaid expenses
14
15     Total current assets
16
17  Fixed assets:
18   Plant, property, and equipment
19   Less: Accumulated depreciation
20
21     Total fixed assets
22
23  Other assets:
24   Investments
25   Goodwill
26
27     Total other assets
28
29       Total assets
30
```

FIGURE 8-2.
The titles and lines on the balance sheet

Now put Multiplan in the alpha/value mode, which will make entering the titles quick and easy.

Leave the cursor where it is:	**Type or press:**
Start the Options command	O
Move the highlight to *alpha/value*	Tab (four times)
Select *Yes*	Y
Execute the command	Enter

```
                    7              8     9     10    11
RPORATION
===================================================================
BALANCE SHEET
-------------------------------------------------------------------
    Liabilities and
    Stockholders' Equity            June 30, 1987  June 30, 1986
-------------------------------------------------------------------
    Current liabilities:
     Notes payable (current portion)
     Accounts payable
     Accrued taxes
     Other accrued liabilities

     Total current liabilities

    Long-term liabilities:
     Notes payable (long-term)

     Total liabilities

    Stockholders' equity
     Common stock ($10 par value,
      40,000 shares outstanding)
     Paid-in capital
     Retained earnings

     Total stockholders' equity

       Total liabilities and
       stockholders' equity
```

ALPHA/VALUE now replaces the command menu and will remain until you turn it off after entering all the titles. If you mistype, press the Backspace key to back up the highlight and erase; or press the F7 through F10 keys to move the highlight without erasing, then type missing characters or press Delete to delete unwanted characters. Now type the titles (but not the lines) for the balance sheet.

Place the cursor on R1C6. Type *AVEN CORPORATION* and move the cursor to R3C5. When you move the cursor, the title you just typed moves from the command line, where Multiplan displays what you type, and appears (partially) in the cell in which it belongs.

Now press the Spacebar five times to center the next title when it's fully displayed. Type *COMPARATIVE BALANCE SHEET* and move the cursor to R6C1. Only the first five characters—*COMPA*—appear in R3C5. Type *Assets* and move the cursor to the next cell. Continue in this way, typing a title and moving the cursor, until you've typed all the titles. Now press Enter.

Press the Escape key to return the command menu to the screen. Now turn off the alpha/value mode: Leave the cursor where it is and type O (Options). Press the Tab key four times to move the highlight to *alpha/value*. Type N to select *No* and press Enter.

Entering the Long Lines

Next, use the REPT function to enter a double line across row 2. Let's begin by filling R2C1 with equal signs (used as text).

Place the cursor on R2C1:	**Type or press:**
Start the Value command	V
Repeat an equal sign 32 times	REPT(" = ",32)
Execute the command	Enter

Now copy the REPT formula in R2C1 into the columns to the right.

Leave the cursor on R2C1:	**Type or press:**
Start the Copy command	C
Select the Right option	R
Specify the number of cells to copy into	10
Execute the command	Enter

The double line now extends through column 11.

Next, use the REPT function to enter a single line across row 4: Place the cursor on R4C1 and type *V* (Value). Type *REPT(" – ",32)* and press Enter. Leave the cursor on R4C1 and type *CR* (Copy Right). The number *10* appears in the *number of cells* field, because Multiplan "remembered" your last Copy command. Since *10* is correct, press Enter.

Next, copy all the REPT formulas from row 4 to row 7. (The F6 key can produce the colon you see in the column on the right of the following instructions, as before the number 11.)

Leave the cursor on R4C1:	**Type or press:**
Start the Copy command	C
Select the From option	F

(Multiplan displays *COPY FROM cells: R4C1*,
the first cell to copy from)

Specify the last cell to copy from	:11
Move the highlight to *to cells*	Tab
Specify the first cell in row 7 to copy into	R7C1
Execute the command	Enter

Formatting the Titles

Now let's open the cell boundaries so the long titles can extend into the empty cells to their right. These titles are *AVEN CORPORATION* in R1C6, *COMPARATIVE BALANCE SHEET* in R3C5, and the dates *June 30, 1987* and *June 30, 1986* in row 6 in the assets and the liabilities sections. You can format them as a group. It doesn't matter that you are including lines and empty cells in the group.

Place the cursor on R1C2:	**Type or press:**
Start the Format command	F
Select the Cells option	C
(Multiplan displays *Format Cells: R1C2*, the first cell to be continuous)	
Specify the last cell to be continuous	:R6C11
Move the highlight to *format code*	Tab Tab
Select *Cont* (continuous)	C
Execute the command	Enter

Next, right-justify the cell that will show the spreadsheet filename.

Place the cursor on R1C11:	**Type or press:**
Start the Format command	F
Select the Cells option	C
(Multiplan displays *FORMAT cells: R1C11*, the cell to right-justify)	
Move the highlight to *alignment*	Tab
Select *Right*	R
Execute the command	Enter

Entering and Formatting the Dollar Signs

Figure 8-3 shows the locations of the dollar signs, the short lines, and the formulas. Each formula is indicated by a zero in the cell and a circled number

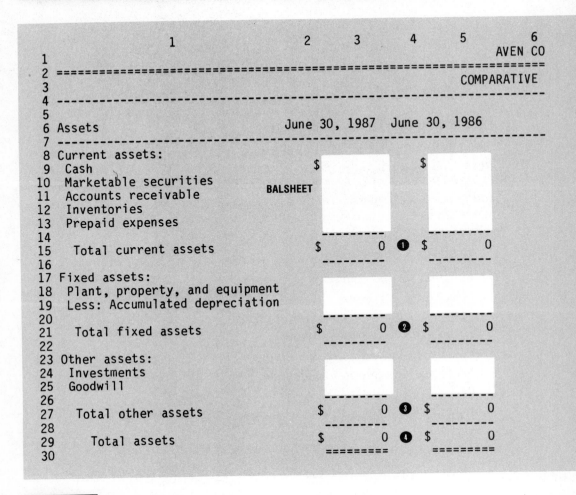

FIGURE 8-3.
Balance sheet dollar signs, dashes, named cells, and formula locations

beside it. Our approach will be to make the 1987 columns in both the assets and liabilities sections complete, then copy the dollar signs, lines, and formulas into the 1986 columns.

Let's begin with the 10 dollar signs in columns 2 and 8. To make entering and formatting them fast and easy, we'll use the master cell technique—we'll enter one dollar sign and right-justify it, and then use Multiplan's ability to copy both the content and format of a cell.

First, place the cursor on R9C2, type *A* for *Alpha*, type a dollar sign, and press Enter. Now right-justify the dollar sign: Leave the cursor on R9C2 and type *FC* (Format Cells). Next, press the Tab key to move the highlight to the *alignment* field. Type *R* to select *Right* and press Enter.

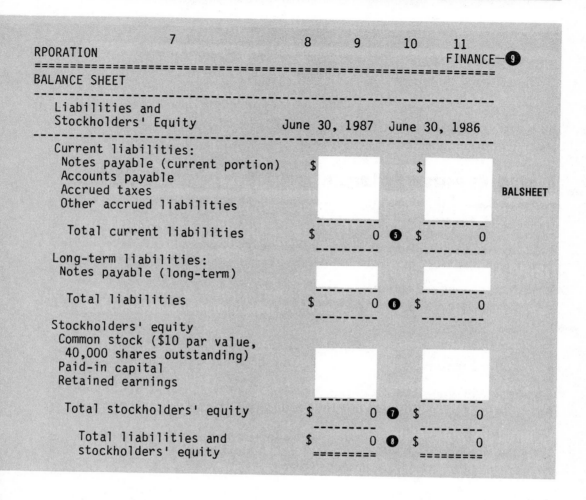

Next, copy this right-justified dollar sign to the dollar sign cells in columns 2 and 8.

Leave the cursor on R9C2:	**Type or press:**
Start the Copy command	C
Select the From option	F
(Multiplan displays *COPY FROM cells:* *R9C2*, the cell to copy from)	
Move the highlight to *to cells*	Tab

Specify the cells to copy into	R15C2,R21C2,R27C2, R29C2,R9C8,R14C8, R19C8,R27C8,R29C8
Execute the command	Enter

You now have all the dollar signs for the 1987 section. This technique is useful for producing any type of financial report that aligns dollar signs and integrates them with the numbers in the next column.

Inserting Commas in the Large Numbers

The next step is to tell Multiplan to insert commas in all the large numbers on the spreadsheet.

Leave the cursor where it is:	Type or press:
Start the Format command	F
Select the Options option	O
(The highlight is on *No* in the *commas* field)	
Select *Yes*	Y
Execute the command	Enter

Multiplan will insert commas only in cells that have a fixed, dollar, percent, or integer format. All the numbers on this spreadsheet are integers, so let's give all the cells the integer code.

Leave the cursor where it is:	Type or press:
Start the Format command	F
Select the Default option	D
Select the Cells option	C
Move the highlight to *format code*	Tab
Select *Int* (integer)	I
Execute the command	Enter

Entering the Short Lines

Let's use the REPT function again, this time to enter the short, single line in R14C3. We'll repeat the minus sign one character less than the full column width, because Multiplan reserves one blank space at the right edge of the cell to allow for a percent sign (if you use it) or for a close parenthesis after a negative number. Therefore, a 9-character line in a 10-character cell aligns the last minus sign with the final digit in the numbers above and below it.

Place the cursor on R14C3:	Type or press:
Start the Value command	V
Repeat a minus sign 9 times	REPT(" – ",9)
Execute the command	Enter

Now copy the short line to the other cells in columns 3 and 9 that need it.

Leave the cursor on R14C3:	Type:
Start the Copy command	C
Select the From option	F
(Multiplan displays *COPY FROM cells:* *R14C3*, the cell to copy from)	
Move the highlight to *to cells*	Tab
Specify the cells to copy into	R16C3,R20C3,R22C3, R26C3,R28C3,R13C9, R15C9,R18C9,R20C9, R26C9,R28C9
Execute the command	Enter

Finally, enter the short, double line: Place the cursor on R30C3 and type *V* (Value). Type *REPT(" = ",9)* and press Enter. Leave the cursor on R30C3 and copy the line to R30C9: Type *CF* (Copy From) and press Tab. Type *R30C9* and press Enter.

NAMING THE CELLS

You will want to get rid of all the old numbers at the start of a new period. You can do this quickly and efficiently by naming the cells that contain those numbers, then using that name in the Blank command. The unshaded areas in Figure 8-3 show the locations of these cells. Let's name them BALSHEET.

Place the cursor on R9C3:	Type or press:
Start the Name command	N
Name the cells	BALSHEET
Move the highlight to *to refer to*	Tab
(Multiplan displays *to refer to: R9C3,* the first cell to name)	

Specify the other cells to name	:R13C3,R18:19C3,R24:25C3, R9:13C5,R18:19C5, R24:25C5,R9:12C9, R17C9,R23:25C9, R9:12C11,R17C11, R23:25C11
Execute the command	Enter

Saving and Naming the Spreadsheet

Now store your spreadsheet on disk with the titles, lines, formats, and cell name, and give the spreadsheet its own filename. If you need to specify which drive contains your data disk or which directory to store the file in, type the appropriate drive letter and press F6 (to produce a colon) or type the pathname before you type *FINANCE*, the filename.

Leave the cursor where it is:	**Type or press:**
Start the Transfer command	T
Select the Save option	S
Name the spreadsheet	FINANCE
Execute the command	Enter

ENTERING THE FORMULAS

The circled numbers in Figure 8-3 show the locations of the formulas that perform your calculations. The formulas require relative cell references only. The left column in the following instructions contains the locations of the cell references and other elements in the formula. The column on the right and the line immediately below the formula heading show the finished formula.

To build a formula, move the cursor to each cell shown in the left column (Multiplan will produce the relative notation) and type everything else—operators, symbols, and function names. When you type a character, the cursor returns to the formula cell so that you can type another character, move the cursor to another cell, or enter the formula.

When your formula agrees with the instructions, press Enter. If Multiplan displays *Not a valid formula*, check each character. Use the F7 through F10 keys to move the highlight, and correct the problem by typing missing characters or pressing the Delete key to delete unwanted characters. If you prefer to start the formula from scratch, simply press the Escape key and begin again.

FORMULA 1: Total Current Assets

SUM(R[-6]C:R[-2]C)

Formula 1 adds the cash, marketable securities, accounts receivable, inventories, and prepaid expenses (rows 9 through 13 of column 3) and enters the total current assets in R15C3.

Place the cursor on R15C3:	Type or move the cursor:
Start the Value command	V
Enter the formula: SUM(R9C3:R13C3)	SUM(R[-6]C:R[-2]C)
Execute the command	Enter

FORMULA 2: Total Fixed Assets

R[-3]C - R[-2]C

Formula 2 deducts the accumulated depreciation (R19C3) from the plant, property, and equipment assets (R18C3) and enters the total fixed assets in R21C3.

Place the cursor on R21C3:	Type or move the cursor:
Start the Value command	V
Enter the formula: R18C3 - R19C3	R[-3]C - R[-2]C
Execute the command	Enter

FORMULA 3: Total Other Assets

R[-3]C + R[-2]C

Formula 3 adds the investments (R24C3) and goodwill (R25C3) to produce the total other assets in R27C3.

Place the cursor on R27C3:	Type or move the cursor:
Start the Value command	V
Enter the formula: R24C3 + R25C3	R[-3]C + R[-2]C
Execute the command	Enter

FORMULA 4: Total Assets

SUM(R[-14]C,R[-8]C,R[-2]C)

Formula 4 adds the total current assets (R15C3), total fixed assets (R21C3), and total other assets (R27C3) to produce the total assets in R29C3.

Place the cursor on R29C3:	Type or move the cursor:
Start the Value command	V
Enter the formula: SUM(R15C3, R21C3,R27C3)	SUM(R[− 14]C,R[− 8]C, R[− 2]C)
Execute the command	Enter

FORMULA 5: Total Current Liabilities

SUM(R[− 5]C:R[− 2]C)

Formula 5 adds the notes payable (current portion), accounts payable, accrued taxes, and other accrued liabilities (rows 9 through 12 of column 9) and enters the total current liabilities in R14C9.

Place the cursor on R14C9:	Type or move the cursor:
Start the Value command	V
Enter the formula: SUM(R9C9:R12C9)	SUM(R[− 5]C:R[− 2]C)
Execute the command	Enter

FORMULA 6: Total Liabilities

R[− 5]C + R[− 2]C

Formula 6 adds the total current liabilities (R14C9) and long-term liabilities (R17C9) to produce the total liabilities in R19C9.

Place the cursor on R19C9:	Type or move the cursor:
Start the Value command	V
Enter the formula: R14C9 + R17C9	R[− 5]C + R[− 2]C
Execute the command	Enter

FORMULA 7: Total Stockholders' Equity

SUM(R[− 4]C:R[− 2]C)

Formula 7 adds the common stock, paid-in capital, and retained earnings (rows 23 through 25 of column 9) to produce the total stockholders' equity in R27C9.

Place the cursor on R27C9:	Type or move the cursor:
Start the Value command	V
Enter the formula: SUM(R23C9:R25C9)	SUM(R[− 4]C:R[− 2]C)
Execute the command	Enter

FORMULA 8: Total Liabilities and Stockholders' Equity

$R[-10]C + R[-2]C$

Formula 8 adds the total liabilities (R19C9) and total stockholders' equity (R27C9) to produce the total liabilities and stockholders' equity in R29C9.

Place the cursor on R29C9:	**Type or move the cursor:**
Start the Value command	V
Enter the formula: R19C9 + R27C9	$R[-10]C + R[-2]C$
Execute the command	Enter

FORMULA 9: Spreadsheet Filename

NAME()

Formula 9 generates the spreadsheet filename in R1C11. Type the function name and parentheses.

Place the cursor on R1C11:	**Type or press:**
Start the Value command	V
Enter the formula: NAME()	NAME()
Execute the command	Enter

Copying the Cells as a Group

The next step is to copy the right-justified dollar signs, lines, and formulas from the 1987 columns to the 1986 columns. Start with the assets section by identifying the first cell (the dollar sign in R9C2) and the last cell (the line in R30C3) to copy from, and then by identifying the first cell (R9C4) to copy into.

Place the cursor on R9C2:	**Type or press:**
Start the Copy command	C
Select the From option	F
(Multiplan displays *COPY FROM cells: R9C2,* the first cell to copy from)	
Specify the last cell to copy from	:R30C3
Move the highlight to *to cells*	Tab
Specify the first cell to copy into	R9C4
Execute the command	Enter

Now let's repeat this procedure in the liabilities and stockholders' equity section by identifying the first cell (the dollar sign in R9C8) and the last cell (the line in R30C9) to copy from and the first cell (R9C10) to copy into.

Place the cursor on R9C8:	**Type or press:**
Start the Copy command	C
Select the From option	F
(Multiplan displays *COPY FROM cells: R9C8*, the first cell to copy from)	
Specify the last cell to copy from	:R30C9
Move the highlight to *to cells*	Tab
Specify the first cell to copy into	R9C10
Execute the command	Enter

Locking the Formulas

To prevent accidental alterations, lock the formulas.

Leave the cursor where it is:	**Type:**
Start the Lock command	L
Select the Formulas option	F
(Multiplan displays *Enter y to confirm*)	
Confirm the lock	Y

Saving the Formulas

Now store all the formulas on disk. Because you saved the spreadsheet before, Multiplan asks you to confirm overwriting the earlier version.

Leave the cursor where it is:	**Type or press:**
Start the Transfer command	T
Select the Save option	S
(Multiplan displays *FINANCE*— there's no need to retype)	
Execute the command	Enter
(Multiplan recalculates the spreadsheet, then displays *Enter Y to overwrite file*)	
Confirm the overwrite	Y

ENTERING THE SAMPLE NUMBERS

Figure 8-4 shows sample numbers on the balance sheet. You can type a number at any time you see the command menu or *ALPHA/VALUE* on the command line. Because of the formatting you did earlier, Multiplan will insert commas in the numbers that need them. Don't bother to press Enter after you type each number. It's just an extra keystroke: Moving the cursor to another cell, as you did when you entered the titles, serves the same purpose.

Now place the cursor on R9C3. Type *185890* and move the cursor to R10C3. Type *36503* and move the cursor to R11C3. Type *771080* and move the cursor to R12C3, the next cell that will contain a number. Continue in this way, typing a number and moving the cursor, until you type all the numbers in columns 3, 5, 9, and 11. After the last number, press Enter.

Now press F4 to recalculate the spreadsheet so that you can see the result of all your work. Your spreadsheet should look like the one in Figure 8-1, at the beginning of this chapter. Store it on disk: Type *TS* (Transfer Save), press Enter, and type *Y*.

PRINTING YOUR SPREADSHEET

This spreadsheet is 139 characters wide, including the five characters Multiplan uses for row numbers and a space. It is printed in 12-pitch type on two consecutive sheets of 8½-by-11-inch paper or, with a wide-carriage printer, on one sheet of 15-by-11-inch paper.

Setting the Print Margins

The first step before printing is to set the margins around your spreadsheet.

Leave the cursor where it is:	**Type or press:**
Start the Print command	P
Select the Margins option	M

Type the following numbers in the margins fields. Tab past any fields that already have the proper settings. If you overshoot a field, press Tab a few times to move full circle through the fields or press Shift-Tab to move backward one field at a time. The highlight is in the *left* field.

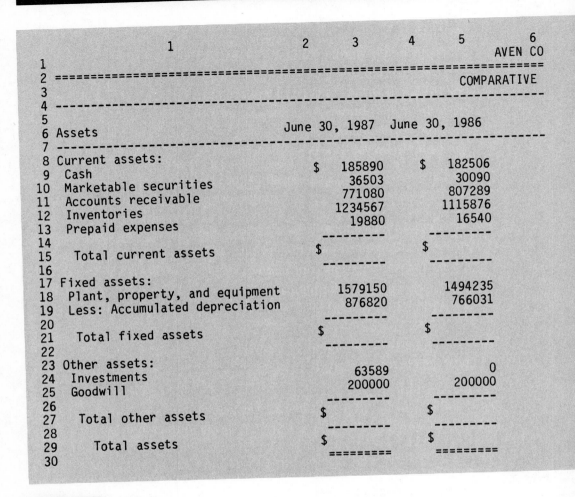

FIGURE 8-4.
Balance sheet sample numbers

To do this:	Type or press:
Specify the number of characters	10
Move the highlight to *top*	Tab
Specify the number of lines	3
Move the highlight to *print width*	Tab
Specify the number of characters:	
For 8½-by-11-inch paper	102
For 15-by-11-inch paper	139

```
                  7                        8      9      10     11
RPORATION                                                        FINANCE
========================================================================
BALANCE SHEET
------------------------------------------------------------------------
      Liabilities and
      Stockholders' Equity           June 30, 1987   June 30, 1986
------------------------------------------------------------------------
   Current liabilities:
     Notes payable (current portion)    $    447500    $    355670
     Accounts payable                        152897         140800
     Accrued taxes                            41234         110560
     Other accrued liabilities               185670         159323
                                        ---------      ---------
     Total current liabilities         $              $
                                        ---------      ---------
   Long-term liabilities:
     Notes payable (long-term)               626017         829371
                                        ---------      ---------
     Total liabilities                 $              $
                                        ---------      ---------
   Stockholders' equity
     Common stock ($10 par value,
      40,000 shares outstanding)             400000         400000
     Paid-in capital                         344550         344550
     Retained earnings                      1015971         740231
                                        ---------      ---------
     Total stockholders' equity        $              $
                                        ---------      ---------
       Total liabilities and           $              $
       stockholders' equity            =========      =========
```

Move the highlight to *print length*	Tab
Specify the number of lines	60
Move the highlight to *page length*	Tab
Specify the number of lines	66
Execute the command	Enter

Setting the Print Options

You are still in the Print command. The next step is to set the print options. The options settings are the same for all the spreadsheets in this book. They tell

Multiplan to print the entire spreadsheet in 12-pitch type with row and column numbers (which help you compare your results with the illustrations). You can find the printer code for 12-pitch type in your printer manual.

Now type O to select the Options option. Type in the following responses. (Tab past any fields that already have the proper settings.) The highlight is in the *area* field.

To do this:	Type or press:
Define the print area	R1:4095
Move the highlight to *setup*	Tab
Enter your printer code for 12-pitch type	(your code)
Move the highlight to *formulas*	Tab Tab
Select *No*	N
Move the highlight to *row-col numbers*	Tab
Select *Yes*	Y
Execute the command	Enter

Now, before you print, store the spreadsheet with the print settings: Exit the Print command by pressing the Escape key. Leave the cursor where it is. Type *TS* (Transfer Save) and press Enter. Type Y to overwrite.

Printing the Spreadsheet

Now turn on your printer and print a copy of your spreadsheet.

Leave the cursor where it is:	Type:
Start the Print command	P
Select the Printer option	P

The printer springs into action, and soon you have your balance sheet.

USING YOUR SPREADSHEET

When you are ready to enter new information, you use the Blank command to erase the old entries. Let's make a practice run now—but don't save the spreadsheet during these steps. You'll want everything exactly as it is now when you add the income statement in the next chapter.

Leave the cursor where it is:	Type or press:
Start the Blank command	B

| Name the cells to blank | BALSHEET |
| Execute the command | Enter |

Instantly, the typed numbers disappear, and only those produced by formulas remain. Now press the F4 (recalculate) key. The formula cells, because they no longer have numbers to work with, now show zeros. Starting fresh is that easy.

Now return the spreadsheet to the screen in its former condition.

Leave the cursor where it is:	**Type or press:**
Start the Transfer command	T
Select the Load option	L
Name of sheet to load	FINANCE
Execute the command	Enter

Multiplan asks you to *Enter Y to save edits, N to lose edits, or cancel.* You want to lose the edits—your blanked out cells—so type N. And the spreadsheet returns with the numbers. Now let's go on to the next chapter and create the income statement.

SPREADSHEET SUMMARY

General: The completed spreadsheet is shown in Figure 8-1. Use Options to set automatic recalculation to *No*. Indent the titles one, two, or four characters. Use Value to enter REPT(" = ",32) and REPT(" − ",32) for the long lines. Use REPT(" = ",9) and REPT(" − ",9) for the short lines. Use Lock Formulas to lock formulas. Use Copy From to copy the right-justified dollar signs, lines, and formulas from the 1987 columns to the 1986 columns as follows: Copy R9C2:R30C3 to R9C4. Copy R9C8:R30C9 to R9C10.

Column Width: Use Format Width as follows: Set columns 1 and 7 to 32 characters wide. Set columns 2, 4, 8, and 10 to 5 characters wide.

Format: Use Format Cells as follows: Continue R1C5:R3C7, R6C2:5 and R6C8:11. Right-justify R1C11 and the dollar signs in R9C2, R15C2, R21C2, R27C2, R29C2, R9C8, R14C8, R19C8, R27C8, and R29C8. Set Format Default Cells to *Int* (integer), then use Format Options to insert commas.

Name: Use Name as follows: R9:13C3,R18:19C3,R24:25C3,R9:13C5, R18:19C5,R24:25C5,R9:12C9,R17C9,R23:25C9,R9:12C11,R17C11, R23:25C11 are named BALSHEET.

Print: Balance Sheet is 139 characters wide, including Multiplan row numbers, and is printed in 12-pitch type. Set Print Margins for 8½-by-11-inch paper as follows: *left* 10, *top* 4, *print width* 102, *print length* 60, and *page length* 66. For 15-by-11-inch paper use the same settings, but set *print width* to 139.

Formulas: Formulas use relative cell references only.

1	R15C3	Total Current Assets SUM(R[−6]C:R[−2]C)
2	R21C3	Total Fixed Assets R[−3]C−R[−2]C
3	R27C3	Total Other Assets R[−3]C+R[−2]C
4	R29C3	Total Assets SUM(R[−14]C,R[−8]C,R[−2]C)
5	R14C9	Total Current Liabilities SUM(R[−5]C:R[−2]C)
6	R19C9	Total Liabilities R[−5]C+R[−2]C
7	R27C9	Total Stockholders' Equity SUM(R[−4]C:R[−2]C)
8	R29C9	Total Liabilities and Stockholders' Equity R[−10]C+R[−2]C
9	R1C11	Spreadsheet Filename NAME()

9

Financial Analysis: Income Statement

The income statement in this chapter summarizes the business activities of the Aven Corporation for one year, although it could just as easily be a report of the activities for one month or one quarter. The income statement lists what came into the business (sales), what went out (cost of goods sold and operating expenses), what income remained after costs and expenses were paid (operating income), and what remained after taxes were paid (net income). Figure 9-1 shows the completed spreadsheet.

■ Sales include all sales of Aven's pet products, adjusted for returns and allowances.

■ Cost of goods sold is the total expenditures needed to produce the products, including the cost of raw materials, factory overhead, factory labor, subcontracting, and such items as freight.

■ Gross profit is the difference between sales and cost of goods sold.

■ Operating expenses include selling costs, general and administrative costs, depreciation, and interest paid.

■ Net income is the difference between gross profit and operating expenses after taxes are deducted.

```
                    1                    2      3      4      5       6
                                                                AVEN CO
 1
 2  ============================================================
 3                                                          COMPARATIVE
 4  ------------------------------------------------------------
 5
 6  Assets                              June 30, 1987  June 30, 1986
 7  ------------------------------------------------------------
 8  Current assets:
 9    Cash                              $  185,890    $  182,506
10    Marketable securities                 36,503        30,090
11    Accounts receivable                   771,080       807,289
12    Inventories                         1,234,567     1,115,876
13    Prepaid expenses                       19,880        16,540
14                                        ---------     ---------
15      Total current assets            $2,247,920    $2,152,301
16                                        ---------     ---------
17  Fixed assets:
18    Plant, property, and equipment      1,579,150     1,494,235
19    Less: Accumulated depreciation        876,820       766,031
20                                        ---------     ---------
21      Total fixed assets              $  702,330    $  728,204
22                                        ---------     ---------
23  Other assets:
24    Investments                            63,589             0
25    Goodwill                              200,000       200,000
26                                        ---------     ---------
27      Total other assets              $  263,589    $  200,000
28                                        ---------     ---------
29      Total assets                    $3,213,839    $3,080,505
30                                        =========     =========
31
32  ============================================================
33                                      Year Ended    Year Ended
34  COMPARATIVE INCOME STATEMENT        June 30, 1987  June 30, 1986
35  ------------------------------------------------------------
36  Sales                               $3,895,870    $3,694,760
37  Cost of goods sold                    2,528,090     2,423,800
38                                        ---------     ---------
39      Gross profit                    $1,367,780    $1,270,960
40                                        ---------     ---------
41  Operating expenses:
42    Selling expense                       377,295       334,890
43    General & admin expense               326,780       292,230
44    Depreciation                          110,789       107,324
45    Interest expense                       93,350       124,406
46                                        ---------     ---------
47      Total operating expenses        $  908,214    $  858,850
48                                        ---------     ---------
49  Operating income before taxes       $  459,566    $  412,110
50    Income taxes                          183,826       164,844
51                                        ---------     ---------
52      Net income                      $  275,740    $  247,266
53                                        =========     =========
54
55  ============================================================
```

FIGURE 9-1.

The completed balance sheet and income statement

```
                          7                    8     9    10    11
RPORATION                                                       FINANCE
===============================================================
BALANCE SHEET
---------------------------------------------------------------
    Liabilities and
    Stockholders' Equity      June 30, 1987  June 30, 1986
---------------------------------------------------------------
    Current liabilities:
     Notes payable (current portion)   $  447,500     $  355,670
     Accounts payable                     152,897        140,800
     Accrued taxes                         41,234        110,560
     Other accrued liabilities           185,670        159,323
                                        ---------      ---------
       Total current liabilities        $ 827,301      $ 766,353
                                        ---------      ---------
    Long-term liabilities:
     Notes payable (long-term)            626,017        829,371
                                        ---------      ---------
       Total liabilities              $1,453,318     $1,595,724
                                        ---------      ---------
    Stockholders' equity
    Common stock ($10 par value,
     40,000 shares outstanding)           400,000        400,000
     Paid-in capital                      344,550        344,550
     Retained earnings                  1,015,971        740,231
                                        ---------      ---------
       Total stockholders' equity     $1,760,521     $1,484,781
                                        ---------      ---------
       Total liabilities and          $3,213,839     $3,080,505
       stockholders' equity           =========      =========

===============================================================


---------------------------------------------------------------




===============================================================
```

A more detailed look at the operating expenses shows the following:

■ Selling expenses include the salaries and commissions of the sales force and other items, such as advertising.

■ General and administrative expenses include rent, utilities, salaries, supplies, and other operating costs needed for the overall administration of the business.

■ Depreciation is the allocation of an asset's cost over its estimated useful life. On this spreadsheet, we'll look at the depreciation for the period reported in the income statement.

■ Interest expense is the cost of borrowing the funds used in business operations.

If you are familiar with Multiplan, you can refer to the summary at the end of this chapter for instructions on creating the spreadsheet.

SETTING UP YOUR SPREADSHEET

Now let's add the income statement to the balance sheet. If you are continuing directly from Chapter 8 and have the balance sheet on your screen, skip to the next step, "Entering the Income Statement Titles." If you are starting up again, bring up the Multiplan screen. Now load the balance sheet.

Leave the cursor where it is:	Type or press:
Start the Transfer command	T
Select the Load option	L
Specify the sheet to load	FINANCE
Execute the command	Enter

Entering the Income Statement Titles

You are about to type the income statement titles shown in Figure 9-2. These titles follow the same indent pattern as the balance sheet: Subtitles such as *Selling expense* in R42C1 are indented one space. Totals such as *Gross profit* in R39C1 are indented two spaces. The final total, *Net income* in R52C1, is indented four spaces. Press the Spacebar the proper number of times before typing each title.

First, copy *June 30, 1987* and *June 30, 1986* from the balance sheet to R34C2 and R34C4. (Remember, pressing F6 produces a colon.)

Place the cursor on R6C2:	**Type or press:**
Start the Copy command	C
Select the From option	F
(Multiplan displays *COPY FROM cells: R6C2,* the first cell to copy from)	
Specify the last cell to copy from	:5
Move the highlight to *to cells*	Tab
Specify the first cell to copy into	R34C2
Execute the command	Enter

Now type the rest of the titles on the income statement.

Place the cursor on R33C2:	**Type:**
Start the Alpha command	A
Type the first title	Year Ended

Move the cursor to R33C4, the next cell that will contain a title. The first five characters of the title you just typed appear in R33C2. (Formatting will let long titles extend into the cells to their right.) Type *Year Ended* again and move the cursor to R34C1. Type *COMPARATIVE INCOME STATEMENT* and move the cursor to the next cell. Continue in this way until you've typed all the titles. After the last title, press Enter.

Entering the Long Lines

Next, copy the double line from row 2 on the balance sheet to rows 32 and 55 on the income statement.

Place the cursor on R2C1:	**Type or press:**
Start the Copy command	C
Select the From option	F
(Multiplan displays *COPY FROM cells: R2C1,* the first cell to copy from)	
Specify the last cell to copy from	:11
Move the highlight to *to cells*	Tab
Specify the first cell in each row to copy into	R32C1,R55C1
Execute the command	Enter

Now copy the single line from row 7 to row 35: Place the cursor on R7C1 and type *CF* (Copy From). Type *:11* and press Tab. Type *R35C1* and press Enter.

```
                    1                    2    3       4    5      6
                                                             AVEN CO
 1
 2  ===============================================================
 3                                                        COMPARATIVE
 4  -------------------------------------------------------------
 5
 6  Assets                        June 30, 1987  June 30, 1986
 7  -------------------------------------------------------------
 8  Current assets:
 9   Cash                           $  185,890     $  182,506
10   Marketable securities              36,503         30,090
11   Accounts receivable               771,080        807,289
12   Inventories                     1,234,567      1,115,876
13   Prepaid expenses                   19,880         16,540
14                                   ---------      ---------
15     Total current assets         $2,247,920     $2,152,301
16                                   ---------      ---------
17  Fixed assets:
18   Plant, property, and equipment  1,579,150      1,494,235
19   Less: Accumulated depreciation    876,820        766,031
20                                   ---------      ---------
21     Total fixed assets           $  702,330     $  728,204
22                                   ---------      ---------
23  Other assets:
24   Investments                        63,589              0
25   Goodwill                          200,000        200,000
26                                   ---------      ---------
27     Total other assets           $  263,589     $  200,000
28                                   ---------      ---------
29     Total assets                 $3,213,839     $3,080,505
30                                   =========      =========
31
32  ===============================================================
33                                   Year Ended    Year Ended
34  COMPARATIVE INCOME STATEMENT     June 30, 1987 June 30, 1986
35  -------------------------------------------------------------
36  Sales
37  Cost of goods sold
38
39     Gross profit
40
41  Operating expenses:
42   Selling expense
43   General & admin expense
44   Depreciation
45   Interest expense
46
47     Total operating expenses
48
49  Operating income before taxes
50   Income taxes
51
52     Net income
53
54  -------------------------------------------------------------
55  ===============================================================
```

FIGURE 9-2.

The titles and lines on the income statement

```
                        7                    8      9     10    11
RPORATION                                                       FINANCE
=================================================================
BALANCE SHEET
-----------------------------------------------------------------
   Liabilities and
   Stockholders' Equity         June 30, 1987   June 30, 1986
-----------------------------------------------------------------
   Current liabilities:
     Notes payable (current portion)  $  447,500    $  355,670
     Accounts payable                    152,897       140,800
     Accrued taxes                        41,234       110,560
     Other accrued liabilities          185,670       159,323
                                      ---------     ---------
     Total current liabilities       $  827,301    $  766,353
                                      ---------     ---------
   Long-term liabilities:
     Notes payable (long-term)          626,017       829,371
                                      ---------     ---------
     Total liabilities               $1,453,318    $1,595,724
                                      ---------     ---------
   Stockholders' equity
     Common stock ($10 par value,
       40,000 shares outstanding)       400,000       400,000
     Paid-in capital                    344,550       344,550
     Retained earnings                1,015,971       740,231
                                      ---------     ---------
     Total stockholders' equity      $1,760,521    $1,484,781
                                      ---------     ---------
     Total liabilities and           $3,213,839    $3,080,505
     stockholders' equity             =========     =========

=================================================================

-----------------------------------------------------------------




=================================================================
```

Formatting the Titles

Now extend the titles *Year Ended* into the cells to their right.

Place the cursor on R33C2:	Type or press:
Start the Format command	F
Select the Cells option	C
(Multiplan displays *FORMAT cells: R33C2,* the first cell to be continuous)	
Specify the last cell to be continuous	:5
Move the highlight to *format code*	Tab Tab
Select *Cont* (continuous)	C
Execute the command	Enter

Copying the Dollar Signs and Short Lines

Figure 9-3 shows the locations of the dollar signs, lines, named cells, and formulas. As we did on the balance sheet, we'll make 1987 (columns 2 and 3) complete, then copy everything into 1986 (columns 4 and 5). Let's begin by copying the right-justified dollar sign from the balance sheet to the income statement.

Place the cursor on R29C2:	Type or press:
Start the Copy command	C
Select the From option	F
(Multiplan displays *COPY FROM cells:* R29C2, the cell to copy from)	
Move the highlight to *to cells*	Tab
Specify the cells to copy into	R36C2,R39C2,R47C2, R49C2,R52C2
Execute the command	Enter

Next, copy the short, single line from the balance sheet to the income statement.

Place the cursor on R28C3:	Type or press:
Start the Copy command	C
Select the From option	F
(Multiplan displays *COPY FROM cells:* R28C3, the cell to copy from)	
Move the highlight to *to cells*	Tab

Specify the cells to copy into	R38C3,R40C3,R46C3, R48C3,R51C3
Execute the command	Enter

And finally, copy the short, double line from R30C3 to R53C3: Place the cursor on R30C3. Type *CF* (Copy From) and press the Tab key. Type *R53C3* and press Enter.

NAMING THE CELLS

Now name the cells that contain the information that changes from one period to the next. Then, at the start of a new period, all you have to do is type one word in the Blank command and all the old entries will be gone. Let's name the cells INCOME.

Place the cursor on R36C3:	**Type or press:**
Start the Name command	N
Name the cells	INCOME
Move the highlight to *to refer to*	Tab
(Multiplan displays *to refer to: R36C3*, the first cell to name)	
Specify the other cells to name	:R37C3,R42:45C3, R50C3,R36:37C5, R42:45C5,R50C5
Execute the command	Enter

Saving the Spreadsheet

Now store your spreadsheet on disk with the income statement titles, formats, lines, and cell names.

Leave the cursor where it is:	**Type or press:**
Start the Transfer command	T
Select the Save option	S
(Multiplan displays *FINANCE*— there's no need to retype)	
Execute the command	Enter
(Multiplan recalculates, then displays *Enter Y to overwrite file*)	
Confirm the overwrite	Y

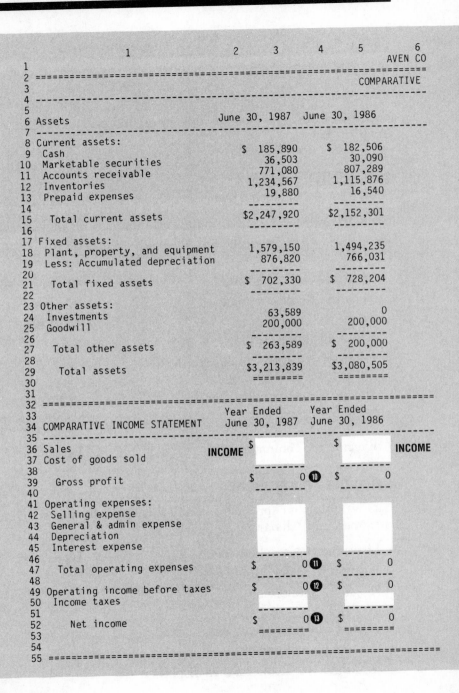

```
                    1              2       3       4       5      6
                                                              AVEN CO
 1
 2  ==============================================================
                                                           COMPARATIVE
 3
 4  --------------------------------------------------------------
 5
 6  Assets                        June 30, 1987  June 30, 1986
 7  --------------------------------------------------------------
 8  Current assets:
 9   Cash                          $  185,890     $  182,506
10   Marketable securities             36,503         30,090
11   Accounts receivable              771,080        807,289
12   Inventories                    1,234,567      1,115,876
13   Prepaid expenses                  19,880         16,540
14                                  ---------      ---------
15      Total current assets        $2,247,920     $2,152,301
16                                  ---------      ---------
17  Fixed assets:
18   Plant, property, and equipment 1,579,150      1,494,235
19   Less: Accumulated depreciation   876,820        766,031
20                                  ---------      ---------
21      Total fixed assets          $  702,330     $  728,204
22                                  ---------      ---------
23  Other assets:
24   Investments                       63,589              0
25   Goodwill                         200,000        200,000
26                                  ---------      ---------
27      Total other assets          $  263,589     $  200,000
28                                  ---------      ---------
29      Total assets                $3,213,839     $3,080,505
30                                  =========      =========
31
32  ==============================================================
33                                  Year Ended     Year Ended
34  COMPARATIVE INCOME STATEMENT    June 30, 1987  June 30, 1986
35  --------------------------------------------------------------
36  Sales                    INCOME  $              $           INCOME
37  Cost of goods sold
38                                  ---------      ---------
39      Gross profit                $        0 ⑩  $         0
40                                  ---------      ---------
41  Operating expenses:
42   Selling expense
43   General & admin expense
44   Depreciation
45   Interest expense
46                                  ---------      ---------
47      Total operating expenses    $        0 ⑪  $         0
48                                  ---------      ---------
49  Operating income before taxes   $        0 ⑫  $         0
50   Income taxes
51                                  ---------      ---------
52      Net income                  $        0 ⑬  $         0
53                                  =========      =========
54
55  ==============================================================
```

FIGURE 9-3.
Income statement dollar signs, lines, named cells, and formula locations

```
RPORATION              7        8     9    10   11
                                               FINANCE
=================================================================
BALANCE SHEET
-----------------------------------------------------------------
  Liabilities and
  Stockholders' Equity      June 30, 1987  June 30, 1986
-----------------------------------------------------------------
  Current liabilities:
   Notes payable (current portion)  $  447,500   $  355,670
   Accounts payable                    152,897      140,800
   Accrued taxes                        41,234      110,560
   Other accrued liabilities          185,670      159,323
                                     ---------    ---------
    Total current liabilities       $  827,301   $  766,353
                                     ---------    ---------
  Long-term liabilities:
   Notes payable (long-term)           626,017      829,371
                                     ---------    ---------
    Total liabilities               $1,453,318   $1,595,724
                                     ---------    ---------
  Stockholders' equity
   Common stock ($10 par value,
    40,000 shares outstanding)         400,000      400,000
   Paid-in capital                     344,550      344,550
   Retained earnings                 1,015,971      740,231
                                     ---------    ---------
    Total stockholders' equity      $1,760,521   $1,484,781
                                     ---------    ---------
    Total liabilities and
    stockholders' equity            $3,213,839   $3,080,505
                                     =========    =========
=================================================================

-----------------------------------------------------------------

=================================================================
```

ENTERING THE FORMULAS

The circled numbers in Figure 9-3 show the locations of the formulas, which require relative cell references only. Use the same techniques to create these formulas as you did on the balance sheet: Move the cursor to the cell locations shown in the left column of the following instructions (Multiplan produces the relative notation) and type the operators, symbols, and function names. The column on the right and the line below the formula heading show the finished formula.

When your formula agrees with the column on the right, press Enter. If Multiplan then displays *Not a valid formula,* check each character. Use the F7 through F10 keys to move the highlight, and correct the problem by typing missing characters or pressing the Delete key to delete unwanted characters. If you prefer to start the formula from scratch, press the Escape key and begin again.

FORMULA 10: Gross Profit

R[−3]C − R[−2]C

Formula 10 deducts the cost of goods sold (R37C3) from the sales (R36C3) to produce the gross profit in R39C3.

Place the cursor on R39C3:	Type or move the cursor:
Start the Value command	V
Enter the formula: R36C3 − R37C3	R[−3]C − R[−2]C
Execute the command	Enter

FORMULA 11: Total Operating Expenses

SUM(R[−5]C:R[−2]C)

Formula 11 adds the selling expense (R42C3), general and administrative expense (R43C3), depreciation (R44C3), and interest expense (R45C3), entering the total operating expenses in R47C3.

Place the cursor on R47C3:	Type or move the cursor:
Start the Value command	V
Enter the formula: SUM(R42C3: R45C3)	SUM(R[−5]C:R[−2]C)
Execute the command	Enter

FORMULA 12: Operating Income Before Taxes

$R[-10]C - R[-2]C$

Formula 12 deducts the total operating expenses (R47C3) from the gross profit (R39C3) to produce the operating income before taxes in R49C3.

Place the cursor on R49C3:	Type or move the cursor:
Start the Value command	V
Enter the formula: R39C3 – R47C3	$R[-10]C - R[-2]C$
Execute the command	Enter

FORMULA 13: Net Income

$R[-3]C - R[-2]C$

Formula 13 deducts the income taxes (R50C3) from the operating income before taxes (R49C3) to produce the net income in R52C3.

Place the cursor on R52C3:	Type or move the cursor:
Start the Value command	V
Enter the formula: R49C3 – R50C3	$R[-3]C - R[-2]C$
Execute the command	Enter

Copying the Cells as a Group

Now copy the dollar signs, lines, and formulas from the 1987 columns to the 1986 columns. Identify the first cell (the dollar sign in R36C2) and the last cell (the double line in R53C3) to copy from, and then identify the first cell (R36C4) to copy into.

Place the cursor on R36C2:	Type or press:
Start the Copy command	C
Select the From option	F
(Multiplan displays *COPY FROM cells:* R36C2, the first cell to copy from)	
Specify the last cell to copy from	:R53C3
Move the highlight to *to cells*	Tab
Specify the first cell to copy into	R36C4
Execute the command	Enter

Locking the Formulas

Although you locked the formulas and titles on the balance sheet, you haven't locked them on the income statement. It's wise to safeguard formulas.

Leave the cursor where it is:	Type:
Start the Lock command	L
Select the Formulas option	F
(Multiplan displays *Enter Y to confirm*)	
Confirm the lock	Y

ENTERING THE SAMPLE NUMBERS

Figure 9-4 shows sample numbers in the income statement. Remember, you can type a number anytime you see the command menu or *ALPHA/VALUE* on the command line, and you don't have to press Enter after typing each one (it's just an extra keystroke). Multiplan will insert the commas because you selected commas formatting in Chapter 8.

Place the cursor on R36C3. Type *3895870* and move the cursor to R37C3. Type *2528090* and move the cursor to R42C3. Continue in this way, typing each number shown in Figure 9-4 and then moving the cursor, until you've typed all the numbers. After the last number, press Enter.

Now store all your work on disk: Leave the cursor where it is and type *TS* (Transfer Save). Press Enter and type *Y* to overwrite the existing file. When Multiplan saves a spreadsheet, it also recalculates it. Your spreadsheet should now look like the one in Figure 9-1, at the beginning of this chapter.

PRINTING YOUR SPREADSHEET

The print margins and options you set on the balance sheet are fine for the income statement. So turn on your printer and print your spreadsheet.

Leave the cursor where it is:	Type:
Start the Print command	P
Select the Printer option	P

And here's your balance sheet and income statement.

USING YOUR SPREADSHEET

To be sure the blanking will work properly when you enter your own numbers, check it now.

Leave the cursor where it is:	Type or press:
Start the Blank command	B
Name the cells to blank	INCOME
Execute the command	Enter

The numbers disappear! Press the F4 (recalculate) key. The formulas no longer have numbers to work with, so the formula cells show zeros. Now return your spreadsheet to the screen in its former condition.

Leave the cursor where it is:	Type or press:
Start the Transfer command	T
Select the Load option	L
Name of sheet to load	FINANCE
Execute the command	Enter

Multiplan asks if you want to save or lose the edits you've made since you last saved. You want to lose them, so type *N*. The original spreadsheet appears. Now let's go on to the next chapter and add the financial ratios.

SPREADSHEET SUMMARY

General: The completed spreadsheet is shown in Figure 9-1. Indent the titles one, two, or four characters. Use Copy From to copy the titles in R6C2:5, long and short lines, and dollar signs from the balance sheet to the income statement. Use Lock Formulas to lock the formulas. Use Copy From to copy the dollar signs, lines, and formulas from R36C2:R53C3 to R36C4.

Format: Use Format Cells to continue R33C2:5.

Name: Use Name as follows: R36:37C3,R42:45C3,R50C3,R36:37C5, R42:45C5, and R50C5 are INCOME.

Formulas: Formulas use relative cell references only.

10	R39C3	Gross Profit
		$R[-3]C - R[-2]C$
11	R47C3	Total Operating Expenses
		$SUM(R[-5]C:R[-2]C)$
12	R49C3	Operating Income Before Taxes
		$R[-10]C - R[-2]C$
13	R52C3	Net Income
		$R[-3]C - R[-2]C$

```
                    1                  2      3      4      5          6
                                                                 AVEN CO
 1
 2  ============================================================================
 3                                                               COMPARATIVE
 4  ----------------------------------------------------------------------------
 5
 6  Assets                                June 30, 1987  June 30, 1986
 7  ----------------------------------------------------------------------------
 8  Current assets:
 9   Cash                                   $  185,890    $  182,506
10   Marketable securities                      36,503        30,090
11   Accounts receivable                       771,080       807,289
12   Inventories                             1,234,567     1,115,876
13   Prepaid expenses                           19,880        16,540
14                                          ---------     ---------
15      Total current assets                $2,247,920    $2,152,301
16                                          ---------     ---------
17  Fixed assets:
18   Plant, property, and equipment          1,579,150     1,494,235
19   Less: Accumulated depreciation            876,820       766,031
20                                          ---------     ---------
21      Total fixed assets                  $  702,330    $  728,204
22                                          ---------     ---------
23  Other assets:
24   Investments                                63,589             0
25   Goodwill                                  200,000       200,000
26                                          ---------     ---------
27      Total other assets                  $  263,589    $  200,000
28                                          ---------     ---------
29      Total assets                        $3,213,839    $3,080,505
30                                          =========     =========
31
32  ============================================================================
33                                         Year Ended    Year Ended
34  COMPARATIVE INCOME STATEMENT           June 30, 1987  June 30, 1986
35  ----------------------------------------------------------------------------
36  Sales                                   $  3895870    $  3694760
37  Cost of goods sold                         2528090       2423800
38                                          ---------     ---------
39      Gross profit                        $             $
40                                          ---------     ---------
41  Operating expenses:
42   Selling expense                           377295        334890
43   General & admin expense                   326780        292230
44   Depreciation                              110789        107324
45   Interest expense                           93350        124406
46                                          ---------     ---------
47      Total operating expenses            $             $
48                                          ---------     ---------
49  Operating income before taxes          $             $
50   Income taxes                              183826        164844
51                                          ---------     ---------
52      Net income                          $             $
53                                          =========     =========
54
55  ============================================================================
```

FIGURE 9-4.
Income statement sample numbers

```
                          7              8      9      10     11
RPORATION                                                    FINANCE
==================================================================
BALANCE SHEET
------------------------------------------------------------------
    Liabilities and
    Stockholders' Equity        June 30, 1987  June 30, 1986
------------------------------------------------------------------
    Current liabilities:
      Notes payable (current portion)  $   447,500    $   355,670
      Accounts payable                     152,897        140,800
      Accrued taxes                         41,234        110,560
      Other accrued liabilities           185,670        159,323
                                        ---------      ---------
        Total current liabilities     $   827,301    $   766,353
                                        ---------      ---------
    Long-term liabilities:
      Notes payable (long-term)            626,017        829,371
                                        ---------      ---------
        Total liabilities            $1,453,318     $1,595,724
                                        ---------      ---------
    Stockholders' equity
      Common stock ($10 par value,
       40,000 shares outstanding)          400,000        400,000
      Paid-in capital                      344,550        344,550
      Retained earnings                  1,015,971        740,231
                                        ---------      ---------
        Total stockholders' equity   $1,760,521     $1,484,781
                                        ---------      ---------
        Total liabilities and
        stockholders' equity         $3,213,839     $3,080,505
                                        =========      =========

==================================================================


------------------------------------------------------------------




==================================================================
```

10
Financial Analysis: Ratios

Financial ratios express the relationship between items on the balance sheet and income statement. For example, dividing current assets by current liabilities gives you the current ratio, a commonly used business barometer. Dividing gross profit by sales gives you a ratio called the gross profit margin. These and other ratios provide a means of making a quick analysis of the financial condition of your business. Ratios are more useful than actual dollar amounts in spotting up and down trends, and they can give you early warnings of problem areas.

Ratio analysis is often used by outsiders—a banker who needs to analyze your company's financial statements before making a loan decision, a trade creditor who wants to determine if your company can pay its bills if credit is extended, or an investor who wants to examine your past, present, and projected earnings.

Though financial ratio analysis can give you valuable insights into the strengths and weaknesses of a company, they do have their limitations. Because some of the information used to derive ratios is based on accounting rules and personal judgments—as well as on facts—ratios should not be considered the final word. They are meaningful tools only when considered in light of the company's past performance, trends over time, and industry norms.

With that in mind, let's add the ratios to the balance sheet and income statement for the Aven Corporation, the spreadsheet we built in Chapter 8 and Chapter 9. If you prefer to create the ratios without following the step-by-step instructions, refer to the summary at the end of this chapter. The completed spreadsheet is shown in Figure 10-1.

```
              1              2      3      4      5      6
                                                    AVEN CO
 1
 2 ====================================================================
 3                                                    COMPARATIVE
 4 --------------------------------------------------------------------
 5
 6 Assets                         June 30, 1987  June 30, 1986
 7 --------------------------------------------------------------------
 8 Current assets:
 9   Cash                          $   185,890    $   182,506
10   Marketable securities              36,503         30,090
11   Accounts receivable               771,080        807,289
12   Inventories                     1,234,567      1,115,876
13   Prepaid expenses                   19,880         16,540
14                                  ---------      ---------
15     Total current assets        $2,247,920     $2,152,301
16                                  ---------      ---------
17 Fixed assets:
18   Plant, property, and equipment  1,579,150      1,494,235
19   Less: Accumulated depreciation    876,820        766,031
20                                  ---------      ---------
21     Total fixed assets          $   702,330    $   728,204
22                                  ---------      ---------
23 Other assets:
24   Investments                        63,589              0
25   Goodwill                          200,000        200,000
26                                  ---------      ---------
27     Total other assets          $   263,589    $   200,000
28                                  ---------      ---------
29     Total assets                $3,213,839     $3,080,505
30                                  =========      =========
31
32 ====================================================================
33                                 Year Ended     Year Ended
34 COMPARATIVE INCOME STATEMENT    June 30, 1987  June 30, 1986
35 --------------------------------------------------------------------
36 Sales                           $3,895,870     $3,694,760
37 Cost of goods sold               2,528,090      2,423,800
38                                  ---------      ---------
39   Gross profit                  $1,367,780     $1,270,960
40                                  ---------      ---------
41 Operating expenses:
42   Selling expense                   377,295        334,890
43   General & admin expense           326,780        292,230
44   Depreciation                      110,789        107,324
45   Interest expense                   93,350        124,406
46                                  ---------      ---------
47     Total operating expenses    $   908,214    $   858,850
48                                  ---------      ---------
49 Operating income before taxes   $   459,566    $   412,110
50   Income taxes                      183,826        164,844
51                                  ---------      ---------
52     Net income                  $   275,740    $   247,266
53                                  =========      =========
54
55 ====================================================================
```

FIGURE 10-1.
The completed financial analysis spreadsheet

```
RPORATION              7          8     9     10    11
                                                    FINANCE
============================================================
BALANCE SHEET
------------------------------------------------------------
  Liabilities and
  Stockholders' Equity        June 30, 1987  June 30, 1986
------------------------------------------------------------
  Current liabilities:
   Notes payable (current portion)  $  447,500   $   355,670
   Accounts payable                    152,897       140,800
   Accrued taxes                        41,234       110,560
   Other accrued liabilities          185,670       159,323
                                    ---------     ---------
     Total current liabilities     $  827,301    $  766,353
                                    ---------     ---------
  Long-term liabilities:
   Notes payable (long-term)          626,017       829,371
                                    ---------     ---------
     Total liabilities             $1,453,318    $1,595,724
                                    ---------     ---------
  Stockholders' equity
   Common stock ($10 par value,
    40,000 shares outstanding)        400,000       400,000
   Paid-in capital                    344,550       344,550
   Retained earnings                1,015,971       740,231
                                    ---------     ---------
     Total stockholders' equity    $1,760,521    $1,484,781
                                    ---------     ---------
     Total liabilities and
     stockholders' equity          $3,213,839    $3,080,505
                                    =========     =========


============================================================

  ** FINANCIAL ANALYSIS RATIOS **        1987        1986
------------------------------------------------------------
  Current Ratio                          2.72        2.81
  Quick Assets or Acid Test Ratio        1.20        1.33
  Cash Ratio                             0.27        0.28
  Net Working Capital ($thousands)       1,421       1,386
  Debt to Assets Ratio                   0.45        0.52
  Debt to Equity Ratio                   0.83        1.07
  Long-term Debt to Equity Ratio         0.36        0.56
  Times Interest Earned                  5.92        4.31
  Avg Collection Period (days)           72          80
  Receivables Turnover Ratio             5.1         4.6
  Inventory Turnover Ratio               2.0         2.2
  Assets Turnover Ratio                  1.2         1.2
  Gross Profit Margin                    35.1%       34.4%
  Net Profit Margin                      7.1%        6.7%
  Return on Assets                       8.6%        8.0%
  Return on Stockholders' Equity         15.7%       16.7%
  Earnings per Share                     $6.89       $6.18


============================================================
```

SETTING UP YOUR SPREADSHEET

If you are continuing directly from Chapter 9 and have the combined balance sheet and income statement on your screen, you can skip the following instruction and go on to entering the titles. If you are starting up Multiplan again, load the spreadsheet: Type *TL* (Transfer Load). Type *FINANCE* and press Enter.

Entering the Titles

Figure 10-2 shows the financial ratio titles. You must type each year— *1987* in R34C9 and *1986* in R34C11—from the Alpha command. Otherwise, Multiplan will treat them as numbers and insert a comma because that's the way we formatted numbers in Chapter 8. Let's enter *1987* first.

Place the cursor on R34C9:	**Type or press:**
Start the Alpha command	A
Type the title	1987
Execute the command	Enter

Now place the cursor on R34C11 and type *A* (Alpha) again. Type *1986*. Don't press Enter yet. Instead, move the cursor to R34C7. Type * * *FINANCIAL ANALYSIS RATIOS* * * and move the cursor to R36C7. Type *Current Ratio* and move the cursor to R37C7. Type the next title. Continue in this way until you've typed all the ratio titles in column 7. After the last title, press Enter.

Formatting the Titles

Next, center the titles 1987 and 1986 to align them with the numbers in the cells below.

Place the cursor on R34C9:	**Type or press:**
Start the Format command	F
Select the Cells option	C
(Multiplan displays *FORMAT cells: R34C9*, the first cell to format)	
Specify the last cell to format	:11
Move the highlight to *alignment*	Tab
Select *Ctr* (center)	C
Execute the command	Enter

Formatting the Number Cells

As we did before, let's complete the 1987 column and then copy everything into the 1986 column at one time. First, give the cells in rows 36 through 38 and 40 through 43 a fixed format with two decimal places.

Place the cursor on R36C9:	**Type or press:**
Start the Format command	F
Select the Cells option	C
(Multiplan displays *FORMAT cells: R36C9*, the first cell to format)	
Specify the other cells to format	:R38C9,R40:43C9
Move the highlight to *format code*	Tab Tab
Select *Fix*	F
Move the highlight to *# of decimals*	Tab
Specify the number of decimals	2
Execute the command	Enter

Now give the cells in rows 39 and 44 an integer format.

Place the cursor on R39C9:	**Type or press:**
Start the Format command	F
Select the Cells option	C
(Multiplan displays *FORMAT cells: R39C9*, the first cell to format)	
Specify the other cell to format	,R44C9
Move the highlight to *format code*	Tab Tab
Select *Int* (integer)	I
Execute the command	Enter

Next, let's give the cells in rows 45 through 47 a fixed format with one decimal place.

Place the cursor on R45C9:	**Type or press:**
Start the Format command	F
Select the Cells option	C
(Multiplan displays *FORMAT cells: R45C9*, the first cell to format)	

```
                    1          2     3     4     5       6
                                                      AVEN CO
 1
 2  ===============================================================
 3                                                   COMPARATIVE
 4  ---------------------------------------------------------------
 5
 6  Assets                        June 30, 1987  June 30, 1986
 7  ---------------------------------------------------------------
 8  Current assets:
 9   Cash                          $  185,890    $  182,506
10   Marketable securities             36,503        30,090
11   Accounts receivable              771,080       807,289
12   Inventories                    1,234,567     1,115,876
13   Prepaid expenses                  19,880        16,540
14                                  ---------     ---------
15      Total current assets       $2,247,920    $2,152,301
16                                  ---------     ---------
17  Fixed assets:
18   Plant, property, and equipment  1,579,150    1,494,235
19   Less: Accumulated depreciation    876,820      766,031
20                                  ---------     ---------
21      Total fixed assets         $  702,330    $  728,204
22                                  ---------     ---------
23  Other assets:
24   Investments                       63,589             0
25   Goodwill                         200,000       200,000
26                                  ---------     ---------
27      Total other assets         $  263,589    $  200,000
28                                  ---------     ---------
29      Total assets               $3,213,839    $3,080,505
30                                  =========     =========
31
32  ===============================================================
33                                 Year Ended    Year Ended
34  COMPARATIVE INCOME STATEMENT   June 30, 1987  June 30, 1986
35  ---------------------------------------------------------------
36  Sales                          $3,895,870    $3,694,760
37  Cost of goods sold              2,528,090     2,423,800
38                                  ---------     ---------
39      Gross profit               $1,367,780    $1,270,960
40                                  ---------     ---------
41  Operating expenses:
42   Selling expense                  377,295       334,890
43   General & admin expense          326,780       292,230
44   Depreciation                     110,789       107,324
45   Interest expense                  93,350       124,406
46                                  ---------     ---------
47      Total operating expenses   $  908,214    $  858,850
48                                  ---------     ---------
49  Operating income before taxes  $  459,566    $  412,110
50   Income taxes                     183,826       164,844
51                                  ---------     ---------
52      Net income                 $  275,740    $  247,266
53                                  =========     =========
54
55  ===============================================================
```

FIGURE 10-2.

The titles and formula locations for the financial ratios

```
                      7                  8     9     10    11
RPORATION                                                  FINANCE
===================================================================
BALANCE SHEET
-------------------------------------------------------------------

     Liabilities and
     Stockholders' Equity        June 30, 1987  June 30, 1986
     ----------------------------------------------------------

     Current liabilities:
       Notes payable (current portion)  $  447,500    $  355,670
       Accounts payable                    152,897       140,800
       Accrued taxes                        41,234       110,560
       Other accrued liabilities           185,670       159,323
                                        ---------     ---------
         Total current liabilities     $  827,301    $  766,353
                                        ---------     ---------
     Long-term liabilities:
       Notes payable (long-term)           626,017       829,371
                                        ---------     ---------
         Total liabilities            $1,453,318    $1,595,724
                                        ---------     ---------
     Stockholders' equity
     Common stock ($10 par value,
       40,000 shares outstanding)          400,000       400,000
       Paid-in capital                     344,550       344,550
       Retained earnings                 1,015,971       740,231
                                        ---------     ---------
         Total stockholders' equity   $1,760,521    $1,484,781
                                        ---------     ---------
         Total liabilities and        $3,213,839    $3,080,505
         stockholders' equity          =========     =========


===================================================================


    ** FINANCIAL ANALYSIS RATIOS **       1987          1986
    ----------------------------------------------------------
     Current Ratio                         ⑭
     Quick Assets or Acid Test Ratio       ⑮
     Cash Ratio                            ⑯
     Net Working Capital ($thousands)      ⑰
     Debt to Assets Ratio                  ⑱
     Debt to Equity Ratio                  ⑲
     Long-term Debt to Equity Ratio        ⑳
     Times Interest Earned                 ㉑
     Avg Collection Period (days)          ㉒
     Receivables Turnover Ratio            ㉓
     Inventory Turnover Ratio              ㉔
     Assets Turnover Ratio                 ㉕
     Gross Profit Margin                   ㉖
     Net Profit Margin                     ㉗
     Return on Assets                      ㉘
     Return on Stockholders' Equity        ㉙
     Earnings per Share                    ㉚


===================================================================
```

Specify the last cell to format	:R47C9
Move the highlight to *format code*	Tab Tab
Select *Fix*	F
Move the highlight to *# of decimals*	Tab
Specify the number of decimals	1
Execute the command	Enter

Now give the cells in rows 48 through 51 of column 9 a percent format with one decimal place.

Place the cursor on R48C9:	**Type or press:**
Start the Format command	F
Select the Cells option	C
(Multiplan displays *FORMAT cells: R48C9,* the first cell to format)	
Specify the last cell to format	:R51C9
Move the highlight to *format code*	Tab Tab
Select *%*	%
Move the highlight to *# of decimals*	Tab
Specify the number of decimals	1
Execute the command	Enter

The last cell to format is in row 52. Let's code this cell for dollars and cents.

Place the cursor on R52C9:	**Type or press:**
Start the Format command	F
Select the Cells option	C
(Multiplan displays *FORMAT cells: R52C9,* the cell to format)	
Move the highlight to *format code*	Tab Tab
Select *$*	$
Execute the command	Enter

This completes the formatting.

Store all the ratio titles and formats on disk: Leave the cursor where it is. Type *TS* (Transfer Save) and press Enter. Type *Y* to confirm the overwrite.

ENTERING THE FORMULAS

Figure 10-2 shows the locations of the ratio formulas, which use relative cell references only. Move the cursor to cells shown in the left column of the following instructions (Multiplan will produce the relative notation) and type only the arithmetic operators. These cells are at a distance from each other, so use the rapid-movement keys (Home, End, PgUp, PgDn, Ctrl-Left Arrow, Ctrl-Right Arrow) to move the cursor. The column on the right shows the finished formula.

When your formula agrees with the instructions, press Enter. If Multiplan then displays *Not a valid formula*, check each character. Use the F7 through F10 keys to move the highlight, and correct the problem by typing missing characters or pressing the Delete key to delete unwanted characters. If you prefer to start the formula from scratch, press the Escape key and begin again. As you enter each formula, compare your results with those shown in Figure 10-1.

FINANCIAL RATIOS—DESCRIPTIONS AND FORMULAS

The financial ratios on this spreadsheet are divided into four categories:

■ Liquidity ratios

■ Debt ratios

■ Funds management ratios

■ Profitability ratios

Liquidity Ratios

Liquidity refers to a company's cash or near-cash position (that is, assets that can be converted to cash quickly). Liquidity ratios measure a company's cash solvency and its ability to remain solvent under adverse conditions. Four commonly used indicators are current ratio, quick assets ratio, cash ratio, and net working capital.

FORMULA 14: Current Ratio

R[−21]C[−6]/R[−22]C

The current ratio indicates a company's ability to meet its short-term obligations, in other words, to pay bills when they're due. The current ratio is calculated by dividing current assets (R15C3) by current liabilities (R14C9). As a rule, a current ratio of at least 2 to 1 is considered desirable. Expressed in other way, at least $2 in current assets should be available for each $1 of current liabilities.

Place the cursor on R36C9:	Type or move the cursor:
Start the Value command	V
Enter the formula: R15C3/R14C9	R[−21]C[−6]/R[−22]C
Execute the command	Enter

FORMULA 15: Quick Assets or Acid Test Ratio

$$(R[-22]C[-6] - R[-25]C[-6] - R[-24]C[-6])/R[-23]C$$

The quick assets, or acid test, ratio measures a company's ability to meet its current obligations with quickly convertible assets if sales revenues suddenly cease. This ratio is calculated by dividing current assets (R15C3), less inventories (R12C3) and prepaid expenses (R13C3), by current liabilities (R14C9). Inventories are excluded because they are subject to a decline in market value and also because it may take time to convert them into cash. In general, a quick assets ratio of at least 1 to 1 is considered desirable.

Formula 15, and several other formulas in the ratios group, starts with an open parenthesis. You can enter it without typing *V* for Value because Multiplan recognizes a parenthesis as the start of a formula.

Place the cursor on R37C9:	Type or move the cursor:

Enter the formula: (R15C3
  − R12C3 − R13C3)/R14C9
	(R[−22]C[−6]
	  − R[−25]C[−6]
	  − R[−24]C[−6])
	  /R[−23]C

Execute the command	Enter

FORMULA 16: Cash Ratio

$$(R[-29]C[-6] + R[-28]C[-6])/R[-24]C$$

The cash ratio measures the ability of a company to service its short-term obligations from cash and marketable securities, the two most liquid assets. This ratio is calculated by dividing cash (R9C3) plus marketable securities (R10C3) by current liabilities (R14C9).

Place the cursor on R38C9:	Type or move the cursor:

Enter the formula: (R9C3
  + R10C3)/R14C9
	(R[−29]C[−6]
	  + R[−28]C[−6])
	  /R[−24]C

Execute the command	Enter

FORMULA 17: Net Working Capital ($ thousands)

$(R[-24]C[-6] - R[-25]C)/1000$

Net working capital is a dollar amount (not a ratio) that results from subtracting the current liabilities (R14C9) from current assets (R15C3). It is used to evaluate the resources readily available to meet current liabilities when they come due. This indicator is particularly significant for small companies that have relatively limited access to long-term capital markets and must rely on trade credit and short-term bank loans, both of which affect net working capital by increasing current liabilities. The result of the calculation is divided by 1000 for convenience.

Place the cursor on R39C9:	**Type or move the cursor:**
Enter the formula: (R15C3 − R14C9)/1000	$(R[-24]C[-6] - R[-25]C)/1000$
Execute the command	Enter

Debt Ratios

Debt is the amount of financing supplied by creditors. Debt ratios measure:

■ The relative proportion of funds supplied by the owners of the company compared with the funds supplied by creditors.

■ The company's ability to meet its long-term obligations to nonequity suppliers of funds.

Four commonly used debt ratios are debt to assets, debt to equity, long-term debt to equity, and times interest earned.

FORMULA 18: Debt To Assets Ratio

$R[-21]C/R[-11]C[-6]$

The debt to assets ratio indicates the percentage of total assets that are financed by creditors. In general, the lower the ratio, the greater the buffer against creditors' losses in case of liquidation. This ratio is calculated by dividing total liabilities (R19C9) by total assets (R29C3).

Place the cursor on R40C9:	**Type or move the cursor:**
Start the Value command	V
Enter the formula: R19C9/R29C3	$R[-21]C/R[-11]C[-6]$
Execute the command	Enter

FORMULA 19: Debt to Equity Ratio

R[− 22]C/R[− 14]C

The debt to equity ratio indicates the relationship of money borrowed to money invested, a measure of a company's ability to meet its total obligations from equity. In general, the lower the ratio, the higher the proportion of equity relative to debt and the better the firm's credit standing. Conversely, the higher the ratio, the lower the proportion of invested money relative to borrowed money and the less solvent the business. As this ratio approaches 100, the proportion of creditor interest in the business approaches that of stockholders. This ratio is calculated by dividing total liabilities (R19C9) by stockholders' equity (R27C9).

Place the cursor on R41C9:	**Type or move the cursor:**
Start the Value command	V
Enter the formula: R19C9/R27C9	R[− 22]C/R[− 14]C
Execute the command	Enter

FORMULA 20: Long-Term Debt to Equity Ratio

R[− 25]C/R[− 15]C

The long-term debt to equity ratio indicates the relative importance of long-term debt in the company's capital structure. The ratio is determined by dividing long-term liabilities (R17C9) by stockholders' equity (R27C9).

Place the cursor on R42C9:	**Type or move the cursor:**
Start the Value command	V
Enter the formula: R17C9/R27C9	R[− 25]C/R[− 15]C
Execute the command	Enter

FORMULA 21: Times Interest Earned Ratio

(R[+ 6]C[− 6] + R[+ 2]C[− 6])/R[+ 2]C[− 6]

The times interest earned ratio measures the ability of a company to pay annual interest obligations out of its earnings. Inability to meet annual interest costs could result in legal action by creditors. The closer the ratio to industry norms, the better the rating. This ratio is calculated by dividing operating income before taxes (R49C3) plus interest expense (R45C3) by interest expense (R45C3).

Place the cursor on R43C9:	Type or move the cursor:
Enter the formula: (R49C3 + R45C3)/R45C3	(R[+6]C[−6] + R[+2]C[−6]) /R[+2]C[−6]
Execute the command	Enter

Funds Management Ratios

Funds management ratios measure how well (or poorly) a company is using its resources. Four commonly used indicators of funds management are: average collection period, accounts receivable turnover ratio, inventory turnover ratio, and assets turnover ratio.

The value of certain assets, such as receivables and inventories, can fluctuate widely during the year. In calculating the ratios for your own company, I recommend you use the average dollar value of the assets for the year (obtained from company records) instead of the dollar value from the balance sheet. If you don't have access to company records, you can use the company's quarterly statements to compute a reasonable average (add the four quarterly figures, then divide by four).

For demonstration purposes, let's use the number from the Aven Corporation balance sheet. I will indicate—in the narrative and in the formula—when to use an annual average.

FORMULA 22: Average Collection Period

R[−33]C[−6]/(R[−8]C[−6]/365)

The average collection period is the average number of days from the date of a sale on credit until the company collects its cash. A longer-than-normal period may mean uncollectable bills. In general, the average collection period should not exceed the net maturity of the selling terms by more than 10 or 15 days. Therefore, if the company offers 60 days to pay, the average collection period should be no longer than 70 to 75 days. Slow collections without adequate financing charges hurt the company's profits and tie up working capital.

The average collection period is calculated by dividing average accounts receivable (R11C3) by credit sales (R36C3) divided by 365 days. In this example, let's assume that all of Aven's sales are on credit.

Place the cursor on R44C9:	Type or move the cursor:
Start the Value command	V
Enter the formula: R11C3 /(R36C3/365)	R[−33]C[−6] /(R[−8]C[−6]/365)
Execute the command	Enter

FORMULA 23: Receivables Turnover Ratio

$R[-9]C[-6]/R[-34]C[-6]$

The receivables turnover ratio indicates the number of days in which receivables are paid off and is a measure of the efficiency of a company's use of the funds invested in receivables. Money tied up in receivables for too long may make a company short of cash and unable to take advantage of cash discounts. The receivables turnover ratio is calculated by dividing credit sales (R36C3) by average receivables (R11C3).

Place the cursor on R45C9:	Type or move the cursor:
Start the Value command	V
Enter the formula: R36C3/R11C3	$R[-9]C[-6]/R[-34]C[-6]$
Execute the command	Enter

FORMULA 24: Inventory Turnover Ratio

$R[-9]C[-6]/R[-34]C[-6]$

The inventory turnover ratio indicates the number of times inventory is turned over, or replaced. Each time inventory turns over, more profit is generated. In general, the higher the ratio, the more efficiently the company is managing its inventory. A downward trend may be a warning signal of obsolete or slow-moving inventory. The ratio is calculated by dividing the cost of goods sold (R37C3) by the average inventory (R12C3) during the period studied.

Place the cursor on R46C9:	Type or move the cursor:
Start the Value command	V
Enter the formula: R37C3/R12C3	$R[-9]C[-6]/R[-34]C[-6]$
Execute the command	Enter

FORMULA 25: Assets Turnover Ratio

$R[-11]C[-6]/R[-18]C[-6]$

The assets turnover ratio indicates the number of times that fixed assets are turned over—a measure of how efficiently a company uses its assets to generate sales. In general, a higher-than-normal ratio (the normal based on a broad economic analysis) indicates that the company is able to generate sales from its assets faster and better than similar companies or industry averages. The ratio is calculated by dividing sales (R36C3) by average total assets (R29C3).

Place the cursor on R47C9:	Type or move the cursor:
Start the Value command	V
Enter the formula: R36C3/R29C3	R[−11]C[−6]/R[−18]C[−6]
Execute the command	Enter

Profitability Ratios

Profitability ratios measure management's effectiveness in using the resources invested in the business to generate a dollar return. These ratios show return on investment in relation to sales, assets, and equity.

Four commonly used indicators of profitability are gross profit margin, net profit margin, return on assets, and return on stockholder equity. Several ratios require that you use average annual dollar amounts. Again, as with the funds management ratios, I will indicate this in the narrative and formula description.

FORMULA 26: Gross Profit Margin

R[−9]C[−6]/R[−12]C[−6]

Gross profit margin indicates profitability in relation to sales after the cost of producing the goods is deducted. It provides a measurement of the company's pricing, purchasing, and production policies. The ratio is calculated by dividing gross profit (R39C3) by sales (R36C3).

Place the cursor on R48C9:	Type or move the cursor:
Start the Value command	V
Enter the formula: R39C3/R36C3	R[−9]C[−6]/R[−12]C[−6]
Execute the command	Enter

FORMULA 27: Net Profit Margin

R[+3]C[−6]/R[−13]C[−6]

Net profit margin indicates the profit per dollar of sales. It is a measure of the relative efficiency of the combined operations of the company after expenses and income taxes are deducted. A higher-than-normal ratio indicates that sales are good, that expenses are low, or both. The ratio is calculated by dividing net income (R52C3) by sales (R36C3).

Place the cursor on R49C9:	Type or move the cursor:
Start the Value command	V
Enter the formula: R52C3/R36C3	R[+3]C[−6]/R[−13]C[−6]
Execute the command	Enter

FORMULA 28: Return on Assets

R[+ 2]C[− 6]/R[− 21]C[− 6]

Return on assets is another indicator of profitability in relation to investment. It measures the efficiency with which the company is able to generate a return on the use of its assets. The ratio is calculated by dividing net income (R52C3) by average total assets (R29C3).

Place the cursor on R50C9:	Type or move the cursor:
Start the Value command	V
Enter the formula: R52C3/R29C3	R[+ 2]C[− 6]/R[− 21]C[− 6]
Execute the command	Enter

FORMULA 29: Return on Stockholders' Equity

R[+ 1]C[− 6]/R[− 24]C

Return on stockholder equity indicates the earnings generated by the capital invested by all owners of the business. It allows management to measure the effects of its policies on the firm's profitability, compared with other types of investments. This ratio is the single most important measure of a firm's financial position—a kind of bottom line for the bottom line. The ratio is calculated by dividing net income (R52C3) by average stockholders' equity (R27C9).

Place the cursor on R51C9:	Type or move the cursor:
Start the Value command	V
Enter the formula: R52C3/R27C9	R[+ 1]C[− 6]/R[− 24]C
Execute the command	Enter

FORMULA 30: Earnings per Share

RC[− 6]/(R[− 29]C/10)

Earnings per share (EPS) is the net income available to common stockholders. This represents the current yearly earnings of the corporation that are attributable to each share of common stock. The denominator of the EPS ratio is usually a weighted average of the amount of stock outstanding during the year. For this example, earnings per share is calculated by dividing net income (R52C3) by the average common shares outstanding (R23C9). We will divide the dollar value of the shares by 10 (par value) to get the number of shares.

Place the cursor on R52C9:	Type or move the cursor:
Start the Value command	V
Enter the formula: R52C3/(R23C9/10)	RC[− 6]/(R[− 29]C/10)
Execute the command	Enter

Your spreadsheet now contains the ratio formulas for 1987.

Copying the Formats and Formulas

Now copy all the ratio formats and formulas from the 1987 column to the 1986 column. Since the formulas are relative, they will also work with the 1986 numbers.

Place the cursor on R36C9:	Type or press:
Start the Copy command	C
Select the From option	F
(Multiplan displays *COPY FROM cells: R36C9*, the first cell to copy from)	
Specify the last cell to copy from	:R52C9
Move the highlight to *to cells*	Tab
Specify the first cell to copy into	R36C11
Execute the command	Enter

Press the F4 key to recalculate the 1986 formulas. Your spreadsheet should look like the one in Figure 10-1. Now lock the formulas: Leave the cursor where it is. Type *LF* (Lock Formulas) and type *Y* to confirm.

Save the spreadsheet in its final form: Leave the cursor where it is, type *TS* (Transfer Save), and press Enter. Type *Y* (for *Yes*) to confirm the overwrite of the earlier version.

PRINTING YOUR SPREADSHEET

Now turn on your printer and print the spreadsheet.

Leave the cursor where it is:	Type:
Start the Print command	P
Select the Printer option	P

And there's your three-in-one financial analysis package.

USING YOUR SPREADSHEET

Before you enter your own information, you can blank out the old numbers in one easy step. Here's how:

Leave the cursor where it is:	Type or press:
Start the Blank command	B
Name the cells to blank	BALSHEET,INCOME
Execute the command	Enter

Now press F4. The error message *#DIV/0!* appears in all the ratio cells except the one for the net working capital, which shows a zero. These error messages will disappear when you enter your numbers. If you want to blank only the balance sheet or income statement, simply enter *BALSHEET* or *INCOME*.

Now reload your spreadsheet with the original entries: Leave the cursor where it is and type *TL* (Transfer Load). Type *FINANCE* and press Enter. Type *N* to lose the edits.

SPREADSHEET SUMMARY

General: The completed spreadsheet is shown in Figure 10-1. Use Lock Formulas to lock the formulas.

Format: Use Format Cells as follows: Center R34C9:11. Fix code with 2 decimal places R36:38C9 and R40:43C9. Integer code R39C9 and R44C9. Fix code with 1 decimal place R45:47C9. Percent code with 1 decimal place R48:51C9. Dollar code R52C9.

Formulas: Formulas use relative cell references only.

14	R36C9	Current Ratio $R[-21]C[-6]/R[-22]C$
15	R37C9	Quick Assets or Acid Test Ratio $(R[-22]C[-6] - R[-25]C[-6]$ $- R[-24]C[-6])/R[-23]C$
16	R38C9	Cash Ratio $(R[-29]C[-6] + R[-28]C[-6])/R[-24]C$
17	R39C9	Net Working Capital ($ thousands) $(R[-24]C[-6] - R[-25]C)/1000$

18	R40C9	Debt to Assets Ratio $R[-21]C/R[-11]C[-6]$
19	R41C9	Debt to Equity Ratio $R[-22]C/R[-14]C$
20	R42C9	Long-Term Debt to Equity Ratio $R[-25]C/R[-15]C$
21	R43C9	Times Interest Earned Ratio $(R[+6]C[-6]+R[+2]C[-6])/R[+2]C[-6]$
22	R44C9	Average Collection Period $R[-33]C[-6]/(R[-8]C[-6]/365)$
23	R45C9	Receivables Turnover Ratio $R[-9]C[-6]/R[-34]C[-6]$
24	R46C9	Inventory Turnover Ratio $R[-9]C[-6]/R[-34]C[-6]$
25	R47C9	Assets Turnover Ratio $R[-11]C[-6]/R[-18]C[-6]$
26	R48C9	Gross Profit Margin $R[-9]C[-6]/R[-12]C[-6]$
27	R49C9	Net Profit Margin $R[+3]C[-6]/R[-13]C[-6]$
28	R50C9	Return on Assets $R[+2]C[-6]/R[-21]C[-6]$
29	R51C9	Return on Stockholders' Equity $R[+1]C[-6]/R[-24]C$
30	R52C9	Earnings per Share $RC[-6]/(R[-29]C/10)$

11

Check Ledger and Reconciliation

A s a dynamic record of your day-to-day transactions, a check ledger shows how much money flowed in and out of your business, where the money came from and where it went, how much cash is lying idle that could be producing income, and what it costs you in service charges to do business with your bank. Comparing one period to another can help you analyze your cash flow, identify income and expense relationships, and serve as the basis for cash budgets and other important cash control documents. Simply put, a check ledger is a good record of how your business is faring financially.

Traditionally, keeping a check ledger has meant a lot of tedious paperwork. For many people, recording checks and deposits, then trying to balance what came in with what went out, is enough to put a glaze over their eyes. But, thanks to Multiplan, that time is past. When you enter your checks, deposits, bank charges and credits, then tick off the transactions listed on the bank statements, the electronic check ledger we'll create in this chapter does the following wondrous things:

- Keeps a running balance.

- Shows which checks and deposits are outstanding.

- Reconciles the check ledger and bank statement.

```
                 1              2                3               4    5        6
                                                                     CHECK LEDGER AND
 1  =============================================================================
 2  =============================================================================
 3  CURRENT PERIOD TRANSACTIONS
 4  ---------------------------------------------------------------------------
 5                     Check                           Check        Allocated
 6  Date             Number  Paid To                   Amount   C    Amount
 7  ---------------------------------------------------------------------------
 8  AUGUST 87                        BALANCE FORWARD----------------------------
 9  Aug 2      203     Nickel Savings Bank             $578.40   1    $578.40
10  Aug 2      204     Holt Stationery                 $161.19   1    $161.19
11  Aug 7      205     Vinicombe Realty                $667.00   1    $667.00
12  Aug 11     206     The Nissen Group              $1,131.00   1  $1,131.00
13  Aug 12     207     Market Newsletter                $75.00   1     $75.00
14  Aug 15     208     VOID
15  Aug 15     209     Don England                   $4,166.66   1  $4,166.66
16  Aug 15     210     DE-Expense Reimbursement        $235.02   1     $88.02
17                                                                     $50.00
18                                                                     $97.00
19  Aug 19     211     Payroll                         $732.90   1    $732.90
20  Aug 27             Deposit
21  Aug 29     212     Pelham U-Drive                  $480.89        $480.89
22  Aug 29     213     Eastern Power                   $125.00   1    $125.00
23  Aug 30     214     NY Telephone Co                 $231.76        $231.76
24  Aug 30     215     Department of Taxation          $146.58        $146.58
25  Aug 30     216     True Blue Medical Plan          $390.00   1    $390.00
26  Aug 30     217     Holt Stationery                  $55.00   1     $55.00
27                                    ENDING BALANCE---------------------------
28  =============================================================================
29  PREVIOUS PERIOD OUTSTANDING                        Check     C
30  ---------------------------------------------------------------------------
31  Jul 7,87   179     Parcel Express                   $15.00   1
32  Jul 10,87  184     Abner Civic Association          $75.00
33  Jul 28,87  199     Pro Advertising                 $456.00   1
34
35
36
37  =============================================================================
38  RECONCILIATION
39  ---------------------------------------------------------------------------
40  Checkbook Balance                               $14,163.93
41    Plus Bank Credits                                  $0.00
42    Less Bank Charges                                 $17.85
43                                                  -----------
44  Adjusted Checkbook Balance                      $14,146.08
45                                                  ===========
46  Bank Statement Balance                          $13,247.99
47    Plus Deposits in Transit                       $1,832.32
48    Less Outstanding Checks                          $934.23
49                                                  -----------
50  Adjusted Bank Statement Balance                 $14,146.08
51                                                  ===========
52  Variance (Checkbook minus Statement)                $0.00
53  =============================================================================
54  Amount of Deposits                              $10,661.43
55  Amount of Checks                                 $9,176.40
56  Checks and Allocation Amounts                      AGREE
57  Maximum Checkbook Balance                       $14,450.50
58  Average Checkbook Balance                       $12,367.83
59  Number of Deposits                                       7
60  Number of Checks                                        14
61  =============================================================================
```

FIGURE 11-1.
The completed check ledger and reconciliation spreadsheet

7	8	9	10	11	12

RECONCILIATION
CHECK

===

Account Number	Deposit Amount	D	Running Balance	***** Outstanding *****	
				Check	Deposit
----------------------->			$12,678.90		
12	$2,350.00	1	$14,450.50	0.00	0.00
6			$14,289.31	0.00	0.00
2	$122.33	1	$13,744.64	0.00	0.00
8	$256.78	1	$12,870.42	0.00	0.00
9			$12,795.42	0.00	0.00
			$12,795.42	0.00	0.00
1			$8,628.76	0.00	0.00
11	$2,350.00	1	$10,743.74	0.00	0.00
3			$10,743.74	0.00	0.00
10			$10,743.74	0.00	0.00
5			$10,010.84	0.00	0.00
	$743.00		$10,753.84	0.00	743.00
16			$10,272.95	480.89	0.00
4	$3,750.00	1	$13,897.95	0.00	0.00
3			$13,666.19	231.76	0.00
7			$13,519.61	146.58	0.00
18	$1,089.32		$14,218.93	0.00	1,089.32
6			$14,163.93	0.00	0.00
----------------------->			$14,163.93		

===

	Deposit	D			
	$432.75	1		0.00	0.00
				75.00	0.00
				0.00	0.00
				0.00	0.00
				0.00	0.00
				0.00	0.00

===

===

■ Totes the number and amount of your checks and deposits—even tells you in plain English when your numbers are off.

■ Calculates the high point and average for the balance each month.

■ Produces an all-in-one record of your monthly transactions.

■ Updates itself, courtesy of a trio of friendly macros.

Figure 11-1 shows the completed spreadsheet.

You can type in your checks and deposits when it suits you: once a month, each time you write a check or make a deposit, or at any time in between. Then, when you receive your bank statement, all you need do is "tick off" each check and deposit listed on the statement. You "tick off" each one by typing a number 1 in the appropriate column of your electronic ledger. These number 1 "tick marks" trigger the reconciliation formulas.

The check ledger works hand-in-hand with the cash disbursements spreadsheet we'll create in the next chapter. The two are linked via Multiplan's *Xternal* command so that all the check dates, numbers, payees, allocated amounts, and account numbers you enter in the ledger are transferred to the disbursements spreadsheet, where the check amounts are distributed in the appropriate expense accounts and totalled. If one check covers several expense accounts, the amount of the check is split into each account.

As a preview of things to come, after you complete the cash disbursements spreadsheet, we'll return to the check ledger spreadsheet and create a cash disbursements module that totals each category. That way, the check ledger becomes an even more powerful, multi-purpose financial record.

If you're familiar with Multiplan and prefer to create the check ledger without following the step-by-step instructions, refer to the summary at the end of this chapter.

SETTING UP YOUR SPREADSHEET

Bring up the Multiplan screen. If you turned off automatic recalculation on your last spreadsheet, you can skip the following step and go on to "Adjusting the Column Widths." Otherwise, to make data entry faster, leave the cursor where it is. Type O to start the Options command, type N for no recalculation, and press Enter. Now we're ready to make your spreadsheet look like the one in Figure 11-2.

Adjusting the Column Widths

Each of Multiplan's columns is now 10 characters wide. Adjusting the width of the columns can give the entries the space they need and produce a spreadsheet that's more pleasing to the eye. Let's start by increasing the width of column 1 to 12 characters.

Leave the cursor on R1C1:	Type or press:
Start the Format command	F
Select the Width option	W
Specify the number of characters in the column	12
Execute the command	Enter

Use the same procedure to adjust the widths of the other columns:

Column number:	Width in characters:
2	7
3	25
4	12
5	4
6	12
7	8
8	12
9	4
10	14
11	12
12	12

Entering the Titles

The next step is to type the titles shown in Figure 11-2, but first a few instructions:

■ Type the entire title * * * * * *Outstanding* * * * * * in R5C11. When you enter this and other long titles in their cells, you will see only as much of the title as will fit in the current cell width. We'll increase the column widths shortly when we format the titles.

■ Type the title *Balance Forward* in R8C3 and *Ending Balance* in R27C3. You will right-justify them later so they look like the ones in Figure 11-2. For now, ignore the long arrows to the right.

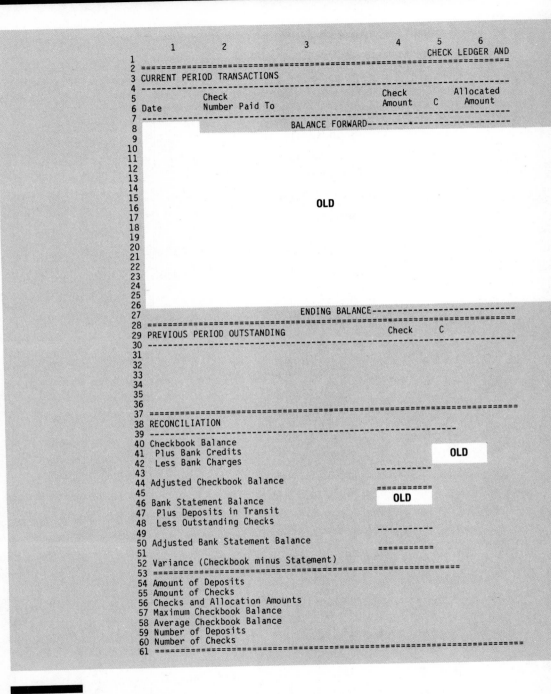

FIGURE 11-2.
The titles, lines, and named cell locations on the check ledger and reconciliation spreadsheet

```
     7        8        9        10         11          12
  RECONCILIATION
  ============================================================

  -----------------------------------------------------------
  Account   Deposit            Running    ***** Outstanding *****
  Number    Amount      D      Balance    Check        Deposit
  -----------------------------------------------------------
  ----------------------->        OLD
```

OLD

```
  ----------------------->
  ============================================================
                  Deposit     D
  -----------------------------------------------------------



  ============================================================




  ============================================================
```

■ Each of the titles in rows 41, 42, 47, and 48 in the reconciliation section is indented one character. Press the Spacebar once before typing each one.

Typically, before you type the first title, you type *A* (Alpha) to prepare the cell, and then you type the title. When you move the cursor to another cell, the title you just typed moves from the command line to its cell and *ALPHA/VALUE* appears on the command line, which means you can type another title or a number.

When you have several titles, you want to keep Multiplan in a constant alpha/value mode. Then, if you happen to press Enter after typing a title, you can type the next title without typing *A* first.

Leave the cursor where it is:	Type or press:
Start the Options command	O
Move the highlight to *alpha/value*	Tab (four times)
Select *Yes*	Y
Execute the command	Enter

ALPHA/VALUE now replaces the command menu and will remain until you deactivate the alpha/value mode.

If you mistype while the title is still on the command line, press the Backspace key (not a direction key) to back up the cursor and erase, or press the F7 through F10 keys to move the highlight without erasing anything, then type a missing character or press Delete to delete an unwanted character.

If you notice an error in a title that is already in its cell, first press Escape to exit the alpha/value mode. This brings up the command menu. Move the cursor to the cell containing the title you want to correct and type *E* (Edit) to put the title on the command line. Then use the F7 through F10 keys to move the highlight and correct the error. When you press Enter to enter the edited title, you'll be back in the alpha/value mode again.

Now start entering the titles. Place the cursor on R1C5. Type *CHECK LEDGER AND RECONCILIATION* and move the cursor to R3C1. Multiplan accepts the entire title but displays only *CHEC* (the first four characters, the width of the cell). Type *CURRENT PERIOD TRANSACTIONS* and move the cursor to R6C1. Multiplan displays *CURRENT PERI* (the first 12 characters, the width of that cell). Type *Date* and move the cursor to the next cell. Continue in this way—typing a title and moving the cursor—until you've typed all the titles. After the last title, press Enter.

Press the Escape key to return the command menu to the screen. Now turn off the alpha/value mode: Leave the cursor where it is. Type *O* (Options) and press the tab key four times. Type *N* to select *No* and press Enter.

Entering the Lines

Lines make a spreadsheet easier to read. Let's start by entering a double line in R2C1. To prevent gaps in the line when you copy it across row 2, we'll use Multiplan's REPT function to repeat an equal sign 25 times—enough to fill even the widest cell.

Place the cursor on R2C1:	**Type or press:**
Start the Value command	V
Repeat an equal sign 25 times	REPT(" = ",25)
Execute the command	Enter

Now copy the formula in R2C1 into the columns to the right.

Leave the cursor on R2C1:	**Type or press:**
Start the Copy command	C
Select the Right option	R
Specify the number of cells to copy into	11
Execute the command	Enter

The double line now extends from column 1 through column 12. Next, copy the entire line from row 2 to rows 28, 37, 53, and 61. Don't be concerned that Figure 11-2 shows a line in row 53 that extends only through column 4— we'll take care of that shortly. Where you see a colon in the column on the right in the following instructions, as before the number 12, you can press the F6 key to produce the colon. It's easier than pressing the Shift key and typing a colon.

Leave the cursor on R2C1:	**Type or press:**
Start the Copy command	C
Select the From option	F
(Multiplan displays *COPY FROM cells: R2C1*, the first cell to copy from)	
Specify the last cell to copy from	:12
Move the highlight to *to cells*	Tab
Specify the first cell in each row to copy into	R28C1,R37C1,R53C1,R61C1
Execute the command	Enter

Now use a REPT formula and a minus sign to enter a single line in row 4: Place the cursor on R4C1 and type *V* (Value). Type *REPT(" – ",25)* and press Enter.

Copy the formula across row 4: Leave the cursor on R4C1 and type *CR* (Copy Right). Multiplan proposes that you copy into 11 cells as you did before. This is correct, so all you do is press Enter. Now copy the entire single line from row 4 to rows 7, 30, and 39 (don't worry about the shorter line in row 39): Leave the cursor on R4C1 and type *CF* (Copy From). Type *:12* and press Tab. Type *R7C1,R30C1,R39C1* and press Enter.

Now blank out the cells in rows 39 and 53 of columns 6 through 12. This will shorten the lines to match the ones in Figure 11-2.

Place the cursor on R39C6:	**Type or press:**
Start the Blank command	B
Specify the cells to blank	:R53C12
Execute the command	Enter

The next step is to enter the short lines in column 4. Let's start with the single line in R43C4, which is one character shy of the full column width, so that it right-aligns with the numbers.

Place the cursor on R43C4:	**Type or press:**
Start the Value command	V
Repeat a minus sign 11 times	REPT(" – ",11)
Execute the command	Enter

Next, enter a short double line in R45C4: Place the cursor on R45C4 and type *V* (Value). Type *REPT("=",11)* and press Enter. Now copy both lines to R49C4 and R51C4: Place the cursor on R43C4 and type *CF* (Copy From). Type *,R45C4* and press Tab. Type *R49C4* and press Enter.

As a gentle reminder to enter an opening balance when you start a new period, create the long arrow pointing to R8C10 and, at the same time, create the arrow pointing to the ending balance in R27C10. An easy way is to copy part of the single line you created in row 7.

Place the cursor on R7C4:	**Type or press:**
Start the Copy command	C
Select the From option	F
(Multiplan displays *COPY FROM cells: R7C4*, the first cell to copy from)	
Specify the last cell to copy from	:8
Move the highlight to *to cells*	Tab
Specify the cells to copy into	R8C4,R27C4
Execute the command	Enter

To complete the arrows, move the cursor to R8C9. Type *A* for Alpha, type three dashes followed by a greater-than sign (>), and press Enter. Now copy it to the other arrow: Leave the cursor on R8C9, type *CF* (Copy From), and press Tab. Type *R27C9* and press Enter.

Formatting the Titles

Now let's continue the long titles across cell boundaries so that they are completely displayed. The group includes *CHECK LEDGER AND RECON-CILIATION* (R1C5), *CURRENT PERIOD TRANSACTIONS* (R3C1), *PRE-VIOUS PERIOD OUTSTANDING* (R29C1), the reconciliation section (rows 38 through 60), and ** * * * * Outstanding * * * * ** (R5C11). To fit them all into the entry field at one time, let's refer to them both by cell locations and by whole columns instead of only by cell locations.

Place the cursor on R1C5:	**Type or press:**
Start the Format command	F
Select the Cells option	C
(Multiplan displays *FORMAT cells: R1C5*, the first cell to be continuous)	
Specify the other cells to be continuous	:8,C1:3,R5C11:12
Move the highlight to *format code*	Tab Tab
Select *Cont* (continuous)	C
Execute the command	Enter

After a few seconds (Multiplan is busily formatting a great many cells), the command menu reappears.

Next, continue and center R56C4, which will contain a formula that produces one of two messages in plain English. The shorter message will be centered in its cell; the longer message will extend across several cells.

Place the cursor on R56C4:	**Type or press:**
Start the Format command	F
Select the Cells option	C
(Multiplan displays *FORMAT cells: R56C4*, the first cell to be continuous)	
Specify the last cell to be continuous	:R56C7
Move the highlight to *alignment*	Tab
Select *Ctr* (center)	C
Move the highlight to *format code*	Tab

Select *Cont* (continuous)	C
Execute the command	Enter

Now center the titles in rows 5 and 6 of columns 4 through 12 (but not * * * * * *Outstanding* * * * * *, which is in a continuous format and can't be centered by formatting) and the titles in row 29 of columns 4 through 9.

	Type or press:
Place the cursor on R5C4:	
Start the Format command	F
Select the Cells option	C
(Multiplan displays *FORMAT cells: R5C4*, the first cell to format)	
Specify the other cells to format	:10,R6C4:12,R29C4:9
Move the highlight to *alignment*	Tab
Select *Ctr* (center)	C
Execute the command	Enter

The next step is to right-justify the titles *Balance Forward* (R8C3), *Ending Balance* (R27C3), and R1C12, which will contain a formula that generates the spreadsheet filename.

	Type or press:
Place the cursor on R8C3:	
Start the Format command	F
Select the Cells option	C
(Multiplan displays *FORMAT cells: R8C3*, the first cell to format)	
Specify the other cells to format	,R27C3,R1C12
Move the highlight to *alignment*	Tab
Select *Right*	R
Execute the command	Enter

Formatting the Number Cells

Now apply the centered format to the cells in column 7 that will contain the account numbers.

	Type or press:
Place the cursor on R9C7:	
Start the Format command	F

Select the Cells option	C
(Multiplan displays *FORMAT cells: R9C7,* the first cell to format)	
Specify the last cell to format	:R26C7
Move the highlight to *alignment*	Tab
Select *Ctr* (center)	C
Execute the command	Enter

Next, left-justify the cells in column 2 that will contain the check numbers. It doesn't matter that the range includes cells other than those we want to format because left-justifying the cells won't affect the appearance.

Place the cursor on R9C2:	**Type or press:**
Start the Format command	F
Select the Cells option	C
(Multiplan displays *FORMAT cells: R9C2,* the first cell to format)	
Specify the other cells to format	:R36C2
Move the highlight to *alignment*	Tab
Select *Left*	L
Execute the command	Enter

Next, let's format cells in column 4 to show the check and other amounts in dollars and cents. Again, the appearance of the empty cells, lines, and text in the ranges won't be affected.

Place the cursor on R9C4:	**Type or press:**
Start the Format command	F
Select the Cells option	C
(Multiplan displays *FORMAT cells: R9C4,* the first cell to format)	
Specify the other cells to format	:R55C4,R57:58C4
Move the highlight to *format code*	Tab Tab
Select *$*	$
Execute the command	Enter

Many other cells need a dollars-and-cents format. Let's use one of the blank cells you just formatted and copy the dollar code.

Leave the cursor on R9C4:	**Type or press:**
Start the Copy command	C
Select the From option	F
(Multiplan displays *COPY FROM cells: R9C4*, the first cell to copy from)	
Move the highlight to *to cells*	Tab
Specify the cells to copy into	R9:26C6,R9:26C8, R31:36C8,R8:27C10
Execute the command	Enter

Now code the outstanding checks and deposits cells in row 9 of columns 11 and 12 for a fixed format with two decimal places. Copying the formulas you will soon enter in these cells will also copy the fixed format.

Place the cursor on R9C11:	**Type or press:**
Start the Format command	F
Select the Cells option	C
(Multiplan displays *FORMAT cells: R9C11*, the first cell to format)	
Specify the last cell to format	:R36C12
Move the highlight to *format code*	Tab Tab
Select *Fix*	F
Move the highlight to *# of decimals*	Tab
Specify the number of decimals	2
Execute the command	Enter

Inserting Commas in the Large Numbers

The next step is to tell Multiplan to insert commas in the large numbers on this spreadsheet.

Leave the cursor where it is:	**Type or press:**
Start the Format command	F
Select the Options option	O
(The highlight is on *No* in the *commas* field)	
Select *Yes*	Y
Execute the command	Enter

NAMING THE CELLS

When you start a new period, you want to start with a clean spreadsheet. By naming the cells containing the information you want to erase, you can type one word in the Blank command and all the old information on the entire spreadsheet will disappear. The locations of these cells—named OLD—are shown in the unshaded areas in Figure 11-2.

Leave the cursor where it is:	Type or press:
Start the Name command	N
Name the cells	OLD
Move the highlight to *to refer to*	Tab
Specify the cells to name	R8C1,R9:26C1:9, R41:42C4, R8C10,R46C4
Execute the command	Enter

You can also use names for groups of cells that are used in formulas to make the formulas easy to enter and understand. The unshaded areas in Figure 11-3 show these locations. Let's start by naming the cells in column 4 CHECKS.

Place the cursor on R9C4:	Type or press:
Start the Name command	N
Name the cells	CHECKS
Move the highlight to *to refer to*	Tab
(Multiplan displays *to refer to: R9C4,* the first cell to name)	
Specify the last cell to name	:R26C4
Execute the command	Enter

Now name the cells in column 6 ALLOCATED.

Place the cursor on R9C6:	Type:
Start the Name command	N
Name the cells	ALLOCATED

Multiplan is keeping track of your actions and, in the *to refer to* field, proposes R9:26C6. This is correct, so press Enter.

Next, name the group in column 8 DEPOSITS: Place the cursor on R9C8 and type *N*. Type *DEPOSITS* and press Enter.

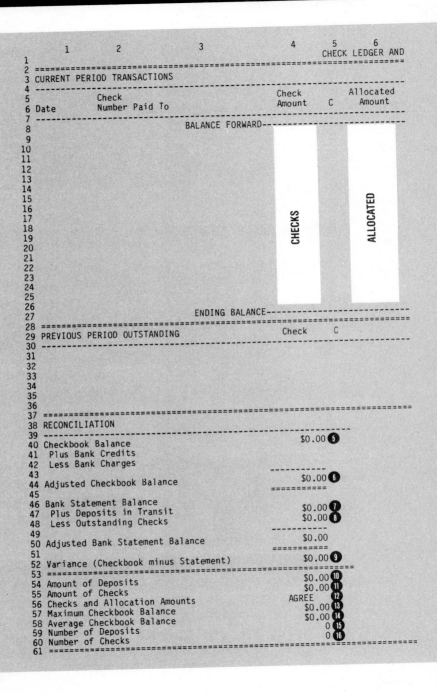

FIGURE 11-3.
Check ledger and reconciliation named cells and formula locations

```
    7        8        9        10           11              12
 RECONCILIATION                                                CHECK 🔟
=================================================================


------------------------------------------------------------------
Account   Deposit                 Running     ***** Outstanding *****
Number    Amount      D           Balance      Check         Deposit
------------------------------------------------------------------
------------------------->
                                  $0.00 ❶        0.00 ❷        0.00 ❸
                                  $0.00          0.00          0.00
                                  $0.00          0.00          0.00
                                  $0.00          0.00          0.00
                                  $0.00          0.00          0.00
                                  $0.00          0.00          0.00
                  D               $0.00          0.00          0.00
                  E               $0.00  O       0.00  O       0.00
                  P       B       $0.00  C       0.00  D       0.00
                  O       A       $0.00  H       0.00  E       0.00
                  S       L       $0.00  E       0.00  P       0.00
                  I       A       $0.00  C       0.00  O       0.00
                  T       N       $0.00  K       0.00  S       0.00
                  S       C       $0.00  S       0.00  I       0.00
                          E       $0.00          0.00  T       0.00
                                  $0.00          0.00  S       0.00
                                  $0.00          0.00          0.00
                                  $0.00          0.00          0.00
                                  $0.00          0.00          0.00
------------------------->        $0.00 ❹    EBALANCE
=================================================================
          Deposit    D
------------------------------------------------------------------
                                             O    0.00     O    0.00
                                             C    0.00     D    0.00
                                             H    0.00     E    0.00
                                             E    0.00     P    0.00
                                             C    0.00     O    0.00
                                             K    0.00     S    0.00
                                             S    0.00     I    0.00
                                                                T    0.00
=================================================================


=================================================================
```

Follow the same procedure to name the other groups:

Place the cursor on:	Type:	Type:	Press:	Type:	Press:
R8C10	N	BALANCE	Tab	R8:26C10	Enter
R9C11	N	OCHECKS	Tab	R9:36C11	Enter
R9C12	N	ODEPOSITS		(R9:36C12 is already entered)	Enter
R27C10	N	EBALANCE	Tab	R27C10	Enter

Saving and Naming the Spreadsheet

Now store your spreadsheet on disk with the titles, lines, formats, and cell names, and give the spreadsheet its own filename. If you need to specify which drive contains your data disk or which directory to store the file in, type the drive letter and press F6 (to produce a colon) or type the pathname before you type CHECK, the filename.

Leave the cursor where it is:	Type or press:
Start the Transfer command	T
Select the Save option	S
Name the spreadsheet	CHECK
Execute the command	Enter

ENTERING THE FORMULAS

The circled numbers in Figure 11-3 show the locations of the formulas that balance your electronic checkbook. These formulas use relative and named cell references. The left column in the following instructions shows cell locations, names of named cells, and other elements in the formula. The column on the right and in the line immediately above the formula description show the finished formula.

To build a formula, move the cursor to each cell location shown in the left column (Multiplan will produce the relative notation) and type everything else —operators, symbols, cell names, and function names. When you type a character, the cursor returns to the formula cell so you can type another character, move the cursor to another cell, or enter the formula.

When your formula agrees with the instructions, press Enter. If Multiplan then displays *Not a valid formula*, check each character. Use the F7 through F10 keys to move the highlight, and correct the problem by typing missing characters or pressing the Delete key to delete unwanted characters. If you prefer to start the formula from scratch, simply press the Escape key and begin again.

FORMULA 1: Running Balance

$$R[-1]C + RC[-2] - RC[-6]$$

Formula 1 adds the balance forward (R8C10) to any deposit in R9C8, then deducts any check amount in R9C4 to start the running balance in R9C10.

Place the cursor on R9C10:	Type or move the cursor:
Start the Value command	V
Enter the formula: R8C10 + R9C8 − R9C4	$R[-1]C + RC[-2] - RC[-6]$
Execute the command	Enter

To keep a running balance throughout the current period, copy Formula 1 down column 10.

Leave the cursor on R9C10:	Type or press:
Start the Copy command	C
Select the Down option	D
Specify the number of cells to copy into	17
Execute the command	Enter

FORMULA 2: Outstanding Check

$$IF(RC[-6] = 1,0,RC[-7])$$

Formula 2 uses the IF function to enter the amount of any outstanding check. The IF function has three parts: the Test statement, the Then statement, and the Else statement. The Test statement looks at R9C5 (the C column). If it finds the number 1—a "tick mark" indicating a check debited to your account—the Then statement enters a zero in the outstanding check cell (R9C11). If R9C5 is empty, the Else statement merely copies the amount of the outstanding check from R9C4 to R9C11.

Place the cursor on R9C11:	Type or move the cursor:
Start the Value command	V
Enter the formula: IF(R9C5 = 1, 0,R9C4)	$IF(RC[-6] = 1,0,RC[-7])$

Translation: IF(C column contains a 1,
then enter zero, else enter the check
amount)

Execute the command   Enter

FORMULA 3: Outstanding Deposit

IF(RC[− 3] = 1,0,RC[− 4])

Formula 3 does for deposits what Formula 2 does for checks. If the Test statement finds a "tick mark" (again, the number 1) in R9C9 (the D column), the Then statement enters a zero in the outstanding deposit cell (R9C12). If R9C9 is empty, the Else statement copies the amount of the outstanding deposit from R9C8 to R9C12.

Place the cursor on R9C12:	Type or move the cursor:
Start the Value command	V
Enter the formula: IF(R9C9 = 1, 0,R9C8)	IF(RC[− 3] = 1, 0,RC[− 4])
Translation: IF(D column contains a 1, then enter zero, else enter the deposit amount)	
Execute the command	Enter

Now let's copy Formulas 2 and 3 down their respective columns into the current and previous period portions of the spreadsheet. We will use a comma (the union operator) to tell Multiplan to skip over the lines and blank cells in rows 27 through 30.

Place the cursor on R9C11:	Type or press:
Start the Copy command	C
Select the From option	F
(Multiplan displays *COPY FROM cells:* R9C11, the first cell to copy from)	
Specify the last column to copy from	:12
Move the highlight to *to cells*	Tab
Specify the first cell in each row to copy into	R10:26C11, R31:36C11
Execute the command	Enter

FORMULA 4: Ending Balance

R[− 1]C

Formula 4 copies the amount in R26C10 to the ending balance cell (R27C10).

Place the cursor on R27C10:	**Type or move the cursor:**
Start the Value command	V
Enter the formula: R26C10	R[− 1]C
Execute the command	Enter

FORMULA 5: Checkbook Balance

EBALANCE

Formula 5 copies the ending balance in the current period (R27C10, EBALANCE) to the checkbook balance cell (R40C4). All you have to do is type the name of the cell.

Place the cursor on R40C4:	**Type or press:**
Start the Value command	V
Enter the formula: EBALANCE	EBALANCE
Execute the command	Enter

FORMULA 6: Adjusted Checkbook Balance

R[− 4]C + R[− 3]C − R[− 2]C

Formula 6 adds the checkbook balance in R40C4 to any bank credits (R41C4) and deducts any bank charges (R42C4) to produce the adjusted checkbook balance in R44C4.

Place the cursor on R44C4:	**Type or move the cursor:**
Start the Value command	V
Enter the formula: R40C4 + R41C4 − R42C4	R[− 4]C + R[− 3]C − R[− 2]C
Execute the command	Enter

Formula 6, when copied to R50C4, also calculates the adjusted bank statement balance. In its new location, it adds the bank statement balance (R46C4) to any deposits in transit (R47C4) and deducts any outstanding checks (R48C4). To copy the formula, leave the cursor on R44C4 and type *CF* (Copy From). Press Tab to move the highlight to *to cells.* Type *R50C4* and press Enter.

FORMULA 7: Deposits in Transit

SUM(ODEPOSITS)

Formula 7 adds the outstanding deposits (R9C12 through R36C12, ODEPOSITS) in the current and previous periods to give you the amount of deposits in transit (R47C4). Type the entire formula.

Place the cursor on R47C4:	Type or press:
Start the Value command	V
Enter the formula: SUM(ODEPOSITS)	SUM(ODEPOSITS)
Execute the command	Enter

FORMULA 8: Outstanding Checks

SUM(OCHECKS)

Formula 8 adds the outstanding checks (R9C11 through R36C11, OCHECKS) in the current and previous periods and enters the result in R48C4. Again, type the entire formula.

Place the cursor on R48C4:	Type or press:
Start the Value command	V
Enter the formula: SUM(OCHECKS)	SUM(OCHECKS)
Execute the command	Enter

FORMULA 9: Variance (Checkbook minus Statement)

R[−8]C − R[−2]C

Formula 9 subtracts the adjusted bank statement balance (R50C4) from the adjusted checkbook balance (R44C4) to show any discrepancy between the two amounts and enters the result in R52C4.

Place the cursor on R52C4:	Type or move the cursor:
Start the Value command	V
Enter the formula: R44C4 − R50C4	R[−8]C − R[−2]C
Execute the command	Enter

FORMULA 10: Total Deposits

SUM(DEPOSITS)

Formula 10 adds the deposits (R9C8 through R26C8, DEPOSITS) and enters the result in R54C4. This is another formula you type.

Place the cursor on R54C4:	Type or press:
Start the Value command	V
Enter the formula: SUM(DEPOSITS)	SUM(DEPOSITS)
Execute the command	Enter

FORMULA 11: Total Checks

SUM(CHECKS)

Formula 11 adds the checks (R9C4 through R26C4, CHECKS) and enters the result in R55C4. Again, type the entire formula.

Place the cursor on R55C4:	Type or press:
Start the Value command	V
Enter the formula: SUM(CHECKS)	SUM(CHECKS)
Execute the command	Enter

FORMULA 12: Checks and Allocation Amounts

IF(SUM(CHECKS) = SUM(ALLOCATED),"AGREE","OFF BY "
&DOLLAR(SUM(CHECKS) − SUM(ALLOCATED))
&" CHECK YOUR NUMBERS")

Formula 12 demonstrates Multiplan's ability to communicate in plain English. The Test statement *IF(SUM(CHECKS) = SUM(ALLOCATED)* compares the sum of the checks in column 4 with the sum of the allocated amounts in column 6. If they are equal, the Then statement enters the message *AGREE* in R56C4. If they are not equal, the *DOLLAR(SUM(CHECKS) − SUM(ALLOCATED))* part of the Else statement calculates the difference and embeds it in the message generated by the *OFF BY $xx.00 CHECK YOUR NUMBERS* part of the Else statement (the amount is indicated by *xx* here).

The DOLLAR function converts the result of the calculation to text and inserts the leading dollar sign and two decimal places. The converted-to-text number can then share the same cell as the real text and still be recalculated as conditions on the spreadsheet change. The & sign (concatenation operator) combines the converted number with the other text in the Else statement. Type the entire formula and press the Spacebar once after each of the following elements: the words *OFF* and *BY*, the fifth set of quotation marks, and the words *CHECK* and *YOUR*.

Place the cursor on R56C4:	Type or move the cursor:
Start the Value command	V

Enter the formula: IF(SUM(CHECKS) = SUM(ALLOCATED), "AGREE","OFF BY " &DOLLAR(SUM(CHECKS) − SUM(ALLOCATED)) &" CHECK YOUR NUMBERS")

IF(SUM(CHECKS) = SUM(ALLOCATED), "AGREE","OFF BY " &DOLLAR (SUM(CHECKS) − SUM(ALLOCATED)) &" CHECK YOUR NUMBERS")

Execute the command

Enter

FORMULA 13: Maximum Checkbook Balance

MAX(BALANCE)

Formula 13 scans the running balance (R8C10 through R26C10, BAL-ANCE), uses the MAX function to extract the largest amount, and enters it in R57C4. If you are letting your money lie idle in a non-interest-bearing account, this can be an eye opener. Type the entire formula.

Place the cursor on R57C4:	**Type or press:**
Start the Value command	V
Enter the formula: MAX (BALANCE)	MAX(BALANCE)
Execute the command	Enter

FORMULA 14: Average Checkbook Balance

AVERAGE(BALANCE)

Formula 14 uses the AVERAGE function to find the average running balance (R8C10 through R26C10, BALANCE), another indicator of how efficiently you are handling your money, and enters the result in R58C4. Again, type the entire formula.

Place the cursor on R58C4:	**Type or press:**
Start the Value command	V
Enter the formula: AVERAGE (BALANCE)	AVERAGE(BALANCE)
Execute the command	Enter

FORMULA 15: Number of Deposits

COUNT(DEPOSITS)

Formula 15 uses the COUNT function to count the deposits (R9C8 through R26C8, DEPOSITS) and enters the result in R59C4. Type the entire formula.

Place the cursor on R59C4:	Type or press:
Start the Value command	V
Enter the formula: COUNT (DEPOSITS)	COUNT(DEPOSITS)
Execute the command	Enter

FORMULA 16: Number of Checks

COUNT(CHECKS)

Formula 16 counts the checks (R9C4 through R26C4, CHECKS) and enters the result in R60C4. Again, type the entire formula.

Place the cursor on R60C4:	Type or press:
Start the Value command	V
Enter the formula: COUNT (CHECKS)	COUNT(CHECKS)
Execute the command	Enter

FORMULA 17: Spreadsheet Filename

NAME()

Formula 17 generates the spreadsheet filename in R1C12. Type the function name and parentheses.

Place the cursor on R1C12:	Type or press:
Start the Value command	V
Enter the formula: NAME()	NAME()
Execute the command	Enter

That's it. You've completed the formulas.

Locking The Formulas

To prevent accidental changes, lock the formulas and titles.

Leave the cursor where it is:	Type:
Start the Lock command	L

Select the Formulas option	F
(Multiplan displays *Enter Y to confirm*)	
Confirm the lock	Y

Saving the Formulas

Now, to safeguard all your work, store the formulas on disk. Because you saved the spreadsheet before, Multiplan asks you to confirm your intention to overwrite the earlier version.

Leave the cursor where it is:	**Type or press:**
Start the Transfer command	T
Select the Save option	S
(Multiplan displays *CHECK* —there's no need to retype)	
Execute the command	Enter
(Multiplan recalculates the spreadsheet, then displays *Enter Y to overwrite file*)	
Confirm the overwrite	Y

ENTERING THE TRANSIENT TEXT AND NUMBERS

You are now ready to enter the practice text and numbers shown in Figure 11-4. Because of the formatting you did earlier, Multiplan will enter the dollar signs and commas in the large numbers. There are many entries so, as you did when you entered the titles, activate the alpha/value mode first: Leave the cursor where it is and type O (Options). Press the Tab key four times to move the highlight to *alpha/value*. Type Y and press Enter. If you need to return to the command menu, press the Escape key.

Now place the cursor on R8C1. Type *AUGUST 87* and move the cursor to the next cell containing text or a number. Type the next entry and move the cursor to the next cell. Continue in this way until you have made all of the following entries:

■ In the current period transactions section, enter the dates in column 1, the check numbers in column 2, the payees in column 3, the check amounts in column 4, the allocated amounts in column 6, the account numbers in column 7, the number 1 "tick marks" in columns 5 and 9, and the balance forward in R8C10.

■ In the previous period outstanding section, enter the dates in column 1, the check numbers in column 2, the payees in column 3, the check amounts in column 4, the deposits in column 8, and the number 1 "tick marks" in columns 5 and 9.

■ In the reconciliation section, enter the bank credits in R41C4, the bank charges in R42C4, and the bank statement balance in R46C4. After you type the last entry, press Enter.

Your spreadsheet should now look like the one in Figure 11-1 at the beginning of this chapter. Press Escape to bring up the command menu. Now deactivate the alpha/value mode: Leave the cursor where it is. Type O (Options) and press Tab four times. Type N (No) and press Enter. Store the spreadsheet on disk: Type TS (Transfer Save), press Enter, and type Y to overwrite.

PRINTING YOUR SPREADSHEET

This spreadsheet can be printed in 12-pitch type either on two consecutive sheets of 8½-by-11-inch paper or, with a wide carriage printer, on one sheet of 15-by-11-inch paper. It is 139 characters wide on a single sheet of paper, including Multiplan row numbers.

Setting the Print Margins

The first step before printing is to set the margins around your spreadsheet.

Leave the cursor where it is:	Type or press:
Start the Print command	P
Select the Margins option	M

Type the following numbers in the margins fields. (Tab past any field that already has the proper setting.) If you overshoot a field, press Tab a few times to move full circle through the fields or press Shift-Tab to move backward one field at a time. The highlight is in the *left* field.

To do this:	Type or press:
Specify the number of characters:	
For 8½-by-11-inch paper	0
For 15-by-11-inch paper	15
Move the highlight to *top*	Tab
Specify the number of lines	0
Move the highlight to *print width*	Tab

```
              1            2                    3              4      5      6
                                                                  CHECK LEDGER AND
 1
 2  ================================================================================
 3  CURRENT PERIOD TRANSACTIONS
 4  --------------------------------------------------------------------------------
 5                      Check                                 Check          Allocated
 6  Date                Number  Paid To                       Amount    C    Amount
 7  --------------------------------------------------------------------------------
 8  AUGUST 87                        BALANCE FORWARD-----------------------------
 9  Aug 2      203      Nickel Savings Bank                    578.4    1    578.4
10  Aug 2      204      Holt Stationery                        161.19   1    161.19
11  Aug 7      205      Vinicombe Realty                       667      1    667
12  Aug 11     206      The Nissen Group                       1131     1    1131
13  Aug 12     207      Market Newsletter                      75       1    75
14  Aug 15     208      VOID
15  Aug 15     209      Don England                            4166.66  1    4166.66
16  Aug 15     210      DE-Expense Reimbursement               235.02   1    88.02
17                                                                           50
18                                                                           97
19  Aug 19     211      Payroll                                732.9    1    732.9
20  Aug 27              Deposit
21  Aug 29     212      Pelham U-Drive                         480.89        480.89
22  Aug 29     213      Eastern Power                          125      1    125
23  Aug 30     214      NY Telephone Co                        231.76        231.76
24  Aug 30     215      Department of Taxation                 146.58        146.58
25  Aug 30     216      True Blue Medical Plan                 390      1    390
26  Aug 30     217      Holt Stationery                        55       1    55
27                                         ENDING BALANCE----------------------------
28  ================================================================================
29  PREVIOUS PERIOD OUTSTANDING                               Check    C
30  --------------------------------------------------------------------------------
31  Jul 7,87   179      Parcel Express                         15       1
32  Jul 10,87  184      Abner Civic Association                75
33  Jul 28,87  199      Pro Advertising                        456      1
34
35
36
37  ================================================================================
38  RECONCILIATION
39  --------------------------------------------------------------------------------
40  Checkbook Balance
41    Plus Bank Credits                                             0
42    Less Bank Charges                                         17.85
43                                                            -----------
44  Adjusted Checkbook Balance
45                                                            ===========
46  Bank Statement Balance                                    13247.99
47    Plus Deposits in Transit
48    Less Outstanding Checks
49                                                            -----------
50  Adjusted Bank Statement Balance
51                                                            ===========
52  Variance (Checkbook minus Statement)
53  ================================================================================
54  Amount of Deposits
55  Amount of Checks
56  Checks and Allocation Amounts
57  Maximum Checkbook Balance
58  Average Checkbook Balance
59  Number of Deposits
60  Number of Checks
61  ================================================================================
```

FIGURE 11-4.
Check ledger and reconciliation transient text and numbers

```
      7          8        9       10          11            12
   RECONCILIATION                                         CHECK
=================================================================

-----------------------------------------------------------------
Account    Deposit            Running    ***** Outstanding *****
Number     Amount      D      Balance      Check       Deposit
-----------------------------------------------------------------
----------------------->       12678.9
   12          2350    1
    6
    2        122.33    1
    8        256.78    1
    9

    1
   11          2350    1
    3
   10
    5
              743
   16
    4          3750    1
    3
    7
   18        1089.32
    6
----------------------->
=================================================================
            Deposit    D
-----------------------------------------------------------------
             432.75    1
```

```
=================================================================
```

```
=================================================================
```

Specify the number of characters:	
For 8½-by-11-inch paper	96
For 15-by-11-inch paper	139
Move the highlight to *print length*	Tab
Specify the number of lines	62
Move the highlight to *page length*	Tab
Specify the number of lines	66
Execute the command	Enter

Setting the Printing Options

You are still in the Print command. The next step is to set the print options. The options settings are the same for every spreadsheet in this book: Print the entire spreadsheet in 12-pitch type with row and column numbers. You can find the printer code for 12-pitch type in your printer manual.

Now type O to select the Options option. Type in the following responses. (Tab past any field that already has the proper setting.) The highlight is in the *area* field.

To do this:	Type or press:
Define the print area	R1:4095
Move the highlight to *setup*	Tab
Enter your printer code for 12-pitch type	(your code)
Move the highlight to *formulas*	Tab Tab
Select *No*	N
Move the highlight to *row-col numbers*	Tab
Select *Yes*	Y
Execute the command	Enter

Now, before you print, store the spreadsheet with the print settings: Press Escape to exit the Print command. Leave the cursor where it is. Type *TS* (Transfer Save) and press Enter. Type Y to overwrite the earlier version.

Printing the Spreadsheet

Now turn on your printer and print a copy of your spreadsheet.

Leave the cursor where it is:	Type:
Start the Print command	P
Select the Printer option	P

CREATING THE MACROS THAT UPDATE THE LEDGER

Updating the ledger spreadsheet at the start of a new period involves copying any outstanding item from the current period (rows 9 to 26) to the previous period (rows 31 to 36) after erasing the information from the previous period. Outstanding items can be one of three kinds:

■ A check, such as for Pelham U-Drive in row 21, which has entries in columns 1 through 4 (date, check number, paid to, and amount).

■ A deposit in its own row, such as the one in row 20, which has entries in column 1 (date), column 3 (the word *Deposit*), and column 8 (amount).

■ A deposit that shares a row with a check, such as the one in R25C8, which has entries only in column 1 (date) and column 8 (amount).

Manually updating several items each month can get tiresome. The process is best left to macros, which are intended for this kind of repetitive activity.

Figure 11-5 shows three macros and two macro subroutines. (A subroutine is a macro that is called by another macro.) The macros in R32C14, R34C14, and R36C14 copy the contents of the following cells: Check entries in columns 1 to 4, deposit entries in columns 1 to 8, or deposit entries in columns 1 and 8 only. The subroutines in R27C14 and R29C14 handle the actions the macros have in common. Separating them from the macros saves time and effort.

For instance, each macro starts with the command code 'CA (call on) and the cell we'll name *A* (together, the command code and cell name appear in the macro as 'CAA'). This tells Multiplan to call on R27C14, the cell named *A*, and run the subroutine there. It's a whole lot easier to type 'CAA' (call on Subroutine A) into each macro than GR'?'TB1'RTCF'RE (which *is* Subroutine A). Each macro also contains 'CAB', which directs Multiplan to the subroutine in R29C14, the cell we'll name *B*.

Subroutine A copies an entry from a row in the current period. Subroutine B copies an entry to a row in the previous period, then moves to the date in column 1 and appends the year. The '? (a "wild card") tells the macro to pause for keyboard input—in this case, so that you can type a row number or cell location. The command code 'RE at the end of the subroutine tells Multiplan to return to the macro that called for the detour and resume running there.

The command code 'GO and the cell location near the end of each macro tells Multiplan to go to the same macro cell, creating a looping pattern that repeats the macro as many times as is necessary. The command code 'QU ends the macro.

Macro number	Cell location:	Contents of cell:
	R26C14:	Subroutine A
	R27C14	GR'?'TB1'RTCF'RE
	R28C14:	Subroutine B
	R29C14	'TB'?'RTGR'?'RTE'CL,87'RT'RE
1	R31C14:	Copy Check Row to Previous Period (Alt-CR)
	R32C14	'CAA':4'CAB''GOR32C14''QU
2	R33C14:	Copy Deposit Row to Previous Period (Alt-DR)
	R34C14	'CAA':8'CAB''GOR34C14''QU
3	R35C14:	Copy Deposit Entry to Previous Period (Alt-DE)
	R36C14	'CAA','RK'RK'RK'RK'RK'RK'RK 'CAB''RK'RKADeposit'RT 'GOR36C14''QU

FIGURE 11-5.
The macros that update the check ledger

Keystrokes are shown by their keycodes (an apostrophe followed by two letters), so 'TB is Tab and 'RT is Return (or Enter). When you are in the Edit Macro mode, Multiplan produces these keycodes automatically. You'll find a detailed description of macros and keycodes in Chapter 18.

Some of this may be difficult to visualize right now. Be patient. Things have a way of becoming clear when you see the macros in action.

Preparing for the Macros

A few preparations have to be made before you enter the macros. First, increase the width of column 14 (the area on the spreadsheet we'll reserve for macros) so that you can see each macro in its entirety (it will make things easier for you): Place the cursor on R26C14 and type *FW* (Format Width). Type *62* and press Enter.

Next, enter the macro descriptions and the keystrokes (shown in parentheses following the descriptions) that get them going: Place the cursor on R26C14 and type *A* (Alpha). Type *Subroutine A* and move the cursor to R28C14. Type *Subroutine B* and move the cursor to R31C14. Type *Copy check row to previous period (Alt-CR)* and move the cursor to R33C14. Type *Copy deposit row to previous period (Alt-DR)* and move the cursor to R35C14. Type *Copy deposit entry to previous period (Alt-DE)* and press Enter.

And finally, name the cells that will contain the macro subroutines: Place the cursor on R27C14 and type *N* (Name). Type *A* and press Enter. Place the cursor on R29C14 and type *N*. Type *B* and press Enter.

WRITING THE MACROS

The left column of the following instructions describes the actions of the macro during its run. (References to the Edit Macro mode are also in the left column, although Edit Macro relates to writing the macro, not how the macro runs). The column on the right contains the keystrokes that cause the macro actions. At several points in the writing, I'll ask you to press the F5 key to activate the Edit Macro mode, which affects the keyboard in a special way: While in this mode, Multiplan enters the keycode for any key you press, which makes writing a macro a breeze.

Keep one thing in mind: If you make a typing mistake or hit the wrong key while in the Edit Macro mode (you'll see *EM* to the right of the *Free* indicator), press F5 to return the keyboard to standard operation before you press any other key. Otherwise, Multiplan will continue to enter the keycodes for the keys you press. If you mistype when you are out of the Edit Macro mode, use Backspace to erase characters, press F5 to reenter the Edit Macro mode, and continue from where you left off.

Macro Subroutine A

GR'?'TB1'RTCF'RE

Subroutine A moves the cursor to the cell you designate, where it starts copying the entry, then returns to the macro that called for the subroutine. Place the cursor on R27C14 and type *A* to start the Alpha command, which is the command you use to enter a macro.

Macro action:	Type or press:
Start the Goto command and select the Row-col option (pause for keyboard input)	GR'?

Activate the Edit Macro mode	F5
Move the highlight to *column*	Tab
Specify column 1	1
Confirm the Goto command	Enter
Start the Copy command and select the From option	CF
Return to the main macro	'RE

Press F5 to exit the Edit Macro mode. There's no need to press Enter. Just move the cursor to R29C14 and Multiplan enters Subroutine A in its cell.

Macro Subroutine B

'TB'?'RTGR'?'RTE'CL,87'RT'RE

Subroutine B copies the items into a cell you designate, edits the date so that the year number *87* appears at the end, then returns to the macro that called for the subroutine. The cursor is now on R29C14. Press F5 to activate the Edit Macro mode.

Macro actions:	Type or press:
Move the highlight to *to cells*	Tab
Pause for keyboard input	'?
Confirm the Copy command	Enter
Start the Goto command and select the Row-col option (pause for keyboard input)	GR'?
Confirm the Goto command	Enter
Start the Edit command	E
Move the highlight one character to the left	F9
Type ,87 at the end of the date	,87
Confirm the Edit command	Enter
Return to the main macro	'RE

Press F5 to exit the Edit Macro mode. Now move the cursor to R32C14 and Multiplan enters Subroutine B in its cell.

Macro 1: Copy Check Row to Previous Period

'CAA':4'CAB''GOR32C14''QU

Macro 1 doesn't contain any keycodes, so you don't have to use the Edit Macro mode. The cursor is on R32C14.

Macro actions:	Type or press:
Call on Subroutine A	'CAA'
Specify the last cell to copy from	:4
Call on Subroutine B	'CAB'
Go to R32C14, the macro cell (this macro calls itself)	'GOR32C14'
End the macro	'QU

Enter the macro by pressing the Enter key.

Macro 2: Copy Deposit Row to Previous Period

'CAA':8'CAB''GOR34C14''QU

Except for the last cell to copy from and the cell where you enter it, Macro 2 is just the same as Macro 1. Instead of starting from scratch, let's just copy, then edit.

Leave the cursor on R32C14:	**Type or press:**
Start the Copy command	C
Select the From option	F
(Multiplan displays *COPY FROM cells: R32C14*, the cell to copy from)	
Move the highlight to *to cells*	Tab
Specify the row to copy into	R34C14
Execute the command	Enter

Now place the cursor on R34C14 and type *E* (Edit). The macro appears on the command line. Press the F9 key nine times, which places the highlight atop the number 2. To change the cell location to R34C14, press the Delete key and type 4. Now press the F7 key six times to place the highlight atop the number 4. To change the range to :8, press the Delete key and type 8. Press Enter.

Macro 3: Copy Deposit Entry to Previous Period

'CAA','RK'RK'RK'RK'RK'RK'RK'CAB''RK
'RKADeposit'RT'GOR36C14''QU

Macro 3 handles a deposit that shares a row with a check. After using the subroutines to copy the date and amount and appending the year, it plunks the word *Deposit* into column 3. Place the cursor on R36C14 and type *A* to start the Alpha command.

Macro actions:	Type or press:
Call on Subroutine A	'CAA'
Type the union operator (,)	,
Activate the Edit Macro mode	F5
Move the cursor seven cells to the right	Right Arrow (seven times)
Call on Subroutine B	'CAB'
Move the cursor two cells to the right	Right Arrow (twice)
Start the Alpha command, type *Deposit*	ADeposit
Confirm the Alpha command	Enter
Go to R36C14, the macro cell (this macro calls itself)	'GOR36C14'
Exit the Edit Macro mode	F5
End the macro	'QU

Press the Enter key to enter the macro. Now check each character—particularly the apostrophes—in the subroutines and macros to make sure everything agrees with the ones in Figure 11-5.

Naming the Macros and Assigning Run Codes

The last step is to name each macro and assign a run code. Then, you can simply hold down the Alt key, type two letters, and the macro will go to work. Let's start with Macro 1, which copies a check row.

Place the cursor on R32C14:	Type or press:
Start the Name command	N
Name the macro	CHECKROW
Move the highlight to *macro*	Tab Tab
Select *Yes*	Y
Move the highlight to *command key(s)*	Tab
Assign the run code	CR
Execute the command	Enter

Now for Macro 2, which copies a deposit row: Place the cursor on R34C14 and type *N* (Name). Type *DEPOSITROW* and press Tab twice. Type *Y* and press Tab again. Type *DR* and press Enter.

And finally, name Macro 3, which copies the deposit entries that share a row with a check: Place the cursor on R36C14 and type *N*. Type the title

DEPOSITENTRY and press Tab twice. Type *Y* and press Tab again. Type *DE* and press Enter.

Safeguard your work. First, lock the macro cells: Place the cursor on R26C14 and type *LC* (Lock Cells). Type *:R36C14* and press Tab. Type *L* (Locked) and press Enter. Next, save the spreadsheet: Type *TS* (Transfer Save), press Enter, and type *Y* to overwrite.

USING YOUR SPREADSHEET

Though it took some effort to create, this check ledger virtually runs itself. In the following practice session, you'll erase the old information, run the macros, and sort the entries. Figure 11-6 shows how things should look when you're finished. Be sure that you don't save the spreadsheet at any time during these steps. You'll want everything exactly as is when you create the cash disbursement spreadsheet in the next chapter.

Let's assume these entries are your own. You've completed the reconciliation and everything checks out perfectly. The first step, as you have already done, is to print a copy of the spreadsheet for your records.

Erasing Old Entries from the Previous Period

The next step is to clean up the section for the previous period by erasing every entry with a "tick mark" beside it—in this case, the check and deposit in row 31 and the check in row 33.

Place the cursor on R31C1:	Type or press:
Start the Blank command	B
(Multiplan displays *BLANK cells: R31C1*, the first cell to blank)	
Specify the other cells to blank	:9,R33C1:5
Execute the command	Enter

Updating with Macros

The next step is to copy the items without a "tick mark"—the checks in rows 21, 23, and 24 and the deposits in row 20 and R25C8—from the current period section to the previous period section. This is when the macros earn their keep. Let's start by copying the entry for Pelham U-Drive from row 21 to row 31. The *CHECKROW* macro (with the run code CR) handles this task: Leave the cursor on R31C1. Hold down the Alt key and type *CR*.

If Multiplan finds an error in a macro or subroutine, it will display the message *Error in Macro* and a cell location. If this happens, compare the macro in

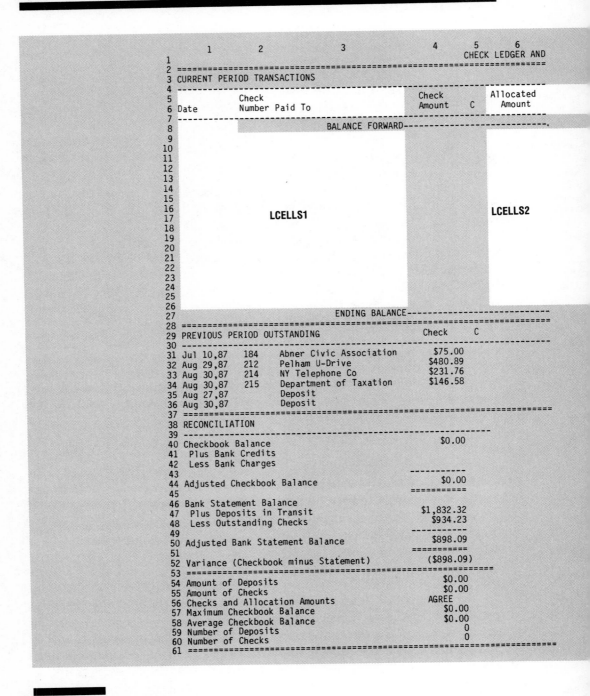

FIGURE 11-6.
Check ledger and reconciliation prepared for new entries

```
    7              8        9        10             11            12
RECONCILIATION                                                         CHECK
===============================================================================


-------------------------------------------------------------------------------
Account    Deposit                 Running     ***** Outstanding *****
Number     Amount        D         Balance         Check        Deposit
-------------------------------------------------------------------------------
-----------------------> 
                                    $0.00          0.00          0.00
                                    $0.00          0.00          0.00
                                    $0.00          0.00          0.00
                                    $0.00          0.00          0.00
                                    $0.00          0.00          0.00
                                    $0.00          0.00          0.00
                                    $0.00          0.00          0.00
                                    $0.00          0.00          0.00
                                    $0.00          0.00          0.00
                                    $0.00          0.00          0.00
                                    $0.00          0.00          0.00
                                    $0.00          0.00          0.00
                                    $0.00          0.00          0.00
                                    $0.00          0.00          0.00
                                    $0.00          0.00          0.00
                                    $0.00          0.00          0.00
                                    $0.00          0.00          0.00
-----------------------> 
                                    $0.00
===============================================================================
            Deposit      D
-------------------------------------------------------------------------------
                                                   75.00         0.00
                                                  480.89         0.00
                                                  231.76         0.00
                                                  146.58         0.00
            $743.00                                 0.00       743.00
          $1,089.32                                 0.00     1,089.32
===============================================================================


===============================================================================
```

the specified cell with the macro listing in Figure 11-5 and correct any errors.

The macro starts its run, then pauses for your input. Type *21* (the row the check is on) and press Enter. The macro breezes into the Copy command, then pauses again. Type *R31C1* (the first cell in the row you want to copy into) and press Enter. The next pause is for the new location, so that the macro can return to edit the date. Type *31* and press Enter. The macro appends the year, then starts the cycle again, so that you can continue with the next outstanding check—for *NY Telephone Co* in row 23.

Type *23* and press Enter. At the pause, type *R33C1* and press Enter. At the next pause, type *33* and press Enter. The next check is to the *Department of Taxation* in row 24. Type *24* and press Enter. At the next pause, type R34C1 and press Enter. At the next pause, type *34* and press Enter. This is the last check to be copied, so press the Escape key to stop the macro.

Now let's work with the deposit in row 20, which will be handled by the *DEPOSITROW* macro (with the run code DR). Hold down the Alt key and type *DR*. At the first pause, type *20* and press Enter. At the next pause, type R35C1 and press Enter. When the macro pauses again, type *35* and press Enter. At the next pause, press Escape to stop the macro.

There's one more deposit to go—the one in R25C8, which is handled by the *DEPOSITENTRY* macro (with the run code DE). Hold down Alt and type *DE*. At the first pause, type *25* and press Enter. The cursor bounces to column 8 to pick up the deposit amount (it happens quickly, so watch carefully). At the next pause, type *R36C1* and press Enter. When the macro pauses again, type *36* and press Enter. At the next pause, press Escape to stop the macro.

Ah, a piece of cake.

Sorting the Copied Items in the Previous Period Section

To keep things tidy, sort the check numbers in the previous period section so that they appear on the spreadsheet in numerical order.

Place the cursor on R31C2:	Type or press:
Start the Sort command	S
Move the highlight to *between rows*	Tab
Specify the first row to sort	31
Move the highlight to *and*	Tab
Specify the last row to sort	34

In the *order* field, the parentheses around > show that ascending order is the current selection. This is what you want, so press Enter. If you enter checks in anything but numerical order, you can use the Sort command in the same way to straighten them out.

Erasing the Rest of the Old Information

Remember all those cells you named OLD? This is when you use that name to blank out the rest of the old information in one easy step.

Leave the cursor where it is:	Type or press:
Start the Blank command	B
Name the cells to blank	OLD
Execute the command	Enter

In the wink of an eye, all the entries in the current period are gone, everything in the previous period is intact, and Multiplan has recalculated every formula. Everything is ready for the start of a new period.

Now restore the spreadsheet containing its original entries: Leave the cursor where it is, type *TL* (Transfer Load), type *CHECK* (the spreadsheet filename), and press Enter. Press *N* to lose the edits.

You could stop now because your check ledger spreadsheet is complete. But let's explore Multiplan's external link instead.

PREPARING THE CHECK LEDGER FOR LINKING

Multiplan's Xternal command links spreadsheets so that you can feed data from one to another without retyping the information. Let's prepare the check ledger now so that we can link it in the next chapter with the cash disbursements spreadsheet.

Naming the Linked Cells

The first step is to name the cells containing the information we want both spreadsheets to share. These cells, shown in the unshaded areas in Figure 11-6, are in columns 1 through 3 and columns 6 through 7 in the current period. The information in columns 4 and 5 isn't needed on the cash disbursements spreadsheet. If we give a different name to each group we want, we can then transfer them into contiguous columns on the cash disbursements spreadsheet.

The first group contains the column headings (rows 5 and 6 of columns 1 through 3), the single line (row 7 of columns 1 through 3), the current month (R8C1), the dates (R9C1 through R26C1), the check numbers (R9C2 through R26C2), and the payees (R9C3 through R26C3). Let's name them LCELLS1 (for Linked CELLS 1).

Place the cursor on R5C1:	Type or press:
Start the Name command	N

Name the cells	LCELLS1
Move the highlight to *to refer to*	Tab
(Multiplan displays *to refer to:* R5C1)	
Specify the other cells to name	:R7C3,R8C1,R9:26C1:3
Execute the command	Enter

The second group contains the column headings (rows 5 and 6 of columns 6 and 7), the single line (row 7 of columns 6 and 7), the allocated amounts (R9C6 through R26C6), and the account numbers (R9C7 through R26C7). Let's name them LCELLS2 (for Linked CELLS 2).

Place the cursor on R5C6:	**Type or press:**
Start the Name command	N
Name the cells	LCELLS2
Move the highlight to *to refer to*	Tab
(Multiplan displays *to refer to:* R5C6)	
Specify the other cells to name	:R7C7,R9:26C6:7
Execute the command	Enter

Store the LCELLS names and cell locations by typing *TS* (Transfer Save) and pressing Enter. Type *Y* to overwrite. The spreadsheet is now all set for linking.

Adding Check Entry Rows

Later, if you need more room for your transactions, this is how to insert rows. If you practice these steps now, don't save the spreadsheet at any time because you'll want it as it is now when you go on to the cash disbursements spreadsheet in Chapter 12. After you finish practicing, reload the original version by using Transfer Load.

Step 1: To be sure that any rows you add are included in the named areas, always insert the new rows between the first and last check or deposit entry rows (at this time, rows 9 and 26 and rows 31 and 36). Let's suppose you want to insert four rows at the bottom of the current period. Place the cursor in row 26 and type *IR* (Insert Row). Type *4* and press Enter.

Step 2: To enter the formulas and formats into the new rows, copy from row 25 of columns 2 through 12: Place the cursor on R25C2 and type *CF* (Copy From). Type *:12* and press Tab. Type *R26:29C2* and press Enter. Multiplan is tracking your actions and will adjust all the cell references in the formulas so that they continue to calculate properly.

Step 3: To check that everything else works as it should, erase the old entries: Type *B* (Blank), then type *OLD* and press Enter. The entries in the previous period are intact, and Multiplan has recalculated all the formulas including those in the reconciliation section.

Use Transfer Save to store these changes on disk. The procedure is the same if you need more rows in the previous period outstanding section. This is important: When you insert rows in the current period of the check ledger, be sure to insert the same number of rows in the cash disbursements spreadsheet so that the linked areas are identical.

SPREADSHEET SUMMARY

General: The completed spreadsheet is shown in Figure 11-1. Use Options to set automatic recalculation to *No.* Use Value to enter REPT(" = ",25) and REPT(" − ",25) for the long lines, REPT(" = ",11) and REPT(" − ",11) for the short lines. Indent the titles one space as shown in Figure 11-1. Use Lock Formulas to lock formulas.

Column Width: Use Format Width as follows: Set columns 1, 4, 6, 8, and 11 to 12 characters wide, column 2 to 7 characters, column 3 to 25 characters, columns 5 and 9 to 4 characters, column 7 to 8 characters, and column 10 to 14 characters.

Format: Use Format Cells as follows: Continue R1C5:8, C1:3, R5C11:12. Continue and center R56C4. Center R5C4:10, R6C4:12, R29C4:9, and R9C7:R26C7. Right-justify R8C3, R27C3, and R1C12. Left-justify R9:R36C2. Dollar code R9:58C4, R9:26C6, R9:36C8, and R8:27C10. Fix code with two decimal places R9C11:R36C12. Use Format Options to insert commas.

Name: Use Name as follows: R8C1,R9:26C1:9, R41:42C4,R8C10, and R46C4 are OLD. R9:26C4 are CHECKS. R9:26C6 are ALLOCATED. R9:26C8 are DEPOSITS. R8:26C10 are BALANCE. R9:36C11 are OCHECKS. R9:36C12 are ODEPOSITS. R27C10 is EBALANCE. R27C14 is A. R29C14 is B. R32C14 is CHECKROW. R34C14 is DEPOSITROW. R36C14 is DEPOSITENTRY. R5C1:R7C3,R8C1,R9:26C1:3 are LCELLS1. R5C6:R7C7,R9:26C6:7 are LCELLS2. The LCELLS groups will be linked to the cash disbursements spreadsheet in Chapter 12.

Print: Check Ledger and Reconciliation is 139 characters wide, including Multiplan row numbers, and is printed in 12-pitch. For 8½-by-11-inch paper, set the following margins: *left 0, top 0, print width 96, print length 62,* and *page length 66.* For 15-by-11-inch paper, set *left* to 15 and *print width* to 139. The other settings are the same as for 8½-by-11-inch paper.

Formulas: Formulas use named and relative cell references.

1   R9C10   Running Balance
             $R[-1]C + RC[-2] - RC[-6]$

2   R9C11   Outstanding Check
             $IF(RC[-6] = 1,0,RC[-7])$

3   R9C12   Outstanding Deposit
             $IF(RC[-3] = 1,0,RC[-4])$

4   R27C10   Ending Balance
             $R[-1]C$

5   R40C4   Checkbook Balance
             EBALANCE

6   R44C4   Adjusted Checkbook Balance
             $R[-4]C + R[-3]C - R[-2]C$

7   R47C4   Deposits In Transit
             SUM(ODEPOSITS)

8   R48C4   Outstanding Checks
             SUM(OCHECKS)

9   R52C4   Variance (Checkbook minus Statement)
             $R[-8]C - R[-2]C$

10 R54C4   Total Deposits
             SUM(DEPOSITS)

11 R55C4   Total Checks
             SUM(CHECKS)

12 R56C4   Checks and Allocation Amounts
             IF(SUM(CHECKS) = SUM(ALLOCATED),
             "AGREE","OFF BY "
             &DOLLAR(SUM(CHECKS)
             - SUM(ALLOCATED))
             &" CHECK YOUR NUMBERS")

13 R57C4   Maximum Checkbook Balance
             MAX(BALANCE)

14 R58C4   Average Checkbook Balance
             AVERAGE(BALANCE)

15	R59C4	Number of Deposits COUNT(DEPOSITS)
16	R60C4	Number of Checks COUNT(CHECKS)
17	R1C12	Spreadsheet Filename NAME()

Macros and Run Codes:

	R27C14	Subroutine A GR'?'TB1'RTCF'RE
	R29C14	Subroutine B 'TB'?'RTGR'?'RTE'CL,87'RT'RE
1	R32C14	Copy Check Row to Previous Period (Alt-CR) 'CAA':4'CAB''GOR32C14''QU
2	R34C14	Copy Deposit Row to Previous Period (Alt-DR) 'CAA':8'CAB''GOR34C14''QU
3	R36C14	Copy Deposit Entry to Previous Period (Alt-DE) 'CAA','RK'RK'RK'RK'RK'RK'RK 'CAB''RK'RKADeposit'RT'GOR36C14''QU

12

Cash Disbursements

Information about how much your business spends by account, or category, is important to you because it can help you analyze the cash flow cycles of your business, plan for expenditures, prepare financial reports, and claim the proper allowances and deductions on your tax statements. This chapter demonstrates three ways to categorize these expenditures.

The first approach uses Multiplan's Xternal command to link the check ledger in Chapter 11 to the cash disbursements spreadsheet you create here. Therefore, you must create the check ledger first. Xternal is one of the marvels of Multiplan and is a real time-saver, because any change you make in the linked area of the source spreadsheet is reflected in the destination spreadsheet. The check ledger, because it feeds information, is the source; the cash disbursements spreadsheet, because it receives information, is the destination.

The linked area contains the dates, check numbers, payees, allocated amounts, and account codes. When the cash disbursements spreadsheet receives this information, it distributes the amounts into expense accounts, totals each account, then calculates the grand total of all the accounts. Figure 12-1 shows the completed cash disbursements spreadsheet.

In the second approach, you tuck a cash disbursements module into the check ledger and use the INDEX function and iteration to create a single source spreadsheet that not only shows each check written in the current period, but also a total of each expense account as well. Figure 12-3 shows the check ledger cum module.

	1	2	3	4	5	6 CASH DISBURSE
1						
2	==					
3		Check		Allocated	Account	1 ❶
4	Date	Number	Paid To	Amount	Number	Draw
5	--					
6	AUGUST 87					❷
7	Aug 2	203	Nickel Savings Bank	$578.40	12	
8	Aug 2	204	Holt Stationery	$161.19	6	
9	Aug 7	205	Vinicombe Realty	$667.00	2	
10	Aug 11	206	The Nissen Group	$1,131.00	8	
11	Aug 12	207	Market Newsletter	$75.00	9	
12	Aug 15	208	VOID			
13	Aug 15	209	Don England	$4,166.66	1	$4,166.66
14	Aug 15	210	DE-Expense Reimbursement	$88.02	11	
15				$50.00	3	
16				$97.00	10	
17	Aug 19	211	Payroll	$732.90	5	
18	Aug 27		Deposit			
19	Aug 29	212	Pelham U-Drive	$480.89	16	
20	Aug 29	213	Eastern Power	$125.00	4	
21	Aug 30	214	NY Telephone Co	$231.76	3	
22	Aug 30	215	Department of Taxation	$146.58	7	
23	Aug 30	216	True Blue Medical Plan	$390.00	18	
24	Aug 30	217	Holt Stationery	$55.00	6	
25	==					
26			Totals	$9,176.40 ❸		$4,166.66

FIGURE 12-1.

The completed cash disbursements spreadsheet showing the formula locations

In the third aproach, you convert the cash disbursements module into the independent spreadsheet shown in Figure 12-4, which uses Xternal Total to keep a year-to-date total of expenditures for each account. A macro menu we'll create makes working with this spreadsheet a breeze.

If you're familiar with Multiplan and prefer to create the module and the spreadsheets without following the step-by-step instructions, refer to the summaries at the end of this chapter.

CREATING THE CASH DISBURSEMENTS SPREADSHEET

We'll be working with both the cash disbursements and check ledger spreadsheets. Since their names are rather long, let's call the check ledger and reconciliation spreadsheet CHECK and the cash disbursements spreadsheet DISBURS. (Later we'll use these names as the filenames.)

In Chapter 11, we began the process of linking CHECK and DISBURS. First, we named the areas to be linked LCELLS1 and LCELLS2. Then, we

```
    7           8         9        10        11        12        13        14
  MENTS                                                                 DISBURS ❹
  ============================================================================
    2           3         4         5         6         7         8         9
  Rent        Phone   Utilities  Payroll  Supplies   Taxes   Technical Dues/Subs
  ----------------------------------------------------------------------------

 $667.00                                   $161.19

                                                              $1,131.00
                                                                        $75.00

              $50.00

                                  $732.90

                         $125.00
             $231.76

                                                     $146.58
                                            $55.00
  ============================================================================
 $667.00     $281.76   $125.00   $732.90   $216.19   $146.58 $1,131.00  $75.00
```

stored the LCELLS names and cell locations on disk. Now let's establish the link between CHECK and DISBURS so that every time you load DISBURS, it contains CHECK's current information.

LINKING DISBURS AND CHECK

We're creating a new spreadsheet, so let's start with a clean screen. If you're starting up again, bring up the Multiplan screen. Be sure your computer can access CHECK, either on a floppy disk now in your data drive or on your hard disk. If you still have CHECK on your screen, clear the screen: Leave the cursor where it is and type *TCA* (Transfer Clear All).

Check to see that automatic recalculation is turned off: Type *O* (Options). The highlight should be on *No* in the *recalc* field. If it's on *Yes*, type *N* and press Enter. If it's on *No*, press the Escape key.

The next few steps load the information in the LCELLS groups from CHECK to your new spreadsheet. After these two steps, your screen should look like the one in Figure 12-2. First, load LCELLS1.

	1	2	3	4	5
1					
2					
3		Check		Allocated	Account
4	Date	Number	Paid To	Amount	Number
5	--				
6	AUGUST 87				
7	Aug 2		203 Nickel Sav	578.4	12
8	Aug 2		204 Holt Stati	161.19	6
9	Aug 7		205 Vinicombe	667	2
10	Aug 11		206 The Nissen	1131	8
11	Aug 12		207 Market New	75	9
12	Aug 15		208 VOID		
13	Aug 15		209 Don Englan	4166.66	1
14	Aug 15		210 DE-Expense	88.02	11
15				50	3
16				97	10
17	Aug 19		211 Payroll	732.9	5
18	Aug 27		Deposit		
19	Aug 29		212 Pelham U-D	480.89	16
20	Aug 29		213 Eastern Po	125	4
21	Aug 30		214 NY Telepho	231.76	3
22	Aug 30		215 Department	146.58	7
23	Aug 30		216 True Blue	390	18
24	Aug 30		217 Holt Stati	55	6

FIGURE 12-2.
The first glimpse of the cash disbursements spreadsheet with the LCELLS loaded

Place the cursor on R3C1:	Type or press:
Start the Xternal command	X
Select the Copy option	C
(The highlight is in *from sheet*)	
Name the source spreadsheet	CHECK
Move the highlight to *name*	Tab
Identify the area to copy	LCELLS1

The *to* field at the bottom of your screen shows R3C1, the upper left corner of the area we want LCELLS1 copied into. The field to the right shows *linked:(Yes)No*. The responses in both fields are correct, so press Enter.

There's a slight delay while Xternal Copy loads LCELLS1 from CHECK. When loading is complete, you see *[CHECK LCELLS1]* on the status line at the bottom of your screen. These names in brackets confirm the spreadsheet link.

Now load LCELLS2 in the same way.

Place the cursor on R3C4:	Type or press:
Start the Xternal command	X
Select the Copy option	C
Name the source spreadsheet	CHECK

Move the highlight to *name*	Tab
Identify the area to copy	LCELLS2
Execute the command	Enter

SETTING UP THE CASH DISBURSEMENTS SPREADSHEET

All the entries are now loaded and your DISBURS spreadsheet is well on its way. Formatting is the only change you can make in these cells. You can enter or delete information only through the source (CHECK) spreadsheet.

Adjusting the Column Widths

Let's set up DISBURS so it looks like the spreadsheet in Figure 12-1. Start by changing the widths of the columns.

Place the cursor on R3C1:	Type or press:
Start the Format command	F
Select the Width option	W
Specify the number of characters in the column	12
Execute the command	Enter

Follow this procedure to change the width of column 2 to 7 characters, column 3 to 25 characters, and columns 4 and 6 to 12 characters each. Column 5 can remain at the default width (10 characters).

Entering the Titles

The next step is to type the new titles shown in Figure 12-1 in rows 1, 4, and 26. Only the first part of the title CASH DISBURSEMENTS will appear at this time because the title is longer than its cell can display. We'll take care of that shortly when we format the titles.

Place the cursor on R1C6:	Type:
Start the Alpha command	A
Type the first title	CASH DISBURSEMENTS

Now move the cursor to R4C6. Type *Draw* and move the cursor to R4C7. Type *Rent* and move the cursor to R4C8. Type *Phone* and move the cursor again. Continue in this way, typing a title and moving the cursor, until you enter the other account names in row 4, columns 9 through 14, and the title *Totals* in R26C3. After you type the last title, press Enter.

Entering the Long Lines

Now, as you did in creating CHECK, use the REPT function to put a double line across row 2. First, press the Home key to jump the cursor to R1C1.

Place the cursor on R2C1:	**Type or press:**
Start the Value command	V
Repeat an equal sign 25 times	REPT(" = ",25)
Execute the command	Enter

Now copy the formula into the columns to the right.

Leave the cursor on R2C1:	**Type or press:**
Start the Copy command	C
Select the Right option	R
Specify the number of cells to copy into	13
Execute the command	Enter

Next, copy the entire row of formulas to row 25.

Leave the cursor on R2C1:	**Type or press:**
Start the Copy command	C
Select the From option	F
(Multiplan displays *COPY FROM cells: R2C1,* the first cell to copy from)	
Specify the last cell to copy from	:14
Move the highlight to *to cells*	Tab
Specify the first cell to copy into	R25C1
Execute the command	Enter

Now extend the single line across row 5. The existing line can't be copied because it's part of the linked area and is locked by Xternal Copy. Let's start a new line by repeating a minus sign enough times to fill the widest column (column 6) in the expense accounts section.

Place the cursor on R5C6:	**Type or press:**
Start the Value command	V
Repeat a minus sign 12 times	REPT(" = ",12)
Execute the command	Enter

Leave the cursor on R5C6 and type *CR* (Copy Right). Type *8* and press Enter.

Formatting the Title and Number Cells

Next, display the title CASH DISBURSEMENTS completely by continuing it into the cells to the right.

Place the cursor on R1C6:	**Type or press:**
Start the Format command	F
Select the Cells option	C
(Multiplan displays *FORMAT cells: R1C6*, the first cell to be continuous)	
Specify the last cell to be continuous	:7
Move the highlight to *format code*	Tab Tab
Select *Cont* (continuous)	C
Execute the command	Enter

Next, center the cells in column 2 (the check numbers and heading), column 5 (the account numbers and heading), and rows 3 and 4 (the expense account numbers and headings in columns 4 to 14). You can center all of them easily by formatting entire columns (it takes Multiplan a tad longer, but it saves you keystrokes) at the same time you format specific cell locations.

Leave the cursor on R1C6:	**Type or press:**
Start the Format command	F
Select the Cells option	C
Specify the cells to format	C2,C5,R3:4C4:14
Move the highlight to *alignment*	Tab
Select *Ctr* (center)	C
Execute the command	Enter

Now right-justify the cell that will contain the formula that generates the spreadsheet filename: Place the cursor on R1C14 and type *FC* (Format Cells). Press Tab to move the highlight to *alignment*. Type *R* (Right) and press Enter.

Formatting the Dollar Cells

The next step is to format the cells that show their contents in dollars and cents—the allocated amounts in column 4, the totals in R26C4, and the amounts in the expense accounts in row 7 of columns 6 through 14. Don't be concerned about the other rows in columns 6 through 14. Copying the formulas you enter in row 7 down the columns will copy the dollar format, too.

Place the cursor on R7C4:	Type or press:
Start the Format command	F
Select the Cells option	C
(Multiplan displays *FORMAT cells: R7C4*, the first cell to format)	
Specify the other cells to format	:R26C4,R7C6:14
Move the highlight to *format code*	Tab Tab
Select *$*	$
Execute the command	Enter

Inserting Commas in the Large Numbers

If you didn't quit Multiplan after creating CHECK, the commas option is still activated, so you can skip this step. Otherwise, tell Multiplan to insert commas in the large numbers on this spreadsheet.

Leave the cursor on where it is:	Type or press:
Start the Format command	F
Select the Options option	O
(The highlight is on *No* in the *commas* field)	
Select *Yes*	Y
Execute the command	Enter

Saving and Naming the Spreadsheet

Now store the spreadsheet on disk with the linked areas and the new titles, lines, and formats, and give the spreadsheet its own filename. If you need to tell Multiplan which drive contains your data disk or which directory you want to store the file in, type the drive letter and press F6 (to produce a colon) or type the pathname before you type DISBURS, the filename.

Leave the cursor on where it is:	Type or press:
Start the Transfer command	T
Select the Save option	S
Name the spreadsheet	DISBURS
Execute the command	Enter

ENTERING THE FORMULAS

The circled numbers in Figure 12-1 show the locations of the formulas, which use relative cell references only. Just as you did when you created the Check Ledger, move the cursor to the cell location in the left column of the following instructions (Multiplan will produce the relative notation) and type the operators, symbols, and function names. The column on the right and the line below the formula heading show the finished formula.

When your formula agrees with the instructions, press Enter. If Multiplan then displays *Not a valid formula*, check each character. Use the F7 through F10 keys to move the highlight, and correct the problem by typing missing characters or pressing the Delete key to delete unwanted characters. If you prefer to start the formula from scratch, press the Escape key and begin again.

FORMULA 1: Account Numbers

COLUMN() − 5

Formula 1 uses the COLUMN function to number the expense accounts in row 3. COLUMN returns the number of the column in which it appears. Because the formula is entered in column 6 of the spreadsheet and we want to start with account 1, the formula subtracts 5 from the current column number. Type the entire formula.

Place the cursor on R3C6:	**Type or press:**
Start the Value command	V
Enter the formula: COLUMN() − 5	COLUMN() − 5
Execute the command	Enter

Now copy Formula 1 to the right: Leave the cursor on R3C6 and type *CR* (Copy Right). Multiplan "remembered" your last copy instruction when you copied the line to the right, and now proposes that you copy 8 cells. This is correct, so press Enter. Press the F4 (recalculate) key so that the account numbers are sequentially arranged.

FORMULA 2: Distribution into Accounts

IF(R C5 = R3 C,R C4, "")

Formula 2 distributes the allocated amounts (column 4) into the expense accounts (columns 6 through 14). The formula uses Multiplan's intersection operator—a space character—in the Test and Then statements of the IF function. The intersection operator combines two cell references: the formula's own row or column, no matter where the formula is located, and a specified row or column. The intersection operator allows us to enter one formula, copy it to many other cells, and have it perform the same function in each cell.

The Test statement $R\ C5 = R3\ C$ compares the account number in the cell at the intersection of the formula's row and column 5 with the account number in the cell at the intersection of row 3 and the formula's column (R signifies the current row, C signifies the current column). If the numbers agree, the Then statement $R\ C4$ enters in the formula cell the allocated amount in the cell at the intersection of the formula's row and column 4. If there is no match, the Else statement (the double quotes) makes the formula cell appear blank. Type the entire formula. Be sure to press the Spacebar (to indicate intersections) after typing the first R, the number 3, and the third R.

Place the cursor on R7C6:	**Type or press:**
Start the Value command	V
Enter the formula: IF(R C5 = R3 C,R C4,"")	IF(R C5 = R3 C,R C4,"")

Translation: IF(the account number in
   the current row of column 5 equals the
   account number in row 3 of the current
   column, then enter the allocated
   amount in the current row of column 4,
   else display nothing)	

Execute the command	Enter

There's no match between the number 12 in R7C5 and the number 1 in R3C6, so Formula 2 does just what you told it to do—it makes the cell appear empty.

Now copy Formula 2 to the right: Leave the cursor on R7C6. Type *CR* (Copy Right). Multiplan again proposes 8 as the number of cells to copy into, which is correct, so press Enter. There's no match between the number 12 in R7C5 and any number in row 3, so every cell appears empty.

Copying the Formulas as a Group

Now copy the formulas in columns 6 through 14 into the other cells in the account columns.

Leave the cursor on R7C6:	**Type or press:**
Start the Copy command	C
Select the Down option	D

Specify the number of cells to copy down	17
Move the highlight to *starting at*	Tab
Specify the last cell to copy from	:14
Execute the command	Enter

Leave the cursor where it is and press F4. As the formulas do their work, the account amounts pop into the categories.

FORMULA 3: Totals

SUM(R[−19]C:R[−1]C)

Formula 3 adds the allocated amounts in column 4 and enters the total in R26C4. Include the double line in R25C4 in the formula. That way, if you later add rows in the check entry area, Multiplan will adjust the formula to include the new amounts.

Place the cursor on R26C4:	Type or move the cursor:
Start the Value command	V
Enter the formula: SUM (R7C4:R25C4)	SUM(R[−19]C:R[−1]C)
Execute the command	Enter

And $9,176.40 appears. Now copy Formula 3 into columns 6 through 14 so that it totals each expense account.

Leave the cursor on R26C4:	Type or press:
Start the Copy command	C
Select the From option	F
(Multiplan displays *COPY FROM cells:* R26C4, the cell to copy from)	
Move the highlight to *to cells*	Tab
Specify the cells to copy into	R26C6:14
Execute the command	Enter

Press F4 and watch the totals of each category appear.

FORMULA 4: Spreadsheet Filename

NAME()

Formula 4 generates the spreadsheet filename in R1C14. Type the function name and parentheses.

Place the cursor on R1C14:	**Type or press:**
Start the Value command	V
Enter the formula: NAME()	NAME()
Execute the command	Enter

Your spreadsheet should now look like the completed one in Figure 12-1 at the beginning of this chapter.

Locking the Formulas

To avoid accidental alteration, lock the formulas.

Leave the cursor where it is:	**Type:**
Start the Lock command	L
Select the Formulas option	F
(Multiplan displays *Enter Y to confirm*)	
Confirm the lock	Y

Saving the Formulas

Now store all the formulas with the spreadsheet on disk and confirm your intention to overwrite the earlier version.

Leave the cursor where it is:	**Type or press:**
Start the Transfer command	T
Select the Save option	S
(Multiplan displays *DISBURS*—there's no need to retype)	
Execute the command	Enter
(Multiplan displays *Enter Y to overwrite file*)	
Confirm the overwrite	Y

PRINTING YOUR SPREADSHEET

This spreadsheet is 163 characters wide, including Multiplan row numbers. It is printed in 12-pitch type on two sheets of 8½-by-11-inch paper or, with a wide carriage printer, on one sheet of 15-by-11-inch paper.

Setting The Print Margins and Print Options

The first step before printing is to set the margins around the spreadsheet.

Leave the cursor where it is:	Type or press:
Start the Print command	P
Select the Margins option	M

Type the following numbers in the margins fields, just as you did on CHECK. (Tab past any field that already has the proper setting.)

For 8½-by-11-inch paper: *left* 0, *top* 6, *print width* 96, *print length* 60, *page length* 66.

For 15-by-11-inch paper: *left* 0, *top* 6, *print width* 163, *print length* 60, *page length* 66.

After you type the last number, press Enter. You are still in the Print command.

The next step is to make sure the Print Options settings are what you want: Type O to select the Options option. The *area* field shows *R1:4095*. The *setup* field contains your printer code for 12-pitch type. The *formulas* field has parentheses around *No*. The *row-col numbers* field has parentheses around *Yes*. If your screen agrees, press the Escape key. If it doesn't, tab to the field with the incorrect setting and change it. When you have finished, press Enter.

Before you print, store the spreadsheet with the print settings: Press Escape to exit the Print command. Leave the cursor where it is. Type *TS* (Transfer Save) and press Enter. Type *Y* to overwrite.

Printing the Spreadsheet

Now turn on your printer and print a copy of your spreadsheet.

Leave the cursor where it is:	Type:
Start the Print command	P
Select the Printer option	P

And there's a copy of your spreadsheet.

USING YOUR SPREADSHEET

Now let's see how the linking between CHECK and DISBURS works:

■ Leave the cursor where it is and type *TL* (Transfer Load). Type *CHECK* and press Enter. And here's that familiar check ledger and reconciliation spreadsheet.

■ Change one or two payee names in column 3 (type *A* for Alpha first) and account numbers in column 7 (any number from 1 to 9, the existing accounts). Don't go overboard; you'll soon have to reenter the original information so that your results continue to agree with these instructions. It's a good idea to jot down your changes.

■ Store these changes on disk: Type *TS* (Transfer Save), press Enter, and then type *Y*.

■ Load the DISBURS spreadsheet: Type *TL* (Transfer Load). Type *DISBURS* and press Enter. You can now see the message *Copying: CHECK LCELLS2*, then *Copying: CHECK LCELLS1* on the status line at the bottom of the screen as Multiplan updates, loads, and recalculates DISBURS. When DISBURS appears on the screen, it contains the new payee names in column 3 and, where you changed account numbers, the amounts are distributed into new accounts.

Viewing the Spreadsheet Relationships

When you are working with linked spreadsheets, Multiplan makes it easy to see their relationship.

Leave the cursor where it is:	Type:
Start the Xternal command	X
Select the List option	L

Multiplan now shows you that CHECK supports DISBURS, but that no spreadsheet depends on DISBURS. You can also see this information by calling up Xternal List from CHECK. Press Enter to bring back DISBURS.

Now load CHECK: Leave the cursor where it is and type *TL* (Transfer Load). Type *CHECK* and press Enter. Type *N* to lose edits. Refer to Figure 12-1 (or your note about which entries you changed) and type in the original entries that you overwrote earlier. When that's done, type *TS*, press Enter, and type *Y*. Resist the temptation to change anything else now; you'll soon be creating a cash disbursements module on this spreadsheet.

Dissolving the Link

Later you may want to dissolve the link between CHECK and DISBURS so that DISBURS becomes an independent spreadsheet. (You will then have to type in the dates, payees, check amounts, and so on instead of having them transferred from the check ledger.) If you remove the Xternal link, the contents of the LCELLS groups will disappear and the expense account titles and the formulas in the unlinked area will remain. With DISBURS on your screen, here's how to unlink when that time comes:

Leave the cursor where it is:	Type or press:
Start the Xternal command	X
Select the Copy option	C
(Multiplan displays *EXTERNAL COPY from sheet:* CHECK)	
Move the highlight to *name*	Tab
Name the linked cells	LCELLS1
Move the highlight to *to*	Tab
(Multiplan displays the LCELLS1 cell locations)	
Delete the cell locations	Del
Execute the command	Enter

Repeat these steps, but type *LCELLS2* in the *name* field to dissolve the link completely. To get a head start on an independent disbursements spreadsheet, you can then bring back the titles, lines, and entries in both groups of LCELLS by following the instructions for linking in Chapter 11 (but be sure to type *N* for No in the *linked* field of the Xternal Copy command). Use the Blank command to blank out the entries you don't need, and you're on your way.

Adding Expense Account Categories

Clearly, you will need more expense account categories on DISBURS when you're ready to play around with this spreadsheet on your own. Here's how:

First, copy everything in column 14 (lines, account number, formats, and formulas) into the new columns. Let's assume you need five more categories: With the cursor on R2C14, type *CF* (Copy From). Type *:R26C14* and press the Tab key to move the highlight to the *to cells* field. Type *R2C15:R2C19* and press Enter. Press the F4 key to recalculate, and the amounts that previously had no accounts appear. Then replace *Due/Subs* with your own expense account names in row 4 of the new columns. If you use different account numbers, replace the formula or type in your own numbers. Then type *TS* (Transfer Save) to save the changes on disk.

CREATING THE CASH DISBURSEMENTS MODULE

Spreading your expenditures on a spreadsheet, as you just did, is a time-honored way to keep track of what you spend in each category. But computers have a way of blazing new paths that are often more efficient. Figure 12-3 shows

```
              1           2             3            4      5        6
                                                          CHECK LEDGER AND
 1  =============================================================================
 2  ======================================================================
 3  CURRENT PERIOD TRANSACTIONS
 4  ----------------------------------------------------------------------
 5                Check                            Check          Allocated
 6  Date          Number  Paid To                 Amount    C      Amount
 7  ----------------------------------------------------------------------
 8  AUGUST 87     MONTH           BALANCE FORWARD------------------------
 9  Aug 2         203     Nickel Savings Bank      $578.40   1     $578.40
10  Aug 2         204     Holt Stationery          $161.19   1     $161.19
11  Aug 7         205     Vinicombe Realty         $667.00   1     $667.00
12  Aug 11        206     The Nissen Group       $1,131.00   1   $1,131.00
13  Aug 12        207     Market Newsletter         $75.00   1      $75.00
14  Aug 15        208     VOID
15  Aug 15        209     Don England            $4,166.66   1   $4,166.66
16  Aug 15        210     DE-Expense Reimbursement  $235.02   1      $88.02
17                                                                  $50.00
18                                                                  $97.00
19  Aug 19        211     Payroll                  $732.90   1     $732.90
20  Aug 27                Deposit
21  Aug 29        212     Pelham U-Drive           $480.89          $480.89
22  Aug 29        213     Eastern Power            $125.00   1      $125.00
23  Aug 30        214     NY Telephone Co          $231.76          $231.76
24  Aug 30        215     Department of Taxation   $146.58          $146.58
25  Aug 30        216     True Blue Medical Plan   $390.00   1      $390.00
26  Aug 30        217     Holt Stationery           $55.00   1       $55.00
27                                ENDING BALANCE---------------------------
28  ======================================================================
29  PREVIOUS PERIOD OUTSTANDING                   Check     C
30  ----------------------------------------------------------------------
31  Jul 7,87      179     Parcel Express            $15.00   1
32  Jul 10,87     184     Abner Civic Association   $75.00
33  Jul 28,87     199     Pro Advertising          $456.00   1
34
35
36
37  ======================================================================
38  RECONCILIATION
39  ----------------------------------------------------------------------
40  Checkbook Balance                           $14,163.93
41   Plus Bank Credits                               $0.00
42   Less Bank Charges                              $17.85
43                                              -----------
44  Adjusted Checkbook Balance                  $14,146.08
45                                              ===========
46  Bank Statement Balance                      $13,247.99
47   Plus Deposits in Transit                    $1,832.32
48   Less Outstanding Checks                       $934.23
49                                              -----------
50  Adjusted Bank Statement Balance             $14,146.08
51                                              ===========
52  Variance (Checkbook minus Statement)            $0.00
53  ======================================================================
54  Amount of Deposits                          $10,661.43
55  Amount of Checks                             $9,176.40
56  Checks and Allocation Amounts               AGREE
57  Maximum Checkbook Balance                   $14,450.50
58  Average Checkbook Balance                   $12,367.83
59  Number of Deposits                                   7
60  Number of Checks                                    14
61  ======================================================================
```

FIGURE 12-3.

The cash disbursements module created on the check ledger

```
     7        8         9       10          11           12
 RECONCILIATION                                                    CHECK
 ===================================================================
```

Account Number	Deposit Amount	D	Running Balance	***** Outstanding ***** Check	Deposit
			--------> $12,678.90		
12	$2,350.00	1	$14,450.50	0.00	0.00
6			$14,289.31	0.00	0.00
2	$122.33	1	$13,744.64	0.00	0.00
8	$256.78	1	$12,870.42	0.00	0.00
9			$12,795.42	0.00	0.00
0			$12,795.42	0.00	0.00
1			$8,628.76	0.00	0.00
11	$2,350.00	1	$10,743.74	0.00	0.00
3			$10,743.74	0.00	0.00
10			$10,743.74	0.00	0.00
5			$10,010.84	0.00	0.00
0	$743.00		$10,753.84	0.00	743.00
16			$10,272.95	480.89	0.00
4	$3,750.00	1	$13,897.95	0.00	0.00
3			$13,666.19	231.76	0.00
7			$13,519.61	146.58	0.00
18	$1,089.32		$14,218.93	0.00	1,089.32
6			$14,163.93	0.00	0.00
			--------> $14,163.93		

```
 ===================================================================
              Deposit    D
 -------------------------------------------------------------------
            $432.75      1                     0.00          0.00
                                              75.00          0.00
                                               0.00          0.00
                                               0.00          0.00
                                               0.00          0.00
                                               0.00          0.00
 ===================================================================
                   ACCOUNT TOTALS                   TRUE ❶
 -------------------------------------------------------------------
```

			DISBURS TOTALS
1	Owner's Draw	$4,166.66 ❷	
2	Rent	$667.00	
3	Phone & Telex	$281.76	
4	Utilities	$125.00	
5	Payroll	$732.90	
6	Office Supplies	$216.19	
7	Payroll Taxes	$146.58	
8	Technical Services	$1,131.00	
9	Dues & Subs	$75.00	
10	Travel & Transportation	$97.00	
11	Business Entertainment	$88.02	
12	Loan Repayment	$578.40	
13	Postage & Shipping	$0.00	
14	Professional Fees	$0.00	
15	Repairs & Maintenance	$0.00	
16	Car Rental	$480.89	
17	Capital Equipment	$0.00	
18	Medical/Dental Insurance	$390.00	
19	Advertising & Promotion	$0.00	
20	Gifts & Contributions	$0.00	
21	Miscellaneous	$0.00	

```
 ===================================================================
```

a powerful cash disbursements module tucked into the check ledger. This combination can eliminate the need for a separate cash disbursements spreadsheet.

The formulas in the module scan the account numbers in column 7, pluck the allocated amounts from column 6 by account number, then internally total each expense account. Multiplan performs these internal calculations by iterating the formulas. Iteration allows a formula to repeat itself, using the result of its previous calculation for its next calculation.

Setting Up the Cash Disbursements Module

First, load CHECK: Type *TL* (Transfer Load). Press any direction key to display a list of your Multiplan files. Use the direction keys to move the highlight to CHECK and press Enter. CHECK is now on your screen. Set up the module as follows:

1. Start by typing the new entries: Place the cursor on R38C10 and type *A* (Alpha). Type the title *ACCOUNT TOTALS* and move the cursor to R40C9. Type *1* and move the cursor to R41C9. Referring to Figure 12-3, continue in this way to enter the numbers in column 9 and the category titles in column 10. (Some of them will be only partially displayed at this time.) Ignore the word *TRUE* in R38C12 and the amounts in column 12—these entries are generated by formulas. After you type the last entry, press Enter.

2. Now copy a piece of the single line in row 30: Place the cursor on R30C9 and type *CF* (Copy From). Type *:12* and press the Tab key. Move the cursor to R39C9 and press Enter.

3. Formatting is next on the agenda. Let's first continue the account titles into column 11: Place the cursor on R40C10. Type *FC* (Format Cells). Type *:R60C11* and press the Tab key twice to move the highlight to *format code*. Type C to select *Cont* (continuous) and press Enter. Next, center the TRUE formula cell: Place the cursor on R38C12. Type *FC* and press the Tab key to move the highlight to *alignment*. Type C to select *Ctr* and press Enter. And finally, format the cells in column 12 to show dollars and cents: Place the cursor on R40C12 and type *FC*. Type *:R61C12* and press Tab twice to move the highlight to *format code*. Type *$* and press Enter.

4. The last set-up step is naming cells. The formulas work with the allocated amounts in column 6 and the account numbers in column 7. You named the allocated amount area when you first created CHECK. Now name the cells that contain the account numbers: Place the cursor on R9C7 and type *N* (Name). Type *ACCOUNT* and press Tab to move the highlight to *to refer to*. Type *:R26C7* and press Enter.

Entering the Formulas

Now enter the iteration formulas, which will make everything run like clockwork.

FORMULA 1: Iteration Completion Test

ITERCNT() = COUNT(ACCOUNT)

Formula 1 controls the iteration process. The ITERCNT function stops the iterations when the number of iterations equals the number of accounts (R9C7 through R26C7, ACCOUNT). Type the entire formula.

Place the cursor on R38C12:	**Type or press:**
Start the Value command	V
Enter the formula: ITERCNT() = COUNT(ACCOUNT)	ITERCNT() = COUNT(ACCOUNT)
Execute the command	Enter

The first iteration pass is coming up, so #N/A appears in the cell.

FORMULA 2: Distribution into Accounts

IF(ISNA(ITERCNT()),0,IF(INDEX(ACCOUNT,ITERCNT()) = RC[− 3],RC + INDEX(ALLOCATED,ITERCNT()),RC))

Formula 2 is a "nested" IF formula (one IF formula within another) that totals each amount by account. Because of the way the iteration process works, ITERCNT isn't available during the first iteration, so the formula produces #NA. The formula needs ITERCNT to move the calculation to the Then statement. The Test statement *IF(ISNA(ITERCNT()))* accounts for this by using the function ISNA (IS Not Available) to send Multiplan to the Then statement *0*, which enters a zero in the formula cell.

During the second and subsequent iterations, the second IF formula does its work. The Test statement *IF(INDEX(ACCOUNT,ITERCNT()) = RC[− 3]* compares each cell containing an account number (R9C7 through R26C7, ACCOUNT) with the account number in R40C9. When they agree, the Then statement *RC + INDEX(ALLOCATED,ITERCNT())* accumulates the corresponding allocated amount (R9C6 through R26C7, ALLOCATED) and enters the result in R40C9. The notation *RC* is the formula cell. When they don't agree, the Else statement *RC* retains the amount currently in R40C9.

Type the entire formula except the relative reference to R40C9. At the proper place, move the cursor to R40C9.

Place the cursor on R40C12:	Type or move the cursor:
Start the Value command	V
Enter the formula: IF(ISNA (ITERCNT()),0, IF(INDEX(ACCOUNT, ITERCNT()) = R40C9,RC +INDEX(ALLOCATED, ITERCNT()),RC))	IF(ISNA(ITERCNT()),0, IF(INDEX(ACCOUNT, ITERCNT()) = RC[−3],RC +INDEX(ALLOCATED, ITERCNT()),RC))

Translation: IF(iteration count is not available, then enter zero, else IF index of cells in column named ACCOUNT is equal to account number in R40C9, then add allocated amount to amount in cell, else keep the amount already in cell)

Execute the command	Enter

To accumulate the amounts in the other accounts, copy Formula 2 into the cells below: Leave the cursor on R40C12 and type *CD* (Copy Down). Type *20* and press Enter.

Filling in the Blanks

To work properly, Formula 2 needs numbers from contiguous cells. If it finds an empty cell in the account column, it will stop before indexing all the account numbers, producing inaccurate results. The simple solution is to fill each empty cell in column 7 of rows 9 to 26 with a zero. So, enter a zero in R14C7 and R20C7.

Turning Iteration On

Now turn iteration on and tell Multiplan the location of the iteration completion test—the ITERCNT formula that counts the iterations.

Leave the cursor where it is:	Type or press:
Start the Options command	O
Move the highlight to *iteration*	Tab Tab
Select *Yes*	Y
Move the highlight to *completion test at*	Tab
Specify the location	R38C12
Execute the command	Enter

Position the cursor in the cash disbursements module so that you can see rows 38 through 57 of column 12. Press F4 to recalculate. As you watch, the completion test in R38C12 changes from #NA to FALSE as Formula 2 scans each account number in column 7 and plunks each allocated amount into the proper cell. A few seconds later, Formula 2 completes its work, and the completion test shows TRUE.

This check ledger contains more than one item for only one account—Holt Stationery (account 6), with two checks written. Multiplan dutifully added both amounts for Holt Stationery, with the result shown in R45C12. Neat.

To see it on paper, be sure your printer is on and type *PP* (Print Printer).

CREATING THE CASH DISBURSEMENTS SUMMARY SPREADSHEET

One thing leads to another and before you know it, you're on the verge of creating yet another spreadsheet to track your cash disbursements. Starting with the traditional DISBURS, then moving to the iterating module on CHECK, you can now use the module to create the stand-alone spreadsheet shown in Figure 12-4.

```
            1            2                         3              4
  1                CASH DISBURSEMENTS YTD AS OF AUGUST 87      CDTOTAL
  2   ================================================================
  3                ACCOUNT                        CUM TOTALS   %GTOTAL ❸
  4   ----------------------------------------------------------------
  5      1         Owner's Draw                   $8333.32      45.4% ❷
  6      2         Rent                           $1334.00       7.3%
  7      3         Phone & Telex                   $563.52       3.1%
  8      4         Utilities                       $250.00       1.4%
  9      5         Payroll                        $1465.80       8.0%
 10      6         Office Supplies                 $432.38       2.4%
 11      7         Payroll Taxes                   $293.16       1.6%
 12      8         Technical Services             $2262.00      12.3%
 13      9         Dues & Subs                     $150.00       0.8%
 14     10         Travel & Transportation         $194.00       1.1%
 15     11         Business Entertainment          $176.04       1.0%
 16     12         Loan Repayment                 $1156.80       6.3%
 17     13         Postage & Shipping               $0.00        0.0%
 18     14         Professional Fees                $0.00        0.0%
 19     15         Repairs & Maintenance            $0.00        0.0%
 20     16         Car Rental                      $961.78       5.2%
 21     17         Capital Equipment                $0.00        0.0%
 22     18         Medical/Dental Insurance        $780.00       4.3%
 23     19         Advertising & Promotion          $0.00        0.0%
 24     20         Gifts & Contributions            $0.00        0.0%
 25     21         Miscellaneous                    $0.00        0.0%
 26   ----------------------------------------------------------------
 27                GRAND TOTAL          GTOTAL  $18352.80 ❶    100.0%
 28   ================================================================
```

FIGURE 12-4.
The cash disbursements spreadsheet that keeps a running total of expenditures

This spreadsheet, which is linked to the CHECK module via Multiplan's Xternal command, accumulates the account totals and calculates the percentage breakdown of each account. The macro menu shown in Figure 12-6 does virtually all the work. Before you blank out CHECK at the start of a new period, all you do is bring up the standalone spreadsheet and type a few keystrokes that run the macros. Multiplan then imports the amount in each account from the CHECK module and adds it to the corresponding cumulative total in column 3.

Naming the Cells

The first step is to name the cells containing the entries we want Xternal to copy from CHECK to the standalone spreadsheet—the month in R8C1, the account totals in R40C12 through R60C12, and the account numbers and titles in R40C9 through R60C11. Let's start with the month.

Place the cursor on R8C1:	**Type:**
Start the Name command	N
Name the cell	MONTH

The correct cell location is already in the *to refer to* field, so press Enter. Now name the totals cells.

Place the cursor on R40C12:	**Type or press:**
Start the Name command	N
Name the cells	TOTALS
Move the highlight to *to refer to*	Tab
(Multiplan displays *to refer to: R40C12*)	
Specify the last cell to name	:R60C12
Execute the command	Enter

And finally, name the cells containing the lines and the account numbers and titles: Place the cursor on R40C9 and type *N*. Type *DISBURS* and press Tab. Type *R40:60C9:11* and press Enter. Save the spreadsheet containing the new names: Leave the cursor on R40C9 and type *TS* (Transfer Save). Press Enter and type *Y*.

We want to start with a new spreadsheet, so type *TCA* (Transfer Clear All) to clear the check ledger and bring up a new Multiplan screen.

Creating the Summary Spreadsheet with Xternal Copy

Now transfer the contents of the cells named DISBURS from the check ledger. We'll keep them unlinked so that the entries on this new spreadsheet won't disappear when you blank out the check ledger each month.

Place the cursor on R5C1:	Type or press:
Start the Xternal command	X
Select the Copy option	C
(The highlight is in *from sheet*)	
Name the source spreadsheet	CHECK
Move the highlight to *name*	Tab
Identify the area to copy	DISBURS
Move the highlight to *linked: (Yes) No*	Tab Tab
Select *No*	N
Execute the command	Enter

Column 2 isn't wide enough to display the longest account names, so some of the names are truncated. We'll take care of that shortly. Now transfer the month from CHECK: Place the cursor on R1C3 and type *XC* (Xternal Copy). Type *CHECK* and press Tab to move the highlight to the *name* field. Type *MONTH* and press Tab twice to move the highlight to the *linked* field. Type *N* for *No* and press Enter.

Setting Up the Spreadsheet

Now set up the rest of the spreadsheet in the following sequence so that it looks like the one in Figure 12-4:

1. Increase the column widths: Leave the cursor on R1C3 and type *FW* (Format Width). Type *14* and press Enter. Now place the cursor on R1C2 and type *FW* again. Type *29* and press Enter. That's more like it. Now you can see all of each title.

2. Now create the double line: Place the cursor on R2C1 and type *V* (Value). Type *REPT(" = ",29)* and press Enter. Type *CR* (Copy Right). Type *3* and press Enter. With the cursor on R2C1, type *CF* (Copy From). Type *:4* and press the Tab key to move the highlight to *to cells*. Type *R28C1* and press Enter.

3. Now for the single line: Place the cursor on R4C1 and type *V* (Value). Type *REPT(" – ",29)* and press Enter. Type *CR* (Copy Right). Multiplan proposes that you copy three cells as you did before, so press Enter. With the cursor on R4C1, type *CF* (Copy From). Type *:4* and press Tab. Type *R26C1* and press Enter. Press the PgDn key so that you can see the lines.

4. Next, enter the new titles: Press the Home key, place the cursor on R1C2, and type *A* (Alpha). Type *CASH DISBURSEMENTS YTD AS OF* and move the cursor to R3C2. Type *ACCOUNT* and move the cursor to R3C3. Type *CUM TOTALS* and move the cursor to R3C4. Type *%GTOTAL* and move the cursor to R27C2. Type *GRAND TOTAL* and press Enter.

5. Right-justify the new titles and the cell that will contain the spreadsheet filename: Place the cursor on R1C4 and type *FC* (Format Cells). Type *,R3C3:4* and press the Tab key to move the highlight to *alignment*. Type *R* (Right) and press Enter.

6. Now for the numbers. First, center the account numbers in column 1: Place the cursor on R5C1 and type *FC* (Format Cells). Type *:R25C1* and press Tab. Type *C* to select *Ctr* and press Enter.

7. Next, format the cells in column 3 to show the totals as dollars and cents: Place the cursor on R5C3 and type *FC*. Type *:R27C3* and press Tab twice to move the highlight to *format code*. Type *$* and press Enter.

8. Format R5C4 to show a percentage with one decimal place: Place the cursor on R5C4 and type *FC*. Press Tab twice. Type *%* and press Tab again. Type *1* and press Enter. Copying the formula you enter in this cell down column 4 will copy the percentage format to the other cells.

9. And finally, name the cell to be used by the formula in column 4: Place the cursor on R27C3 and type *N* (Name). Type *GTOTAL* and press Enter.

This completes the setup, so save all your work and name the spreadsheet: Leave the cursor where it is and type *TS* (Transfer Save). Type *CDTOTAL* (short for Cash Disbursements TOTAL), and press Enter.

Entering the Formulas

Now enter the formulas. The formulas contain relative and named cell references. The locations of the formulas are shown in Figure 12-4.

FORMULA 1: Grand Total

SUM(R[−22]C:R[−1]C)

Formula 1 adds the allocated amounts in column 3 and enters the grand total in R27C3. Include the line in R26C3 in the formula. That way, if you later add rows for more accounts, Multiplan will adjust the formula to include the new amounts.

Leave the cursor on R27C3:	Type or move the cursor:
Start the Value command	V
Enter the formula: SUM(R5C3:R26C3)	SUM(R[−22]C:R[−1]C)
Execute the command	Enter

Now copy Formula 1 to R27C4, where it can calculate the total of the percentages: Leave the cursor on R27C3 and type *CR* (Copy Right). Type *1* and press Enter. Copying the SUM formula copied its dollar format, so reformat the percentage cell: Place the cursor on R27C4. Type *FC* (Format Cells) and press Tab twice. Type % and press Tab again. Type *1* and press Enter.

FORMULA 2: Account Totals as a Percent of Grand Total

RC[−1]/GTOTAL

Formula 2 divides the owner's total draw in R5C3 by the grand total (R27C3, GTOTAL) and enters its percentage of the grand total in R5C4.

Place the cursor on R5C4:	Type or move the cursor:
Start the Value command	V
Enter the formula: R5C3/GTOTAL	RC[−1]/GTOTAL
Execute the command	Enter

Formula 2 has no grand total to work with yet, so the error message *#DIV/0!* (can't divide by zero) appears. To calculate each account total as a percentage of the grand total, copy Formula 2 down the column: Leave the cursor on R5C4 and type *CD* (Copy Down). Type *20* and press Enter. You now have a string of *#DIV/0!* error messages.

FORMULA 3: Spreadsheet Filename

NAME()

Formula 3 enters the spreadsheet filename in R1C4. Type the function name and the parentheses.

Place the cursor on R1C4:	Type or press:
Start the Value command	V
Enter the formula: NAME()	NAME()
Execute the command	Enter

Accumulating the Totals

Multiplan's Xternal Total command lets you import numbers from other spreadsheets and have Multiplan perform arithmetic calculations (addition, subtraction, multiplication, or division) on them as they are imported. This feature makes it easy to keep running totals of the expenditures in each category. Let's import all the current totals from the check ledger.

Place the cursor on R5C3:	Type or press:
Start the Xternal command	X
Select the Total option	T
(The highlight is next to *from sheet*)	
Name the source spreadsheet	CHECK
Move the highlight to *name*	Tab
Identify the area name	TOTALS

The proposed response in the *starting at* field is *R5C3*, and parentheses enclose the plus sign in the *operation* field. Both responses are correct, so press Enter. In a flash, Multiplan loads the account totals from CHECK into the empty cells. Press F4 to calculate the formulas in column 4.

Now import the totals again so that you can see the addition process: Leave the cursor on R5C3 and type *XT* (Xternal Total). Type *CHECK* and press the Tab key. Type *TOTALS* and press Enter. Multiplan instantly adds the account totals to the amounts already in the cells and produces a grand total. Press F4 to recalculate. Your spreadsheet now looks like the one in Figure 12-4. Save your work: Leave the cursor where it is and type *TS* (Transfer Save) and press Enter. Type *Y* to overwrite.

With Xternal Total, you can import text and numbers together, text only, or numbers only. You can even combine several spreadsheets by entering their filenames in the *sheet* field. For example, type the range *CHECK1:CHECK4* to combine spreadsheets CHECK1, CHECK2, CHECK3, and CHECK4. The incoming numbers can be added to, subtracted from, multiplied by, or divided by the current numbers.

As with Xternal Copy, Xternal Total imports only the results of formulas, not the formulas themselves. If you have a conditional formula that produces a TRUE or FALSE answer, that result is imported as text.

Multiplan won't let you import information under either of the following conditions:

- You try to import text into a cell that contains a value, formula, or text.

- You try to import a value into a cell that contains text or a formula.

Instead, Multiplan displays the message *Incoming data mismatched in:* and gives the cell location. Any other information not considered a "mismatch" is imported on cue. To remedy a mismatch, you can blank out the mismatched cell, reenter matching information, or redefine the export or import area.

PRINTING YOUR SPREADSHEET

The cash disbursements summary spreadsheet is 68 characters wide, including Multiplan row numbers. It is printed, like the others in this book, in 12-pitch type. To set the margins, leave the cursor where it is and type *PM* (Print Margins). Type the following numbers in the margins fields (tabbing past any field that already has the proper setting): *Left* 10, *top* 6, *print width* 96, *print length* 60, and *page length* 66. After you type the last number, press Enter.

Now check the print options: Type O to select the Options option. The *area* field should show *R1:4095*. The *setup* field should contain your printer code for 12-pitch type. The *formulas* field should have parentheses around *No*. The *row-col numbers* field should have parentheses around *Yes*. If your screen agrees, press the Escape key. If not, type in the correct setting (tabbing past any fields with the proper settings), then press Enter.

Now store the spreadsheet with the print settings: Press Escape to exit the *Print* command. Leave the cursor where it is and type *TS*. Press Enter and type *Y*. Now turn on your printer. Print the spreadsheet by typing *PP* (Print Printer).

CREATING A MACRO MENU

Multiplan lets you create macro menus that appear in place of, and operate the same as, the Multiplan command menu. A macro menu consists of three rows of information entered in contiguous columns on the spreadsheet with no empty or continuous cells between them. To give you an idea of how it looks, Figure 12-5 shows a macro menu in rows 4, 5, and 6.

■ Row 4 contains the macro names. These names are the same as, or similar to, the ones in Multiplan's command menu.

■ Row 5 contains a description of what each macro does. The description appears on the message line when you step through the menu.

■ Row 6 contains the macros. These macros are a short version of the ones you'll soon create on the cash disbursements summary spreadsheet. You can see them in their entirety in Figure 12-6.

When you work with a macro menu, you need a traffic manager, a function ably performed by the macro in R2C6. The traffic macro contains the command code '*MN*, which directs Multiplan to the starting point—the top left

```
          6              7              8            9            10
 1 Menu
 2 'HM'MNR4C7'
 3
 4 Month          Total          Save         Print        Exit
 5 Enters month   Adds totals    Saves spread Prints spread Exits to Check
 6 GR1'TB4'RT     GR5'tbr'rtXT   TS'RTY'GOMENU PP'GOMENU''QU TLCHECK'RT'QU
 7
 8
 9
10
```

FIGURE 12-5.
The layout of a macro menu

cell in the menu, which contains the name of the first macro. The way things are set up, the five macros in this menu and the traffic macro address all the activities you are likely to perform on this spreadsheet.

Preparing for the Macros

You don't have to see all or even part of a macro for it to work, but seeing it will make things easier. So, let's increase the width of columns 6 through 10 to 51 characters each, which allows ample room for the descriptions and macros.

Place the cursor on R1C6:	Type or press:
Start the Format command	F
Select the Width option	W
Specify the number of characters in each column	51
Move the highlight to *through*	Tab Tab
Specify column 6 through 10	10
Execute the command	Enter

Next, refer to Figure 12-6 and enter only the macro names and descriptions: Place the cursor on R1C6 and type A (Alpha). Now type *Autoexec and Menu (Alt-M)* and move the cursor to R4C6. Type *Month* and move the cursor to R5C6. Type *Enters the Checkbook month in R1C3* and move the cursor to the next cell. Continue in this way, typing and moving the cursor, until you type all the names and descriptions that belong in rows 4 and 5, columns 7 through 10. After the last entry, press Enter.

MACRO 1: Traffic Macro

R1C6:   Autoexec and Menu (Alt-M)

R2C6:   'HM'MNR4C6'

MACRO 2: Month Macro

R4C6:   Month

R5C6:   Enters the Checkbook month in R1C3

R6C6:   GR1'TB3'RTB'RTXCCHECK'TBMONTH
           'TB'TBN'RT'GOMENU''QU

MACRO 3: Total Macro

R4C7:   Total

R5C7:   Adds the Checkbook totals to the current totals

R6C7:   GR5'tb3'rtXTCHECK'tbTOTALS'rt'rc'GOMENU''qu

MACRO 4: Save Macro

R4C8:   Save

R5C8:   Saves the spreadsheet

R6C8:   TS'RTY'GOMENU''QU

MACRO 5: Print Macro

R4C9:   Print

R5C9:   Prints the spreadsheet

R6C9:   PP'GOMENU''QU

MACRO 6: Exit Macro

R4C10:   Exit

R5C10:   Exits this spreadsheet and returns to the Checkbook

R6C10:   TLCHECK'RT'QU

FIGURE 12-6.

The macro menu on the cash disbursements summary spreadsheet

WRITING THE MACROS

Multiplan provides two ways to write a macro: Edit Macro and Record Macro. Though the results are the same, the means are quite different.

When you work in the Edit Macro mode, Multiplan records your keystrokes in a cell without you actually seeing the action you specify take place. When you work in the Record Macro mode, Multiplan both records your keystrokes and lets you see the actions as you specify them.

We'll use both approaches to write the macros. We'll use Edit Macro for the traffic macro and the Month, Save, Print, and Exit menu macros. To demonstrate the difference, we'll use Record Macro for the Total menu macro.

Let's start by using Edit Macro here in the same way as we did on the Check Ledger. Remember, if you make a typing error while in the Edit Macro mode (you can tell you're in Edit Macro mode by the *EM* to the right of the *Free* indicator), be sure to press F5 to exit Edit Macro before you hit a key. Otherwise, Multiplan will enter the key code for the key you hit. Then use Backspace to erase the error, press F5 to reenter the Edit Macro mode, and continue from there.

MACRO 1: Traffic Macro

'HM'MNR4C6'

The traffic macro sends the cursor to the home position (R1C1) where you can see the macro actions as they happen, and then identifies the top left cell in the macro menu (R4C6). Place the cursor on R2C6 and type *A* to start the Alpha command. Press F5 to activate the Edit Macro mode.

Macro actions:	Type or press:
Send the cursor to the home position	Home
Exit the Edit Macro mode	F5
The macro menu is in R4C6	'MNR4C6'

Don't bother to press Enter. Simply move the cursor to R6C6 and Macro 1 enters its cell.

MACRO 2: Month—Enters the Checkbook month in R1C3

GR1'TB3'RTB'RTXCCHECK'TBMONTH'TB
'TBN'RT'GOMENU''QU

The first macro in the menu sends the cursor to R1C3 where it blanks out the month, then uses Xternal Copy to import the new month from CHECK. It leaves the cell unlinked so that the month remains when you blank out CHECK. The macro then brings up the macro menu so that you can select another command. The cursor is on R6C6.

Macro actions:	Type or press:
Start the Goto command and select the Row-col option, row 1	GR1
Activate the Edit Macro mode	F5

Move the highlight to *column*	Tab
Specify column *3*	3
Confirm the Goto Row-col command	Enter
Start the Blank command	B
Confirm the blanking of R1C3	Enter
Start the Xternal command and select the Copy option, sheet named *CHECK*	XCCHECK
Move the highlight to *name*	Tab
Copy from the cell named *MONTH*	MONTH
Move the highlight to *linked: (Yes) No*	Tab Tab
Select *No*	N
Confirm the Xternal command	Enter
Exit the Edit Macro mode	F5
Go to the macro menu	'GOMENU'
End the macro	'QU

Press the Enter key to move Macro 2 into its cell.

MACRO 3: Total—Adds the Checkbook totals to the current totals

GR5'tb3'rtXTCHECK'tbTOTALS'rt'rc'GOMENU''qu

Macro 3 (the second macro in the menu) sends the cursor to R5C3, and then uses Xternal Total to add each expense account total from CHECK (R40C12 through R60C12, TOTALS) to the current totals on this spreadsheet. It then recalculates the spreadsheet to produce the percentages and grand total.

Macro 3 is written by using Multiplan's Record Macro mode. In this mode, Multiplan captures your keystrokes while showing on the screen exactly what you specify as if you were working in normal mode. When you turn off the recording, Multiplan enters the command code 'qu at the end of the macro.

To display the macro menu when it completes its run, the macro needs the command code *GO* and the named cell *MENU* (all together, the command is 'GOMENU'). With Record Macro, you edit in command codes afterward.

First, tell Multiplan where to record the macro: Place the cursor on R6C7 and type *N* (Name). Type *RECORD* and press the Tab key twice to move the cursor to *macro: Yes(No)*. Type *Y* and press Enter.

Now press the Home key to jump the cursor to R1C1, a good place to start. If you make a typing mistake during recording, ignore it. Afterward, when you edit in the command code, you can correct the typing error, too.

To start recording, hold down the Shift key and press F9. You can now see *RM* on the status line to the right of the *Free* indicator.

Macro actions:	Type or press:
Start the Goto command and select the Row-col option, row 5	GR5
Move the highlight to *column*	Tab
Specify column 3	3
Confirm the Goto command	Enter
Start the Xternal command and select the Total option, sheet named *CHECK*	XTCHECK
Move the highlight to *name*	Tab
Copy from the cell named *TOTALS*	TOTALS
Confirm the Xternal command	Enter
Recalculate the spreadsheet	F4

Now end the recording by pressing Shift-F9 again (*RM* disappears from the status line at the bottom of the screen).

Tell the macro to bring up the macro menu when it completes its work so that you can select another command: Move the cursor to R6C7 and type *E* (Edit). The macro appears on the command line. Press the F9 key four times to place the highlight on top of the apostrophe before *qu*. Type 'GOMENU' and press Enter.

If you mistyped anything, leave the cursor on R6C7 and type *E* again. Use the F7 through F10 keys to move the highlight, and correct any mistakes by typing the missing characters or using the Delete key to delete unwanted characters. Then press Enter.

You can record as many macros as you wish. Just be sure to tell Multiplan the new cell location before each recording session.

Now that you've seen how Record Macro works, let's go back to using Edit Macro for the last three macros.

MACRO 4: Save—Saves the spreadsheet

TS'RTY'GOMENU''QU

Macro 4 saves the spreadsheet after confirming an overwrite of the earlier version, then brings up the macro menu so that you can select another command. The cursor is on R6C8. Type *A* to start the Alpha command.

Macro actions:	Type or press:
Start the Transfer command and select the Save option	TS
Activate the Edit Macro mode	F5
Confirm the Transfer command	Enter
Exit the Edit Macro mode	F5
Select *Y* to overwrite file	Y
Go to the macro menu	'GOMENU'
End the macro	'QU

Move the cursor to R6C9 and Macro 4 enters its cell.

MACRO 5: Print—Prints the spreadsheet

PP'GOMENU' 'QU

Macro 5 sends the spreadsheet to the printer, then brings up the macro menu. The cursor is on R6C9.

Macro actions:	Type or press:
Start the Print command and select the Printer option	PP
Go to the macro menu	'GOMENU'
End the macro	'QU

Move the cursor to R6C10 and Macro 5 enters its cell.

MACRO 6: Exit—Exits this spreadsheet and returns to the Checkbook

TLCHECK'RT'QU

The last macro in the menu loads the check ledger spreadsheet. It assumes you've saved the spreadsheet first, so there's no built-in response to any request to save the edits, lose the edits, or cancel. The cursor is on R6C10.

Macro actions:	Type or press:
Start the Transfer command, select the Load option, and load *CHECK*	TLCHECK
Activate the Edit Macro mode	F5
Confirm the Transfer command	Enter

Exit the Edit Macro mode	F5
End the macro	'QU

Press Enter to enter Macro 6 in its cell.

Naming the Menu Cell

To give the macros a map to the menu, name the menu cell and assign a macro run code.

Place the cursor on R2C6:	Type or press:
Start the Name command	N
Name the cell	MENU
Move the highlight to *macro: Yes (No)*	Tab Tab
Select *Yes*	Y
Move the highlight to *command key(s)*	Tab
Assign the run code	M
Execute the command	Enter

Now save the macro menu on your spreadsheet: Leave the cursor on R2C6. Type *TS* (Transfer Save) and press Enter. Type *Y* to overwrite.

Running the Macro Menu

Here comes the fun part—using the macro menu you've created. Hold down the Alternate key and type *M.* Multiplan immediately sends the cursor to R1C1 and displays *Month Total Save Print Exit* on the command line with the highlight on *Month.* The message line shows what this macro does: *Enters the Checkbook month in R1C3.* Press the Tab key to move the highlight to *Total.* You now see *Adds the Checkbook totals to the current totals* on the message line. Press Tab a few times to see the other descriptions.

The clear advantage to a macro menu is that all your command choices are on the screen at one time. You have only to name and give a run code to the traffic macro, not the menu macros. To run a menu macro, all you do is type its first letter, just as on Multiplan's menu. Try it now. Type *M* to run the Month macro. As you watch, Multiplan blanks out *AUGUST 87* in R1C3, then imports the same month (since you haven't updated CHECK yet) and brings back the macro menu.

Now type *T* to run the Total macro. Multiplan instantly adds the numbers from CHECK to the current numbers, recalculates, and again brings up the macro menu. Next, try Save (type *S*), then Print (turn on your printer, then type *P*). You now have a printout of the spreadsheet and the macros. (If you don't want to see the macros on a printout, simply change the setting in the *area* field of Print Options Area to *R1C1:R28C4*.) You're not ready to leave this spreadsheet yet, so reserve Exit for later. Press the Escape key to bring up the Multiplan menu.

WORKING WITH AN AUTOEXEC MENU

The first thing Multiplan looks for when it loads a spreadsheet is an autoexec (automatic execution) macro. An autoexec macro instructs Multiplan to perform certain tasks as soon as it loads the spreadsheet. You want Multiplan to display the macro menu immediately, because it contains all the commands you will need for this spreadsheet. All you have to do is name the traffic macro AUTOEXEC. It doesn't matter that it already has the name *Menu*.

Place the cursor on R2C6:	Type or press:
Start the Name command	N
Name the cell	AUTOEXEC
Move the highlight to *macro: Yes (No)*	Tab Tab
Select *Yes*	Y
Execute the command	Enter

Now hold down the Alternate key and type *M* to bring up your macro menu. Type *S* to save the spreadsheet with AUTOEXEC.

To see how AUTOEXEC works, we need to clear this spreadsheet from the screen so we can load it again. This is a good time to check out the Exit macro, so type *E* to exit and bring up the check ledger spreadsheet. Now, reload the cash disbursements summary spreadsheet: Type *TL* (Transfer Load). Type *CDTOTAL* and press Enter. And here's the macro menu.

If you had other work to do, you would now press Escape to bring up the Multiplan command menu. You can have one autoexec macro on each spreadsheet and it can be any kind of macro, not just one that brings up a macro menu.

And Here's Another Idea. . .

With a bit more work, you can have a month-by-month summary that looks like the one in Figure 12-7. When you insert columns (use the Insert command, Columns option) for August, September, and October, the macros will shift into columns 9 through 13. You can still use the macro menu, but you will have to change the cell locations in the Autoexec, Month, and Total macros. As an

	1	2	3	4	5	6	7 CDTOTAL1
1		CASH DISBURSEMENTS FOR 1987					
2	===
3		ACCOUNT		AUGUST	SEPTEMBER	OCTOBER	TOTALS	%GTOTAL
4		---
5	1	Owner's Draw		$4,166.66	$4,166.66	$4,166.66	$12,499.98	49.0%
6	2	Rent		$667.00	$667.00	$667.00	$2,001.00	7.8%
7	3	Phone & Telex		$281.76	$324.60	$203.11	$809.47	3.2%
8	4	Utilities		$125.00	$0.00	$118.00	$243.00	1.0%
9	5	Payroll		$732.90	$732.90	$1,234.56	$2,700.36	10.6%
10	6	Office Supplies		$216.19	$56.25	$58.00	$330.44	1.3%
11	7	Payroll Taxes		$146.58	$0.00	$0.00	$146.58	0.6%
12	8	Technical Services		$1,131.00	$500.00	$0.00	$1,631.00	6.4%
13	9	Dues & Subs		$75.00	$0.00	$24.50	$99.50	0.4%
14	10	Travel & Transportation		$97.00	$90.00	$105.00	$292.00	1.1%
15	11	Business Entertainment		$88.02	$245.00	$90.00	$423.02	1.7%
16	12	Loan Repayment		$578.40	$578.40	$578.40	$1,735.20	6.8%
17	13	Postage & Shipping		$0.00	$25.00	$5.00	$30.00	0.1%
18	14	Professional Fees		$0.00	$0.00	$0.00	$0.00	0.0%
19	15	Repairs & Maintenance		$0.00	$0.00	$75.00	$75.00	0.3%
20	16	Car Rental		$480.89	$480.89	$480.89	$1,442.67	5.7%
21	17	Capital Equipment		$0.00	$0.00	$0.00	$0.00	0.0%
22	18	Medical/Dental Insurance		$390.00	$0.00	$0.00	$390.00	1.5%
23	19	Advertising & Promotion		$0.00	$575.00	$0.00	$575.00	2.3%
24	20	Gifts & Contributions		$0.00	$0.00	$0.00	$0.00	0.0%
25	21	Miscellaneous		$0.00	$79.83	$0.00	$79.83	0.3%
26		--
27		TOTALS		$9,176.40	$8,521.53	$7,806.12	$25,504.05	100.0%
28	===

FIGURE 12-7.
The month-by-month cash disbursements summary spreadsheet

alternative to changing the cell locations, you can replace the row and column numbers in your macros with cell names, cursor movements, or the '? "wild card" command code. Then, no matter how many more columns you insert, your macros will continue to work properly. Just use the techniques you learned in this chapter and you should have no trouble at all.

CASH DISBURSEMENTS SPREADSHEET SUMMARY

General: The completed spreadsheet is shown in Figure 12-1. Use Options to set automatic recalculation to *No*. Use Value to enter REPT(" = ",25) and REPT(" − ",12) for long lines. Use Lock Formulas to lock formulas. Use Xternal Copy to load the following cells from the Check Ledger: LCELLS1 into R3C1 and LCELLS2 into R3C4.

Column Width: Use Format Width as follows: Set column 1 to 12 characters, column 2 to 7 characters, column 3 to 25 characters, and columns 4 and 6 to 12 characters each.

Format: Use Format Cells as follows: Continue R1C6:7. Center C2, C5, and R3:4C4:14. Right-justify R1C14. Dollar code R7:26C4 and R7C6:14. Use Format Options to insert commas throughout the spreadsheet.

Print: Cash Disbursements is 163 characters wide, including Multiplan row numbers, and is printed in 12-pitch. For 8½-by-11-inch paper, set the following margins: *left* 0, *top* 6, *print width* 96, *print length* 60, and *page length* 66. For 15-by-11-inch paper, set *print width* to 163. The other settings are the same as for 8½-by-11-inch paper.

Formulas: Formulas use relative cell references only.

1	R3C6	Account Numbers	COLUMN() − 5
2	R7C6	Disbursements into Accounts	IF(R C5 = R3 C,R C4,"")
3	R26C4	Totals	SUM(R[−19]C:R[−1]C)
4	R1C14	Spreadsheet Filename	NAME()

CASH DISBURSEMENTS MODULE SUMMARY

General: The completed spreadsheet is shown in Figure 12-3. Use Copy to copy the lines from the Check Ledger. Turn on iteration. The completion test is in R38C12.

Format: Use Format Cells as follows: Continue R40:60C10:11. Center R38C12. Dollar code R40:61C12.

Name: R9:26C7 are ACCOUNT. R8C1 is MONTH. R40:60C12 are TOTALS. R40:60C9:11 are DISBURS.

Formulas: Formulas use relative and named cell references.

1 R38C12   Iteration Completion Test
   ITERCNT() = COUNT(ACCOUNT)

2 R40C12   Distribution Into Accounts
   IF(ISNA(ITERCNT()),0,IF(INDEX(ACCOUNT, ITERCNT()) = RC[−3],RC + INDEX (ALLOCATED,ITERCNT()),RC))

CASH DISBURSEMENTS SUMMARY SPREADSHEET SUMMARY

General: The completed spreadsheet is shown in Figure 12-4. Use Xternal Copy to load the following from Check: DISBURS to R5C1, MONTH to R1C3, and TOTALS to R5C3. Use Value to enter REPT(" = ",29) and REPT(" − ",29) for long lines.

Column Width: Use Format Width to increase column 2 to 29 characters and column 3 to 14 characters.

Format: Use Format Cells as follows: Right-justify R1C4 and R3C3:4. Center R5:25C1. Dollar code R5:R27C3. Percent code with one decimal place R5C4.

Name: R27C3 is GTOTAL.

Formulas: Formulas use relative and named cell references.

1	R27C3	Grand Total
		SUM(R[− 22]C:R[− 1]C)
2	R5C4	Account Totals as a Percent of Grand Total
		RC[− 1]/GTOTAL
3	R1C4	Spreadsheet Filename
		NAME()

Print: The Cash Disbursements Summary is 68 characters wide, including Multiplan row numbers, and is printed in 12-pitch on 8½-by-11-inch paper. Set the following margins: *left* 10, *top* 6, *print width* 96, *print length* 60, and *page length* 66.

Macro Menu: Name R2C6 MENU and assign the run code M, then name R2C6 AUTOEXEC.

1	R1C6	Autoexec and Menu (Alt − M)
	R2C6	'HM'MNR4C6'
2	R4C6	Month
	R5C6	Enters the Checkbook month in R1C3
	R6C6	GR1'TB3'RTB'RTXCCHECK'TBMONTH
		'TB'TBN'RT'GOMENU''QU
3	R4C7	Total
	R5C7	Adds the Checkbook totals to the current totals
	R6C7	GR5'tb3'rtXTCHECK'tbTOTALS
		'rt'rc'GOMENU''qu

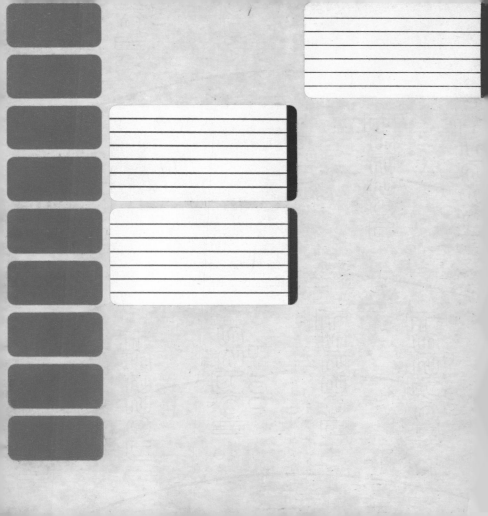

4	R4C8	Save
	R5C8	Saves the spreadsheet
	R6C8	TS'RTY'GOMENU''QU
5	R4C9	Print
	R5C9	Prints the spreadsheet
	R6C9	PP'GOMENU''QU
6	R4C10	Exit
	R5C10	Exits this spreadsheet and returns to the Checkbook
	R6C10	TLCHECK'RT'QU

13

Five-in-one Depreciation Analysis

The determination of depreciation policies is one of the most important decisions a business manager can make. When a business purchases equipment, buildings, and other fixed assets, except land, the cost of these assets can be depreciated ("written off") over a period of years. In accounting terms, depreciation is simply the allocation of the cost of a capital asset less estimated salvage value (if any) to each year of the asset's estimated useful life. Depreciation allowances are deductible when the taxable income of a business is computed and they affect the amount of tax to be paid. All else being equal, the greater the depreciation allowance, the lower the tax paid.

The following discussion summarizes five of the depreciation methods currently being used: straight line, sum-of-the-years'-digits, units of production, declining balance, and modified accelerated cost recovery system (MACRS). Figure 13-1 shows the result of all five methods for one asset, an offset press. Because tax laws governing depreciation are varied and complex, you should consult your accountant or tax advisor to determine the specific regulations and tax implications of each method.

```
              1          2          3          4           5
                                             DEPRECIATION ANALYSIS
 1
 2 ===================================================================:
 3 Equipment Description        Offset Press #1255A
 4 Date of Purchase                Feb 23, 1984
 5 Today's Date                    Sep 17, 1987
 6 Service to Date in Years              3.57
 7 Original Cost                   $36,000.00
 8 Estimated Salvage Value          $4,000.00
 9 Depreciable Cost                $32,000.00
10 Term in Years                          10
11 ===================================================================:
12                    Straight    Sum-of-the   Units of    Estimated
13           Year      Line      Years'-Digits Production     Hours
14 ---------------------------------------------------------------------
15            1      $3,200.00    $5,818.18    $8,000.00      3000
16            2      $3,200.00    $5,236.36    $6,400.00      2400
17            3      $3,200.00    $4,654.55    $5,066.67      1900
18            4      $3,200.00    $4,072.73    $3,466.67      1300
19            5      $3,200.00    $3,490.91    $2,666.67      1000
20            6      $3,200.00    $2,909.09    $2,133.33       800
21            7      $3,200.00    $2,327.27    $1,600.00       600
22            8      $3,200.00    $1,745.45    $1,333.33       500
23            9      $3,200.00    $1,163.64      $800.00       300
24           10      $3,200.00      $581.82      $533.33       200
25 ===================================================================:
26         Totals   $32,000.00   $32,000.00   $32,000.00     12000
27                                                          AGREE
```

FIGURE 13-1.

The completed five-in-one depreciation analysis spreadsheet

Straight Line: Under the straight line method, the cost of the asset, minus its estimated salvage value, is deducted in equal amounts during each year of the asset's estimated useful life. The rate and the base on which depreciation is computed remain the same each year.

Sum-of-the-Years'-Digits: Under the sum-of-the-years'-digits method, a diminishing distribution of the asset's cost, less its estimated salvage value, is allocated over the asset's estimated useful life. The term "digits" refers to each year of the asset's estimated useful life. An estimated useful life of 10 years, for example, is computed as $1+2+3+4+5+6+7+8+9+10$, for a total of 55 digits. Sum-of-the-years'-digits is represented as a fraction. The numerator of the fraction each year represents the remaining years in the asset's useful life, and the denominator is the sum of the years' digits. For example, if an asset's useful life is 10 years, 10/55 of the depreciable cost is deducted in the first year, 9/55 in the second year, 8/55 in the third year, and so on. The rate changes each year, but the base on which the depreciation is computed remains the same.

Units of Production: Under the units of production method, the cost of the asset, less its estimated salvage value, is deducted in proportion to the number of hours of the asset's estimated use each year. Therefore, the depreciation allowance varies from year to year.

6	7	8	9
			DEPREC

==

Units of Production Method Only:
Estimated Useful Life in Hours   12000
Hourly Depreciation Rate $2.67

==

Declining Balance	MACRS (3 years)	MACRS (5 years)	MACRS (7 years)
$7,200.00	$11,988.00	$7,200.00	$5,148.00
$5,760.00	$15,984.00	$11,520.00	$8,820.00
$4,608.00	$5,328.00	$6,912.00	$6,300.00
$3,686.40	$2,700.00	$4,140.00	$4,500.00
$2,949.12		$4,140.00	$3,204.00
$2,359.30		$2,088.00	$3,204.00
$1,887.44			$3,204.00
$1,509.95			$1,620.00
$1,207.96			
$831.84			

==

$32,000.00	$36,000.00	$36,000.00	$36,000.00

Declining Balance (DB): Under the declining balance method, depreciation is greatest in the first year and is smaller in each succeeding year. Salvage value is not taken into account. DB uses an accelerated rate of depreciation, which is usually a percentage of the straight line rate. The most frequently used DB rate is 200 percent (the maximum permitted for tax purposes), commonly called the double declining balance method. The depreciable basis of the asset is reduced each year by the amount of the depreciation already taken. The rate remains the same each year, but the base on which the depreciation is computed changes (declines) each year.

Modified Accelerated Cost Recovery System (MACRS): Under the MACRS method of depreciation, the cost of an eligible asset is deducted over a period of 3, 5, 7, 10, 15, 20, 27.5, or 31.5 years, depending on the type of property. Property in the 3-, 5-, 7-, or 10-year class is depreciated using a rate of 200 percent (double declining balance), and property in the 15- or 20-year class, 150 percent (one and one-half declining balance). Under both methods, the depreciation is switched to straight line when this will maximize deductions. Straight line depreciation is the only method allowed for 27.5- and 31.5-year property.

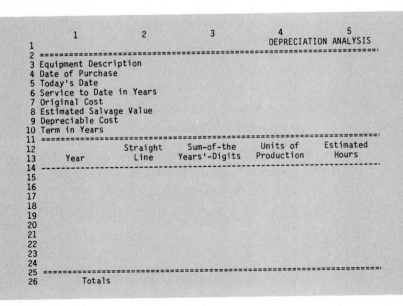

FIGURE 13-2.
The titles and lines on the depreciation analysis spreadsheet

The depreciation analysis spreadsheet in this chapter shows clearly the practicality of using electronic spreadsheets for business. Anyone who has labored over depreciation schedules knows the time it takes to calculate the method with the greatest tax advantages manually. With this spreadsheet, you type only a few numbers—the original cost of the asset, its estimated salvage value at the end of the depreciation period, the number of years over which you will depreciate the asset, and an estimate of its useful life—and the spreadsheet instantly calculates the allowances for each of the five depreciation methods.

If you're familiar with Multiplan and prefer to create this spreadsheet without following the step-by-step instructions, refer to the summary at the end of this chapter.

SETTING UP YOUR SPREADSHEET

Bring up the Multiplan screen. If you've already turned off automatic recalculation, you can skip the following instructions and go to "Adjusting the Column Widths." Otherwise, to make data entry faster, leave the cursor on R1C1. Type O to start the Options command, type N for no recalculation, and press Enter. Now we're ready to make your spreadsheet look like the one shown in Figure 13-2.

```
        6            7            8            9
=====================================================================


Units of Production Method Only:
 Estimated Useful Life in Hours
 Hourly Depreciation Rate
=====================================================================
 Declining      MACRS        MACRS        MACRS
  Balance     (3 years)    (5 years)    (7 years)
---------------------------------------------------------------------




=====================================================================
```

Adjusting the Column Widths

Each of Multiplan's columns is now 10 characters wide. To give the entries the space they need, increase the default width of every column to 14 characters:

Leave the cursor where it is:	Type or press:
Start the Format command	F
Select the Default option	D
Select the Width option	W
Specify the number of characters in each column	14
Execute the command	Enter

Entering the Titles

The next step is to type the titles you see in Figure 13-2. Before you begin, here are a few instructions on indenting and other matters:

■ The titles *Estimated Useful Life in Hours* in R8C6 and *Hourly Depreciation Rate* in R9C6 are indented one space. Press the Spacebar once before typing each title.

■ Type *Totals* in R26C1 without any indent. You'll right-justify it later so that it looks like the one in Figure 13-2.

■ The titles *(3 years)*, *(5 years)*, and *(7 years)* in row 13 of columns 7 through 9 start with an open parenthesis. When you type an open parenthesis, Multiplan assumes you're starting a formula. Clearly, you need to do something special to tell Multiplan that each of these entries is a title, not a formula. Enter them later with the Alpha command when you are instructed to do so.

■ Some of the titles are longer than their cells can display. Don't be concerned. We'll take care of that shortly when we format the titles.

■ If you mistype, you can press the Backspace key to erase. You can also use the F7 through F10 keys to move the highlight through the title without erasing, then type a missing character or press the Delete key to erase an unwanted character.

Let's start with the spreadsheet title, *DEPRECIATION ANALYSIS*, in R1C4, which is indented five spaces to center it in the two cells it occupies.

Place the cursor on R1C4:	**Type:**
Start the Alpha command	A
Indent five spaces	Spacebar (five times)
Type the spreadsheet title	DEPRECIATION ANALYSIS

The title appears on the command line, which is where Multiplan displays what you type. You don't have to press Enter to enter it in its cell. Just use the direction keys to move the cursor to R3C1, the next cell that will contain a title. When you move the cursor, *DEPRECIATION ANALYSIS* disappears from the command line and appears (partially) in the cell in which it belongs.

Type *Equipment Description* and move the cursor to R4C1. Type *Date of Purchase* and again move the cursor to the next cell. Continue in this way — typing a title and moving the cursor — until you type every title except the three in parentheses in row 13. After the last title, press Enter.

Now that the command menu is back on the screen, enter the three titles in parentheses: Place the cursor on R13C7 and type *A* for Alpha. Type *(3 years)* and press Enter. Now do it again. Place the cursor on R13C8 and again type *A*. Type *(5 years)* and press Enter. Let's do it one more time. Place the cursor on R13C9 and type *A*. Type *(7 years)* and press Enter.

Entering the Long Lines

Now let's enter a double line across row 2. In R2C1, enter a REPT formula that repeats an equal sign 14 times—enough to fill any cell in row 2. The quotation marks tell Multiplan the equal sign is text.

Place the cursor on R2C1:	**Type or press:**
Start the Value command	V
Repeat an equal sign 14 times	REPT(" = ",14)
Execute the command	Enter

Now copy the REPT formula into the columns to the right:

Leave the cursor on R2C1:	**Type or press:**
Start the Copy command	C
Select the Right option	R
Specify the number of cells to copy into	8
Execute the command	Enter

Rows 11 and 25 need the same kind of line, so copy it from row 2. You can press F6 to produce a colon, as shown in the column on the right of the following instructions before the number 9.

Leave the cursor on R2C1:	**Type or press:**
Start the Copy command	C
Select the From option	F
(Multiplan displays *COPY FROM cells: R2C1*, the first cell to copy from)	
Specify the last cell to copy from	:9
Move the highlight to *to cells*	Tab
Specify the first cell in each row to copy into	R11C1,R25C1
Execute the command	Enter

Now use the REPT function and a minus sign to enter a single line across row 14: Place the cursor on R14C1 and type *V* (Value). Type *REPT(" – ",14)* and press Enter. Type *CR* (Copy Right). Multiplan proposes to copy 8 cells, a repeat of your last Copy instruction. Since this is correct, press Enter.

Formatting the Title Cells

The easy way to display all of the wide titles completely is to give every cell a continuous format.

Leave the cursor where it is:	Type or press:
Start the Format command	F
Select the Default option	D
Select the Cells option	C
Move the highlight to *format code*	Tab
Select *Cont* (continuous)	C
Execute the command	Enter

Now center the titles in rows 12 and 13 and cell R27C5, which will contain a message-producing formula. Using *R12, R13* to indicate rows 12 and 13 instead of *R12:13C1:9* will reduce the number of characters you type.

Place the cursor on R27C5:	Type or press:
Start the Format command	F
Select the Cells option	C
(Multiplan displays *FORMAT cells: R27C5,* the first cell to format)	
Specify the other cells to format	,R12,R13
Move the highlight to *alignment*	Tab
Select *Ctr* (center)	C
Execute the command	Enter

Now right-justify the title *Totals* in R26C1 and the contents of R1C9, which will contain the spreadsheet filename.

Place the cursor on R26C1:	Type or press:
Start the Format command	F
Select the Cells option	C
(Multiplan displays *FORMAT cells: R26C1,* the first cell to format)	
Specify the last cell to format	,R1C9
Move the highlight to *alignment*	Tab
Select *Right*	R
Execute the command	Enter

Formatting the Date Cells

Next, format R4C3 and R5C3 to show the date of purchase and today's date as a three-letter month, one- or two-digit day, and four-digit year, a custom format. All you need do is use Multiplan's date format symbols in the configuration you choose. Be sure to type the spaces as shown.

Place the cursor on R4C3:	**Type or press:**
Start the Format command	F
Select the Time-Date option	T
Select the Cells option	C
(Multiplan displays *FORMAT TIME-DATE cells:* R4C3, the first cell to format)	
Specify the last cell to format	:R5C3
Move the highlight to *format*	Tab
Specify the format	mmm d, yyyy
Execute the command	Enter

Formatting the Number Cells

Now center the cells that will contain the year numbers in column 1 (rows 15 through 24) and the estimated hours in column 5 (rows 15 through 24).

Place the cursor on R15C1:	**Type or press:**
Start the Format command	F
Select the Cells option	C
(Multiplan displays *FORMAT cells: R15C1,* the first cell to format)	
Specify the other cells to format	:R24C1,R15:24C5
Move the highlight to *alignment*	Tab
Select *Ctr* (center)	C
Execute the command	Enter

Many cells on this spreadsheet contain dollar values. The easy way to handle them all is to format one cell for dollars and cents, then copy the contents of that cell to the other cells that need it. Let's start by formatting R7C3, which will contain the original cost of the asset.

Place the cursor on R7C3:	**Type or press:**
Start the Format command	F
Select the Cells option	C
(Multiplan displays *FORMAT cells: R7C3*, the cell to format)	
Move the highlight to *format code*	Tab Tab
Select *$*	$
Execute the command	Enter

Now copy the dollar format from R7C3 to the following cells: Estimated Salvage Value (R8C3), Depreciable Cost (R9C3), Hourly Depreciation Rate (R9C9), Straight Line (R15:16C2), Sum-of-the-Years'-Digits (R15:16C3), Units of Production (R15:16C4), Declining Balance (R15:24C6), MACRS (R15C7), and Totals (R26C2). Several cells that need the dollar format aren't included in this group because copying the formulas down the columns will carry the dollar format to them.

Leave the cursor on R7C3:	**Type or press:**
Start the Copy command	C
Select the From option	F
(Multiplan displays *COPY FROM cells: R7C3*, the first cell to copy from)	
Move the highlight to *to cells*	Tab
Specify the cells to copy into	R8:9C3,R9C9,R15:16C2:4, R15:24C6,R15C7,R26C2
Execute the command	Enter

The last cell to format is R6C3, which will contain the number of years the asset is in service. Have Multiplan show it as a fixed number with two decimal places.

Place the cursor on R6C3:	**Type or press:**
Start the Format command	F
Select the Cells option	C
(Multiplan displays *FORMAT cells: R6C3*, the cell to format)	
Move the highlight to *format code*	Tab Tab
Select *Fix*	F

Move the highlight to *# of decimals*	Tab
Specify the number of decimals	2
Execute the command	Enter

Inserting Commas in the Large Numbers

Commas in the large numbers will make this spreadsheet easier to read.

Leave the cursor where it is:	Type or press:
Start the Format command	F
Select the Options option	O
(The highlight is on *No* in the *commas* field)	
Select *Yes*	Y
Execute the command	Enter

NAMING THE CELLS

Let's now name the cells that the formulas refer to. Using names will make the formulas easy to create and understand. The unshaded areas in Figure 13-3 show the locations of the named cells. DBYEAR1 (R15C6) refers to the declining balance in year 1, and DRATE (R9C9) is for the depreciation rate. The first named cell contains the original cost of the asset.

Leave the cursor on R7C3:	Type:
Start the Name command	N
Name the cell	ORIGINAL

The *to refer to* field shows R7C3, which is correct. So all you do is press Enter.
Use this same procedure to name the following cells. (Be sure to press Enter after you type each name.)

Place the cursor on:	Name the cell:
R8C3	SALVAGE
R9C3	DEPRECIABLE
R10C3	TERM
R8C9	LIFE
R9C9	DRATE
R15C6	DBYEAR1

```
                    1              2              3              4              5
                1                                              DEPRECIATION ANALYSIS
                2 ================================================================:
                3 Equipment Description
                4 Date of Purchase        ❶ Feb 23, 1984
                5 Today's Date            ❷ Sep 17, 1987
                6 Service to Date in Years             3.57
                7 Original Cost                                  ORIGINAL
                8 Estimated Salvage Value                        SALVAGE
                9 Depreciable Cost        ❸        $0.00         DEPRECIABLE
               10 Term in Years                       10         TERM
               11 ================================================================:
               12                 Straight     Sum-of-the     Units of      Estimated
               13      Year        Line     Years'-Digits    Production       Hours
               14 ----------------------------------------------------------------
               15       1          $0.00 ❺    $0.00 ❻       $0.00 ❾      3000
               16       2  ❹       $0.00      $0.00 ❼       $0.00        2400
               17       3          $0.00      $0.00         $0.00        1900
               18       4          $0.00      $0.00         $0.00        1300
               19       5          $0.00      $0.00         $0.00        1000
               20       6          $0.00      $0.00         $0.00         800
               21       7          $0.00      $0.00         $0.00         600
               22       8          $0.00      $0.00         $0.00         500
               23       9          $0.00      $0.00         $0.00         300
               24      10          $0.00      $0.00         $0.00         200
               25 ================================================================:
               26      Totals      $0.00 ⓯    $0.00         $0.00       12000
               27                                                        AGREE ⓰
```

FIGURE 13-3.
Depreciation analysis named cells and formula locations

Saving and Naming the Spreadsheet

Now store the spreadsheet on disk with the titles, lines, formats, and cell names, and give the spreadsheet its own filename. If you need to tell Multiplan which drive contains your data disk or which directory to store the file in, type the drive letter and press F6 (to produce a colon) or type the pathname before you type *DEPREC*, the filename.

Leave the cursor where it is:	Type or press:
Start the Transfer command	T
Select the Save option	S
Name the spreadsheet	DEPREC
Execute the command	Enter

ENTERING THE PRACTICE NUMBERS AND A DATE

Figure 13-3 shows practice numbers. Entering these numbers now will prevent error messages from appearing in the cells when you enter the formulas. You can type a number any time you see the command menu or *ALPHA/*

```
        6              7              8              9
                                               DEPREC 🔟
=====================================================================
Units of Production Method Only:
  Estimated Useful Life in Hours       LIFE      12000
  Hourly Depreciation Rate             DRATE     $0.00  8

=====================================================================
     Declining      MACRS          MACRS          MACRS
      Balance      (3 years)      (5 years)      (7 years)
     ----------------------------------------------------------------
DBYEAR1   $0.00 🔟     $0.00 🔟      $0.00          $0.00
          $0.00 🔟     $0.00         $0.00          $0.00
          $0.00 🔟     $0.00         $0.00          $0.00
          $0.00        $0.00         $0.00          $0.00
          $0.00                      $0.00          $0.00
          $0.00                      $0.00          $0.00
          $0.00                                     $0.00
          $0.00                                     $0.00
          $0.00                                     $0.00
          $0.00 🔟
=====================================================================
          $0.00        $0.00         $0.00          $0.00
```

VALUE on the command line. Just type the number and move the cursor to another cell. When you do so, the number you typed is placed in its cell.

Place the cursor on R8C9 (Estimated Useful Life in Hours). Type *12000* and move the cursor to R10C3 (Term in Years). Type *10* and move the cursor to R15C1 (Year 1). Type *1* and move the cursor to R15C5. Now type the estimated hours in rows 15 through 24 of column 5, moving the cursor down from one cell to the next. When you've finished, press Enter.

Now move the cursor to R4C3 and type *A* (Alpha). Type *2/23/84* and press the Enter key. Multiplan, in keeping with the custom time-date format you entered in the cell, displays the date as *Feb 23, 1984*. Because Multiplan stores dates and times as serial numbers, the status line displays *30735*, the serial number of this date.

ENTERING THE FORMULAS

The next step is to enter the formulas that perform your calculations. Their locations are numbered in Figure 13-3. The formulas use relative and named cell references. The left column in the following instructions contains the cell locations, the names of named cells, and other elements that the formula works with. The column on the right and the line below the formula heading show the finished formula.

To build a formula, move the cursor to each cell location shown in the left column (Multiplan will produce the relative notation) and type everything else—operators, symbols, function names, and cell names. When you type a character, the cursor returns to the formula cell. This lets you type another character, move the cursor to another cell location, or enter the formula.

When your formula agrees with the instructions, press Enter. If Multiplan then displays *Not a valid formula,* check each character. Use the F7 through F10 keys to move the highlight, and correct the problem by typing missing characters or pressing the Delete key to delete unwanted characters. If you prefer to start the formula from scratch, press the Escape key and begin again.

FORMULA 1: Today's Date

NOW()

Formula 1 enters the serial number of the current date kept by your computer's clock. The date is based on the one you typed at the DOS prompt when you turned on your computer or by your battery-powered clock, if you have one. Type the function name and the parentheses at the end.

Place the cursor on R5C3:	Type or press:
Start the Value command	V
Enter the formula: NOW()	NOW()
Execute the command	Enter

Changing Today's Date in DOS

So that your results agree with the figures in this chapter, let's pretend that today's date is Sept. 17, 1987. Leave Multiplan for a few seconds to visit MS-DOS and change your date.

Leave the cursor where it is:	Type or press:
Start the Run command	R
Select the Dos option	D
Enter the DOS command	DATE
Execute the command	Enter

DOS now displays your current date and invites you to enter a new date. Type *9-17-87* and press Enter twice, once to enter the date and the second time to resume Multiplan. Now press the F4 key to recalculate the NOW formula to show the date. Multiplan updates the value of NOW to reflect the current date each time it recalculates the spreadsheet.

FORMULA 2: Service to Date in Years

$(R[-1]C - R[-2]C)/365$

Formula 2 subtracts the serial number of the purchase date (R4C3) from the serial number of today's date (R5C3), divides the result by 365 days, and enters the years that the asset has been in service in R6C3. The formula starts with an open parenthesis, so there's no need to type *V* (Value) first.

Place the cursor on R6C3:	**Type or move the cursor:**
Enter the formula: (R5C3 − R4C3)/365	$(R[-1]C - R[-2]C)/365$
Execute the command	Enter

FORMULA 3: Depreciable Cost

ORIGINAL − SALVAGE

Formula 3 subtracts the estimated salvage value (R8C3, SALVAGE) from the original cost of the asset (R7C3, ORIGINAL) and enters the depreciable cost in R9C3. Type the entire formula.

Place the cursor on R9C3:	**Type or press:**
Start the Value command	V
Enter the formula: ORIGINAL − SALVAGE	ORIGINAL − SALVAGE
Execute the command	Enter

FORMULA 4: Year Numbers

$1 + R[-1]C$

Formula 4 adds 1 to the number in the cell above it (R15C1). When it is copied down column 1, it generates sequential year numbers. The formula starts with a number, so there's no need to type *V*.

Place the cursor on R16C1:	**Type or move the cursor:**
Enter the formula: 1 + R15C1	$1 + R[-1]C$
Execute the command	Enter

Now copy Formula 4 down the column.

Leave the cursor on R16C1:	**Type:**
Start the Copy command	C
Select the Down option	D

Multiplan proposes 8—a repeat of your last Copy command when you copied the line to the right. This is the correct number, so press Enter.

Now press F4 to recalculate so that the year numbers appear in the proper sequence.

FORMULA 5: Straight Line Method

IF(RC[−1]< = TERM,DEPRECIABLE/TERM,0)

Formula 5 calculates the straight line depreciation allowances. The tax laws permit the use of different terms for depreciating an asset with this method, so the formula calculates the allowances only for the term you select, and enters a zero between the last year of the term and 10 years (the limit for calculations by this spreadsheet).

The IF function has three parts: the Test statement, the Then statement, and the Else statement. The Test statement compares the year number (R15C1) with the length of term (R10C3, TERM). If the year number is less than or equal to the term, the Then statement divides the depreciable cost (R9C3, DEPRECIABLE) by the term, and enters the result in R15C2. If the year number is greater than the term, the Else statement enters a zero in the formula cell.

Place the cursor on R15C2:	Type or move the cursor:
Start the Value command	V

Enter the formula: IF(R15C1
  < = TERM,
  DEPRECIABLE
  /TERM,0)
	IF(RC[−1]< = TERM,
	  DEPRECIABLE/TERM,0)

Translation: IF(year is less than or
  equal to length of term, then enter
  depreciable cost divided by length
  of term, else enter zero)	

Execute the command	Enter

The Then statement produces $0.00 because R9C3 (DEPRECIABLE) is empty.

Now copy Formula 5 down the column: Leave the cursor on R15C2 and type CD (Copy Down). Type 9 as the number of cells to copy down and then press Enter.

Sum-of-the-Years'-Digits Method

Formulas 6 and 7 calculate the depreciation allowances for the sum-of-the-years'-digits method. As mentioned at the beginning of this chapter, the sum of the digits is determined by adding the years of useful life in this fashion: $1+2+3+4$ and so on. Each formula uses the equation $Sum = T(T+1)/2$, where T is Term, the life of the asset. In Multiplan notation, this appears as *(TERM * (TERM + 1)/2)* on our spreadsheet. Each formula then divides the remaining years by this figure and multiplies the resulting fraction by the depreciable cost of the asset.

FORMULA 6: Sum-of-The-Years'-Digits — Year 1

TERM * DEPRECIABLE/(TERM * (TERM + 1)/2)

Formula 6 calculates the sum-of-the-years'-digits allowance in year 1 and enters the result in R15C3. We will assume that year 1 is a full 12 months. Type the entire formula.

Place the cursor on R15C3:	Type or press:
Start the Value command	V
Enter the formula: TERM * DEPRECIABLE/ (TERM * (TERM + 1)/2)	TERM * DEPRECIABLE/ (TERM * (TERM + 1)/2)
Translation: Length of term times depreciable cost divided by (length of term times (length of term + 1) divided by 2)	
Execute the command	Enter

FORMULA 7: Sum-of-The-Years'-Digits — Year 2

IF(RC[− 2]< = TERM,(TERM − R[− 1]C[− 2]) * DEPRECIABLE/(TERM * (TERM + 1)/2),0)

Formula 7 calculates the sum-of-the-years'-digits allowances in year 2. The Test statement compares the year number (R16C1) with the length of term (R10C3, TERM). If the year number is less than or equal to the term, the Then statement calculates the depreciation allowance and enters the result in R16C3. If the year number is greater than the term, the Else statement enters a zero.

Place the cursor on R16C3:	Type or move the cursor:
Start the Value command	V
Enter the formula: IF(R16C1 < = TERM, (TERM − R15C1) * DEPRECIABLE/ (TERM * (TERM + 1)/2),0)	IF(RC[− 2]< = TERM, (TERM − R[− 1]C[− 2]) * DEPRECIABLE/ (TERM * (TERM + 1)/2),0)

Translation: IF(year is less than or equal
   to length of term, then enter (length of
   term minus previous year) times
   depreciable cost divided by (length of
   term times (length of term + 1) divided
   by 2), else enter zero)

Execute the command   Enter

To calculate the sum-of-the-years'-digits allowances in the remaining years,
copy Formula 7 down the column: Leave the cursor on R16C3 and type *CD*
(Copy Down). Type *8* and press Enter.

FORMULA 8: Hourly Depreciation Rate

DEPRECIABLE/LIFE

Formula 8 divides the depreciable cost (R9C3, DEPRECIABLE) by the estimated useful life (in hours) of this asset (R8C9, LIFE) and enters the hourly
depreciation rate in R9C9. This figure is needed for the units of production
method. Type the entire formula.

Place the cursor on R9C9:	**Type or press:**
Start the Value command	V
Enter the formula: DEPRECIABLE /LIFE	DEPRECIABLE/LIFE
Execute the command	Enter

FORMULA 9: Units of Production Method

RC[+ 1] * DRATE

Formula 9 calculates the allowance for the units of production method. The
formula multiplies the estimated hours in year 1 (R15C5) by the hourly depreciation rate (R9C9, DRATE) and enters the allowance in R15C4.

Place the cursor on R15C4:	**Type or move the cursor:**
Start the Value command	V
Enter the formula: R15C5 * DRATE	RC[+ 1] * DRATE
Execute the command	Enter

To calculate the allowances in the remaining years, copy Formula 9 down
the column: Leave the cursor on R15C4 and type *CD* (Copy Down). Type *9* and
press Enter.

Declining Balance Method

Formulas 10 through 13 calculate the declining balance (DB) depreciation allowances. With this method, the estimated salvage value is not deducted from the original cost of the asset. DB depreciation is calculated by multiplying the original cost (R7C3, ORIGINAL), less accumulated depreciation, by a fixed rate. As mentioned earlier, the most commonly used rate is 200 percent (double declining), the maximum permitted. A rate of 200 percent over a 10-year period is 20 percent per year.

FORMULA 10: Declining Balance — Year 1

ORIGINAL * 20%

Formula 10 calculates the declining balance allowance in the first year. The formula multiplies the original cost (R7C3, ORIGINAL) by 20% and enters the result in R15C6. Type the entire formula.

Place the cursor on R15C6:	Type or press:
Start the Value command	V
Enter the formula: ORIGINAL * 20%	ORIGINAL * 20%
Execute the command	Enter

FORMULA 11: Declining Balance — Year 2

(ORIGINAL – DBYEAR1) * 20%

Formula 11 calculates the declining balance allowance in year 2. The formula subtracts the amount in year 1 (R15C6, DBYEAR1) from the original cost (R7C3, ORIGINAL), multiplies the result by 20% and enters that result in R16C6. This formula starts with an open parenthesis — there's no need to type V first. Type the entire formula.

Place the cursor on R16C6:	Type or press:
Enter the formula: (ORIGINAL – DBYEAR1) * 20%	(ORIGINAL – DBYEAR1) * 20%
Execute the command	Enter

FORMULA 12: Declining Balance — Year 3

(ORIGINAL – SUM(R[– 1]C:DBYEAR1)) * 20%

Formula 12 calculates the declining balance allowance in year 3. The formula subtracts the sum of the prior years' allowances (R16C6 to R15C6,

DBYEAR1) from the original cost (R7C3, ORIGINAL), multiplies the result by 20%, and enters that amount in R17C6. Again, there's no need to type V.

Place the cursor on R17C6:	Type or move the cursor:
Enter the formula: (ORIGINAL − SUM(R16C6:DBYEAR1)) * 20%	(ORIGINAL − SUM (R[− 1]C:DBYEAR1)) * 20%
Execute the command	Enter

Now copy Formula 12 down the column so that it calculates the allowances in years 4 through 9: Leave the cursor on R17C6 and type CD (Copy Down). Type 6 and press Enter.

FORMULA 13: Declining Balance — Year 10

DEPRECIABLE − SUM(DBYEAR1:R[− 1]C)

Formula 13 calculates the DB allowance for year 10 and enters the result in R24C6. Although the declining balance method doesn't take salvage value into account in determining the initial allowances, an asset cannot be depreciated below its estimated salvage value. Therefore, the formula deducts the allowances in years 1 through 9 (R15C6, named DBYEAR1, through R23C6) from the depreciable cost of the asset (R7C3, DEPRECIABLE), thereby ensuring that the depreciation amount for the last year won't put the total depreciation under the salvage value.

Place the cursor on R24C6:	Type or move the cursor:
Start the Value command	V
Enter the formula: DEPRECIABLE − SUM(DBYEAR1:R23C6) *Translation:* Depreciable cost minus the sum of (allowances in years 1 through 9)	DEPRECIABLE − SUM(DBYEAR1: R[− 1]C)
Execute the command	Enter

Modified Accelerated Cost Recovery System (MACRS) Method

The MACRS (Modified Accelerated Cost Recovery System) calls for a variety of percentage rates in each of seven different schedules. To keep this spreadsheet neat and trim, we'll include only the 3-, 5-, and 7-year schedules. Once you know the techniques, you can enter the schedules for the other years. Salvage value is disregarded in computing MACRS.

FORMULA 14: MACRS Base Formula

ORIGINAL

Formula 14 calculates the MACRS depreciation allowances based on the original cost of the asset (R7C3, ORIGINAL). To save keystrokes, we'll make Formula 14 a base formula, copy it into the other MACRS cells, then append the appropriate rate for each year. Type the one-word formula.

Place the cursor on R15C7:	Type or press:
Start the Value command	V
Enter the formula: ORIGINAL	ORIGINAL
Execute the command	Enter

Now copy this base formula into the other MACRS cells.

Leave the cursor on R15C7:	Type or press:
Start the Copy command	C
Select the From option	F
(Multiplan displays *COPY FROM cells: R15C7*, the cell to copy from)	
Move the highlight to *to cells*	Tab
Specify the cells to copy into	R16:18C7,R15:20C8, R15:22C9
Execute the command	Enter

Next, use Multiplan's Edit command to append a multiplication sign and a percentage according to the chart in Figure 13-4. Federal tax regulations say, "first and last depreciation allowances reflect half-year conventions," which has been interpreted as providing allowances for six months during the first year and six months in the year following the last year of the schedule. To account for these partial years, the chart shows the schedule plus one year (for example, a 3-year schedule with a fourth year).

Let's start the editing with year 1 of the 3-year schedule.

Leave the cursor on R15C7:	Type or press:
Start the Edit command	E
(Multiplan displays *ORIGINAL* on the command line)	
Append the multiplication symbol and the appropriate percentage	*33.3%
Execute the command	Enter

Row	Length of Term	3-Year (Column 7)	5-Year (Column 8)	7-Year (Column 9)
15	Year 1	33.3%	20%	14.3%
16	Year 2	44.4%	32%	24.5%
17	Year 3	14.8%	19.2%	17.5%
18	Year 4	7.5%	11.5%	12.5%
19	Year 5		11.5%	8.9%
20	Year 6		5.8%	8.9%
21	Year 7			8.9%
22	Year 8			4.5%

FIGURE 13-4.

MACRS depreciation schedule

You now have *33.3% at the end of the formula. Move the cursor to R16C7 (year 2 of the 3-year schedule) and type E (Edit). Type *44.4% and press Enter.

Before you continue, look again at the MACRS schedules. Years 4 and 5 in the 5-year schedule use 11.5%, and years 5, 6, and 7 in the 7-year schedule use 8.9%. You can speed up your editing a bit by editing the first formula in this group, then using Copy Down to copy it into the other cell or cells. Now continue editing until all the MACRS formulas have their proper percentages.

FORMULA 15: Totals

SUM(R[-11]C:R[-1]C)

Formula 15 adds the straight line entries in rows 15 through 24 of column 2 and enters the result in R26C2. The formula includes the line in row 25. This lets you insert rows between rows 25 and 26 to expand the number of years your depreciation spreadsheet can handle.

Place the cursor on R26C2:	Type or move the cursor:
Start the Value command	V
Enter the formula: SUM (R15C2:R25C2)	SUM(R[-11]C:R[-1]C)
Execute the command	Enter

To produce the total in each column, leave the cursor on R26C2 and type *CR* (Copy Right). Type 7 and press Enter. Now press F4 to recalculate.

Uh-oh! The estimated hours in R26C5 are now shown as dollars. When you copied Formula 15, you also copied its dollar format. No problem. Let's reformat the cell: Place the cursor on R26C5. Type *FC* (Format Cells) and press the Tab key to move to the *alignment* field. Type C to select *Ctr* (Center) and press the Tab key again to move to the *format code* field. Type D to select *Def* (Default) and press Enter. You now have the SUM formula and the correct format in the cell.

FORMULA 16: Recheck Flag

IF(R[− 1]C = LIFE, "AGREE", "CHECK YOUR NUMBERS")

Formula 16 produces one of two messages. The Test statement compares the estimated hours of useful life (R8C9, LIFE) and the total in R26C5. If the two numbers agree, the Then statement enters the word *AGREE* in R27C5. If they don't agree, which causes the units of production numbers to be off, the Else statement flags you with the message *CHECK YOUR NUMBERS*.

Place the cursor on R27C5:	**Type or move the cursor:**
Start the Value command	V
Enter the formula: IF(R26C5 = LIFE, "AGREE", "CHECK YOUR NUMBERS") *Translation:* IF(total of column 5 equals estimated useful life, then enter AGREE, else enter CHECK YOUR NUMBERS)	IF(R[− 1]C = LIFE, "AGREE", "CHECK YOUR NUMBERS")
Execute the command	Enter

Cells R26C5 and R8C9 both contain *12000*, so *AGREE* appears on cue.

FORMULA 17: Spreadsheet Filename

NAME()

Formula 17 generates the spreadsheet filename in R1C9. Type the function name and parentheses.

Place the cursor on R1C9:	**Type or press:**
Start the Value command	V
Enter the formula: NAME()	NAME()
Execute the command	Enter

Locking the Formulas

Now, to prevent accidental changes, lock the formula cells.

Leave the cursor where it is:	Type:
Start the Lock command	L
Select the Formulas option	F
(Multiplan displays *Enter Y to confirm*)	
Confirm the lock	Y

Saving the Formulas

Now store all your work on disk. Because you saved the spreadsheet before, Multiplan asks you to confirm your intention to overwrite the earlier version.

Leave the cursor where it is:	Type or press:
Start the Transfer command	T
Select the Save option	S
(Multiplan displays *DEPREC*—there's no need to retype)	
Execute the command	Enter
(Multiplan recalculates the spreadsheet, then displays *Enter Y to overwrite file*)	
Confirm the overwrite	Y

ENTERING THE TRANSIENT TEXT AND MORE NUMBERS

Now complete this spreadsheet by entering the transient text (text you plan to change regularly) and the remaining numbers. Place the cursor on R3C3 and type *A* (Alpha). Now type *Offset Press #1255A* and move the cursor to R7C3. Type *36000* and move the cursor to R8C3. Type *4000* and press Enter.

Now for the fun stuff. Move the cursor to R26C8 so that you have a good view of the action. Press F4 and watch your spreadsheet come alive! Move the cursor around the spreadsheet to bring other areas of it into view. Your spreadsheet should now look just like the one in Figure 13-1, at the beginning of this chapter.

PRINTING YOUR SPREADSHEET

This spreadsheet is 131 characters wide on a single sheet of paper, including Multiplan row numbers, and is printed in 12-pitch type. Using a wide-carriage printer and 15-by-11-inch paper, it prints across the page. Using 8½-by-11-inch paper, you can print the spreadsheet in one of two ways: on two consecutive sheets or on one sheet, with columns 1 through 5 printed on the top half and columns 6 through 9 printed immediately below.

Setting the Print Margins

The first step before printing is to set the margins around your spreadsheet.

Leave the cursor where it is:	Type or press:
Start the Print command	P
Select the Margins option	M

Type the following numbers in the margins fields. (Tab past any field that already has the proper setting.) If you overshoot a field, press Tab a few times to move full circle through the fields or press Shift-Tab to move backward one field at a time. The highlight is in the *left* field.

To do this:	Type or press:
For one sheet of 8½-by-11-inch paper:	
Specify the number of characters	10
Move the highlight to *top*	Tab
Specify the number of lines	2
Move the highlight to *print width*	Tab
Specify the number of characters	75
Move the highlight to *print length*	Tab
Specify the number of lines	28
Move the highlight to *page length*	Tab
Specify the number of lines	30
Execute the command	Enter

If you want this spreadsheet to print on two consecutive sheets of 8½-by-11-inch paper, use 60 for *print length* and 66 for *page length*. Use the following settings for a wide-carriage printer.

To do this:	Type or press:
For 15-by-11-inch paper:	
Specify the number of characters	15
Move the highlight to *top*	Tab
Specify the number of lines	6

Move the highlight to *print width*	Tab
Specify the number of characters	131
Move the highlight to *print length*	Tab
Specify the number of lines	60
Move the highlight to *page length*	Tab
Specify the number of lines	66
Execute the command	Enter

Setting the Print Options

You are still in the Print command. The next step is to set the print options. These settings (the same for every spreadsheet in this book) print the entire spreadsheet in 12-pitch type with row and column numbers, which helps you compare your results with the figures in this chapter. You can find the printer code for 12-pitch type in your printer manual.

Now type O to select the Options option. Type in the following responses. (Tab past any field that already has the proper setting.) The highlight is in the *area* field.

To do this:	Type or press:
Define the print area	R1:4095
Move the highlight to *setup*	Tab
Enter your printer code for 12-pitch type	(your code)
Move the highlight to *formulas*	Tab Tab
Select *No*	N
Move the highlight to *row-col numbers*	Tab
Select *Yes*	Y
Execute the command	Enter

Now, before you print, store the spreadsheet with the print settings: Exit the Print command by pressing the Escape key. Leave the cursor where it is. Type *TS* and press Enter. Type Y.

Printing the Spreadsheet

Now turn on your printer and print a copy of your spreadsheet.

Leave the cursor where it is:	Type:
Start the Print command	P
Select the Printer option	P

USING YOUR SPREADSHEET

You can now try out your "What if?" assumptions to your heart's content. Enter another type of asset, change the original cost, enter another estimated salvage value, modify the length of term, or change the estimated useful life. A feast of five different methods of depreciation is spread out before you. Enjoy!

Printing Different Kinds of Reports

Multiplan can produce a variety of printed reports, including the ones shown in Figures 13-5 and 13-6, so leave your printer on and ready to print. The Run command, which you used earlier to enter a new date in DOS, can print a list of all the names you've assigned to cells, as shown in Figure 13-5, which is useful for troubleshooting a spreadsheet and for documentation. If you need to, align the paper in your printer so that the top of the page is at the proper place.

```
DBYEAR1:                    Macro - No        Command Code -  none
    R15C6

DEPRECIABLE:                Macro - No        Command Code -  none
    R9C3

DRATE:                      Macro - No        Command Code -  none
    R9C9

LIFE:                       Macro - No        Command Code -  none
    R8C9

ORIGINAL:                   Macro - No        Command Code -  none
    R7C3

SALVAGE:                    Macro - No        Command Code -  none
    R8C3

TERM:                       Macro - No        Command Code -  none
    R10C3
```

FIGURE 13-5.

A report listing the cell names on the five-in-one depreciation analysis spreadsheet

```
0 Cells have a value of #NULL!.
0 Cells have a value of #DIV/0!.
0 Cells have a value of #VALUE!.
0 Cells have a value of #REF!.
0 Cells have a value of #NAME?.
0 Cells have a value of #NUM!.
0 Cells have a value of #N/A.
3 Formulas that reference blank cells.
R26C7      R26C8      R26C9
0 Cells with formats but no value.
0 Named areas that overlap.
0 Names are partially locked.
0 Cells contain a Circular Reference.
```

FIGURE 13-6.

A report summarizing existing conditions on the five-in-one depreciation analysis spreadsheet

Leave the cursor where it is:	Type:
Start the Run command	R
Select the Report option	R
Select the Print option	P
Select the Names option	N
Select the All option	A

Let's do it again, this time printing a summary of conditions on your spreadsheet, which can pinpoint existing problems or flag potential ones: Leave the cursor where it is and type *RRPSF* (Run Report Print Summary Full). Your report should look like the one in Figure 13-6.

Several other reports you can produce with the Run command provide information that is just as valuable and far-reaching. One of them, a comprehensive cross-reference report, identifies the format, contents, and name of every active cell on the spreadsheet and the relationship of each to the others. The pages run on and on, so it will take a long time to print. To start printing it, type *RRPC* (Run Report Print Cross-Ref) and press Enter. It's a guaranteed eye-opener. Try it.

SPREADSHEET SUMMARY

General: The completed spreadsheet is shown in Figure 13-1. Use Options to set automatic recalculation to *No*. Use Value to enter REPT(" = ",14) and REPT(" − ",14) for long lines. Use Lock Formulas to lock formulas.

Column Width: Use Format Default Width to set all columns to 14 characters wide.

Format: Use Format Default Cells to continue all the titles. Use Format Cells as follows: Center R27C5, R12, R13, R15C1:R24C1, R15:26C5. Right-justify R26C1 and R1C9. Dollar code R7:9C3, R9C9, R15:16C2, R15:16C3, R15:16C4, R15:24C6, R15C7, and R26C2. Give R6C3 the fixed format with two decimal places. Use Format Time-Date Cells to enter the custom format mmm d, yyyy in R4C3:R5C3. Use Format Options to insert commas in the large numbers.

Name: Use Name as follows: R7C3 is ORIGINAL. R8C3 is SALVAGE. R9C3 is DEPRECIABLE. R10C3 is TERM. R8C9 is LIFE. R9C9 is DRATE. R15C6 is DBYEAR1.

Print: Depreciation Analysis is 131 characters wide on one sheet of paper, including Multiplan row numbers, and is printed in 12-pitch type. The following settings print the spreadsheet on one sheet of 8½-by-11-inch paper: *left* 10, *top* 2, *print width* 75, *print length* 28, and *page length* 30. To print on two consecutive sheets of 8½-by-11-inch paper, use the previous settings for *left*, *top*, and *print width*, but set *print length* to 60 and *page length* to 66. On 15-by-11-inch paper, the following settings print the spreadsheet across the page: *left* 15, *top* 6, *print width* 131, *print length* 60, and *page length* 66.

Formulas: Formulas use relative and named cell references.

1	R5C3	Today's Date NOW()
2	R6C3	Service to Date in Years (R[−1]C−R[−2]C)/365
3	R9C3	Depreciable Cost ORIGINAL − SALVAGE
4	R16C1	Year Numbers 1+R[−1]C
5	R15C2	Straight-Line Method IF(RC[−1]<=TERM,DEPRECIABLE /TERM,0)
6	R15C3	Sum-of-The-Years'-Digits Method—Year 1 TERM * DEPRECIABLE /(TERM * (TERM + 1)/2)

7	R16C3	Sum-of-The-Years'-Digits — Year 2 IF(RC[− 2] < = TERM,(TERM − R[− 1]C[− 2]) * DEPRECIABLE /(TERM * (TERM + 1)/2),0)
8	R9C9	Hourly Depreciation Rate DEPRECIABLE/LIFE
9	R15C4	Units of Production Method RC[+ 1] * DRATE
10	R15C6	Declining – Balance — Year 1 ORIGINAL * 20%
11	R16C6	Declining-Balance — Year 2 (ORIGINAL − DBYEAR1) * 20%
12	R17C6	Declining-Balance — Year 3 (ORIGINAL − SUM(R[− 1]C:DBYEAR1)) * 20%
13	R24C6	Declining-Balance — Year 10 DEPRECIABLE − SUM(DBYEAR1:R[− 1]C)
14	R15C7	MACRS Base Formula ORIGINAL (See schedules in Figure 13-4 for percentage rates)
15	R26C2	Totals SUM(R[− 11]C:R[− 1]C)
16	R27C5	Recheck Flag IF(R[− 1]C = LIFE,"AGREE","CHECK YOUR NUMBERS")
17	R1C9	Spreadsheet Filename Name()

14

Cash Flow Analysis

areful financial planning is a continuing necessity for the business manager. Knowing your cash flow, forecasting your cash needs, planning to borrow at the proper time, and substantiating your firm's payback ability are all factors of sound cash management—and profitability.

Cash flow is the difference between receipts and disbursements for a given period. Cash flow analysis involves the assessment of all elements of a business on an after-tax basis. Tracking these elements can help to eliminate errors in judgment made in haste or based on assumptions rather than facts.

Even with sound cash management, there will be times when inflow will not cover the cost of everyday operations, major improvements, or expansion. Borrowing can then provide the money needed. But first you must know how much money you need to borrow and whether the cash flow of the business will be sufficient to pay back the loan. This is when cash flow projection becomes critical to survival.

For the example in this chapter, let's suppose you run a firm that manufactures and sells telecommunications equipment. You are considering buying a small company that manufactures fiber optic products. The purchase will require a significant outlay of funds. You need to know how much cash flow this expansion will generate and if you can reasonably expect it to cover the operating costs of a new division plus repayment of a sizable loan.

The cash flow spreadsheet in Figure 14-1 can answer these questions. It's designed to give you far-reaching flexibility in analyzing the financial condition of an existing business and any enticing investment opportunities that come

	1	2	3	4	5	6 CASH FLOW
1						
2	==
3	Cash Invested	$200,000.00				
4	Amount Financed	$800,000.00				
5	Term in Years	10				
6	Annual Interest Rate (%)	15.00				
7	Annual Loan Payment	$154,881.56				
8	Total Loan Payment	$1,548,815.59				
9						
10		YEAR 1	%Sales	%Inc	YEAR 2	%Sales
11		----------------------			-----------------------	
12	Cash Sales	900,000	100.0%	20	1,080,000	100.0%
13	Cost of Goods Sold	315,000	35.0%	35	378,000	35.0%
14		---------	-----		---------	-----
15	Gross Profit	585,000	65.0%		702,000	65.0%
16						
17	Cash Disbursements					
18	Salaries	150,000	16.7%	11	166,500	15.4%
19	Payroll Taxes	30,000	3.3%		33,300	3.1%
20	Rent	36,000	4.0%	15	41,400	3.8%
21	Advertising	55,000	6.1%	15	63,250	5.9%
22	Insurance	30,000	3.3%	10	33,000	3.1%
23	Office Expenses	18,000	2.0%	12	20,160	1.9%
24	Professional Fees	25,000	2.8%	15	28,750	2.7%
25	Utilities/Phone	15,000	1.7%	8	16,200	1.5%
26		---------	-----		---------	-----
27	Total Operating Expenses	359,000	39.9%		402,560	37.3%
28	Loan Repayment	154,882	17.2%		154,882	14.3%
29		---------	-----		---------	-----
30	Total Cash Disbursements	513,882	57.1%		557,442	51.6%
31		---------	-----		---------	-----
32	Cash Flow before Taxes	71,118	7.9%		144,558	13.4%
33		=========	=====		=========	=====
34	Less: Income Tax	22,345	2.5%		3,900	0.4%
35		---------	-----		---------	-----
36	Cash Flow after Taxes	48,773	5.4%		140,658	13.0%
37		=========	=====		=========	=====
38	Return on Capital Invested	4.9%			14.1%	
39						
40	==
41	Loan Summary-Approximate					
42	Principal Remaining	765,118			725,005	
43	Annual Interest Paid	120,000			114,768	
44	Annual Principal Paid	34,882			40,114	
45	==
46	***** WORK AREA *****					
47	Cost of Property Acquired	400,000				
48	MACRS Depreciation (5-Year)	80,000			128,000	
49	Taxable Income				26,000	
50	Income Tax if Taxable >=75000				0	
51	Income Tax if Taxable <75000				3,900	
52	==

FIGURE 14-1.

The completed cash flow analysis spreadsheet

```
  7          8           9    10      11          12    13      14           15
ANALYSIS                                                     CASHFLOW
===========================================================================================
```

%Inc	YEAR 3	%Sales	%Inc	YEAR 4	%Sales	%Inc	YEAR 5	%Sales
20	1,296,000	100.0%	20	1,555,200	100.0%	20	1,866,240	100.0%
35	453,600	35.0%	35	544,320	35.0%	35	653,184	35.0%
	842,400	65.0%		1,010,880	65.0%		1,213,056	65.0%
11	184,815	14.3%	11	205,145	13.2%	11	227,711	12.2%
	36,963	2.9%		41,029	2.6%		45,542	2.4%
15	47,610	3.7%	15	54,752	3.5%	15	62,964	3.4%
15	72,738	5.6%	15	83,648	5.4%	15	96,195	5.2%
10	36,300	2.8%	10	39,930	2.6%	10	43,923	2.4%
12	22,579	1.7%	12	25,289	1.6%	12	28,323	1.5%
15	33,063	2.6%	15	38,022	2.4%	15	43,725	2.3%
8	17,496	1.4%	8	18,896	1.2%	8	20,407	1.1%
	451,563	34.8%		506,709	32.6%		568,791	30.5%
	154,882	12.0%		154,882	10.0%		154,882	8.3%
	606,445	46.8%		661,591	42.5%		723,673	38.8%
	235,955	18.2%		349,289	22.5%		489,383	26.2%
	9,168	0.7%		58,047	3.7%		109,405	5.9%
	226,787	17.5%		291,242	18.7%		379,978	20.4%
	22.7%			29.1%			38.0%	

```
===========================================================================================

       678,874                   625,823                   564,815
       108,751                   101,831                    93,873
        46,131                    53,050                    61,008
===========================================================================================

        76,800                    46,000                    46,000
        56,672                   205,286                   356,339
             0                    58,047                   109,405
         9,168                         0                         0
===========================================================================================
```

your way. When you enter your estimates on loans, investments, sales, and disbursements, the spreadsheet presents this dazzling array of features and formulas for a five-year period:

■ A loan amortization formula that calculates the precise annual payments on a prospective loan.

■ Formulas that show the mix of interest and principal paid each year and the principal remaining. Later in this chapter, you'll replace these formulas with others that employ Multiplan's powerful iteration feature to produce to-the-penny results.

■ A 5-year MACRS (Modified Accelerated Cost Recovery System) depreciation schedule.

■ Before- and after-tax cash flows.

■ Taxable income each year and formulas that calculate corporate taxes.

■ A group of "What if?" cells with which you can project the inflow and outflow of funds.

Good estimates, even when they are truly informed projections, are still subject to uncontrollable influences. One of the great advantages of this spreadsheet is the speed with which you can change your estimates as conditions change so that you can instantly see the effects on cash flow and return on capital investment.

If you're familiar with Multiplan and prefer to create the cash flow spreadsheet without following the step-by-step instructions, refer to the summary at the end of this chapter.

SETTING UP YOUR SPREADSHEET

Bring up the Multiplan screen. If you turned off automatic recalculation on your last spreadsheet, you can skip the following instructions and go on to "Adjusting the Column Widths." Otherwise, to make data entry faster, leave the cursor where it is. Type O to start the Options command, type N for no recalculation, and press Enter. Now let's make your spreadsheet look like the one in Figure 14-2.

Adjusting the Column Widths

This spreadsheet has 15 columns filled with information. We can adjust the width of every column to give the entries the space they need and still print the spreadsheet on one 15-by-11-inch or two 8½-by-11-inch sheets of paper. Let's start by increasing the width of column 1 to 29 characters.

Leave the cursor on R1C1:	Type or press:
Start the Format command	F
Select the Width option	W
Specify the number of characters in the column	29
Execute the command	Enter

Use the same procedure to change the widths of the other columns, according to the following table:

Column Number:	Width in Characters:
2	14
3	7
4	6
5	14
6	7
7	6
8	14
9	7
10	6
11	14
12	7
13	6
14	14
15	7

Entering the Titles

The next step is to type the titles shown in Figure 14-2. The titles in rows 18 through 25, 28, and 34 in column 1 are indented one space. Press the Spacebar once before typing each one. Otherwise, type the titles without indents.

If you mistype, press the Backspace key, not a direction key, to back up the highlight and erase; or use the F7 through F10 keys to move the highlight through the text, then press the Delete key to delete unwanted characters or type missing characters.

First, put Multiplan in the alpha/value mode. Then, you can use either a direction key or the Enter key to enter a title, and Multiplan will keep *ALPHA/VALUE* on the command line ready for your next title (you won't have to type *A* for Alpha each time). Let's activate this mode now.

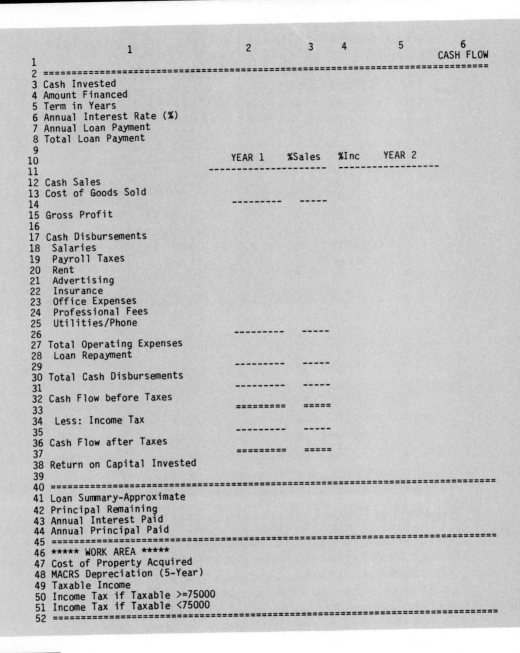

```
                      1                    2        3    4      5        6
                                                                    CASH FLOW
 1
 2 =====================================================================
 3 Cash Invested
 4 Amount Financed
 5 Term in Years
 6 Annual Interest Rate (%)
 7 Annual Loan Payment
 8 Total Loan Payment
 9
                                    YEAR 1    %Sales  %Inc    YEAR 2
10                                  --------------------    ------------------
11
12 Cash Sales
13 Cost of Goods Sold
14                                  ---------  -----
15 Gross Profit
16
17 Cash Disbursements
18   Salaries
19   Payroll Taxes
20   Rent
21   Advertising
22   Insurance
23   Office Expenses
24   Professional Fees
25   Utilities/Phone
26                                  ---------  -----
27 Total Operating Expenses
28   Loan Repayment
29                                  ---------  -----
30 Total Cash Disbursements
31                                  ---------  -----
32 Cash Flow before Taxes
33                                  =========  =====
34   Less: Income Tax
35                                  ---------  -----
36 Cash Flow after Taxes
37                                  =========  =====
38 Return on Capital Invested
39
40 =====================================================================
41 Loan Summary-Approximate
42 Principal Remaining
43 Annual Interest Paid
44 Annual Principal Paid
45 =====================================================================
46 ***** WORK AREA *****
47 Cost of Property Acquired
48 MACRS Depreciation (5-Year)
49 Taxable Income
50 Income Tax if Taxable >=75000
51 Income Tax if Taxable <75000
52 =====================================================================
```

FIGURE 14-2.

The titles and lines on the cash flow analysis spreadsheet

```
7            8             9   10         11         12   13         14         15
ANALYSIS
==============================================================================
```

                    YEAR 3   YEAR 4   YEAR 5

```
==============================================================================


==============================================================================


==============================================================================
```

Leave the cursor where it is:	**Type or press:**
Start the Options command	O
Move the highlight to *alpha/value*	Tab (four times)
Select *Yes*	Y
Execute the command	Enter

ALPHA/VALUE is now on the command line and will remain until you restore the standard setting after you type all the titles. If you need to work with a command other than Alpha or Value, press Escape to return the command menu to the screen. When you press Enter to execute that command, Multiplan returns to the alpha/value mode.

Now move the cursor to R1C6. Type the spreadsheet title *CASH FLOW ANALYSIS* and move the cursor to R3C1. Only the first part of the title appears in the cell. Don't be concerned. We'll take care of that shortly. Now type *Cash Invested* and move the cursor to R4C1. Type *Amount Financed* and move the cursor to the next cell down. Type *Term in Years* and move the cursor again. Continue in this way, moving the cursor and typing a title, until you type all the titles shown in Figure 14-2. Now press Enter.

Leave the cursor where it is and press Escape to return the command menu to the screen. Next, restore Multiplan's standard command mode: Type O (Options) and press Tab four times to move the highlight to *alpha/value*. Type N to select *No* and press Enter.

Entering the Lines

The next step is to use a formula containing the REPT function and an equal sign to enter a double line across row 2. Let's start by filling cell R2C1 with 29 equal signs.

Place the cursor on R2C1:	**Type or press:**
Start the Value command	V
Repeat an equal sign 29 times	REPT(" = ",29)
Execute the command	Enter

Now copy the formula in R2C1 into the columns to the right.

Leave the cursor on R2C1:	**Type or press:**
Start the Copy command	C
Select the Right option	R
Specify the number of cells to copy into	14
Execute the command	Enter

Rows 40, 45, and 52 need the same kind of line, so copy the formula from row 2. Where you see a colon in the column on the right side of the following instructions, as before the number 15, press the F6 key to produce the colon.

Leave the cursor on R2C1:	**Type or press:**
Start the Copy command	C
Select the From option	F
(Multiplan displays *COPY FROM cells: R2C1*, the first cell to copy from)	
Specify the last cell to copy from	:15
Move the highlight to *to cells*	Tab
Specify the first cell in each row to copy into	R40C1,R45C1, R52C1
Execute the command	Enter

There are many short lines on this spreadsheet. We'll use Copy From as much as possible to make entering these lines as easy as possible. Let's first create the line under the title *YEAR 1* in column 2:

Place the cursor on R11C2:	**Type or press:**
Start the Value command	V
Repeat a minus sign 14 times	REPT(" – ",14)
Execute the command	Enter

Now copy this formula to underline the titles *%Sales* (percent of sales) in column 3 and *YEAR 2* in column 5.

Leave the cursor on R11C2:	**Type or press:**
Start the Copy command	C
Select the From option	F
(Multiplan displays *COPY FROM cells: R11C2*, the cell to copy from)	
Move the highlight to *to cells*	Tab
Specify the cells to copy into	R11C3,R11C5
Execute the command	Enter

Next, create a line under the title *%Inc* (percent increase) in column 4. To produce a line that aligns nicely with the numbers above and below it, indent two spaces before typing the minus signs.

Place the cursor on R11C4:	Type or press:
Start the Alpha command	A
Indent two spaces	Spacebar Spacebar
Type four minus signs	$-\ -\ -\ -$

Don't bother to press Enter. Just move the cursor to R14C2. To create a line in this cell, press the Spacebar four times and type nine minus signs. Now move the cursor to R14C3. To create this line, press the Spacebar twice, type five minus signs, and press Enter. Now, copy these lines to the other cells in columns 2 and 3.

Leave the cursor on R14C3:	Type or press:
Start the Copy command	C
Select the From option	F
(Multiplan displays *COPY FROM cells: R14C3*, the first cell to copy from)	
Specify the last cell to copy from	:2
Move the highlight to *to cells*	Tab
Specify the first cell in each row to copy into	R26C2,R29C2, R31C2,R35C2
Execute the command	Enter

Now for the double lines in columns 2 and 3: Place the cursor on R33C2 and type *A*. Press the Spacebar four times and type nine equal signs. No need to press Enter. Move the cursor to R33C3. Press the Spacebar twice, type five equal signs, and press Enter.

And finally, copy these lines from row 33 to row 37: Leave the cursor on R33C3 and type *CF* (Copy From). Type *:2* and press Tab. Type *R37C2* and press Enter.

Formatting the Titles

The next step is to display the title *CASH FLOW ANALYSIS* in full by continuing it into the two cells to its right.

Place the cursor on R1C6:	Type or press:
Start the Format command	F
Select the Cells option	C
(Multiplan displays *FORMAT cells: R1C6*, the first cell to be continuous)	
Specify the last cell to be continuous	:8

Move the highlight to *format code*	Tab Tab
Select *Cont* (continuous)	C
Execute the command	Enter

Next, center the titles in row 10.

Place the cursor on R10C2:	**Type or press:**
Start the Format command	F
Select the Cells option	C
(Multiplan displays *FORMAT cells: R10C2*, the first cell to format)	
Specify the last cell to format	:15
Move the highlight to *alignment*	Tab
Select *Ctr* (center)	C
Execute the command	Enter

Now right-justify the title *%Inc* in R10C4 and the empty R1C14, which will soon contain the spreadsheet filename. You will later copy *%Inc* to years 3, 4, and 5. When you do, it will copy the right-justified format.

Place the cursor on R10C4:	**Type or press:**
Start the Format command	F
Select the Cells option	C
(Multiplan displays *FORMAT cells: R10C4*, the first cell to format)	
Specify the other cell to format	,R1C14
Move the highlight to *alignment*	Tab
Select *Right*	R
Execute the command	Enter

Formatting the Number Cells

Now format the cells that will contain the cash invested (R3C2), amount financed (R4C2), annual loan payment (R7C2), and total loan payment (R8C2) to show their contents in dollars and cents.

Place the cursor on R3C2:	**Type or press:**
Start the Format command	F
Select the Cells option	C

(Multiplan displays *FORMAT cells: R3C2*, the first cell to format)

Specify the other cells to format	:R4C2,R7:8C2
Move the highlight to *format code*	Tab Tab
Select *$*	$
Execute the command	Enter

Now format the annual interest rate cell (R6C2) to show a fixed number with two decimal places.

Place the cursor on R6C2:	**Type or press:**
Start the Format command	F
Select the Cells option	C
(Multiplan displays *FORMAT cells: R6C2*, the cell to format)	
Move the highlight to *format code*	Tab Tab
Select *Fix*	F
Move the highlight to *# of decimals*	Tab
Specify the number of decimals	2
Execute the command	Enter

Next, format the percent of sales cells in column 3 to show their contents as percentages with one decimal place. For simplicity, let's treat these cells as a range even though some of them won't contain anything and others contain a line. We need the same format in R38C2 (return on capital invested), so include it in the group.

Place the cursor on R12C3:	**Type or press:**
Start the Format command	F
Select the Cells option	C
(Multiplan displays *FORMAT cells: R12C3*, the first cell to format)	
Specify the other cells to format	:R36C3,R38C2
Move the highlight to *format code*	Tab Tab
Select *%*	%
Move the highlight to *# of decimals*	Tab
Specify the number of decimals	1
Execute the command	Enter

Inserting Commas in the Large Numbers

Large numbers are easier to read when commas separate the digits. Before that can occur, however, the numbers must be in a dollar, percent, fixed, or integer format. Many cells already have one of these formats. Let's format the rest for integers.

Leave the cursor where it is:	Type or press:
Start the Format command	F
Select the Default option	D
Select the Cells option	C
Move the highlight to *format code*	Tab
Select *Int* (integer)	I
Execute the command	Enter

Now tell Multiplan to insert commas in all large numbers: Leave the cursor where it is and type *FO* (Format Options). Type *Y* to select *Yes* in the *commas* field, and press Enter.

NAMING THE CELLS

The unshaded areas in Figure 14-3 show the locations of the named cells that the formulas use in their calculations. Named cell references make the formulas easy to enter and understand. Let's start by naming R3C2, the cell containing the cash invested, INVEST.

Place the cursor on R3C2:	Type:
Start the Name command	N
Name the cell	INVEST

In the *to refer to* field to the right, you see R3C2. This location is correct, so simply press Enter. Use the same procedure to name the following cells (be sure to press Enter after you type each name):

Place the cursor on:	Type the name:
R4C2	LOAN
R5C2	TERM
R6C2	RATE
R7C2	PAY
R47C2	PROPERTY

```
                    1                    2        3      4       5        6
 1                                                                     CASH FLOW
 2 ============================================================================
 3 Cash Invested                      200000  INVEST
 4 Amount Financed                    800000  LOAN
 5 Term in Years                          10  TERM
 6 Annual Interest Rate (%)               15  RATE
 7 Annual Loan Payment                  ①      PAY
 8 Total Loan Payment                   ②
 9
10                                 YEAR 1   %Sales   %Inc   YEAR 2
11                                 ---------------------  -----------------
12 Cash Sales                      900000      1      20            ⑫
13 Cost of Goods Sold                 ③               35            ⑬
14                                 --------- ------         ---------
15 Gross Profit                       ④
16
17 Cash Disbursements
18   Salaries                      150000             11
19   Payroll Taxes                    ⑤
20   Rent                           36000             15
21   Advertising                    55000             15
22   Insurance                      30000             10
23   Office Expenses                18000             12
24   Professional Fees              25000             15
25   Utilities/Phone                15000              8
26                                 --------- ------         ---------
27 Total Operating Expenses           ⑥
28   Loan Repayment                   ⑦
29                                 --------- ------         ---------
30 Total Cash Disbursements           ⑧
31                                 --------- ------         ---------
32 Cash Flow before Taxes             ⑨
33                                 ========= =====         =========
34   Less: Income Tax              22345                        ⑭
35                                 --------- ------         ---------
36 Cash Flow after Taxes             ⑩
37                                 ========= =====         =========
38 Return on Capital Invested        ⑪
39
40 ============================================================================
41 Loan Summary-Approximate
42 Principal Remaining                ⑮                       ⑯
43 Annual Interest Paid               ⑰                       ⑱
44 Annual Principal Paid              ⑲
45 ============================================================================
46 ***** WORK AREA *****
47 Cost of Property Acquired       400000  PROPERTY
48 MACRS Depreciation (5-Year)        ⑳
49 Taxable Income                                             ㉑
50 Income Tax if Taxable >=75000                              ㉒
51 Income Tax if Taxable <75000                               ㉓
52 ============================================================================
```

FIGURE 14-3.

Cash flow analysis named cells, practice numbers, and formula locations

```
7         8         9   10        11        12   13        14        15
ANALYSIS
========================================================================
```

```
          YEAR 3                  YEAR 4                  YEAR 5
```

```
========================================================================
```

```
========================================================================
```

```
========================================================================
```

Saving and Naming the Spreadsheet

Now store the spreadsheet on disk with the titles, lines, formats, and cell names, and give it a filename. If you need to specify which drive contains your data disk or which directory to store the file in, type the drive letter and press F6 (to produce a colon) or type the pathname before you type *CASHFLOW*, the filename.

Leave the cursor where it is:	Type or press:
Start the Transfer command	T
Select the Save option	S
Name the spreadsheet	CASHFLOW
Execute the command	Enter

ENTERING THE PRACTICE NUMBERS

Figure 14-3 contains estimates of what it will take to run this business (when you enter numbers for your business, the estimates will be your own). A cash investment of $200,000 and a loan of $800,000 are needed to get the business off to a good start. The 10-year loan at 15 percent interest reflects assumptions on the cost of cash and payback time.

Column 2 shows the projected sales and most of the expenses for the first year of operation. The amount in R34C2 (*22,345*) is the income tax paid on the preceding year's profits. The tax figure is not calculated by this spreadsheet. The amount in R47C2 (*$400,000*) is the depreciable property acquired with the company. The entries in column 4 (where you will do most of your "What if?" experimenting) are estimated increases in sales and expenses during the second year of operation.

You can type a number any time you see the command menu on the screen or *ALPHA/VALUE* on the command line. Simply type the number, then move the cursor to the next cell that will contain a number. Type that number, move the cursor again, and so on. Because of the formatting you did earlier, Multiplan will enter the dollar signs, commas, and decimal places. Now enter the numbers as follows:

1. Place the cursor on R3C2. Type *200000* and move the cursor to R4C2. Type *800000* and move the cursor to R5C2. Type the next number and move the cursor again. Continue typing numbers and moving the cursor down column 2 until you type the number in R47C2.

2. Move the cursor to R12C3 and type the number *1*. (When you move the cursor away, the entry appears in the cell as *100.0%*.)

3. Type the numbers in column 4 in rows 12, 13, 18, and 20 through 25. After you type the last number, press Enter. You will enter the short lines in column 5 after you enter the formulas.

ENTERING THE FORMULAS

The circled numbers in Figure 14-3 show the locations of the formulas that perform the calculations. The formulas use relative and named cell references. The left column in the following instructions contains the locations of the relative references, names of named cells, and other elements in the formula. The column on the right side of the instructions and the line before the formula description show the finished formula.

To build a formula, move the cursor to each cell location shown in the left column (Multiplan will produce the relative notation) and type everything else—operators, symbols, function names, and cell names. Each time you type a character, the cursor returns to the formula cell so that you can type another character, move the cursor to another cell, or enter the formula.

When your formula agrees with the instructions, press Enter. If Multiplan then displays *Not a valid formula*, check each character. Use the F7 through F10 keys to move the highlight, and correct the problem by typing missing characters or pressing the Delete key to erase unwanted characters. If you prefer to start the formula from scratch, simply press the Escape key and begin again. After you enter each formula, compare your results with those shown in Figure 14-4.

Because of the large number of formulas on this spreadsheet and the complexity of some of them, save your spreadsheet often, even when the instructions don't tell you to do so. Just type *TS* (Transfer Save), press Enter, and type *Y* to overwrite.

FORMULA 1: Annual Loan Payment

ABS(PMT(RATE%/12,TERM*12,LOAN))*12

Formula 1 amortizes the loan in equal monthly installments (including principal and interest), then it multiplies the result by 12 to produce the annual loan payment in R7C2. The PMT (payment) function calculates the payments based on the annual interest rate (R6C2, RATE) divided by 12 to get the monthly interest rate, the term in years (R5C2, TERM) multiplied by 12 to get the number of payments, and the amount financed (R4C2, LOAN). A payment is an outflow of funds (a negative number). The ABS (absolute) function converts the negative result produced by PMT to a positive result. All the cell locations are named, so type the entire formula.

	1	2	3	4	5	6 CASH FLOW

```
 1  
 2  ============================================================================
 3  Cash Invested                    $200,000.00
 4  Amount Financed                  $800,000.00
 5  Term in Years                           10
 6  Annual Interest Rate (%)             15.00
 7  Annual Loan Payment             $154,881.56
 8  Total Loan Payment            $1,548,815.59
 9  
10                                   YEAR 1    %Sales   %Inc    YEAR 2
11                                 -----------          --------  ----------
12  Cash Sales                       900,000   100.0%    20    1,080,000
13  Cost of Goods Sold               315,000     ㉕      35      378,000
14                                 ----------   -----            ----------
15  Gross Profit                     585,000                      702,000
16  
17  Cash Disbursements
18    Salaries                       150,000              11      166,500
19    Payroll Taxes                   30,000                       33,300
20    Rent                            36,000              15       41,400
21    Advertising                     55,000              15       63,250
22    Insurance                       30,000              10       33,000
23    Office Expenses                 18,000              12       20,160
24    Professional Fees               25,000              15       28,750
25    Utilities/Phone                 15,000               8       16,200
26                                 ----------   -----            ----------
27  Total Operating Expenses         359,000                      402,560
28    Loan Repayment                 154,882                      154,882
29                                 ----------   -----            ----------
30  Total Cash Disbursements         513,882                      557,442
31                                 ----------   -----            ----------
32  Cash Flow before Taxes            71,118                      144,558
33                                 ========    =====            =========
34    Less: Income Tax                22,345                        3,900
35                                 ----------   -----            ----------
36  Cash Flow after Taxes             48,773                      140,658
37                                 ========    =====            =========
38  Return on Capital Invested         4.9%                        14.1%
39  
40  ============================================================================
41  Loan Summary-Approximate
42  Principal Remaining              765,118                      725,005
43  Annual Interest Paid             120,000                      114,768
44  Annual Principal Paid             34,882                       40,114
45  ============================================================================
46  ***** WORK AREA *****
47  Cost of Property Acquired        400,000
48  MACRS Depreciation (5-Year)       80,000                      128,000
49  Taxable Income                                                 26,000
50  Income Tax if Taxable >=75000                                       0
51  Income Tax if Taxable <75000                                    3,900
52  ============================================================================
```

FIGURE 14-4.

Cash flow analysis formula results and the locations of two more formulas: spreadsheet filename and percent of sales

```
7              8        9    10       11         12    13     14            15
ANALYSIS                                                     CASHFLOW ㉔
=============================================================================
```

%Inc	YEAR 3	%Inc	YEAR 4	%Inc	YEAR 5
20	1,296,000	20	1,555,200	20	1,866,240
35	453,600	35	544,320	35	653,184
	---------		---------		---------
	842,400		1,010,880		1,213,056
11	184,815	11	205,145	11	227,711
	36,963		41,029		45,542
15	47,610	15	54,752	15	62,964
15	72,738	15	83,648	15	96,195
10	36,300	10	39,930	10	43,923
12	22,579	12	25,289	12	28,323
15	33,063	15	38,022	15	43,725
8	17,496	8	18,896	8	20,407
	---------		---------		---------
	451,563		506,709		568,791
	154,882		154,882		154,882
	---------		---------		---------
	606,445		661,591		723,673
	---------		---------		---------
	235,955		349,289		489,383
	=========		=========		=========
	9,168		58,047		109,405
	---------		---------		---------
	226,787		291,242		379,978
	=========		=========		=========
	22.7%		29.1%		38.0%

```
=============================================================================
```

	678,874		625,823		564,815
	108,751		101,831		93,873
	46,131		53,050		61,008

```
=============================================================================
```

	76,800		46,000		46,000
	56,672		205,286		356,339
	0		58,047		109,405
	9,168		0		0

```
=============================================================================
```

Place the cursor on R7C2:	Type or press:
Start the Value command	V
Enter the formula: ABS(PMT (RATE%/12, TERM * 12,LOAN)) * 12	ABS(PMT(RATE%/12, TERM * 12,LOAN)) * 12
Execute the command	Enter

You now see *$154,881.56* in R7C2.

FORMULA 2: Total Loan Payment

PAY * TERM

Formula 2 multiplies the annual loan payment (R7C2, PAY) by the term (R5C2, TERM) and enters the total payment during the life of the loan in R8C2. Type the entire formula.

Place the cursor on R8C2:	Type or press:
Start the Value command	V
Enter the formula: PAY * TERM	PAY * TERM
Execute the command	Enter

FORMULA 3: Cost of Goods Sold

R[−1]C * 35%

Formula 3 multiplies the cash sales in year 1 (R12C2) by 35%, and enters the cost of goods sold in R13C2.

Place the cursor on R13C2:	Type or move the cursor:
Start the Value command	V
Enter the formula: R12C2 * 35%	R[−1]C * 35%
Execute the command	Enter

FORMULA 4: Gross Profit

R[−3]C − R[−2]C

Formula 4 subtracts the cost of goods sold (R13C2) from the cash sales (R12C2) to produce the projected gross profit for year 1 in R15C2.

Place the cursor on R15C2:	Type or move the cursor:
Start the Value command	V
Enter the formula: R12C2 − R13C2	R[−3]C − R[−2]C
Execute the command	Enter

FORMULA 5: Payroll Taxes

R[−1]C* 20%

Formula 5 multiplies the projected salaries (R18C2) by 20%, and enters the payroll taxes in R19C2. The 20% figure approximates the amount an employer pays for mandated employee benefits, such as social security, unemployment insurance, disability insurance, and so on.

Place the cursor on R19C2:	Type or move the cursor:
Start the Value command	V
Enter the formula: R18C2* 20%	R[−1]C* 20%
Execute the command	Enter

FORMULA 6: Total Operating Expenses

SUM(R[−10]C:R[−1]C)

Formula 6 adds the projected operating expenses in year 1 (rows 18 through 25 of column 2) and enters the result in R27C2. The formula includes the empty cell in R17C2 and the line in R26C2. In this way, you can later insert rows anywhere between these two cells and Multiplan will adjust Formula 6 to include the new items.

Place the cursor on R27C2:	Type or move the cursor:
Start the Value command	V
Enter the formula: SUM (R17C2:R26C2)	SUM(R[−10]C:R[−1]C)
Execute the command	Enter

FORMULA 7: Loan Repayment

PAY

Formula 7 doesn't calculate anything. It simply copies the annual loan payment from R7C2 (PAY) to the loan repayment cell at R28C2. Because cell

R28C2 is formatted to show an integer, the payment amount is rounded to the nearest dollar. Type the one-word formula.

Place the cursor on R28C2:	Type or press:
Start the Value command	V
Enter the formula: PAY	PAY
Execute the command	Enter

FORMULA 8: Total Cash Disbursements

$R[-3]C + R[-2]C$

Formula 8 adds the total operating expenses (R27C2) and loan repayment (R28C2) to produce the total cash disbursements in R30C2.

Place the cursor on R30C2:	Type or move the cursor:
Start the Value command	V
Enter the formula: R27C2 + R28C2	$R[-3]C + R[-2]C$
Execute the command	Enter

FORMULA 9: Cash Flow Before Taxes

$R[-17]C - R[-2]C$

Formula 9 subtracts the total cash disbursements (R30C2) from the gross profit (R15C2) to produce the cash flow before taxes in R32C2.

Place the cursor on R32C2:	Type or move the cursor:
Start the Value command	V
Enter the formula: R15C2 − R30C2	$R[-17]C - R[-2]C$
Execute the command	Enter

FORMULA 10: Cash Flow After Taxes

$R[-4]C - R[-2]C$

Formula 10 subtracts the income tax (R34C2) from the cash flow before taxes (R32C2) and enters the cash flow after taxes in R36C2.

Place the cursor on R36C2:	Type or move the cursor:
Start the Value command	V
Enter the formula: R32C2 − R34C2	$R[-4]C - R[-2]C$
Execute the command	Enter

FORMULA 11: Return on Capital Invested

R[−2]C/(INVEST+LOAN)

Formula 11 divides the cash flow after taxes (R36C2) by the sum of the cash invested (R3C2, INVEST) and amount financed (R4C2, LOAN) and enters the return on capital invested in R38C2.

Place the cursor on R38C2:	Type or move the cursor:
Start the Value command	V
Enter the formula: R36C2 /(INVEST+LOAN)	R[−2]C/(INVEST +LOAN)
Execute the command	Enter

Saving the Formulas

Column 2 now contains the formulas needed in the cash flow section in year 1. So, even if you've been doing so periodically, this is a good time to store all the formulas on disk:

Leave the cursor where it is:	Type or press:
Start the Transfer command	T
Select the Save option	S
(Multiplan displays *CASHFLOW*— there's no need to retype)	
Execute the command	Enter
(Multiplan recalculates the spreadsheet, then displays *Enter Y to overwrite file*)	
Confirm the overwrite	Y

Copying the Formulas from Year 1 to Year 2

Let's make year 2 as complete as possible so that we can copy everything from year 2 to years 3, 4, and 5. We'll start by copying the lines, formulas, and numbers (but not the cash sales in R12C2, the cost of goods sold in R13C2, or the income tax in R34C2) from year 1 to year 2.

Place the cursor on R14C2:	Type or press:
Start the Copy command	C
Select the From option	F
(Multiplan displays *COPY FROM cells: R14C2*, the first cell to copy from)	

Specify the other cells to copy from	:R33C2,R35:38C2
Move the highlight to *to cells*	Tab
Specify the first cell to copy into	R14C5
Execute the command	Enter

FORMULA 12: Sales Projections

RC[− 3] + RC[− 3] * RC[− 1]%

Formula 12 adds the sales in year 1 (R12C2) to the percentage increase in sales (R12C2 times R12C4) and enters the projected sales for year 2 in R12C5. Be sure to type the percent sign at the end of the formula.

Place the cursor on R12C5:	**Type or move the cursor:**
Start the Value command	V
Enter the formula: R12C2 + R12C2 * R12C4%	RC[− 3] + RC[− 3] * RC[− 1]%
Execute the command	Enter

Formula 12 can calculate the dollar amount of each disbursement based on the percentage increase in column 4, so copy it into the cash disbursements cells in year 2 (rows 18 and 20 through 25 in column 5). Formula 12 will replace the numbers now in these cells.

Leave the cursor on R12C5:	**Type or press:**
Start the Copy command	C
Select the From option	F
(Multiplan displays *COPY FROM cells: R12C5*, the cell to copy from)	
Move the highlight to *to cells*	Tab
Specify the cells to copy into	R18C5,R20:25C5
Execute the command	Enter

FORMULA 13: Cost of Goods Sold

R[− 1]C * RC[− 1]%

Formula 13 calculates the cost of goods sold (R13C5) as a percent of sales in year 2 (R12C5), based on the percentage increase you enter in R13C4. Again, don't forget the percent sign at the end of the formula.

Place the cursor on R13C5:	Type or move the cursor:
Start the Value command	V
Enter the formula: R12C5∗R13C4%	R[−1]C∗RC[−1]%
Execute the command	Enter

Now press the F4 (recalculate) key to produce the correct numbers.

FORMULA 14: Income Tax

IF(R[+16]C>0,R[+16]C,R[+17]C)

Formula 14 doesn't calculate anything. It simply copies the income tax in year 2 from one of two cells—R50C5 or R51C5—and enters the amount in R34C5. Cells R50C5 and R51C5 will soon contain formulas that calculate the company's income tax based on its taxable income. The formula in cell R50C5 does its work when taxable income is $75,000 or more; the formula in cell R51C5 does its work when taxable income is less than $75,000.

The IF formula has three parts: the Test statement, the Then statement, and the Else statement. The Test statement looks at R50C5. If the amount in R50C5 is greater than zero (taxable income is $75,000 or more), the Then statement copies that amount from R50C5 to R34C5. If it finds a zero (taxable income is less than $75,000), the Else statement copies the amount from R51C5 instead. These concepts will make more sense when you enter the formulas in the work area.

Place the cursor on R34C5:	Type or move the cursor:
Start the Value command	V
Enter the formula: IF(R50C5>0, R50C5,R51C5)	IF(R[+16]C>0,R[+16]C, R[+17]C)
Translation: IF(income tax in R50C5 is greater than 0, then copy tax in R50C5 for taxable income of $75,000 or more, else copy tax in R51C5 for taxable income of less than $75,000)	
Execute the command	Enter

A zero appears in R34C5 and will remain until you enter the income tax formulas in the work area.

All the entries except income tax (R34C5), cash flow after taxes (R36C5), and return on capital invested (R38C5) should match those in Figure 14-4. Store the spreadsheet on disk: Leave the cursor where it is and type *TS* (Transfer Save), press Enter, and type *Y* to overwrite the earlier version.

Loan Summary—Approximate

The formulas in the loan summary are intended to closely approximate the principal remaining, interest paid, and principal paid each year. They are not designed to produce precise figures. They let you recalculate the spreadsheet quickly, which is a great advantage when you are busily exploring a variety of "What if?" situations. The iteration formulas you'll find later in this chapter will give you precise, though less rapid, results.

FORMULA 15: Principal Remaining—Year 1

LOAN − R[+ 2]C

Formula 15 deducts the principal paid in year 1 (R44C2) from the amount of the loan (R4C2, LOAN) and enters the principal remaining in year 1 in R42C2.

Place the cursor on R42C2:	Type or move the cursor:
Start the Value command	V
Enter the formula: LOAN − R44C2	LOAN − R[+ 2]C
Execute the command	Enter

The full amount of the loan—*800,000*—appears in R42C2, because the principal paid is not yet entered.

FORMULA 16: Principal Remaining—Year 2

RC[− 3] − R[+ 2]C

Formula 16 deducts the principal paid in year 2 (R44C5) from the principal remaining at the end of year 1 (R42C2) to produce the principal remaining at the end of year 2 in R42C5.

Place the cursor on R42C5:	Type or move the cursor:
Start the Value command	V
Enter the formula: R42C2 − R44C5	RC[− 3] − R[+ 2]C
Execute the command	Enter

Again, *800,000* appears.

FORMULA 17: Annual Interest Paid — Year 1

LOAN * RATE%

Formula 17 multiplies the amount financed (R4C2, LOAN) by the interest rate (R6C2, RATE) and enters the interest paid on the loan in year 1 in R43C2. Type the entire formula (remember the percent sign at the end).

Place the cursor on R43C2:	Type or press:
Start the Value command	V
Enter the formula: LOAN * RATE%	LOAN * RATE%
Execute the command	Enter

FORMULA 18: Annual Interest Paid — Year 2

R[−1]C[−3] * RATE%

Formula 18 multiplies the principal remaining at the end of year 1 (R42C2) by the annual interest rate (R6C2, RATE) and enters the interest paid on the loan in year 2 (R43C5). Again, don't forget the percent sign at the end.

Place the cursor on R43C5:	Type or move the cursor:
Start the Value command	V
Enter the formula: R42C2 * RATE%	R[−1]C[−3] * RATE%
Execute the command	Enter

Both interest paid cells (R43C2 and R43C5) now display *120,000*.

FORMULA 19: Annual Principal Paid

PAY − R[−1]C

Formula 19 deducts the interest paid (R43C2) from the annual loan payment (R7C2, PAY) and enters the principal paid at the end of the year in R44C2.

Place the cursor on R44C2:	Type or move the cursor:
Start the Value command	V
Enter the formula: PAY − R43C2	PAY − R[−1]C
Execute the command	Enter

Let's copy Formula 19 to year 2: Leave the cursor on R44C2. Type *CF* (Copy From) and press Tab to move the highlight to *to cells*. Type *R44C5* (the cell to copy into) and press Enter. Press F4 to recalculate. The numbers in the loan summary should now agree with Figure 14-4. If you haven't saved your formulas lately, use Transfer Save now.

FORMULA 20: MACRS Depreciation

PROPERTY * 20%

Formula 20 calculates MACRS (Modified Accelerated Cost Recovery System) depreciation on the property acquired with the company. Depreciation, which is not a cash item, doesn't appear on a cash flow statement. (For a detailed discussion of MACRS, see Chapter 13.) It is needed, however, to compute taxable income. The MACRS 5-year depreciation schedule is: Year 1 at 20%, year 2 at 32%, year 3 at 19.2%, and years 4 and 5 at 11.5%. In year 1, Formula 20 multiplies the amount in the cell named PROPERTY (R47C2) by 20%. Type the entire formula.

Place the cursor on R48C2:	Type or press:
Start the Value command	V
Enter the formula: PROPERTY * 20%	PROPERTY * 20%
Execute the command	Enter

Now enter the depreciation formula for year 2 in the same way: Place the cursor on R48C5 and type *V* (Value). Type *PROPERTY* 32%* and press Enter.

FORMULA 21: Taxable Income from Prior Year

R[−17]C[−3] + R[−5]C[−3] − R[−1]C[−3]

Formula 21 calculates the year 1 taxable income (R49C5) to determine the income taxes paid in year 2 (R34C5). Taxable income is computed by adding the cash flow before taxes (R32C2) and principal paid (R44C2) in year 1, then deducting the depreciation allowance (R48C2) in year 1.

Place the cursor on R49C5:	Type or move the cursor:
Start the Value command	V
Enter the formula: R32C2 + R44C2 − R48C2	R[−17]C[−3] + R[−5]C[−3] − R[−1]C[−3]
Execute the command	Enter

FORMULA 22: Tax on Corporate Income of $75,000 or More

IF(R[−1]C>=75000,13750+34%*(R[−1]C−75000),0)

Formula 22 calculates the corporate income tax on taxable income of $75,000 or more, based on current tax laws. The Test statement looks at taxable income in R49C5. If this amount is $75,000 or more, the Then statement calculates $13,750 plus 34% of taxable income over $75,000, and enters the result in R50C5. If the amount is less than $75,000, the Else statement enters a zero in cell R50C5.

Place the cursor on R50C5:	Type or move the cursor:
Start the Value command	V
Enter the formula: IF(R49C5 >=75000,13750+34% *(R49C5−75000),0) *Translation:* IF(taxable income is greater than or equal to 75000, then calculate 13750 plus 34% of taxable income minus 75000), else enter 0)	IF(R[−1]C>=75000, 13750+34% *(R[−1]C−75000),0)
Execute the command	Enter

Taxable income in R49C5 is less than $75,000, so Formula 22 enters a zero.

FORMULA 23: Tax on Corporate Income of Less than $75,000

IF(AND(R[−2]C>0,R[−2]C<75000),MIN(50000,R[−2]C)
 *15%+MAX(0,MIN(50000,R[−2]C−50000))*25%,0)

Formula 23 calculates the income tax when taxable income is less than $75,000. The current corporate tax schedule is:

Taxable Income:	Tax Rate:
First $50,000	15%
Second $25,000	25%

Formula 23 must discern how much of the taxable income falls within each level and apply the proper rate to the amount in each level. For example, with a taxable income of $38,000, it must calculate a straight 15% of the amount. With a taxable income of $58,000, it must add 15% of $50,000 and 25% of $8,000. The MIN (minimum) and MAX (maximum) functions define the upper and lower limits. MIN selects the smallest value in parentheses and MAX the largest value in parentheses. The AND function limits the calculations to only those times when taxable income is between $0 and $75,000.

The Test statement looks at the taxable income in R49C5. If this amount is greater than $0 and less than $75,000, the formula performs its computations and enters the result in R51C5. If the amount is less than $0 (a negative taxable income) or $75,000 or more (the province of Formula 22), Formula 23 enters a zero in its cell.

Place the cursor on R51C5:	Type or move the cursor:
Start the Value command	V
Enter the formula: IF(AND (R49C5>0,R49C5<75000), MIN(50000,R49C5) * 15% + MAX(0,MIN(50000,R49C5 − 50000)) * 25%,0)	IF(AND(R[− 2]C>0, R[− 2]C<75000),MIN (50000,R[− 2]C) * 15% + MAX(0,MIN(50000, R[− 2]C − 50000)) * 25%,0)
Translation: IF(taxable income is greater than 0 AND less than 75000, then enter MIN(50000 or taxable income) times 15% plus MAX(0 or MIN(50000 or taxable income minus 75000))times 25%), else enter 0)	
Execute the command	Enter

Formula 23 calculates a tax of $3,900, which is copied by the formula in R34C5 when the spreadsheet is recalculated.

This completes the formulas for year 2. Use Transfer Save to store the spreadsheet on disk.

Copying Year 2 to Years 3, 4, and 5

Now let's copy the title *%Inc* and all the formulas, numbers, formats, and lines from year 2 (columns 4 and 5) to year 3 (columns 7 and 8), year 4 (columns 10 and 11), and year 5 (columns 13 and 14). To do this, identify the first cell in column 4 and the last cell in column 5 that you want to copy from. Then specify only the first cell in columns 7, 10, and 13 that you want to copy to.

Place the cursor on R10C4:	Type or press:
Start the Copy command	C
Select the From option	F
(Multiplan displays *COPY FROM cells: R10C4*, the first cell to copy from)	
Specify the other cells to copy from	:R25C4,R11:51C5

Move the highlight to *to cells*	Tab
Specify the first cell in each column to copy into	R10C7,R10C10, R10C13
Execute the command	Enter

Editing the MACRS Depreciation Rates

Recall that the MACRS 5-year depreciation schedule requires the use of varying percentage rates during the depreciation term. Copying this formula along with all the others was efficient, but you now have the wrong percentage in years 3, 4, and 5. The correct formula in year 3 is PROPERTY * 19.2%. It's easy to make amends: Place the cursor on R48C8 and type *E* for Edit. Press the F9 key three times to move the highlight atop the *3* in *32%*. Press Delete. Type *19* and a decimal point, then press Enter.

Now change the percentage in year 4 to *11.5%*: Place the cursor on R48C11 and type *E*. Press the F9 key three times. Press the Delete key twice to delete the number *32*. Type *11.5* and press Enter.

Year *5* needs the same formula as year 4: Leave the cursor on R48C11, type *CF* (Copy From), and press Tab. Type *R48C14* and press Enter. Now press F4 to recalculate. Your spreadsheet should now look like the one in Figure 14-4.

FORMULA 24: Spreadsheet Filename

NAME()

Formula 24 generates the spreadsheet filename in R1C14. Simply type the function name and parenthesis.

Place the cursor on R1C14:	**Type or press:**
Start the Value command	V
Enter the formula: NAME()	NAME()
Execute the command	Enter

FORMULA 25: Percent of Sales

RC[− 1]/R12 C[− 1]

Formula 25 calculates the year 1 cost of goods sold (R13C2) as a percent of year 1 sales (R12C2). This formula uses R12 C[− 1] to indicate the sales cell. The space between R12 and C[− 1] is Multiplan's intersection operator. This handy half-absolute/half-relative cell notation tells Multiplan to use the cell in row 12 that intersects with the cell one column to the left of the formula cell.

When you copy Formula 25 to years 2, 3, 4, and 5, it will find the sales figure for the correct year. To build the formula, move the cursor to R13C2 and type everything else, including the C[− 1] notation. Be sure to press the Spacebar between R12 and C[− 1].

Place the cursor on R13C3:	Type or move the cursor:
Start the Value command	V
Enter the formula: R13C2/R12 C[− 1] *Translation:* Year 1 cost of goods sold divided by year 1 sales	RC[− 1]/R12 C[− 1]
Execute the command	Enter

And *35.0%* appears.

To calculate each entry in year 1 as a percent of sales, copy Formula 25 into the other cells in column 3.

Leave the cursor on R13C3:	Type or press:
Start the Copy command	C
Select the From option	F
(Multiplan displays *COPY FROM cells: R13C3*, the cell to copy from)	
Move the highlight to *to cells*	Tab
Specify the cells to copy into	R15C3,R18:25C3,R27:28C3, R30C3,R32C3,R34C3, R36C3
Execute the command	Enter

Now copy the title *%Sales*, and the lines, formats, and formulas from column 3 to columns 6, 9, 12, and 15.

Place the cursor on R10C3:	Type or press:
Start the Copy command	C
Select the From option	F
(Multiplan displays *COPY FROM cells: R10C3*, the first cell to copy from)	
Specify the last cell to copy from	:R37C3
Move the highlight to *to cells*	Tab
Specify the first cell in each column to copy into	R10C6,R10C9,R10C12, R10C15
Execute the command	Enter

Your spreadsheet is complete. Press F4 to see the result of all your work. When recalculation stops, your spreadsheet should look like the one in Figure 14-1, at the beginning of this chapter.

Locking and Saving the Formulas

You wouldn't want anything to happen to your formulas, so lock them: Leave the cursor where it is, type *LF* (Lock Formulas), and type *Y* to confirm the lock. Now save your spreadsheet by typing *TS* and pressing Enter. Type *Y* to confirm the overwrite.

PRINTING YOUR SPREADSHEET

This spreadsheet can be printed in 12-pitch type either on two sheets of 8½-by-11-inch paper or, with a wide-carriage printer, on one sheet of 15-by-11-inch paper. It is 163 characters wide on a single sheet of paper, including Multiplan row numbers.

Setting the Print Margins

The first step before printing is to set the margins around your spreadsheet.

Leave the cursor where it is:	Type or press:
Start the Print command	P
Select the Margins option	M

Type the following numbers in the margins fields. Tab past any field that already has the proper setting. If you overshoot a field, press Tab a few times to move full circle through the fields or press Shift-Tab to move backward one field at a time. The highlight is in the *left* field.

To do this:	Type or press:
Specify the number of characters	0
Move the highlight to *top*	Tab
Specify the number of lines	3
Move the highlight to *print width*	Tab
Specify the number of characters:	
For 8½-by-11-inch paper	102
For 15-by-11-inch paper	163
Move the highlight to *print length*	Tab
Specify the number of lines	60

Move the highlight to *page length*	Tab
Specify the number of lines	66
Execute the command	Enter

Setting the Print Options

You are still in the Print command. The next step is to set the print options. The options settings are the same for every spreadsheet in this book: Print the entire spreadsheet in 12-pitch type with row and column numbers. You can find the printer code for 12-pitch type in your printer manual.

Now type O to select the Options option. Type in the following responses. Tab past any field that already has the proper setting. The highlight is in the *area* field.

To do this:	**Type or press:**
Define the print area	R1:4095
Move the highlight to *setup*	Tab
Enter your printer code for 12-pitch type	(your code)
Move the highlight to *formulas*	Tab Tab
Select *No*	N
Move the highlight to *row-col numbers*	Tab
Select *Yes*	Y
Execute the command	Enter

Now, before you print, store the spreadsheet with the print settings: Press the Escape key to exit the Print command. Leave the cursor where it is. Type *TS*, press Enter, and type *Y*.

Printing the Spreadsheet

Now turn on your printer and print your spreadsheet.

Leave the cursor where it is:	**Type:**
Start the Print command	P
Select the Printer option	P

And here's a copy of your spreadsheet.

USING THE SPREADSHEET

Let's take a closer look at how this spreadsheet works. But don't save any changes because we're going to add iteration formulas and you'll want the spreadsheet exactly as it is now when we do.

For year 1, you enter only your estimated sales and disbursements. The formulas use these estimates to calculate the cost of goods sold, gross profit, total operating expenses, payroll taxes, loan repayment, total cash disbursements, cash flow before and after taxes, return on capital invested, and percent of sales for each year. When you change an estimate, the results change.

In years 2, 3, 4, and 5, the situation is quite different. You enter only your estimated percentage increases (as integers) in columns 4, 7, 10, and 13. The formulas then use these estimates to calculate all the other numbers for you.

Everything in the loan summary and work area except property acquired (R47C2) is generated by formulas. If you change the amount financed, term, or interest rate on a loan, the loan payment is recalculated and the change is reflected in the cash flow. If taxable income changes, corporate taxes are recalculated and the change is reflected in the cash flow. If you change the amount of cash invested, the return on capital invested changes.

Let's say you project a 25% growth in sales and a 12% increase in salaries in year 2. Try it now. Type 25 in R12C4 and 12 in R18C4. Press the F4 (recalculate) key. Instantly, your year 2 sales become 1,125,000, salaries become 168,000, and salaries as a percentage of sales become 14.9%. But that's only the tip of the iceberg. Since what you do in one year affects what happens in the future, Multiplan recalculates the formulas in each succeeding year to reflect your estimates. You can try endless "What if?" combinations to see the effect on your cash flow for the next five years.

Using Multiplan's Windows

Suppose you want to try some "What if?" tests with the interest rate and term of a loan and at the same time see the effect on the payments of interest and principal. The rate and term are at the top of the spreadsheet. The loan summary is at the bottom. Let's use Multiplan's Window command to split the screen into three windows.

Window #1 will contain the investment and loan information in rows 1 through 8. Since you want to make changes in the interest rate and term in this area of the spreadsheet, you want window #1 to remain fixed while you scroll through the other areas. You do this by not linking window #1 to the other windows when you split the screen the first time.

Place the cursor on R9C1:	Type or press:
Start the Window command	W
Select the Split option	S
Select Horizontal	H
(Multiplan displays *WINDOW SPLIT HORIZONTAL at row:* 9. The *linked* field shows *No*)	
Execute the command	Enter

Rows 9 through 19 are now displayed in window #2. To the right of #2 are the column numbers 1 through 5. The presence of these numbers indicates that windows #1 and #2 are not linked. Window #1 will remain fixed when you scroll through window #2. This is called unsynchronized scrolling.

We'll view the year titles in window #2 and the loan summary in window #3, linking window #3 and window #2 so that the year titles scroll together with the loan entries. This is called synchronized scrolling, because the contents of one window remain in a constant relationship with the contents of the other. To open window #3:

Place the cursor on R11C1:	Type or press:
Start the Window command	W
Select the Split option	S
Select Horizontal	H
(Multiplan displays *WINDOW SPLIT HORIZONTAL at row:* 11)	
Move the highlight to *linked*	Tab
Select *Yes*	Y
Execute the command	Enter

On the left side of the screen, you can see #3, the start of the new window. The absence of column numbers to the right of #3 indicates that windows #2 and #3 are linked. The cursor is in window #3 in row 11. Move the cursor to row 40. You now have your "What if?" area in window #1, year titles in window #2, and the loan summary in window #3—all at one time.

You can make changes only in the window the cursor is in, so press the F1 key to move the cursor to window #1. Change the interest rate and the term of the loan. Now press the F4 key. In a flash, the loan summary reflects your changes. Press Shift-F1 to move the cursor to window #3. Move the cursor to the right. The "What-if?" area is fixed in place, the titles and loan numbers scroll together, and the results in years 3, 4, and 5 are visible at all times. Now close window #3:

Leave the cursor in window #3:	Type or press:
Start the Window command	W
Select the Close option	C
Execute the command	Enter

To close window #2, type *WC* and press Enter.

You can use the Window command to display as many as eight areas of your spreadsheet. You can clear a window with the Transfer Clear command, and then enter new information in that window. It's worthwhile to play around with windows so that you become familiar with how they work.

Now load the spreadsheet with the original entries: Leave the cursor where it is and type *TL* (Transfer Load). Type *CASHFLOW* and press Enter. When Multiplan asks if you want to save or lose the edits, type *N* to tell Multiplan to disregard the changes.

REFINING YOUR CASH FLOW SPREADSHEET

As the spreadsheet now exists, the calculations for interest, principal paid, and the principal remaining on a loan are not precise. Since principal paid is part of taxable income, the taxable income calculations—corporate income taxes, cash flow after taxes, and return on capital invested—are also not precise. The following section explains how to refine your cash flow spreadsheet by using iteration, Multiplan's powerful problem-solving feature, to calculate the precise figures.

Iteration permits a formula to make repeated passes on itself, using the result of the previous pass for its next calculation. Each pass (each monthly calculation in these particular formulas) refines the answer until the result (annual totals) achieves the required degree of accuracy.

Because of the increased number of calculations, a spreadsheet that uses iteration formulas takes longer to recalculate than one that does not. The best approach is to have two versions—the one you've just created, which you can use as your workhorse when you want instant answers to "What if?" questions, and another, which you can use when you require exact numbers. Figure 14-5 shows the iterating spreadsheet.

	1	2	3	4	5	6
						CASH FLOW
1						
2	===
3	Cash Invested	$200,000.00				
4	Amount Financed	$800,000.00				
5	Term in Years	10				
6	Annual Interest Rate (%)	15.00				
7	Annual Loan Payment	$154,881.56				
8	Total Loan Payment	$1,548,815.59				
9		YEAR 1	%Sales	%Inc	YEAR 2	%Sales
10						
11		--------	-----	----	--------	-----
12	Cash Sales	900,000	100.0%	20	1,080,000	100.0%
13	Cost of Goods Sold	315,000	35.0%	35	378,000	35.0%
14		--------	-----		--------	-----
15	Gross Profit	585,000	65.0%		702,000	65.0%
16						
17	Cash Disbursements					
18	Salaries	150,000	16.7%	11	166,500	15.4%
19	Payroll Taxes	30,000	3.3%		33,300	3.1%
20	Rent	36,000	4.0%	15	41,400	3.8%
21	Advertising	55,000	6.1%	15	63,250	5.9%
22	Insurance	30,000	3.3%	10	33,000	3.1%
23	Office Expenses	18,000	2.0%	12	20,160	1.9%
24	Professional Fees	25,000	2.8%	15	28,750	2.7%
25	Utilities/Phone	15,000	1.7%	8	16,200	1.5%
26		--------	-----		--------	-----
27	Total Operating Expenses	359,000	39.9%		402,560	37.3%
28	Loan Repayment	154,882	17.2%		154,882	14.3%
29		--------	-----		--------	-----
30	Total Cash Disbursements	513,882	57.1%		557,442	51.6%
31		--------	-----		--------	-----
32	Cash Flow Before Taxes	71,118	7.9%		144,558	13.4%
33		========	=====		========	=====
34	Less: Income Tax	22,345	2.5%		4,275	0.4%
35		--------	-----		--------	-----
36	Cash Flow After Taxes	48,773	5.4%		140,283	13.0%
37		========	=====		========	=====
38	Return on Capital Invested	4.9%			14.0%	
39						
40	===
41	Loan Summary-Actual					
42	Monthly Interest Rate	0.0125	❸ MRATE			
43	Principal Remaining	762,618			719,226	
44	Interest Paid (final month)	9,574	❹		9,039	❼
45	Principal Paid (final month)	3,332	❺		3,868	❽
46	Annual Interest Paid	117,499	❻		111,490	
47	Annual Principal Paid	37,382			43,392	
48	===
49	***** WORK AREA *****					
50	Cost of Property Acquired	400,000			128,000	
51	MACRS Depreciation (5-Year)	80,000			28,501	
52	Taxable Income				0	
53	Income Tax if Taxable >=75000				4,275	
54	Income Tax if Taxable <75000					
55	===

FIGURE 14-5.
Completed iterating version of cash flow analysis

7	8	9	10	11	12	13	14	15
ANALYSIS							CASHFLOW.1	

%Inc	YEAR 3	%Sales	%Inc	YEAR 4	%Sales	%Inc	YEAR 5	%Sales
20	1,296,000	100.0%	20	1,555,200	100.0%	20	1,866,240	100.0%
35	453,600	35.0%	35	544,320	35.0%	35	653,184	35.0%
	842,400	65.0%		1,010,880	65.0%		1,213,056	65.0%
11	184,815	14.3%	11	205,145	13.2%	11	227,711	12.2%
	36,963	2.9%		41,029	2.6%		45,542	2.4%
15	47,610	3.7%	15	54,752	3.5%	15	62,964	3.4%
15	72,738	5.6%	15	83,648	5.4%	15	96,195	5.2%
10	36,300	2.8%	10	39,930	2.6%	10	43,923	2.4%
12	22,579	1.7%	12	25,289	1.6%	12	28,323	1.5%
15	33,063	2.6%	15	38,022	2.4%	15	43,725	2.3%
8	17,496	1.4%	8	18,896	1.2%	8	20,407	1.1%
	451,563	34.8%		506,709	32.6%		568,791	30.5%
	154,882	12.0%		154,882	10.0%		154,882	8.3%
	606,445	46.8%		661,591	42.5%		723,673	38.8%
	235,955	18.2%		349,289	22.5%		489,383	26.2%
	9,988	0.8%		59,488	3.8%		111,246	6.0%
	225,968	17.4%		289,801	18.6%		378,137	20.3%
	22.6%			29.0%			37.8%	

668,858		610,394		542,532	
8,417		7,695		6,857	
4,490		5,212		6,050	
104,514		96,418		87,019	59 ❷
50,367		58,464		67,862	TRUE ❶

76,800		46,000		46,000	
59,950		209,523		361,753	
0		59,488		111,246	
9,988		0		0	

THE LOAN SUMMARY FORMULAS

The loan summary for each of the five years contains four iteration formulas: The one in row 44 calculates the interest paid each month; the one in row 45 calculates the principal paid each month; the one in row 46 adds the interest paid for the year; and the one in row 47 adds the principal paid for the year. Therefore, each formula performs 12 internal calculations, one for each month in the year.

Each formula contains the ITERCNT (iteration count) function and specific month parameters that tell it when to start and stop its calculations. ITERCNT controls the iteration process in two ways:

■ It limits the calculations performed by each iteration formula to 12 in each year.

■ It limits the total number of iterations to 60 in all five years.

During the first calculation (the first month), ITERCNT displays #N/A (not available). The ISNA (is not available) function interacts with ITERCNT in the first year so that the formulas start calculating at the proper time—when ITERCNT is #N/A.

The formulas in the first year calculate the results for the 12 months from #N/A to 11. The formulas in the second year calculate the results for the 12 months from 12 to 23. The formulas in the third year calculate from 24 to 35. The fourth year goes from 36 to 47, and the fifth year from 48 to 59. This cycle accounts for all 60 months. When the cycle is complete, ITERCNT stops any further calculations.

Used in another way, the ITERCNT function in R46C15 displays a counter so that you can see where the calculations are in the iteration process.

How the Formulas Calculate

The loan summary formulas work as a team, using the results of their own and each other's calculations. This is what happens during the first pass:

■ The interest paid formula in R44C2 calculates the first month's interest payment by multiplying the amount of the loan by the monthly interest rate.

■ The principal paid formula in R45C2 simultaneously takes the annual loan payment, divides it by 12 to get the monthly loan payment, and subtracts the interest paid that has just been calculated by the formula in R44C2.

■ Meanwhile, the annual interest paid formula in R46C2 accumulates the amount calculated by the interest paid formula, and the annual principal paid formula in R47C2 accumulates the amount that is calculated by the principal paid formula.

■ The principal remaining formula in R43C2 uses the amount calculated by the principal paid formula in R47C2 to calculate the principal remaining in the first month.

After the first pass, the formulas start the next pass for the second month of the first year. The interest paid formula in R44C2 takes the current principal remaining in R43C2 and multiplies that amount by the monthly interest rate. The other formulas make their calculations accordingly.

The formulas cycle back repeatedly on their previous calculations until, after 12 passes, ITERCNT determines that the first-year calculations are complete. The monthly interest paid and principal paid formulas then display the amounts as of the final month of the cycle. The annual interest paid and annual principal paid formulas display the amounts accumulated during the 12 calculations, and the principal remaining formula displays the amount remaining after the first year. The formulas in the second and succeeding years take their turns until the 60-month cycle is complete.

MODIFYING THE CASH FLOW SPREADSHEET

Now, let's modify the cash flow spreadsheet to perform these calculations. If you prefer to skip the step-by-step instructions, refer to the summary, "Modified Cash Flow Analysis," at the end of this chapter.

1. The first step is to save CASHFLOW under a different name so that you have two versions—the original CASHFLOW for quick calculations and the new version we'll call CASHFLOW.1 for precise loan numbers. Leave the cursor where it is, type *TS* (Transfer Save), and press the F10 key to move the cursor to the space after the *W* in *CASHFLOW*. Type *.1* and press Enter.

2. Next, make room for the new formulas: Place the cursor on R42C1 and type *IR* (Insert Row). Multiplan proposes one row, which is what you want, so press Enter. Now place the cursor on R44C1 and type *IR*. Type 2 and press Enter. Multiplan will adjust the cell locations in the existing formulas so that they continue to refer to the proper information.

3. Now, type the new titles: Place the cursor on R42C1 and type *A* to start the Alpha command. Type *Monthly Interest Rate* and move the cursor to R44C1. Type *Interest Paid (final month)* and move the cursor down to R45C1. Type *Principal Paid (final month)* and press Enter.

4. The next step is to format R42C2 to show the monthly interest rate as a fixed number with four decimal places: Place the cursor on R42C2 and type *FC* (Format Cells). Press Tab twice to move the highlight to *format code*. Type *F* for *Fix* and tab to *# of decimals*. Type 4 and press Enter.

5. Now, name the monthly interest rate cell MRATE so that you can use this name in the formulas: Leave the cursor on R42C2 and type *N* to start the Name command. Type *MRATE* and press Enter.

6. Next, unlock the cells in the loan summary: Place the cursor on R41C1 and type *LC* (Lock Cells). Type *:R47C14* and tab to the *status* field. Type *U* for *unlocked* and press Enter.

7. Finally, make the loan summary title more precise: Leave the cursor on R41C1 and type *E* to start the Edit command. Use the Backspace key to erase *Approximate*. Type *Actual"* (the quotation mark belongs at the end of the word) and press Enter.

Use Transfer Save to store the spreadsheet on disk. Since Multiplan recalculates when it stores, the NAME function in R1C14 now displays *CASH-FLOW.1*, the name of your new spreadsheet.

ENTERING THE LOAN FORMULAS

Figure 14-5 shows the location of the new loan formulas. Enter them the same way you entered the earlier ones. One important note: Don't recalculate or save this spreadsheet until later, when the instructions tell you to do so.

FORMULA 1: Iteration Completion Test

ITERCNT() = 59

Formula 1, in R47C15, starts and stops the formulas in each year and limits the overall iterations in the five years covered by this spreadsheet. We want the formulas to perform 12 iterations per year, a total of 60 for five years. Since ITERCNT returns the message #N/A during the first calculation, we'll tell Formula 1 to iterate another 59 times, then stop the calculations. Type the entire formula.

Place the cursor on R47C15:	**Type or press:**
Start the Value command	V
Enter the formula: ITERCNT() = 59	ITERCNT() = 59
Execute the command	Enter

#N/A now appears in R47C15.

FORMULA 2: Iteration Counter

ITERCNT()

Formula 2 displays the iteration count in R46C15 so that you can see where the calculations are in the iteration cycle. This formula isn't vital—it's simply nice to have for keeping track. Type the entire formula.

Place the cursor on R46C15:	Type or press:
Start the Value command	V
Enter the formula: ITERCNT()	ITERCNT()
Execute the command	Enter

Again, #N/A appears.

Later, if you prefer not to have Formulas 1 and 2 appear on the printed spreadsheet, you can blank them out temporarily before printing or move them permanently out of the print area, say to column 16.

FORMULA 3: Monthly Interest Rate

RATE%/12

Formula 3 divides the annual interest rate (R6C2, RATE) by 12 to produce the monthly interest rate in R42C2 (MRATE). Type the entire formula.

Place the cursor on R42C2:	Type or press:
Start the Value command	V
Enter the formula: RATE%/12	RATE%/12
Execute the command	Enter

You now see the monthly interest rate 0.0125 in R42C2. This percentage is based on the annual interest rate of 15% in R6C2, the interest rate cell.

FORMULA 4: Year 1—Interest Paid (final month)

IF(ISNA(ITERCNT()),LOAN * MRATE,
    IF(ITERCNT()>11,RC,R[− 1]C* MRATE))

Formula 4 is a "nested" IF formula that internally calculates the interest paid during each month of the first year, then displays in R44C2 the interest paid in the twelfth month of the year.

The Test statement in the first IF formula checks the ITERCNT function. If ITERCNT is #N/A (the first month), the Then statement multiplies the amount of the loan (R4C2, LOAN) by the monthly interest rate (R42C2, MRATE) to get the first month's interest payment. If this is not the first month, the formula evaluates the Else statement (the second IF formula).

The Test statement in the second IF formula checks to see if ITERCNT is greater than 11, indicating that the count is past the first year. If the test is true, the Then statement displays the current contents of the cell (RC).

If ITERCNT is not past the first year, the Else statement of the "nested" IF formula multiplies the principal remaining from the last calculation (R43C2) by the monthly interest rate (MRATE) to get the current month's interest payment. It keeps calculating the interest amounts, based on the prior calculation, until the ITERCNT completion test is greater than 11. At that point, the calculations for the first year stop.

Type everything in the formula except the relative notation R[− 1]C, which refers to R43C2. The RC in the formula refers to R44C2, the formula cell. You can either type *RC* yourself or move the cursor away from R44C2, then back again, and Multiplan will type it for you.

Place the cursor on R44C2:	**Type or move the cursor:**
Start the Value command	V
Enter the formula: IF(ISNA (ITERCNT()),LOAN * MRATE,IF(ITERCNT()>11, RC,R43C2 * MRATE))	IF(ISNA(ITERCNT()), LOAN * MRATE, IF(ITERCNT()>11, RC,R[− 1]C * MRATE))
Execute the command	Enter

The number *10,000* now appears in R44C2. This is the interest paid in the first month of the loan.

FORMULA 5: Year 1—Principal Paid (final month)

$$(PAY/12) − R[− 1]C$$

Formula 5 divides the annual loan payment (R7C2, PAY) by 12 to get the monthly loan payment and then subtracts the current interest paid (R44C2). When the calculations stop, the result in R45C2 is the principal paid in the twelfth month of the year. Formula 5 begins with an open parenthesis, which Multiplan recognizes as the start of a formula, so there's no need to type *V* to start the Value command.

Place the cursor on R45C2:	**Type or move the cursor:**
Enter the formula: (PAY/12) – R44C2	(PAY/12) – R[–1]C
Execute the command	Enter

You can now see 2,907 in R45C2. This is the principal paid in the first month of the loan.

Now copy Formula 5 to the second year: Leave the cursor on R45C2. Type CF (Copy From) and tab to the *to cells* field. Type *R45C5* and press Enter.

FORMULA 6: Year 1—Annual Interest Paid

IF(ISNA(ITERCNT()),R[–2]C,IF(ITERCNT()>11,RC,RC + R[–2]C))

Formula 6, another "nested" IF formula, accumulates the monthly interest payments calculated in the interest paid cell (R44C2) and enters the annual interest paid in R46C2. It replaces the formula currently in R46C2.

The Test statement in the first IF formula checks ITERCNT. If ITERCNT is not available (the first month), the Then statement displays the current interest paid (R44C2). If ITERCNT is available (past the first month), the formula moves to the Else statement and evaluates the second IF formula.

The Test statement in the second IF formula looks to see if ITERCNT is greater than 11 (past the first year). If this is true, the Then statement stops the calculations and displays the amount accumulated in the cell (RC). If ITERCNT is not greater than 11, the Else statement takes the amount in its cell (R46C2) and repeatedly adds the current interest paid, which is being calculated by the formula in R44C2, until ITERCNT is greater than 11. The formula then stops and displays the accumulated monthly calculations.

Formula 6 contains two RC references. As you did with Formula 4, type *RC* or move the cursor away from R46C2, then back at both points in the formula.

Place the cursor on R46C2:	**Type or move the cursor:**
Start the Value command	V
Enter the formula: IF(ISNA (ITERCNT()),R44C2, IF(ITERCNT()>11, RC,RC + R44C2))	IF(ISNA(ITERCNT()), R[–2]C, IF(ITERCNT() >11,RC,RC + R[–2]C))
Execute the command	Enter

The number *10,000* in the cell is the accumulation of the monthly interest calculations in R44C2. Since no iterations have taken place yet, the amounts in R44C2 and R46C2 are the same.

FORMULA 7: Year 2 — Interest Paid (final month)

IF(OR(ITERCNT()<12,ITERCNT()>23),RC,
    IF(ITERCNT() = 12,R[− 1]C[− 3] * MRATE,R[− 1]C * MRATE))

Formula 7, in R44C5, is a more complex "nested" IF formula that includes Multiplan's OR function. This formula calculates the interest paid during the second year, then shows the interest paid in the twenty-fourth month. As with the other nested IF formulas, the Test statement in the first IF formula looks at ITERCNT (R47C15). The formula then uses the OR function to determine the start and stop parameters. If ITERCNT is less than 12 (the first month of the second year) or is greater than 23 (the last month of the second year), the Then statement displays the current contents of the cell (RC). If ITERCNT is between 12 and 23, the formula evaluates the second IF formula.

The Test statement in the second IF formula checks to see if ITERCNT is equal to 12. If it is, the Then statement multiplies the principal remaining from the first year (R43C2) by MRATE (R42C2) and enters the result in R44C5. If ITERCNT is not equal to 12, the Else statement takes the principal remaining from the last calculation (R43C5) and multiplies it repeatedly by MRATE until ITERCNT is greater than 23, at which point the calculations stop.

Place the cursor on R44C5:	Type or move the cursor:
Start the Value command	V
Enter the formula: IF(OR (ITERCNT()<12, ITERCNT()>23),RC, IF(ITERCNT() = 12,R43C2 * MRATE,R43C5 * MRATE))	IF(OR(ITERCNT()<12, ITERCNT()>23),RC, IF(ITERCNT() = 12, R[− 1]C[− 3] * MRATE, R[− 1]C * MRATE))
Execute the command	Enter

The message #N/A appears in R44C5 because the results for the first year are not yet calculated.

FORMULA 8: Year 2 — Annual Interest Paid

IF(ITERCNT()<12,0,IF(ITERCNT()>23,RC,RC + R[− 2]C))

Formula 8 is a "nested" IF formula that calculates the annual interest paid in the second year. It replaces the formula currently in R46C5.

The Test statement in the first IF formula checks ITERCNT to see if it is less than 12 (the first month of the second year). If it is, the Then statement simply enters a zero in R46C5. If ITERCNT is not less than 12, the formula moves to the Else statement and evaluates the second IF formula.

The Test statement in the second IF formula sees if ITERCNT is greater than 23. If it is, the iteration cycle is past the second year. Calculation stops, and the Then statement displays the current contents of the cell (*RC*). If ITERCNT is not greater than 23, the Else statement accumulates the results of the interest calculations in R44C5 and enters the annual interest paid in R46C5.

Place the cursor on R46C5:	**Type or move the cursor:**
Start the Value command	V
Enter the formula: IF(ITERCNT() <12,0, IF(ITERCNT()>23, RC,RC + R44C5))	IF(ITERCNT()<12,0, IF(ITERCNT()>23, RC,RC + R[− 2]C))
Execute the command	Enter

And again, *#N/A* appears in R46C5 because the results for the first year are not yet calculated.

Copying Formulas in Groups

Now let's copy the formulas in the second year in rows 44 through 46 to the third, fourth, and fifth years: Place the cursor on R44C5 and type *CF* (Copy From). Now type *:R46C5* and press Tab to move the highlight to the *to cells* field. Type *R44C8,R44C11,R44C14* and press Enter.

EDITING THE FORMULAS

You now have the correct formulas for every year, but the wrong start and stop numbers for years 3, 4, and 5. So, the next step is to edit the formulas. Let's begin with R44C8, the final month of interest paid for year 3. Place the cursor on R44C8 and type *E* to start the Edit command.

The formula now on the command line is as follows (the numbers you need to change are shown in boldface type):

IF(OR(ITERCNT()<**12**,ITERCNT()>**23**),RC,
    IF(ITERCNT() = **12**,R[− 1]C[− 3]∗ MRATE,R[− 1]C∗ MRATE))

Change the number following each occurrence of *ITERCNT* in this way: Working from right to left in the formula, press F7 until the highlight rests on the number *12* (the one preceded by the equal sign). Press the Delete key to delete *12*, and type *24* in its place. Now press the F7 key until the highlight rests on the number *23*, press the Delete key, and type *35*. Next, press F7 until the highlight rests on the number *12*, press the Delete key, and type *24*. Your formula now looks like this (the changes are in boldface type):

IF(OR(ITERCNT()<**24**,ITERCNT()>35),RC,
   IF(ITERCNT()=**24**,R[−1]C[−3]∗MRATE,R[−1]C∗MRATE))

If yours does, press Enter. If it doesn't, press Escape and start again.

Now follow the same procedure to edit the other formulas in row 44. Be sure to press Enter after you edit and verify each formula.

Place the cursor on R44C11 and change the formula to:

IF(OR(ITERCNT()<**36**,ITERCNT()>47),RC,
   IF(ITERCNT()=**36**,R[−1]C[−3]∗MRATE,R[−1]C∗MRATE))

Place the cursor on R44C14 and change the formula to:

IF(OR(ITERCNT()<**48**,ITERCNT()>59),RC,
   IF(ITERCNT()=**48**,R[−1]C[−3]∗MRATE,R[−1]C∗MRATE))

Next, follow the same procedure to edit the annual interest paid formulas in years 3, 4, and 5 in row 46. Again the changes are in the numbers shown in boldface type following each occurrence of *ITERCNT*.

Place the cursor on R46C8 and change the formula to:

IF(ITERCNT()<**24**,0,IF(ITERCNT()>35,RC,RC+R[−2]C))

Place the cursor on R46C11 and change the formula to:

IF(ITERCNT()<**36**,0,IF(ITERCNT()>47,RC,RC+R[−2]C))

Place the cursor on R46C14 and change the formula to:

IF(ITERCNT()<**48**,0,IF(ITERCNT()>59,RC,RC+R[−2]C))

Copying Another Group of Formulas

Now copy the annual interest paid formulas from row 46 to row 47 where they can perform the same calculations to produce the annual principal paid: Place the cursor on R46C2 and type *CF* (Copy From). Type *:14* and press Tab to move the highlight to the *to cells* field. Type *R47C2* and press Enter. You now have all the new formulas in place.

TURNING ITERATION ON

Now tell Multiplan to turn on iteration and tell it the location of the completion test, so that it knows when to stop all the calculations.

Leave the cursor where it is:	**Type or press:**
Start the Options command	O
Move the highlight to *iteration*	Tab Tab

Select *Yes*	Y
Move the highlight to *completion test at*	Tab
Enter the location of the ITERCNT control formula	R47C15
Execute the command	Enter

Both of these settings will be saved when you store the spreadsheet on disk.

NOW...

This is the moment when all your work pays off. Position the spreadsheet so that you have a good view of columns 8 through 15 in the loan summary. Press the F4 key. Now settle back and relax while Multiplan does its job.

As the calculations start, #N/A appears in the loan summary cells. Though you can't see it on the screen right now, the formulas in years 1 and 2 go through their calculations. While this is happening, the ITERCNT counter in R46C15 shows the current iteration number. The formulas for years 3, 4, and 5 now take their turn, and you can see successive calculations in each cell. The ITERCNT completion test in R47C15 shows *FALSE* throughout this time. After a short while, when the count reaches 59, iteration stops and the ITERCNT formula shows *TRUE*.

Your spreadsheet now looks like the one in Figure 14-5. Lock the new formulas by typing *LF* (Lock Formulas), then *Y* to confirm. Use Transfer Save to store the spreadsheet on disk. Now print your spreadsheet just as you did the earlier, non-iterating version.

Your cash flow analysis spreadsheet is now pure precision!

SPREADSHEET SUMMARY—CASH FLOW ANALYSIS

General: The completed spreadsheet is shown in Figure 14-1. Use Options to set automatic recalculation to *No*. Use Value to enter REPT(" = ",29) for long lines. See the step-by-step instructions for entering the short lines. Use Lock Formulas to lock the formulas.

Column Width: Use Format Width to set the column widths.

Column Number:	Width in Characters:
1	30
2	14
3	7

4	6
5	14
6	7
7	6
8	14
9	7
10	6
11	14
12	7
13	6
14	14
15	7

Format: Use Format Cells as follows: Continue R1C6:8. Center R10C2:15. Right-justify R10C4 and R1C14. Dollar code with 2 decimal places R3:4C2, R7:8C2. Fix code with 2 decimal places R6C2. Percent code with 1 decimal place R12:36C3 and R38C2. Use Format Default Cells to integer code the other cells. Use Format Options to insert automatic commas.

Name: Use Name as follows: R3C2 is INVEST. R4C2 is LOAN. R5C2 is TERM. R6C2 is RATE. R7C2 is PAY. R47C2 is PROPERTY.

Print: Cash Flow Analysis is 163 characters wide, including Multiplan row numbers, and is printed in 12-pitch type. For 8½-by-11-inch paper, use Print Margins to make the following margin settings: *left* 0, *top* 3, *print width* 102, *print length* 60, and *page length* 66. Use the same margins for 15-by-11-inch paper, but set the print width to 163.

Formulas: The formulas use relative and named cell references.

1	R7C2	Annual Loan Payment ABS(PMT(RATE%/12,TERM * 12,LOAN)) * 12
2	R8C2	Total Loan Payment PAY * TERM
3	R13C2	Cost of Goods Sold R[-1]C * 35%
4	R15C2	Gross Profit R[-3]C - R[-2]C

5	R19C2	Payroll Taxes R[−1]C * 20%
6	R27C2	Total Operating Expenses SUM(R[−10]C:R[−1]C)
7	R28C2	Loan Repayment PAY
8	R30C2	Total Cash Disbursements R[−3]C + R[−2]C
9	R32C2	Cash Flow Before Taxes R[−17]C − R[−2]C
10	R36C2	Cash Flow After Taxes R[−4]C − R[−2]C
11	R38C2	Return on Capital Invested R[−2]C/(INVEST + LOAN)
12	R12C5	Sales Projections RC[−3] + RC[−3] * RC[−1]%
13	R13C5	Cost of Goods Sold R[−1]C * RC[−1]%
14	R34C5	Income Tax IF(R[+16]C>0,R[+16]C,R[+17]C)
15	R42C2	Principal Remaining—Year 1 LOAN − R[+2]C
16	R42C5	Principal Remaining—Year 2 RC[−3] − R[+2]C
17	R43C2	Annual Interest Paid—Year 1 LOAN * RATE%
18	R43C5	Annual Interest Paid—Year 2 R[−1]C[−3] * RATE%
19	R44C2	Annual Principal Paid PAY − R[−1]C
20	R48C2	MACRS Depreciation PROPERTY * 20%
21	R49C5	Taxable Income from Prior Year R[−17]C[−3] + R[−5]C[−3] − R[−1]C[−3]
22	R50C5	Tax on Corporate Income of $75,000 or More IF(R[−1]C> = 75000,13750 + 34% * (R[−1]C − 75000),0)

23	R51C5	Tax on Corporate Income of Less Than $75,000
		IF(AND(R[−2]C>0,R[−2]C<75000),
		  MIN(50000, R[−2]C)∗15%
		  +MAX(0,MIN(50000, R[−2]C−50000))
		  ∗25%,0)

24	R1C14	Spreadsheet Filename NAME()
25	R13C3	Percent of Sales RC[−1]/R12 C[−1]

SPREADSHEET SUMMARY—MODIFIED CASH FLOW ANALYSIS

General: The completed spreadsheet is shown in Figure 14-5. Use Transfer Save to name this version CASHFLOW.1. Use Options to turn on iteration and specify a completion test at R47C15. Use Insert Row to insert rows 42, 44, and 45. See the step-by-step instructions for editing the formulas. Use Lock Formulas to lock the new formulas.

Format: Use Format Cells to format R42C2 to a fixed code with 4 decimal places.

Name: R42C2 is MRATE.

Formulas: The formulas use relative and named cell references.

1	R47C15	Iteration Completion Test ITERCNT()=59
2	R46C15	Iteration Counter ITERCNT()
3	R42C2	Monthly Interest Rate RATE%/12

4	R44C2	Year 1—Interest Paid (final month)
		IF(ISNA(ITERCNT()),LOAN∗MRATE,
		  IF(ITERCNT()>11,RC,
		  R[−1]C∗MRATE))

5	R45C2	Year 1—Principal Paid (final month) $(PAY/12) - R[-1]C$
6	R46C2	Year 1—Annual Interest Paid $IF(ISNA(ITERCNT()),R[-2]C,$ $IF(ITERCNT()>11,RC,RC+R[-2]C))$
7	R44C5	Year 2—Interest Paid (final month) $IF(OR(ITERCNT()<12,ITERCNT()>23),$ $RC,IF(ITERCNT()=12,R[-1]C[-3]$ $* MRATE,R[-1]C * MRATE))$
8	R46C5	Year 2—Annual Interest Paid $IF(ITERCNT()<12,0,$ $IF(ITERCNT()>23,RC,RC+R[-2]C))$

PART 3

Using Multiplan
to the Fullest

15

Multiplan's Built-in Functions

Multiplan's dazzling array of functions lets you work with numbers and text in special ways. Functions are shortcuts built into the program to make it easy for you to perform common and complex calculations, extract information from cells, produce words from formulas, and select one of several possible answers. The spreadsheets in Chapters 3 through 14 demonstrate many of these functions. This chapter describes them all.

The function name tells Multiplan the kind of operation to perform. For example, the SUM function adds a list of numbers. The function name is always followed by parentheses that enclose the variables the function works with (altogether known as the argument). A variable can be:

- A reference to a cell that contains a number.

- A reference to a cell containing a formula that yields a number.

- A number that you supply.

- An arithmetic operator.

- A comparison operator.

- A symbol.

- A reference to a cell that contains text.

- Text that you supply.

- A cell name.

In some cases, no variables are required, but you must still provide the parentheses. Spaces are allowed only within text or as intersection operators.

You build a formula that contains a function the same way you build any other formula: Type *V* to start the Value command. Move the cursor to the cell references and type all the other elements, including the function name (in uppercase or lowercase), the parentheses, and any text, operators, and symbols that the formula needs. When the formula is complete, you press Enter.

In the following examples, the function names, text, and cell names are in uppercase. You can tell which is which by keeping this in mind: Function names are always followed by an open parenthesis, such as *SUM(*. Text, such as *"CHECK YOUR NUMBERS"*, is always enclosed in quotation marks. Cell names, such as *SALARIES*, stand alone with neither an open parenthesis nor quotation marks. The type of argument that a function requires is shown within the parentheses with initial letters capitalized.

ABS(Number)

ABS produces the absolute value of the number in parentheses. An absolute value is a number without a plus or minus sign. For example, *ABS(50 − 370)* produces *320*, not *− 320*.

AND(List)

AND, like OR and NOT, is a logical function. It is typically combined with the IF function to produce the logical value *TRUE* or *FALSE*. An AND list can contain two to five comparison tests at a time. If every test is true (correct), AND produces the true value. If even one test is false (incorrect), AND produces the false value. Here's an example of AND syntax:

IF(AND(PROFIT>15%,SALES>20000),COMMISSION + 250,0)

If both tests are true—that is, if profit is greater than 15% and sales are greater than 20000—the formula calculates the commission plus 250. If either test fails, the formula produces a zero.

If the AND list contains no comparison tests, the formula produces the error message *#VALUE!* (wrong type of value). AND is discussed further in Chapter 16.

ATAN(Number)

COS(Number)

SIN(Number)

TAN(Number)

These trigonometric functions deal with the relation of the sides and angles of triangles. COS, SIN, and TAN calculate the ratio of the relevant triangle sides when the argument is entered as an angle in radians. ATAN calculates the angle in radians when the ratio of the relevant triangle sides is entered. To convert angles from degrees to radians, multiply the degrees of the angle by .0174533. To convert angles from radians to degrees, multiply radians by 57.29578. For example, *SIN(45* * *.0174533)* produces *0.707107* (ratio). *ATAN(1)* * *57.29578* produces *45* (degrees). You can also use ATAN to calculate arcsine and arccosine.

AVERAGE(List)

AVERAGE adds the number values in the list and divides the result by a count of the entries, including cells containing zeros, to get the average. Blank cells and text cells are ignored. For example, *AVERAGE(1,5,6,5,5)* produces *4.4*. Other variations include *AVERAGE(SALES)*, *AVERAGE(SALES86, SALES87)*, and *AVERAGE(R1C1:10)*.

CHAR(Number)

CHAR produces the character represented by the ASCII code number in parentheses. ASCII stands for American Standard Code for Information Interchange. The number can be from 1 to 255. For example, *CHAR(82)* produces the letter *R*, and *CHAR(155)* produces the cents sign. If the number contains decimal places, Multiplan truncates it to an integer. If the number is negative, Multiplan treats it as if it were positive. If the number is outside the range of 1 to 255, Multiplan displays the error message *#VALUE!*.

CODE(Text)

CODE produces the ASCII code of the first character of text specified. The argument can be text enclosed in quotation marks or a reference to a cell containing text. For example, *CODE("Ruth")* produces *82* and *CODE("ruth")* produces *114*. The formula *CODE([RC−1])* produces the ASCII code of the

	1	2	3	4	5	6	7	8	9	10	11
1											
2			1	2	3	4					
3											
4											12
5		1									15
6		2			1988	1989	1990	1991	1992		18
7		3									21
8		4									
9		5									
10		6		6	5	4	3	2	1		
11											
12											

FIGURE 15-1.
Results generated by the COLUMN and ROW functions

first character of text in the referenced cell (in this case, the cell above the formula cell). If the referenced cell is empty or contains a number, the formula cell displays the error message #VALUE!.

COLUMN()

ROW()

COLUMN and ROW enter the column or row number of the cell containing the function. This is not the same as using the Print command to print column and row numbers along the top and left sides of a spreadsheet.

In Figure 15-1, the formula ROW() − 4 is entered in R5C2 and copied down five cells to generate the series of ascending numbers in column 2. The formula COLUMN() − 2 is entered in R2C3 and copied right three cells to produce the ascending series in row 2. 1988 + COLUMN() − 5 is copied right four cells from R6C5 to produce the series of years. To generate the descending numbers in row 10, 10 − COLUMN() is copied right five cells from R10C4. To generate the incremental numbers in column 11, 3 * ROW() is copied down three cells from R4C11. A multiplier can be one to several digits or a decimal fraction.

COS(Number)

See ATAN.

COUNT(List)

COUNT counts the number values in the list, including cells containing zeros. Blank cells and text cells are ignored. For example, *COUNT(14,7,9,1,6)* produces *5. COUNT(R1C1:10)*, where each cell in the range contains a number, produces *10. COUNT(SALARIES)* produces a count of the numbers in the cells named SALARIES.

DATE(Year,Month,Day)

DATE produces the serial number of the year, month, and day specified. The serial number is an integer from 1 to 65380 corresponding to the dates from January 1, 1900, to December 31, 2078. *DATE(1900,1,1)* produces *1* and *DATE(2078,12,31)* produces *65380*. The year, month, and day must be in the valid range—that is, a year from 1900 to 2078 (or, alternately, a number from 0 to 178), a month from 1 to 12, and a day from 1 to 31. If you use an invalid date, such as *DATE(2386,12,30)*, Multiplan displays the error message *#NUM!*. To show the serial number as a date, use the Format Time-Date Cells option.

DATEVALUE(Text)

DATEVALUE produces the serial number of the date specified. The date must be enclosed in quotation marks. For example, *DATEVALUE("6/21/31")* produces *11495*.

DAY(SerialNumber)

MONTH(SerialNumber)

WEEKDAY(SerialNumber)

YEAR(SerialNumber)

Each of these date functions produces an integer that corresponds to the serial number specified. DAY produces a number from 1 to 31; MONTH, a number from 1 to 12; WEEKDAY, a number from 1 to 7 (1 is Sunday and 7 is Saturday); and YEAR, a number from 1900 to 2078. For example, *DAY(3456)* produces *17* and *YEAR(36990)* produces *2001*. Valid serial numbers are in the range from 1 to 65380.

Combining the DAY and DATE functions converts a date into a serial number, then into an integer. For example, *DAY(DATE(1987,5,23))* produces *23*, and *WEEKDAY(DATE(87,10,15))* produces *5*, the number corresponding to Thursday. The WEEKDAY function, combined with the DATE function, simplifies the task of scheduling project deadlines to fall on business days, not weekends. For example, the spreadsheet in Chapter 7 uses the WEEKDAY function to calculate the weekdays remaining between the current date and a project deadline date.

DELTA()

DELTA is used with Multiplan's iteration feature to return the maximum change in values between iterations. You can use DELTA in a convergence test formula to calculate the results of an iteration process to any desired precision. For example, *DELTA()<0.000001* produces *TRUE* when convergence results are less than 0.000001.

DOLLAR(Number,NumberOfDecimals)

DOLLAR converts the number specified to text and adds Multiplan's default currency format. You can specify from 0 to 14 decimal places. If you omit decimal places, Multiplan rounds the number to two decimal places. A number in the default currency format is preceded by a dollar sign and followed by a decimal point and two decimal places. For example, *DOLLAR(5.256)* produces *$5.26* and *DOLLAR(5.256,0)* produces *$5*. If the number is less than 1, a zero appears in the position to the immediate left of the decimal point. If the number is negative, the result is enclosed in parentheses.

The DOLLAR function allows Multiplan to combine text and a calculated number in the same cell. After conversion to text, the number is treated as text and is no longer usable in arithmetic operations such as addition or subtraction. What makes this text-number so special is that it continues to be recalculated when the numbers it relates to in other cells change. The DOLLAR function is illustrated in Chapter 16.

EXP(Number)

EXP calculates the natural logarithm's base value e (2.7182818...) raised to the power of the number specified. This is the inverse of the function LN. Powers of other bases are calculated with the exponentiation operator $\wedge$. For example, *EXP(1)* produces *2.7182818* and *EXP(3)* produces *20.085537*.

FALSE()

TRUE()

FALSE and TRUE each produce their corresponding logical value. These two functions are often used with the IF function. They are handy to test the workings of a formula. For example, TRUE and FALSE are used as the Then and Else statements in the following formula:

IF(COSTS> = 453,TRUE(),FALSE())

If the entry in the COSTS cell is greater than or equal to 453, the formula enters the word *TRUE* in the formula cell. Otherwise, it enters the word *FALSE*. When your formula is working properly, replace *TRUE()* and *FALSE()* with actual Then and Else statements.

FIXED(Number,NumberOfDigits)

FIXED rounds the number specified to the number of digits (decimal places) specified and converts the result to text. The number of digits must be an integer between 0 and 14, inclusive. A negative number is preceded by a minus sign.

Like DOLLAR, the FIXED function allows Multiplan to combine text and a calculated number in the same cell. After conversion to text, the number is treated as text. Though it is no longer usable in arithmetic operations, it continues to be recalculated when the numbers it relates to on the spreadsheet change. The FIXED function is illustrated in Chapter 16.

FV(Rate,NPer,Pmt,PV,TimeOfPmt)

FV calculates the future value of an investment. *Rate* is the interest rate per period, *NPer* is the number of periods, *Pmt* is the periodic payment, *PV* (present value) is the amount, and *TimeOfPmt* is the time that payment is made, either at the end or at the beginning of the period. If payments are made at the end of each period, *TimeOfPmt* is 0; if payments are made at the beginning of each period, *TimeOfPmt* is 1.

Unless you specify otherwise, Multiplan assumes *PV* is 0 and *TimeOfPmt* is 0. Enter cash received as a positive value and cash paid out as a negative value. The rate and the number of periods must correspond to the same period. *Rate* can be either a decimal fraction or a whole number, depending on how you construct the formula. (See the discussion of the internal rate function, IRR, later in this chapter for an example.)

HOUR(SerialNumber)

MINUTE(SerialNumber)

SECOND(SerialNumber)

These three time functions produce an integer corresponding to the serial number specified. HOUR produces a number from 0 to 23. MINUTE and SECOND each produce a number from 0 to 59. Since the serial number for a unit of time smaller than a day is a decimal fraction between 0 and 1, HOUR, MINUTE, and SECOND use only the fractional part of the serial number you specify. For example, *HOUR(.9)* equals *21*. Combining time functions converts the time into a serial number, then into an integer. For example, if the current time is 4:15:37, the formula *MINUTE(NOW())* produces *15*, and *SECOND(TIME(4,48,25))* produces *25*.

IF(Test,Then,Else)

IF is a conditional function that establishes an either/or test condition. The Test statement compares two or more variables. If the result is true (correct), the Then statement produces the answer. If the result is false (incorrect), the Else statement produces the answer. For a complete discussion of the IF function, refer to Chapter 16.

INDEX(Area,Row,Column)

INDEX extracts values or text from the specified area of cells on the spreadsheet, based on the values in *Row* and *Column*. *Area* can be in a single row, a single column, or several rows and columns. *Row* and *Column* each must be a value or a reference to a cell containing a value.

Figure 15-2 shows a commission schedule consisting of three rows and four columns, which is the area R7C3:R9C6. In an INDEX formula, this area becomes a spreadsheet-within-a-spreadsheet that is independent of the spreadsheet row and column numbers. For example, the cells from R7C3 to R7C6 become row 1, and the cells from R7C3 to R9C3 become column 1. The formula *INDEX(R7C3:R9C6,2,3)* in R12C1 extracts *1.8%*—the entry in row 2 column 3 of the area. If you name the area COMMTABLE, you can use the formula *INDEX(COMMTABLE,2,3)*.

If *Area* is a single row, you can omit the *Row* reference; if *Area* is a single column, you can omit the *Column* reference. If the *Row* or *Column* numbers fall outside the *Area*, Multiplan displays the error message *#REF!*. You can see the INDEX function in glorious action in Chapter 11.

	1	2	3	4	5	6
1						
2						
3				Commission Schedule		
4				===		
5			Sales	Year 1	Year 2	Year 3
6			---			
7			$10,000	1.0%	1.2%	1.7%
8			$15,000	1.5%	1.8%	2.4%
9			$20,000	1.7%	2.5%	2.8%
10						
11						
12	1.8%					
13						
14						

FIGURE 15-2.

Commission table used by the INDEX function

INT(Number)

INT produces the largest whole number that is less than or equal to the number specified. For example, INT(3) produces 3, INT(19.7) produces 19, and INT(−1.999) produces −2.

IRR(List,Guess)

IRR calculates the internal rate of return of the cash flows in the list. The internal rate of return is the interest rate that equates the present value of the expected future cash flow to the initial outlay of funds making the net present value equal to zero. Multiplan produces the internal rate of return by the process of iteration, which bases the next calculation on the result of the previous calculation.

If you don't specify a guess, Multiplan provides an initial guess of 0% internal rate of return. If the formula can't produce an answer accurate to 0.00001% within 20 iterations, Multiplan displays #NUM! in the formula cell. Then it's your turn to guess. Try numbers between 0 and 100 until you get a percentage, not #NUM!.

Two techniques can make working with these types of functions easier. First, keep your guess in a separate cell instead of in a formula. By doing so, you can simply type in numbers instead of editing a formula repeatedly. Second, include % in the formula and format the formula cell for percentage. That way,

```
              1                    2
 1 Internal Rate of Return
 2 ===============================
 3 Cash Flow 1              ($75,000)
 4 Cash Flow 2               $60,000
 5 Cash Flow 3              ($12,500)
 6 Cash Flow 4               $41,000
 7 Cash Flow 5               $28,500
 8 Cash Flow 6              ($12,500)
 9 Cash Flow 7               $15,000
10
11 GUESS (%)                      15
12 IRR                         22.9%
```

FIGURE 15-3.
Cash flows illustrating the IRR function

you can type a whole number as your guess instead of a decimal fraction—say, 15 instead of .15.

Let's assume you're considering investing in a franchise operation. Your spreadsheet is shown in Figure 15-3. You expect to make an initial investment of $75,000 and two further payments of $12,500. You enter each cash outflow as a negative number (for example, −75000). Your Guess cell is R11C2. You enter this formula in R12C2:

IRR(R3C2:R9C2,R11C2%)

Multiplan calculates the internal rate of return as 22.9%. The first entry in the list must be a negative cash flow.

ISBLANK(Item)

ISBLANK produces a logical value of true if the item specified is a reference to a blank cell. Otherwise, it produces a logical value of false. For example, if cell R5C10 is empty, the formula ISBLANK(R5C10) displays the word TRUE. If R5C10 contains information, the formula displays the word FALSE. ISBLANK is often combined with the IF function. For example:

IF(ISBLANK(R5C10),"NEED NUMBER","OKAY")

If R5C10 is blank, the formula displays the message NEED NUMBER (the true value). Otherwise, it displays OKAY (the false value). In addition to their use in standard operations, ISBLANK and the other IS functions are handy in macros.

ISERROR(Item)

ISERROR produces a logical value of true if the item specified will generate an error message (#DIV/0!, #N/A, #NAME?, #NULL!, #NUM!, #REF!, or #VALUE!). Otherwise, it produces the logical value of false. ISERROR is often combined with the IF function to test for error conditions. For example:

IF(ISERROR(RATIO),"CHECK YOUR NUMBERS","")

If the cell named RATIO produces an error message, the formula displays the advice *CHECK YOUR NUMBERS* (the true value). If there is no error message, the text "" (the false value) makes the cell appear blank.

ISNA(Item)

ISNA produces the logical value of true if the item specified produces the error message *#N/A* (not available). Otherwise, it produces the logical value of false. Use ISNA in logical formulas to test for data that is not available.

Let's say you have a cell named BALANCE. If the balance isn't available yet, you enter the formula *NA()* in the BALANCE cell, which Multiplan translates into *#N/A*. The formula *ISNA(BALANCE)* produces *TRUE*. If you leave the BALANCE cell empty—without *NA()* in it—the formula produces *FALSE*. Now let's suppose you enter *IF(ISNA(BALANCE),0,BALANCE)*. If the BALANCE cell produces *#N/A*, the formula produces *0* (the true value). Otherwise, it copies the amount from the BALANCE cell (the false value).

ISNUMBER(Item)

ISNUMBER produces the logical value of true if the item specified is a number or a reference to a cell containing a number. Otherwise, it produces the logical value of false. For example, if cell R2C5 contains a number, the formula *ISNUMBER(R2C5)* displays the word *TRUE*. If R2C5 is empty or contains text, the formula displays *FALSE*. Use ISNUMBER in logical formulas to test for numbers.

ISREF(Item)

ISREF produces the logical value of true if the item specified is a reference to a defined name. Otherwise, it produces the logical value of false. Let's suppose you give cells C1 through C6 the name SALES, then enter *IF(ISREF (SALES),"ENTER THE NUMBERS","")*. Since the cells are named, the formula produces the test result *ENTER THE NUMBERS* (the true value). Otherwise, the double quotes (the false value) make the formula cell appear blank.

ISSTRING(Item)

ISSTRING produces the logical value of true if the item specified is text. Otherwise, it produces the logical value of false. For example, if cell R44C5 contains text, the formula *ISSTRING(R44C5)* produces the word *TRUE*. If R44C5 is empty or contains a value or text result of a logical formula, the formula produces *FALSE*.

ITERCNT()

ITERCNT returns the current iteration count and can be used to control the number of times Multiplan iterates (repeats) a formula's calculations. At the end of the first iteration after you make a change to the spreadsheet, ITERCNT produces the message #N/A. At the end of the second iteration, it produces a count of 1 and continues the count until the calculations are concluded. ITERCNT is used in the cash flow spreadsheet created in Chapter 14.

LEFT(Text,NumberOfCharacters)

RIGHT(Text,NumberOfCharacters)

LEFT produces the string of text specified by the number of characters you supply, starting with the leftmost character. RIGHT produces the string of text specified by the number of characters you supply, starting with the rightmost character. The argument can contain the text itself enclosed in quotation marks or a reference to a cell containing text. The number of characters must be greater than zero. The default is one. If the number of characters is greater than the length of text, Multiplan returns the entire string.

For example, *LEFT("WELCOME TO THE WORLD OF MULTI-PLAN",20)* produces *WELCOME TO THE WORLD* and *RIGHT("WEL-COME TO THE WORLD OF MULTIPLAN",22)* produces *THE WORLD OF MULTIPLAN*. As another example, if R5C3 contains the word *Sales*, the formula *IF("Sal" = LEFT(R5C3,3),1,0)* produces *1*, the true value.

LEN(Text)

LEN produces a count of the characters in the specified text. For example, the formula *LEN("Your report has been accepted.")* produces *30*—that is, 26 letter characters plus four space characters. The argument must be text enclosed in quotation marks or a reference to a cell containing text.

LN(Number)

LN computes the natural logarithm, to the base e, of the number in parentheses. The number must be greater than zero. This is the inverse of the function EXP. For example, $LN(2.7182818)$ produces 1.

LOG10(Number)

LOG10 computes the value of the common (base 10) logarithm of the number specified. The number must be greater than zero. For example, the formula $LOG10(100)$ produces 2, $LOG10(150)$ produces 2.1760913, and $LOG10(1000)$ produces 3.

LOOKUP(SearchValue, Table)

LOOKUP searches for the specified value in the specified table and retrieves the corresponding number, text, or logical value. For a complete discussion of the LOOKUP function, refer to Chapter 17.

LOWER(Text)

UPPER(Text)

LOWER converts uppercase letters to lowercase, and UPPER converts lowercase letters to uppercase. The argument can contain the text itself enclosed in quotation marks or a cell reference. For example, if R7C2 contains the text *E.E.Cummings*, the formula *LOWER(R7C2)* produces *e.e.cummings*. If R3C4 contains the text *Quarterly Sales Report*, the formula *UPPER(R3C4)* produces *QUARTERLY SALES REPORT*. These functions are useful when you download files from other programs or redo a spreadsheet created by someone else.

Using the LOWER and UPPER functions is a simple three-step process: Enter the formula in another cell, convert the resulting value to text, then copy the text to the original cell. Let's suppose you want to convert *Quarterly Sales Report* in R3C4 to uppercase. In R5C4, you enter the formula *UPPER(R3C4)*. Though R5C4 displays *QUARTERLY SALES REPORT*, it stores the formula *UPPER(R3C4)*. To convert the formula to its text result, leave the cursor on R5C4, type *E* (Edit), press the F4 key, and press Enter. Cell R5C4 now displays and stores the text *QUARTERLY SALES REPORT*. You can copy this text to R3C4, then blank out R5C4.

MAX(List)

MIN(List)

MAX extracts the largest number in the list, and MIN extracts the smallest number. Blank cells and text cells are ignored. If the list contains no numbers, MAX and MIN produce a zero. For example, *MAX(SALARIES)* extracts the largest number from the cells named SALARIES. The formula *10% * MIN(25000 − SALES,COST)* produces 10% of either 25000 minus SALES or the value of COST, whichever is less.

MID(Text,Start,NumberOfCharacters)

MID extracts the specified characters from the specified text. The text must be enclosed in quotation marks. *Start* is the starting position counting from the first character of the specified text. *NumberOfCharacters* is the number of characters to extract. For example:

    MID("10/07/88",4,2)

The start position of 4 translates into the fourth character (the 0) after the opening quotation marks. The number of characters is 2, so the formula extracts 07. If the start number is greater than the length of text or the number of characters is 0, no characters are returned. The MID function is shown combined with the VALUE function later in this chapter.

MIN(List)

See MAX.

MINUTE(SerialNumber)

See HOUR.

MIRR(List,Safe,Risk)

MIRR calculates the modified internal rate of return of the cash flows in the list, using a safe interest rate returned by the investment to finance the negative cash flows, and a risk interest rate to reinvest the positive cash flows. Figure 15-4 uses the same cash flows, formula structure, and formatting as the example in Figure 15-3, which demonstrates IRR (internal rate of return). You enter the safe interest rate in R11C2, and the risk interest rate in R12C2. The formula in R13C2 is:

    MIRR(R3C2:R9C2,R11C2%,R12C2%)

Assuming a safe interest rate of 13% and a risk interest rate of 19%, Multiplan calculates the modified rate of return at 19.6%.

```
               1                    2
 1 Modified Internal Rate of Return
 2 =====================================
 3 Cash Flow 1              ($75,000)
 4 Cash Flow 2               $60,000
 5 Cash Flow 3              ($12,500)
 6 Cash Flow 4               $41,000
 7 Cash Flow 5               $28,500
 8 Cash Flow 6              ($12,500)
 9 Cash Flow 7               $15,000
10
11 SAFE RATE (%)                  13
12 RISK RATE (%)                  19
13 MIRR                        19.6%
```

FIGURE 15-4.
Cash flows illustrating the MIRR function

MOD(Numerator,Denominator)

MOD calculates the remainder (modulus) of the numerator divided by the denominator. The result has the same sign as the denominator. Both the numerator and denominator must be numbers or references to cells that produce numbers.

For example, the formula *MOD(65,9)* produces *2* (*65* divided by *9* equals *7*, with 2 remaining). If R[− 6]C contains *12* and R3C7 contains *7*, the formula *MOD(R[− 6]C,R3C7)* produces *5* (12 divided by 7 equals 1, with 5 remaining). To illustrate the sign characteristics: *MOD(− 3,2)* produces *1*, and *MOD(3, − 2)* produces *− 1*. If the denominator is zero, Multiplan produces the error message *#DIV/0!* (can't divide by zero).

MONTH(SerialNumber)

See DAY.

N(Range)

N retrieves a value from either a single cell or a cell in the upper left corner of a range, whichever is specified. If the cell doesn't contain a numeric value, N returns a zero. Let's suppose you have a range from R5C5 to R5C7. The formula *N(R5C5:7)* looks at R5C5. If R5C5 contains a number, a formula that produces a number, or a reference to a cell containing a number or formula, Multiplan enters that value in the formula cell. If R5C5 contains text or a logical value such as *TRUE* or *FALSE*, Multiplan enters *0* instead.

NA()

NA produces #N/A when information is not yet available. Let's suppose your spreadsheet needs an interest rate you don't know yet, so you enter NA() in the interest rate cell as a reminder. Multiplan then displays #N/A in the interest rate cell and in every cell that refers to it until you enter the rate.

NAME()

NAME generates the filename of the spreadsheet in the cell in which you enter this function. For example, if you save your spreadsheet under the name STARTUP, then enter NAME() in R1C12, Multiplan displays STARTUP in that cell. If you later rename the spreadsheet, the cell will display the new name.

NOT(Logical)

NOT is a logical function that reverses the result of the comparison test in parentheses. If the test condition is true (correct), NOT produces FALSE. If the test condition is false (incorrect), NOT produces TRUE. NOT is typically used with the IF function to return the logical value of TRUE or FALSE.

NOW()

NOW enters in a cell the serial number for the current date and time, based on the date and time you set at the DOS prompt at start-up or on the date and time kept by your computer's battery-powered clock. This result is updated at every recalculation. The serial number has an integer part and a decimal part. The integer part is in the range from 0 to 65380, corresponding to the dates from January 1, 1900, to December 31, 2078. The decimal part is in the range between 0 and 1, corresponding to the times from 12:00:00 AM (midnight), or 0:00:00 on the 24-hour clock, to 11:59:59 PM, or 23:59:59 on the 24-hour clock.

Let's assume the current date and time are June 21, 1987, at 10:20:45 in the morning. Enter NOW() and Multiplan produces the serial number 31949.431. To show the serial number as a date and time, you use the Format Time-Date Cells option and select format m/d/yy h:mm (month/day/year hour:minute). Multiplan now produces 6/21/87 10:20.

NPER(Rate,Pmt,PV,FV,TimeOfPmt)

NPER produces the number of payments required for an investment. *Rate* is the interest rate per period, *Pmt* is the periodic payment, *PV* (present value) is the amount, *FV* is the future value of the investment, and *TimeOfPmt* is the time that the payment is made, either at the end or beginning of the period. If payments are made at the end of each period, *TimeOfPmt* is 0; if payments are made at the beginning of each period, *TimeOfPmt* is 1.

Unless you specify otherwise, Multiplan assumes *FV* is 0 and *TimeOfPmt* is 0. The rate can be either a decimal fraction or a whole number, depending on how you construct the formula. (See the discussion of IRR earlier in this chapter for an example).

NPV(Rate,List)

NPV calculates the net present value of the specified list. This list contains a series of dollar amounts that will be received at future intervals. Future dollars are not equivalent to present dollars because of the time difference and are, therefore, discounted at the constant interest rate specified in *Rate*.

NPV uses the following formula:

$$\sum_{i=1}^{n} \frac{\text{list}_i}{(1+\text{rate})^i}$$

where: n sigma $i=1$ is the sum of discounted cash flows from period 1 through n.
      list   is the expected net cash flow per year from the project.
      rate   is the required rate of return.

The list can contain numbers or references to cells containing numbers. Multiplan ignores text, blank, and logical cells. The interest rate is expressed as a decimal fraction.

Let's suppose your company is considering investing $45,000 in a project estimated to yield $13,500 after income taxes each year for five years. Your spreadsheet looks like the one in Figure 15-5. You require a 12% rate of return, which you enter in R12C2. With the rate in a separate cell, you can simply type in a new rate you want to test instead of editing the formula. When you enter NPV(R12C2%,R6:10C2) in R13C2, the formula calculates the expected cash flows to a present value of $48,664.48.

```
                    1                2
 1 Net Present Value
 2 ===================================
 3 Investment              $45,000
 4
 5 Cash Flows:
 6   Year 1                $13,500
 7   Year 2                $13,500
 8   Year 3                $13,500
 9   Year 4                $13,500
10   Year 5                $13,500
11
12 RATE OF RETURN (%)         12.0
13 NET PRESENT VALUE     $48,664.48
```

FIGURE 15-5.
Cash flows illustrating the NPV function

OR(List)

OR, like AND and NOT, is a logical function. It is typically combined with the IF function. An OR list can contain two to five comparison tests at a time. Only one of the tests needs to be true (correct) for OR to return *TRUE*. If every test is false (incorrect), OR produces *FALSE*. Here's an example of OR syntax:

IF(OR(PROFIT>15%,SALES>20000),COMMISSION + 100,0)

If either test is true—profit is greater than 15% or sales are greater than 20000—the formula calculates the commission plus 100. If both tests fail, the formula produces a zero.

PI()

PI() produces the value *3.14159265358979*, which approximates the mathematical constant pi (π). For example, *PI() * 2* produces *6.28318530717959*. The circumference of a circle equals two times pi times the radius. If the radius is 6 inches, *PI() * 2 * 6* yields approximately 37.7 inches.

PMT(Rate,NPer,PV,FV,TimeOfPmt)

PMT calculates the payments on a loan for a given period of time at a given interest rate. *Rate* is the interest rate per period, *NPer* is the number of periods or term of the loan, *PV* (present value) is the amount of the loan, *FV* is the future value of the loan, and *TimeOfPmt* is the time each payment is made, either at the end or at the beginning of the period. If payments are made at the end of each period, *TimeOfPmt* is 0; if payments are made at the beginning of each period, *TimeOfPmt* is 1. Unless you specify otherwise, Multiplan assumes *FV* is 0 at the end of the loan, and *TimeOfPmt* is 0. Your entry of *FV* and *TimeOfPmt* is optional, but if you change the *TimeOfPmt* entry to 1, enter an *FV* number (normally 0). Enter cash received as a positive value and cash paid out as a negative value. *Rate* and *NPer* must correspond to the same period. You can see an example of the PMT function in the loan amortization spreadsheet in Chapter 5.

PROPER(Text)

PROPER capitalizes certain characters of the specified text, namely the first letter and each letter that follows a space or a punctuation mark, and converts all other letters to lowercase. Any non-text characters are ignored. The text must be enclosed in quotation marks. For example, *PROPER("LOVE is a 4-letter word")* produces *Love Is A 4-Letter Word*. PROPER is handy when you download files that are in a different format than your own.

PV(Rate,NPer,Pmt,FV,TimeOfPmt)

PV calculates the present value of an investment. *Rate* is the interest rate per period, *NPer* is the number of periods, *Pmt* is the periodic payment, *FV* is the future value of the investment, and *TimeOfPmt* is the time each payment is made, either at the end or at the beginning of the period. If payments are made at the end of each period, *TimeOfPmt* is 0; if payments are made at the beginning of each period, *TimeOfPmt* is 1.

Unless you specify otherwise, Multiplan assumes *FV* is 0 and *TimeOfPmt* is 0. Enter cash received as a positive value and cash paid out as a negative value. *Rate* and *NPer* must correspond to the same period. *Rate* can be either a decimal fraction or a whole number, depending on how you construct the formula. (See the discussion of IRR earlier in this chapter for an example.)

RAND()

RAND generates random numbers between 0 and 1. Entering *RAND()* in a cell causes the cell to display a new random number every time Multiplan recalculates the spreadsheet. For example, in a cell formatted for two decimal places, *RAND()* may produce *0.87* one time, *0.39* the next, and *0.55* the time after that. The RAND function is useful to simulate business models.

```
                   1                        2      3    4
 1 Rate
 2 ==================================================
 3 Initial Investment              ($175,000)  PV
 4 Annual Income                    $35,000    PMT
 5 Time of Year (0=Start, 1=End)         0     TIMEOFPMT
 6 Number of Years Held                  5     NPER
 7 Future Value of Investment      $250,000    FV
 8 Est Annual Rate of Return (%)        15     GUESS
 9
10 Annual Rate of Return               25.2%   RATE
```

FIGURE 15-6.
Investment spreadsheet illustrating the RATE function

RATE(NPer, Pmt, PV, FV, TimeOfPmt, Guess)

RATE calculates the interest rate per period. *NPer* is the number of periods, *Pmt* is the periodic payment, *PV* (present value) is the amount, *FV* is the future value, *TimeOfPmt* is the time each payment is made, either at the end or at the beginning of the period, and *Guess* is what you think the interest rate might be. If payments are made at the end of each period, *TimeOfPmt* is 0; if payments are made at the beginning of each period, *TimeOfPmt* is 1. Unless you specify otherwise, Multiplan assumes *FV* is 0 at the end of the term, *TimeOfPmt* is 0, and *Guess* is 0.

Suppose you are considering investing in real estate for income purposes. Your spreadsheet is shown in Figure 15-6. The number of periods (*NPer*) is in R6C2, the payment (*Pmt*) is in R4C2, the amount (*PV*) is in R3C2, the future value (*FV*) is in R7C2, the time (*TimeOfPmt*) is in R5C2, and the guess (*Guess*) is in R8C2. You enter the following formula in R10C2:

RATE(R6C2,R4C2,R3C2,R7C2,R5C2,R8C2%)

The % in the formula and the percentage format in the formula cell let you type a whole number as your guess instead of a decimal fraction—for example, *15* instead of *.15*. If *#NUM!* appears in the formula cell, try different numbers between 0 and 100 in the guess cell until the result is a percentage. If you name each cell as shown in column 4, you can even use the formula:

RATE(NPER,PMT,PV,FV,TIMEOFPMT,GUESS%)

Looks familiar, doesn't it?

```
              1         2         3         4         5       6             7
 1                        QUARTERLY SALES BY TERRITORY
 2                               (in thousands)
 3    =======================================================================
 4                     Qtr 1     Qtr 2     Qtr 3    Qtr 4     YTD
 5    ------------------------------------------------------------------------
 6    East            123       314       476               913  ******************
 7    West            117       284       201               602  ************
 8    Middle           78        80        98               256  *****
 9    North            95       117       105               317  ******
10    South           130       155       201               486  *********
```

FIGURE 15-7.
Bar graph created with the REPT function

REPT(Text,Count)

REPT repeats the text specified the number of times specified by *Count*. The text, which can consist of one or more characters, must be enclosed in quotation marks or be contained in a cell reference. If *Count* is a number with decimal places, Multiplan truncates the number to an integer. The REPT function is used to create the lines on the spreadsheets in Chapters 3 through 14.

In Figure 15-7, the REPT function creates a bar graph. The formula *REPT(" * ",RC[− 1]/50)* is copied down four cells from R6C7. The numbers in column 6 are divided by 50 to reduce the number of repetitions proportionally. Here, the numbers are represented by asterisks, but you can repeat any character or symbol.

RIGHT(Text,NumberOfCharacters)

See LEFT.

ROUND(Number,NumberOfDecimals)

ROUND produces a number rounded to the number of decimals specified. For example, *ROUND(3.1416,3)* produces *3.142*. When the number of decimals specified is 0, the number is rounded to an integer. For example, *ROUND(3.1416,0)* produces *3*.

When the number of decimals is negative, the integer portion of the number is rounded. With − 1 as the number of decimals, the integer is rounded up when the number is 5 or more, and rounded down when it is less than 5. For example, *ROUND(25, − 1)* produces *30* and *ROUND(3.1416, − 1)* produces *0*. With *− 2* as the number of decimals, the integer is rounded up when the number is 50 or more, and rounded down when it is less than 50. For example, *ROUND(52, − 2)* produces *100* and *ROUND(49, − 2)* produces *0*.

ROW()

See COLUMN.

S(Range)

S retrieves text from either a single cell or a cell in the upper left corner of a range, whichever is specified. If the cell doesn't contain text, S enters "" in the formula cell, which makes the cell appear empty.

Let's suppose you have a range from R3C9 through R5C13. The formula *S(R3:5C9:13)* looks at R3C9. If R3C9 contains text, Multiplan enters that text in the formula cell. If R3C9 contains a number, a formula, a reference to a cell containing a number or formula, or a logical value such as *TRUE* or *FALSE*, Multiplan enters "" instead.

SECOND(SerialNumber)

See HOUR.

SIGN(Number)

SIGN produces a 1, 0, or − 1 to represent the algebraic sign of the number specified. If the number is positive, SIGN produces a 1. If the number is zero, SIGN produces a 0. If the number is negative, SIGN produces a − 1. For example, *SIGN(34)* produces *1*, *SIGN(0)* produces *0*, and *SIGN(− 34)* produces *− 1*.

SIN(Number)

See ATAN.

SQRT(Number)

SQRT produces the square root of the number specified. For example, the formula *SQRT(576)* produces *24*, *SQRT(SUM(4,3,7,6,5))* produces *5*, and *SQRT(ABS(− 4) + 1)* produces *2.236*, rounded to three decimal places. If the number is negative, Multiplan produces the error message *#NUM!* (illegal use of an arithmetic function) in the formula cell.

STDEV(List)

STDEV calculates the standard deviation of the numbers in the list—in other words, how far away these values are from their average. STDEV is represented by the following formula:

$$ s = \sqrt{\frac{\sum x^2 - \frac{(\Sigma x)^2}{n}}{n-1}} $$

where: $\text{sigma } x^2$ is the sum of a list of squared numbers,
         $(\text{sigma } x)^2$ is the sum of the numbers, squared,
            n is the count of the numbers in the list,

To clarify the mechanics of the calculation, assume that 1, 2, 3, 3, and 6 are the numbers in the list. The sum of each number squared is 59. The sum of all the numbers, squared, is 225. The count of the numbers is 5. The count of the numbers minus 1 is 4. Therefore, the formula is:

$$ \text{Standard deviation} = \sqrt{\frac{59 - \frac{225}{5}}{4}} $$

The rounded result of this calculation is a standard deviation of *1.871*, which is the number returned when you use the simple Multiplan formula *STDEV(1,2,3,3,6)* and format for three decimal places. The list can consist of named cells, such as *STDEV(SALARIES)*, or cell locations, such as *STDEV(R1C1:R6C1)*.

SUM(List)

SUM adds the numbers in the list. The list can contain numbers or cell references. Text cells are ignored. For example, *SUM(51,36,25,24,15)* produces *151*. *SUM(RC[+ 5],R6:16C3,R23C10)* adds the numbers in these cells. *SUM(RECEIPTS)* adds the numbers in the cells named RECEIPTS.

TAN(Number)

See ATAN.

TIME(Hour, Minute, Second)

TIME produces the serial number of the *Hour*, *Minute*, and *Second* specified. The serial number is expressed as a decimal between 0 and 1, corresponding to the time from 12:00:00 AM (midnight), 0:00:00 on the 24-hour clock, to 11:59:59 PM, 23:59:59 on the 24-hour clock. For example, *TIME(6,0,0)* produces *0.25* (one-quarter of a day) and *TIME(15,45,0) + TIME(9,45,0)* produces *1.0625* (a bit more than one full day). If you specify an invalid time, Multiplan displays the error message *#NUM!*.

TIMEVALUE(Text)

TIMEVALUE produces the serial number of the specified text. The time can be in any of Multiplan's time formats and must be enclosed in quotation marks. For example, *TIMEVALUE("12:00 PM")* produces *0.5*.

TRIM(Text)

TRIM removes the extra spaces where more than one space exists between the words in the text. The text must be enclosed in quotation marks. TRIM is handy when you download data such as stock market reports from an information service. For example, the formula *TRIM("The X Y Z Company")* produces *The X Y Z Company*.

TRUE()

See FALSE.

UPPER(Text)

See LOWER.

VALUE(Text)

VALUE converts the specified text to a number. The text must be enclosed in quotation marks and can contain a dollar sign, minus sign, commas, or decimal places. It can even be written in scientific notation. For example, each of these formulas produces the number *10*: *VALUE("10")*, *VALUE("$10.00")*, and *VALUE("1E1")*. Both of these formulas return *−10*: *VALUE("−10")* and *VALUE("−1E1")*.

If the text contains non-numeric characters, Multiplan displays the error message *#VALUE!* (wrong type of value) in the formula cell. You can prevent this by isolating the numbers from the non-numeric characters. For example, assume you get a discount if you pay a bill by a certain date, say the 30th of the

	1 Discount Date	2 Current Date	3 Days Remaining
1			
2			
3	--		
4	30	11-12-85	18
5	30	11-21-85	9
6	30	11-25-85	5
7	30	11-28-85	2

FIGURE 15-8.
The VALUE function

month. Your spreadsheet looks like the one in Figure 15-8. The dates in column 2 are text (each was entered directly from the Alpha command). You enter the following formula in R4C3 and copy it down three cells:

$$RC[-2] - VALUE(MID(RC[-1],4,2))$$

The formula uses the MID function to select two characters from the current date, starting with the fourth character. The VALUE function converts the result to a number, which is subtracted from the discount date to give you the days remaining for discount.

WEEKDAY(SerialNumber)

See DAY.

YEAR(SerialNumber)

See DAY.

16

The Versatile IF Function

You make decisions every day, setting conditions and selecting between alternative actions. At the supermarket, for example, you may tell yourself, "If steak is $3.50 or less per pound, I'll buy two pounds, but if steak is more than $3.50 per pound, I'll buy only one pound." Or, "If there's no line at the movie house, I'll buy a ticket, otherwise I'll just go home and watch TV." Or, "If they have that beige suit in my size and the price is right, I'll buy the beige suit, otherwise I'll buy only a sports jacket." These are all examples of your logical decision-making process, based on whether the condition you set turns out to be true or false.

In the wonderful world of electronic spreadsheets, the IF function lets you write a formula that produces an answer to either-or questions. You probably won't want to use an IF formula to decide whether to buy one or two pounds of steak although you could, as you'll soon see, but you do need to understand how IF formulas can help you analyze business problems and decide between logical alternatives. These are the elements of IF formulas:

■ An IF formula begins with the word IF and an open parenthesis, and ends with a close parenthesis. Within the parentheses are three statements: Test, Then, and Else, separated by commas.

■ The Test statement can use one of six symbols known as logical operators to compare two variables. These symbols are: $<$ (less than), $>$ (greater than), $=$ (equal to), $<=$ (less than or equal to), $>=$ (greater than or equal to), and $<>$ (not equal to).

■ If the Test condition is true (that is, correct), the Then statement, the first alternative, produces your answer. If the Test condition is false (that is, incorrect), the Else statement, the second alternative, produces your answer.

The steak example in the form of an IF formula (not an actual IF formula the way Multiplan can use it) would look like this:

IF(STEAK<=3.50,BUY 2 POUNDS,BUY 1 POUND)

The Test statement *Steak is less than or equal to $3.50 per pound* is followed by the Then statement *Buy 2 pounds* which is followed by the Else statement *Buy 1 pound*. If the Test statement is true, you'll buy two pounds of steak. If the Test statement is false, you'll buy only one pound.

I'll get back to the steak example shortly and turn it into an actual IF formula, but first let's take a closer look at the Test, Then, and Else statements.

THE TEST STATEMENT

The Test statement compares two variables, usually values. For example, R23C10>R10C7 compares the number in R23C10 to see if it is greater than the number in R10C7. Both cells happen to be absolute references (they have row and column coordinates) but they can just as easily be relative references such as RC[-3]<=R[+4]C, named references such as SALES>TOTAL, any combination of references such as R23C10<RC[-3] or SALES>R23C10 or RC[-3]=SALES, or a cell reference and a number you supply such as R23C10>100.

You can also compare the results of calculations. Let's suppose you're working with these cell locations:

■ Cell R5C4 contains the number *5*

■ Cell R2C7 contains the number *44*

■ Cell R1C5 contains the number *6*

■ Cell R10C12 contains the number *7*

You want the Test statement to add the numbers in the first two cells to see if the result is greater than multiplying the numbers in the last two cells. Your Test statement, therefore, looks like this:

IF(R5C4+R2C7>R1C5*R10C12

Since the Test statement is true (5+44 is greater than 6*7), whatever you defined as the Then statement produces your answer.

Multiplan can also compare the text in a Test statement and a cell. You must use an equal sign as the logical operator and enclose the text in the Test statement in quotation marks. Let's suppose you are working on tax forms for your clients and you enter either *Married* or *Single* in R3C5. Your Test statement can then be *IF(R3C5 = "Married"* followed by Then and Else statements. If R3C5 contains *Married*, the Then statement produces your answer. If R3C5 contains *Single*, the Else statement produces your answer. The text in the cell must match the formula perfectly (uppercase and lowercase, as well as spelling) for it to work properly. Multiplan can even compare the text in two cells. Again, the equal sign must be the logical operator.

THE THEN AND ELSE STATEMENTS

IF formulas produce either a numeric or a text answer, depending on how you construct the Then and Else statements. The syntax for a numeric answer is IF(Test,Then,Else). To see how Then and Else statements work, let's assume you enter the price of a pound of steak, say *3.39*, in R5C6. In another cell, you enter the formula:

IF(R5C6< = 3.50,2,1)

The Test statement looks at the price of steak in R5C6 and finds *3.39*. Because 3.39 is less than 3.50, the Test condition is true. Therefore, the Then statement produces *2*, the true answer. If R5C6 contained a value larger than 3.50, for example *3.75*, the Else statement would produce *1*, the false answer.

Now, suppose you want an answer in plain English. The syntax for a text answer is IF(Test,"Then","Else"). Notice that the Then and Else statements are enclosed in quotation marks. The formula now looks like this:

IF(R5C6< = 3.50,"BUY 2 POUNDS","BUY 1 POUND")

The Test statement looks at the price of steak in R5C6. If the Test statement is true, the Then statement produces *BUY 2 POUNDS*. If the Test statement is false, the Else statement produces *BUY 1 POUND*. The quotation marks don't appear in the answer.

If you name the price cell STEAK, the formula is even simpler and more readable. It works the same way and looks like this:

IF(STEAK< = 3.50,"BUY 2 POUNDS","BUY 1 POUND")

You can construct your Then and Else statements so that one produces a number and the other text. The syntax is IF(Test,Then,"Else") or IF(Test,"Then",Else).

If you use double quotation marks as your Then or Else statement, you can make the formula cell appear empty, depending on which statement produces the answer. The syntax is IF(Test," ",Else) or IF(Test,Then," ").

SPACES IN AN IF FORMULA

There are no spaces between the statements in an IF formula. The Test statement ends with a comma, followed immediately by the Then statement, another comma, and the Else statement. The only place you can use a space is between words in a text statement. The spaces in the Then statement "*BUY 2 POUNDS*" in the preceding formula are fine. The space between the comma and the *100* in *IF(R[−3]>15, 100∗R[+4],0)* isn't.

ENTERING AN IF FORMULA

You enter an IF formula the same way you enter any other formula: Place the cursor on the cell that will receive the formula and type V to start the Value command. Move the cursor to the cell locations you want in the formula and type everything else. When the formula is complete, press Enter.

SUGGESTIONS FOR BUILDING YOUR OWN IF FORMULAS

The IF function is a valuable asset and a great timesaver, but you may need to practice a little before you feel totally comfortable with it. Here are some suggestions when you can't get your IF formula to work (and there will be those times):

■ Carefully rethink what you want the formula to do. Plan each statement in the formula step by step.

■ Experiment with a similar but simpler problem to which you already know the answer.

■ Review the formula syntax: Did you include Then and Else statements? Are there any spaces between statements? Did you use a comma between statements? Are there an equal number of open and close parentheses? Did you put quotation marks around text?

■ Try out your Test statement by first using 1 and 0 for the Then and Else statements. It's much easier (and less frustrating) than retyping long or complicated statements. When the formula works, replace the 1 and 0 with the real statements.

■ Try reversing the comparison operator in the Test statement (for example, change < to >). This process sometimes helps identify the problem.

■ Try revising your Then and Else statements.

A few words of caution, though: Don't reverse or revise the entire formula at once. Try one change at a time so that you can check each result separately.

THE MINI-SPREADSHEETS

The mini-spreadsheets in the following section explore a few of the virtually unlimited ways to use IF formulas. Some formulas use more than one Multiplan function, others produce answers in everyday English, and still others contain a second, or nested, IF formula in their Then or Else statements.

Each example includes a description of the hypothetical situation, the formula itself, a description of the formula concept (in Multiplan terminology), and an explanation of the formula. At the end of each example, you'll find a summary that explains how to create the spreadsheet. Take it one step at a time and you should have no trouble at all.

SALES BONUS

Your company pays each salesperson a 5% bonus on sales over $5,000 per month. You need a formula that covers both the salespeople who are eligible for the bonus and those who aren't. The spreadsheet is shown in Figure 16-1. The bonus formula is in column 3. It uses relative cell references only.

Formula: IF(RC[−1]>5000,5% * (RC[−1]−5000),0)

Concept: IF Sales is greater than $5,000, Then give a 5% bonus on anything over $5,000, Else no bonus.

Explanation: The Test statement checks the sales in column 2 for each salesperson. If sales are greater than $5,000, the Then statement (5% of sales minus 5000) calculates the bonus. If sales are less than or equal to $5,000, the Else statement enters a zero.

	1 Employee	2 Sales	3 Bonus
1	Employee	Sales	Bonus
2	==		
3	Karen	$5,500	$25
4	Elizabeth	$4,500	$0
5	David	$8,000	$150
6	Clark	$5,000	$0

FIGURE 16-1.
Sales bonus calculations

Multiplan's normal order of calculation is multiplication and division, then addition and subtraction. The parentheses around *(RC[−1]−5000)* change this order so that *5000* is subtracted from the sales figure before the result is multiplied by 5%.

Spreadsheet Summary: Use Format Width to increase columns 2 and 3 to 13 characters each. For the double line, use Value to enter REPT(" = ",13) in R2C1, then Copy Right two cells. Use Format Cells to right-justify the titles *Sales* and *Bonus* in row 1 and dollar code with no decimal places the sales and bonus amounts in columns 2 and 3. Use Format Options to insert commas in the large numbers. Use Value to enter the formula in R3C3, then Copy Down 3 cells and recalculate by pressing F4.

INVENTORY CONTROL

You need a formula on your inventory control spreadsheet that shows in plain English how much to reorder when stocks are running low. You also want to know the status of every item, whether you must reorder it or not. The spreadsheet in Figure 16-2 shows how to use an IF function to do this. The formula, which is in column 4, uses relative cell references only.

Formula: IF(RC[−2]<RC[−1],"REORDER "
&FIXED(RC[−1]−RC[−2],0),"No Action")

Concept: IF Stock on Hand is less than Optimum Level, Then tell me the amount to REORDER, Else tell me No Action is needed.

Explanation: The Test statement compares the stock on hand in column 2 and the optimum level in column 3 for each item in your inventory. If the stock on hand is less than the optimum level, the Then statement subtracts the stock on hand from the optimum level and displays the result, preceded by the word *REORDER*. If the stock is equal to or greater than the optimum level, the Else statement displays the words *No Action*. The quotation marks in the formula tell Multiplan which words are text.

The Then statement is particularly interesting. The FIXED function converts the result of the subtraction to a text number with no decimal places (that's the 0 in the Then statement) so that Multiplan can display the text number and the text *REORDER* in the same cell. The converted number still looks like a number to us, but Multiplan treats it like a word made up of alphabetic characters. If you change the amount of stock or the optimum level, Multiplan recalculates the number accordingly. You can't use this text number in any arithmetic calculations. You cannot, for example, add it to another number.

```
        1           2          3          4
1                 Stock    Optimum
2 Item            on Hand   Level      Status
3 ==================================================
4 Widgets           30       55       REORDER 25
5 Gadgets           16       10        No Action
6 Gidgets           41       73       REORDER 32
```

FIGURE 16-2.
Inventory control information

The & sign in the Then statement links *REORDER* and the converted-to-text number and treats them as a unit. The & sign is Multiplan's concatenation operator, and the process is called concatenation. The space between the final *R* in *REORDER* and the closing quotation marks in the Test statement produces the space between *REORDER* and the reorder number in the answer.

Spreadsheet Summary. Use Format Width to increase columns 1 through 3 to 11 characters, and column 4 to 15 characters. For the double line, use Value to enter REPT(" = ",15) in R3C1, then use Copy Right to copy it 3 cells to the right. Use Format Cells to center the titles and numbers in columns 2 through 4. Use Value to enter the formula in R4C4 and Copy Down 2 cells.

TRAVEL EXPENSES

Employees who travel on company business receive a cash advance to cover expenses. When you get the trip report, you want to calculate how much money your company owes the employee over the amount of the advance or how much the employee must repay. Figures 16-3 and 16-4 show two versions of the spreadsheet. The three IF formulas use relative cell references only. The SUM formulas in R10C4 and R10C5 add the entries in each column.

FORMULA 1

Formula: IF(RC[−2]−RC[−1]<0,RC[−1]−RC[−2]," ")

Concept: IF Advance minus Expenses is less than 0, Then enter the difference between Expenses and Advance, Else employee is due nothing, so enter nothing.

Explanation: Formula 1 is in the Due Employee column in rows 3 through 8. The Test statement subtracts the expenses (in column 3) from the advance (in

	1	2	3	4	5
1	Trip	Advance	Expenses	Due Employee	Due Company
2	===
3	Boston	$300.00	$365.75	$65.75 ❶	❷
4	Plainview	$0.00	$23.50	$23.50	
5	Ashville	$175.00	$120.00		$55.00
6	Orlando	$125.00	$97.20		$27.80
7	Tampa	$30.00	$30.00		
8	Miami	$60.00	$118.30	$58.30	
9				----------	----------
10			Totals	$147.55	$82.80
11					
12	Due Employee: $64.75 ❸				

FIGURE 16-3.
Travel expenses: Due employee

column 2) for each trip. If the result is less than zero (expenses are greater than the advance), the Then statement (expenses minus advance) enters the difference in the Due Employee column (column 4). If the advance equals or exceeds the expenses (the company advanced either the exact amount or more than the employee spent), the double quotes in the Else statement make the cell appear empty. These invisible answers help keep your spreadsheet uncluttered.

A formula that adds a list of numbers (such as the formulas in R10C4 and R10C5) simply ignores the cells that return the invisible double quotes. A formula that tries to perform any other type of calculation with a cell returning the double quotes will produce the error message *#VALUE!* because the quotes are text characters and text can't be calculated. If you run into this situation, replace the double quotes in your statement with a zero. That way, some of the cells containing your IF formula will display a zero instead of looking empty, but your other formula will run smoothly.

FORMULA 2

Formula: $IF(RC[-3] - RC[-2] > 0, RC[-3] - RC[-2], " ")$

Concept: IF Advance minus Expenses is greater than 0, Then enter the difference between Advance and Expenses, Else the company is due nothing, so enter nothing.

Explanation: Formula 2 is in the Due Company column in rows 3 through 8. The Test statement subtracts the expenses from the advance for each trip.

If the result is greater than zero (expenses are less than the advance), the Then statement (advance minus expenses) enters the difference in the Due Company column (column 5). If the expenses equal or exceed the advance (the employee spent as much as or more than the company advanced), the Else statement makes the cell appear empty.

FORMULA 3

Formula: IF(R[−2]C[+3]>R[−2]C[+4],"Due Employee: " &DOLLAR(R[−2]C[+3]−R[−2]C[+4]),"Due Company: " &DOLLAR(R[−2]C[+4]−R[−2]C[+3]))

Concept: IF total of Due Employee column exceeds total of Due Company column, Then enter the words *Due Employee:* and the amount due, Else enter the words *Due Company:* and the amount due.

Explanation: Formula 3, in R12C1, produces an answer that shows who owes whom and how much. The Test statement compares the amounts in R10C4 and R10C5. If the total due the employee is greater than the total due the company, the Then statement displays *Due Employee:* and a number. If the total due the employee is less than the total due the company, the Else statement displays *Due Company:* and a number. If both totals are the same, the Test statement is false and the Else statement displays *Due Company $0.00.*

The Then and Else statements resemble the Then statement in the inventory control example. Here *"Due Employee: "* and *"Due Company: "* are enclosed in quotes to tell Multiplan to use this text in the answer. The space before the closing quotes produces the space you see in the result in R12C1. The & sign (concatenation operator) links the text to the amount calculated by the Then and Else statements.

The DOLLAR function converts the calculation to text in much the same way as the FIXED function did in the inventory example. In this case, however, the DOLLAR function adds a dollar sign and two decimal places. As with the FIXED function, when an answer in the Due Employee or Due Company column changes, Multiplan will recalculate the converted-to-text number, but the result can't be used in any arithmetic calculations.

The double parentheses at the end of the formula are in keeping with the rule that every open parenthesis must be closed. One parenthesis closes the DOLLAR function and the other parenthesis closes the IF function.

The spreadsheet in Figure 16-4 is similar to the one in Figure 16-3. It has different expense amounts so that you can see the result when the employee owes the company money.

	1	2	3	4	5
1	Trip	Advance	Expenses	Due Employee	Due Company
2	===
3	Boston	$500.00	$365.75	①	$134.25 ②
4	Plainview	$0.00	$23.50	$23.50	
5	Ashville	$175.00	$120.00		$55.00
6	Orlando	$125.00	$97.20		$27.80
7	Tampa	$30.00	$30.00		
8	Miami	$60.00	$118.30	$58.30	
9				----------	----------
10			Totals	$81.80	$217.05
11					
12	Due Company: $135.25 ③				

FIGURE 16-4.
Travel expenses: Due company

Spreadsheet Summary: Use Format Width to increase columns 2 through 5 to 13 characters each. For the double line, enter REPT(" = ",13) in R2C1 and use Copy Right to copy it right 4 cells. For the line in R9C4, type *A* for Alpha, press the Spacebar twice, and type 10 minus signs. Then use Copy Right to copy it right 1 cell. Use Format Cells as follows: Center the titles in row 1 (columns 2 through 5); right-justify the title in R10C3; continue R12C1 one cell to the right; code the numbers in columns 2 through 5 for dollars and cents. Use Value to enter Formula 1 in R3C4 and Formula 2 in R3C5. Copy both formulas Down five cells. Enter Formula 3 in R12C1. To total the numbers in columns 4 and 5, enter *SUM(R[− 7]C:R[− 1]C)* in R10C4, then Copy Right 1 cell.

WAGE INCREASES

Your company grants a 5% wage increase to employees who (1) haven't received an increase in 12 months, (2) are below the maximum rate established for their job, and (3) attain a certain level of competence in their work, as measured by a performance points system. Figure 16-5 shows the spreadsheet. The formula is in column 5 and uses relative cell references only.

This example combines the IF and AND functions. The IF/AND combination establishes a condition that says, "If this is true AND this is true AND this is true, then return the true statement. If even one test is false, return the false statement." You can include two to five Test statements in an IF/AND formula. The basic syntax is *IF(AND(Test1,Test2,...Test5),Then,Else)*.

	1	2	3	4	5
1		Last Raise	Hourly	Performance	
2	Employee	(months)	Wage	Points	Action
3	==
4	Norm Lundgren	12	$8.00	53	$8.40
5	Judy Stein	6	$5.50	65	No Raise
6	Bill Vanderite	15	$8.50	43	No Raise
7	Deena Holsberg	12	$9.75	58	$10.24
8	Craig Park	12	$10.75	62	No Raise

FIGURE 16-5.
Employee wage increases

To complicate matters a bit, this formula must satisfy three conditions: calculate the 5% wage increase for eligible employees, prevent any increase from exceeding the maximum rate, and identify those employees who don't qualify for an increase. To accomplish this, you need a "nested" IF formula—that is, one IF formula contained within another. A single IF formula can satisfy only one of two conditions: either/or or true/false. "Nesting" several IF formulas lets you create one formula that satisfies multiple conditions.

Formula: IF(AND(RC[−3]>=12,RC[−2]<10.75,RC[−1]>=45),
IF(RC[−2]*105%>10.75,10.75,RC[−2]*105%),"No Raise")

Concept: IF Last Raise is greater than or equal to 12 months ago, AND Hourly Wage is less than $10.75 an hour (the predetermined maximum for the job), AND Performance Points are greater than or equal to 45 (the predetermined measure of competence), Then IF Hourly Wage with a 5% raise is greater than $10.75, Then $10.75, Else give employee a 5% raise, Else no raise.

Explanation: The first IF formula checks each of the three Test statements in the AND list. If the employee meets every criterion for a raise, the first Else statement (Hourly Wage times 105%) calculates the new wage. The Test statement in the nested IF formula looks at the new wage. If that amount exceeds 10.75, the maximum for the job, the second Then statement enters 10.75. If the new wage does not exceed 10.75, the formula enters the new wage that is calculated. If the employee fails to meet even one of the criteria in the AND list, the second Else statement merely produces no raise. The AND function requires its own set of parentheses, which open before the first Test statement and close after the last Test statement.

Spreadsheet Summary: Use Format Default Width to increase every column to 12 characters, then use Format Width to increase column 1 to 15 characters. For the double line, use Value to enter REPT(" = ",15) in R3C1, then use Copy

Right to copy it right 4 cells. Use Format Cells to center the titles in rows 1 and 2 (columns 2 through 5), center the numbers in columns 2 and 4, and center and code the entries in columns 3 and 5 to dollars and cents. Use Value to enter the formula in R4C5 and use Copy Down to copy it down 4 cells.

The IF/OR Combination

The IF and OR combination of functions is a close companion to the IF/AND combination. Where IF/AND requires every test to be true in order to produce the Then statement, IF/OR requires only one test to be true. What IF/OR says is: "If this is true OR this is true OR this is true, use the Then statement. If none are true, use the Else statement." As with IF/AND, you can include two to five tests in an IF/OR formula. The basic syntax is:

IF(OR (Test1,Test2,...Test5),Then,Else)

By way of example, we can rewrite the IF/AND formula for wage increases as an IF/OR formula, as follows:

IF(OR(RC[− 3]<12,RC[− 2]>10.75,RC[− 1]<45),"No Raise",
IF(RC[− 2] * 105%<10.75,10.75,RC[− 2] * 105%))

The concept here is: IF the interval since the employee's last raise is less than 12 months, OR the employee's wage is greater than $10.75 an hour, OR the employee has less than 45 performance points, Then give no raise, Else IF Hourly Wage with a 5% raise is greater than $10.75, Then $10.75, Else give a 5% raise.

BILLING RATES

You run the accounting department for a heating oil distributor. The rate is determined by the amount of oil used by the customer each month. If a customer uses less than 100 gallons, the rate is $1.15 per gallon. If a customer uses 250 gallons or more, the rate is $1.05 per gallon. If a customer's oil usage is anywhere between these amounts, the rate is $1.10 per gallon. You want one formula that can calculate billing charges under any one of these three conditions.

The mini-spreadsheet in Figure 16-6 contains another example of a "nested" IF formula, which is in column 3 and uses relative cell references only.

Formula: IF(RC[− 1]<100,RC[− 1] * 1.15,
IF(RC[− 1]> = 250,RC[− 1] * 1.05,RC[− 1] * 1.10))

Concept: IF Gallons is less than 100, Then multiply Gallons by 1.15, Else IF Gallons is greater than or equal to 250, Then multiply Gallons by 1.05, Else multiply Gallons by 1.10.

Explanation: The formula is in the Billing column (column 3) in rows 3 through 8. The Test statement in the first IF formula looks at the gallons used by each customer during the billing period (column 2). If the amount is less

	1 Customer	2 Gallons	3 Billing
1	Customer	Gallons	Billing
2	===		
3	Ron Lamb	123	$135.30
4	Mike Halvorson	76	$87.40
5	Chris Kinata	172	$189.20
6	Roger Shanafelt	97	$111.55
7	Patricia Pratt	305	$320.25
8	Dale Christensen	252	$264.60

FIGURE 16-6.
Billing rates

than 100, the Then statement (number of gallons times 1.15) calculates the billing. If the number of gallons is 100 or more, the formula moves to the Else statement, the "nested" IF formula.

The Test statement in the "nested" IF formula again checks the gallons used by each customer. If the number of gallons is greater than or equal to 250, the "nested" IF formula uses its own Then statement (gallons times 1.05) to calculate the billing. If the number of gallons is neither less than 100 nor greater than or equal to 250, the Else statement in the "nested" IF formula (gallons times 1.10) calculates the answer.

Spreadsheet Summary. Use Format Default Width to increase the columns to 13 characters, then use Format Width to increase column 1 to 17 characters. For the double line, use Value to enter REPT(" = ",17) in R2C1, then use Copy Right to copy it right 2 cells. Use Format Cells to right-justify the titles *Gallons* and *Billing* and code the numbers in column 3 to dollars and cents. Use Value to enter the formula in R3C3 and use Copy Down to copy it down 5 cells.

TRADE DISCOUNTS

Your publishing company gives a 30% discount to book dealers who order less than $1,000 worth of books, and a 40% discount to book dealers who order $1,000 worth of books or more at one time. Books sold to the general public are not offered at discount. You want to prepare invoices that distinguish between the two types of customers (dealers and the public) and that calculate the different discount rates for dealers. Figures 16-7 and 16-8 show two versions of the spreadsheet, each containing titles, quantities, and prices of fictitious books, a number in R13C2 identifying the type of customer (1 is a dealer, 0 is the public), and the locations of three "nested" IF formulas. A SUM formula in R9C4 totals the order.

```
                  1              2          3          4
 1 Title                        Qty    Unit Price Total Price
 2 ==========================================================
 3 Annual Report Handbook        6         $9.95     $59.70
 4 Managing Your Business        30        $17.95    $538.50
 5 The Money Book                12        $15.95    $191.40
 6 Computing For Profit          24        $19.95    $478.80
 7 Executive Compensation        15        $14.95    $224.25
 8 ---------------------------------------------------------
 9                                     Total Order   $1492.65
10                                     Discount 40%❷ $597.06❶
11                                     Total Due     $895.59❸
12
13 Customer Code:            1
```

FIGURE 16-7.
Customer code 1: Trade discount

```
                  1              2          3          4
 1 Title                        Qty    Unit Price Total Price
 2 ==========================================================
 3 Annual Report Handbook        1         $9.95      $9.95
 4 Managing Your Business        2         $17.95     $35.90
 5 The Money Book                1         $15.95     $15.95
 6 Computing For Profit          1         $19.95     $19.95
 7 Executive Compensation        1         $14.95     $14.95
 8 ---------------------------------------------------------
 9                                     Total Order    $96.70
10                                         ❷             ❶
11                                     Total Due      $96.70❸
12
13 Customer Code:            0
```

FIGURE 16-8.
Customer code 0: No Discount

Cells are named to make the formulas easy to enter: The customer code (R13C2) is named CODE, the order amount (R9C4) is named TOTAL, and the discount amount (R10C4) is named DISCOUNT.

FORMULA 1

Formula: IF(CODE = 1,IF(TOTAL> = 1000,TOTAL* 40%, TOTAL* 30%)," ")

Concept: IF Customer Code is 1 and IF Total Order is $1,000 or more, Then give a 40% discount, Else give a 30% discount. IF Customer Code is not 1, give no discount.

Explanation: Formula 1 is in R10C4. The Test statement in the first IF formula looks at the code number in R13C2. If the code is 1 (a book dealer), the Then statement—a complete, "nested" IF formula—calculates the answer. If the code is 0 (the public), the Else statement—the double quotation marks—makes the cell appear empty.

When it's called upon to calculate a dealer's discount, the Test statement in the "nested" IF formula checks the total order. If the total order is greater than or equal to $1,000, the Then statement (TOTAL* 40%) calculates your answer. If the amount is less than $1,000, the Else statement (TOTAL* 30%) calculates your answer.

FORMULA 2

Formula: IF(CODE = 1,IF(TOTAL> = 1000,"Discount 40%", "Discount 30%")," ")

Concept: IF Customer Code equals 1 and IF Total Order is $1,000 or more, Then display the words *Discount 40%*, Else display the words *Discount 30%*. IF Customer Code is not 1, display nothing.

Explanation: Formula 2, in R10C3, complements Formula 1. Formula 1 calculates the amount of the dealer discount; Formula 2 displays the percentage used in the calculation. The Test statement in the first IF formula checks the customer code. If the code is 1, the formula evaluates the Then statement, the "nested" IF formula. If the code is 0, the double quotes in the Else statement make the cell appear empty. When the "nested" IF formula is called upon to do its work, The Test statement checks the total in R9C4. If the total order is greater than or equal to $1,000, the Then statement displays *Discount 40%*. If the amount is less than $1,000, the Else statement displays *Discount 30%*.

FORMULA 3

Formula: IF(CODE = 1,TOTAL − DISCOUNT,TOTAL)

Concept: IF Customer Code equals 1, Then subtract Discount from Total Order, Else copy Total Order.

Explanation: Formula 3 is in R11C4. At first glance, it might appear that simple subtraction could do the job as well—simply subtract the discount in R10C4 from the total order in R9C4. Well, not this time. Subtraction would work only when R10C4 contains a number. When there's no discount, as in Figure 16-8, R10C4 only looks empty. The formula in R10C4 is actually returning the invisible double quote marks, which are text. If a formula in R11C4 tried to subtract the text quote marks, Multiplan would display #VALUE! in R11C4 to tell you to use a number instead.

Therefore, the Test statement in Formula 3 checks the customer code number. If the code is 1, the Then statement (TOTAL – DISCOUNT) subtracts the discount from the total order. If the code is 0, the Else statement (TOTAL) merely copies the total order from R9C4 to R11C4.

Spreadsheet Summary: Use Format Width to increase column 1 to 23 characters, and columns 2 through 4 to 12 characters each. For the long lines, use Value to enter REPT(" = ",23) in R2C1 and REPT(" – ",23) in R8C1, then use Copy Right to copy each formula right 3 cells. Use Format Cells to center the titles in row 1 and the numbers in column 2, left-justify the code number in R13C2, and code the numbers in columns 3 and 4 to dollars and cents. Use the Name command as follows: R9C4 is TOTAL, R10C4 is DISCOUNT, and R13C2 is CODE.

Use Value to enter Formula 1 in R10C4, Formula 2 in R10C3, and Formula 3 in R11C4. To calculate the total price for each book, enter $RC[-2] * RC[-1]$ in R3C4 and use Copy Down to copy it down 4 cells. To get the total order, enter $SUM(R[-6]C:R[-1]C)$ in R9C4. You may want to create a formula to calculate sales tax and other charges.

INCOME TAXES

As the head of your own accounting firm, you need to estimate your clients' income tax quickly. Among the sweeping changes in the Tax Reform Act of 1986 is the establishment of two tax brackets, effective for 1988. The schedules are:

Married Filing Jointly

Taxable Income	Amount of Tax	Rate on Excess
$0 to $29,750	0	15%
Over $29,750	$4,663	28%

Single

Taxable Income	Amount of Tax	Rate on Excess
$0 to $17,850	0	15%
Over $17,850	$2,678	28%

	1	2	3	4
1		Filing	Taxable	1988
2	Name	Status	Income	Income Tax
3	--			
4	R Cutsforth	2	$14,000	$2,100
5	P Morris	1	$17,850	$2,678
6	E Snyder	2	$35,000	$6,133
7	H Schlossberg	1	$43,575	$9,881
8	L Summit	1	$29,750	$6,010
9	C Swensen	2	$54,750	$11,663

FIGURE 16-9.
1988 income tax rates

This example illustrates a nested formula that uses the IF/AND combination. In Figure 16-9, column 2 shows the filing status of each client: A 1 is for a married couple filing jointly and a 2 is for a single person. The formula, which uses relative cell references only, is in column 4.

Formula: IF(AND(RC[− 2] = 2,RC[− 1]>29750),4663 + 28%
* (RC[− 1] − 29750),IF(AND(RC[− 2] = 1,RC[− 1]>17850),2678 + 28%
* (RC[− 1] − 17850),15% * RC[− 1]))

Concept: IF Filing Status equals 2 AND Taxable Income is greater than $29,750, Then calculate Income Tax according to that schedule, Else IF Filing Status equals 1 AND Taxable Income is greater than $17,850, Then calculate Income Tax according to that schedule, Else calculate 15% of Income Tax.

Explanation: The first IF formula checks both Test statements in the AND list. If the client is married and filing jointly (filing status is 2) and has a taxable income greater than $29,750, the Then statement calculates the income tax ($4,663 plus 28% of the difference between taxable income and $29,750). If either Test statement is false, the formula moves to the "nested" IF formula and checks both Test statements in that AND list.

If the client is single (filing status is 1) and taxable income is greater than $17,850, the Then statement calculates the income tax ($2,678 plus 28 percent of the difference between taxable income and $17,850). If either statement is false, this means that the client is a married couple filing jointly with a taxable income of $29,750 or less or is a single person with a taxable income of $17,850 or less. In either case, the Else statement takes over and calculates 15% of taxable income.

Spreadsheet Summary: Use Format Default Width to increase the width of every column to 14 characters. For the line, use Value to enter REPT(" – ",14) in R3C1, then use Copy Right to copy it right 3 cells. Use Format Cells to center the titles in rows 1 and 2 (columns 2 through 4) and the numbers in column 2, and code the numbers in columns 3 and 4 to dollars. Enter the formula in R4C4 and use Copy Down to copy it down 5 cells.

17

A Look at the LOOKUP Function

Imagine that you and a friend are in a restaurant ordering dinner. You scan the menu, find the meal you want, and order a "number 3." Your friend orders a "number 12." A short time later, you are dining on enchiladas and refried beans, and your friend is enjoying arroz con pollo with extra-hot sauce. You and your friend have made use of an everyday equivalent of a lookup table—a menu. You chose a number from the menu and received the food corresponding to the number. The same principle applies to a spreadsheet lookup table. You use a formula to choose a number from a lookup table "menu" and retrieve the information corresponding to that number.

A lookup table consists of at least two rows or two columns of information. One row or column serves as the search cells (the numbers on the menu) and the other serves as the corresponding cells (the food corresponding to the number). The search cells always contain values; the corresponding cells can contain either values or text.

You can keep any kind of information in a lookup table. For instance, you might have part numbers with the corresponding number of pieces in stock, item numbers with their corresponding descriptions, salaries with corresponding employee names, code numbers with corresponding real estate locations, or serial numbers with the corresponding technical drawings.

LOOKUP FORMULAS

The syntax of a LOOKUP formula is LOOKUP(SearchValue,Table). The search value can be either a number or a reference to a cell containing a number. The table consists of the search cells and corresponding cells. A LOOKUP formula scans the search cells in the table for the search value and retrieves the value or text in the corresponding cell. This information is then entered directly in the formula cell or is used to perform calculations.

THE SHAPE OF THE LOOKUP TABLE

The amount of information you want to keep in a lookup table and the available space on your spreadsheet often determine the shape of the table. You can lay out a lookup table in a vertical pattern (with more rows than columns), as a square (with an equal number of rows and columns), or in a horizontal pattern (with more columns than rows). The shape of the table doesn't matter to Multiplan, but it matters to you, because a LOOKUP formula searches in a particular direction according to the shape.

Vertical or Square Lookup Tables

Figure 17-1 shows a lookup table that is laid out vertically, with more rows than columns. The search cells are in column 1 and the corresponding cells are in column 2. With a vertical or square table, a LOOKUP formula scans the first column in the table until it finds the cell that contains the largest number that is less than or equal to the search value. It then retrieves the contents of the rightmost corresponding cell.

```
        1         2
 1   LOOKUP TABLE
 2   ====================
 3    Part #     Cost
 4   --------------------
 5     110      $17.75
 6     112      $21.50
 7     123      $32.75
 8     165      $12.50
 9     232       $5.75
```

FIGURE 17-1.

A vertical lookup table (more rows than columns)

	1	2	3	4	5	6
1	LOOKUP TABLE					
2	==					
3	Part #	110	112	123	165	233
4	Cost	$17.75	$21.50	$32.75	$12.50	$5.75

FIGURE 17-2.
A horizontal lookup table (more columns than rows)

If your number is less than all the numbers in the search column, the formula displays the *#N/A* (not available) error message. If your number is greater than all the numbers in the search column, the function retrieves the contents of the corresponding cell in the last row of the table.

Horizontal Lookup Tables

Figure 17-2 shows a lookup table containing the same information as the table in Figure 17-1. This table is laid out horizontally, with more columns than rows. The search cells are in row 3 and the corresponding cells are in row 4. With a horizontal lookup table, a LOOKUP formula scans the first row in the table until it finds the cell that contains the largest number that is less than or equal to the search value. The formula then retrieves the contents of the lowest corresponding cell.

If your number is less than all the numbers in the search row, the formula displays *#N/A* (not available). If your number is greater than all the numbers in the search row, the function retrieves the contents of the corresponding cell in the last column of the table.

Sequence of Search Numbers

The most important rule to follow in setting up a lookup table is to arrange the numbers in the search cells in ascending order, from smallest to largest. Therefore, in a vertical or square table, the smallest number will be in the topmost search cell, as you see in Figure 17-1. In a horizontal table, the smallest number will be in the leftmost search cell, as you see in Figure 17-2. Blank cells among the search cells don't affect the lookup process.

DEFINING THE LOOKUP TABLE

The best way to work with a lookup table is to name it. That way, you can use the name as the Table reference in your formula. To name the table, place the cursor on the first search cell (the top left cell, regardless of the shape of the table), type *N* to start the Name command, and type the name you've chosen for the table. Then enter the cell locations in the *to refer to* field and press Enter.

Another way of defining the table is by using the beginning and ending cell location. Let's say you set up a lookup table in rows 40 through 50 of columns 1 and 2. You want your formula to scan column 1 and retrieve the contents of the corresponding cell in column 2, so you specify the range R40C1:R50C2 as the Table reference.

Instead of using a name or a range of cells, you can use C1:C2 as the Table reference, but this is risky. Your formula will scan every cell in column 1, starting with row 1, to find your number. If you have numbers in column 1 above or below the actual lookup information, your formula can retrieve the contents of the wrong corresponding cells.

Instead of creating a new lookup table, you can sometimes designate existing information as a table. The spreadsheet in Chapter 6 shows how it works.

LOOKUP TABLES WITH MANY ROWS OR COLUMNS

The table in Figure 17-3 should look familiar. It's the same table you saw in Figure 17-1, but with one more column of information. It still has more rows than columns, so it is still a vertical lookup table.

Let's say you need to retrieve two different kinds of information from this table: The cost of a part from column 2 or the pieces in stock from column 3. How do you tell a LOOKUP formula which column to use?

In vertical tables, LOOKUP retrieves the contents of the rightmost cell. So, with tables of more than two columns, you group the search column with each corresponding column. For example, you can name column 1 and 2 COST, and columns 1, 2, and 3 STOCK. You don't need column 2 in the STOCK table, but you must name it with the others because lookup tables consist of contiguous columns and column 2 is between the search cells and the corresponding cells.

When you want to know the cost of part #110, the formula *LOOKUP (110,COST)* gets it from column 2, the rightmost column in the COST table. When you want to know the stock status of part #110, *LOOKUP(110,STOCK)* gets it from column 3, the rightmost column in the STOCK table. The principle is the same with horizontal tables containing more than two rows: The formula retrieves the contents of the bottommost corresponding cell in the named table.

```
            1            2            3
1                   LOOKUP TABLE
2        ==================================
3        Part #      Cost      In Stock
4        ----------------------------------
5         110       $17.75        43
6         112       $21.50        12
7         123       $32.75        17
8         165       $12.50         6
9         232        $5.75        34
```

FIGURE 17-3.
Vertical lookup table with three columns

THE MINI-SPREADSHEETS

Now let's look at the LOOKUP function in action. Each of the following business-oriented examples ends with a summary of how to set up the mini-spreadsheet. If you are new to Multiplan, it's wise to go through some of the step-by-step instructions in Chapters 3 through 14 before tackling the summaries in this chapter.

MATERIAL COSTS

The material costs spreadsheet in Figure 17-4 puts the lookup table in Figure 17-3 to work. The spreadsheet contains part numbers, costs, stock on hand, and order status of parts needed by an auto repair shop—all geared to prepare job estimates. This kind of table can easily be updated so that the information is always current. Rows 3 through 5 are where entries are made, formulas are entered, and calculations are performed. The search value in each formula is contained in a relative cell reference.

Formula 1: LOOKUP(RC[– 1],COST)

Formula 2: LOOKUP(RC[– 2],STOCK)

Formula 3: LOOKUP(RC[– 3],ORDER)

Explanation: The table is in rows 14 through 18. In the table, columns 1 and 2 are named COST, columns 1, 2, and 3 are named STOCK, and columns 1, 2, 3, and 4 are named ORDER. Each LOOKUP formula scans column 1 of the table for the part number you enter above the table in column 1. Formula 1 retrieves

```
            1            2            3            4
  1      Part #     Unit Cost     In Stock     On Order
  2      --------------------------------------------------
  3       123         $32.75 ❶    17 ❷         0 ❸
  4       232          $5.75      34           20
  5       110         $17.75      43           22
  6
  7
  8
  9
 10                   COST-STOCK-ORDER TABLE
 11      ==================================================
 12      Part #      Unit Cost     In Stock     On Order
 13      --------------------------------------------------
 14       110         $17.75      43           22
 15       112         $21.50      12           18
 16       123         $32.75      17            0
 17       165         $12.50       6           12
 18       232          $5.75      34           20
```

FIGURE 17-4.
Material cost

the corresponding unit cost from column 2 in the table, Formula 2 retrieves the corresponding number of pieces of stock from column 3, and Formula 3 retrieves the corresponding number of pieces on order from column 4.

Spreadsheet Summary: Use Format Default Width to increase the width of every column to 12 characters. For the lines, enter REPT(" – ",12) in R2C1 and REPT(" = ",12) in R11C1, then use Copy Right to copy each line to the right 3 cells. Use Copy From to copy the single line from row 2 to row 13.

Use Format Cells as follows: Continue the title COST-STOCK-ORDER TABLE one cell to the right; center the titles in rows 1 and 12 and the numbers in columns 1, 3, and 4; code the numbers in column 2 to dollars and cents. Name the entries in rows 14 through 18 as follows: Columns 1 and 2 are COST, columns 1 through 3 are STOCK, and columns 1 through 4 are ORDER. Enter Formula 1 in R3C2, Formula 2 in R3C3, and Formula 3 in R3C4, then use Copy Down to copy the formulas down 2 cells.

INVENTORY AND ORDER COSTS

The spreadsheet in Figure 17-5 contains the same COST-STOCK-ORDER table as in Figure 17-4. The top half of the spreadsheet now keeps track of

```
             1              2            3            4
 1                      Inventory    On Order
 2       Part #          Cost         Cost
 3     ------------------------------------------
 4        123           $556.75❶      $0.00 ❷
 5        232           $195.50      $115.00
 6        110           $763.25      $390.50
 7
 8
 9
10                  COST-STOCK-ORDER TABLE
11     ==========================================
12      Part #     Unit Cost    In Stock    On Order
13     ------------------------------------------
14        110         $17.75       43          22
15        112         $21.50       12          18
16        123         $32.75       17           0
17        165         $12.50        6          12
18        232          $5.75       34          20
```

FIGURE 17-5.
Cost of inventory and orders

inventory and order costs. Two LOOKUP formulas calculate the cost of the current inventory and future disbursements. Each formula uses a relative cell reference for its search number.

Formula 1: LOOKUP(RC[− 1],COST) * LOOKUP(RC[− 1],STOCK)

Formula 2: LOOKUP(RC[− 2],COST) * LOOKUP(RC[− 2],ORDER)

Explanation: The cells in the table in Figure 17-5 have the same names as the table in Figure 17-4: COST, STOCK, and ORDER. Each formula scans column 1 in the table for the part number and uses the retrieved information to perform its calculations. Formula 1 multiplies the unit cost in column 2 by the result of the second LOOKUP formula, which retrieves the number of units in stock in column 3. Formula 2 multiplies the unit cost in column 2 by the number of units on order in column 4. When the calculations are complete, the results are displayed in the formula cells.

Spreadsheet Summary: Using the material costs spreadsheet (Figure 17-4) as a base, modify the top half to look like the spreadsheet in Figure 17-5. Format rows 4 through 6 in column 3 for dollars and cents. Enter Formula 1 in R4C2 and Formula 2 in R4C3, and use the Copy Down command to copy both formulas down 2 cells.

ITEM DESCRIPTION AND PRICE FOR AN INVOICE

Figure 17-6 shows an invoice containing a table of items available in Alfie's stereo store. Two LOOKUP formulas combined with the IF function enter the description and price of the item. (The IF function is discussed in Chapter 16.) The search value in each formula is a relative cell reference.

Formula 1: IF(RC[− 2]>0,LOOKUP(RC[− 2],DESCRIP)," ")

Formula 2: IF(RC[− 3]>0,LOOKUP(RC[− 3],PRICE)," ")

Explanation: The table is in rows 23 through 30. In the table, columns 1, 2, and 3 are named DESCRIP, and columns 1, 2, 3, and 4 are named PRICE. (Column 2 is unused, but must be named as part of the table for the LOOKUP formula to work.) To prepare an invoice, Alfie simply types in reference numbers in rows 6 through 12 of column 1 and quantities in column 2. Formula 1 then looks at the reference number. If this number is greater than zero (that is, the cell isn't empty), Formula 1 searches the table and retrieves the description corresponding to the number. Formula 2 retrieves the unit price in the same way.

If the reference number cell in column 1 is empty, as in R12C1, the Else statement in each formula uses quotation marks (" ") to make the description cell in column 3 and the unit price cell in column 4 appear empty, while preventing the message #N/A (not available) from appearing in column 5.

Spreadsheet Summary: Use Format Width to reduce the width of columns 1 and 2 to 8 characters, increase column 3 to 30 characters, and increase columns 4 and 5 to 11 characters. For the lines, enter REPT(" = ",30) in R3C1 and REPT(" − ",30) in R5C1, then use Copy Right to copy the formulas right 4 cells. Use Copy From to copy the double line from row 3 to row 20 and the single line from row 5 to row 22. For the short line, enter REPT(" − ",10) in R13C5, then use Copy From to copy it from row 13 to row 16.

To center the title *Our Prices Will Be Music To Your Ears* in R2C2, press the Spacebar 5 times before typing, then use Format Cells to continue the title 2 cells to the right. Use Format Cells to continue *DESCRIPTION-PRICE TABLE* 2 cells to the right; center the title in row 1 and the numbers in column 1; left-justify the numbers in column 2; right-justify the titles *Subtotal, Sales Tax (%),* and *Total Due* in column 3; code the dollar figures in columns 4 and 5 to dollars and cents. Name the entries in rows 23 through 30 as follows: Columns 1, 2, and 3 are *DESCRIP,* and columns 1, 2, 3, and 4 are *PRICE.*

Enter Formula 1 in R6C3 and Formula 2 in R6C4. Use Copy Down to copy each formula down 6 cells. To total each item, enter IF(RC[− 4]>0,RC[− 3] * RC[− 1]," ") in R6C5 and use Copy Down to copy the formula down 6 cells. The IF function prevents an error message if there is no reference number in

```
         1        2             3                    4         5
 1                      Alfie's DISCOUNT STEREO
 2                  Our Prices Will Be Music To Your Ears
 3  ==========================================================================
 4  Ref#     Qty    Description                    Unit Price Total Price
 5  --------------------------------------------------------------------------
 6   3        1     Turntable-Braddock 1768-9 ❶      $124.95 ❷ $124.95
 7   1        1     Amplifier-Fischer 203            $375.50    $375.50
 8   6        2     Speakers-JBL456B78               $122.50    $245.00
 9   4        1     Tuner-Harwood 189A               $314.95    $314.95
10   5        1     Recorder-Harvey AB-567           $478.95    $478.95
11   7        1     Installation                      $75.00     $75.00
12
13
14                                    Subtotal                 ----------
15                               Sales Tax (%)       8.25      $1614.35
16                                                              $133.18
17                                   Total Due                 ----------
18                                                             $1747.53
19  DESCRIPTION-PRICE TABLE
20  ==========================================================================
21  Ref#            Description                    Unit Price
22  --------------------------------------------------------------------------
23   1              Amplifier-Fischer 203            $375.50
24   2              Amplifier-Fischer 332            $249.95
25   3              Turntable-Braddock 1768-9        $124.95
26   4              Tuner-Harwood 189A               $314.95
27   5              Recorder-Harvey AB-567           $478.95
28   6              Speakers-JBL456B78               $122.50
29   7              Installation                      $75.00
30   8              Installation                     $135.00
```

FIGURE 17-6.
Alfie's invoice

column 1. To calculate the subtotal, enter *SUM(R[−8]C:R[−1]C)* in R14C5. To calculate the total, enter *R[−3]C+R[−2]C* in R17C5. To calculate the effect of an 8.25% sales tax, enter *8.25* in R15C4 and enter *R[−1]C * RC[−1]%* in R15C5.

18

Making Macros Work for You

A macro is a set of instructions that tell Multiplan to perform spreadsheet tasks automatically and in a particular sequence. You store these instructions in a cell in the form of keystrokes. You can write a macro, for example, to switch between formats (dollars to integers), to jump the cursor from the bottom of one column to the top of the next, to skip the cursor to a cell containing a number you change often, to trigger the actions of other macros, or even to pause at a particular point for input from the keyboard.

Macros are especially handy when you need to perform a procedure involving several commands in a particular order on a frequent basis. Instead of typing the same sequence of keys over and over, you can write a macro, hit a couple of keys to start the macro, and Multiplan will enter the keystrokes for you. Simply put, macros give you a way to automate repetitive operations, design spreadsheet shortcuts, and eliminate keyboard tedium.

Other than making life easier for you, macros can enable you to develop a sophisticated spreadsheet that someone else—even a new user—can work on. This technique can reduce training time and keep the spreadsheet virtually foolproof. Once you've written the macro, just about anyone can input the repetitive information.

AN EXAMPLE: FROM MANUAL ENTRY TO MACRO

Let's say you regularly switch the format of the numbers on your spread-sheet from integers to dollars and cents and back again. Starting from integers, you would hit the following keys to format manually for dollars and cents:

FDC Tab $ Enter

The following sequence of keystrokes in a macro would produce the same result:

FDC'TB$'RT'QU

Let's look at a side-by-side comparison of the manual and macro keystrokes for our integer-to-dollars example:

Action:	Manual:	Macro:
Start the Format command	F	F
Select the Default option	D	D
Select the Cells option	C	C
Move the highlight to *format code*	Tab	'TB
Select $ (dollars and cents)	$	$
Confirm the command	Enter	'RT
End the macro		'QU

Writing and Naming the Macro

Macros, which always begin with a letter or an apostrophe, are text. They are entered in a cell in the same way you enter any text. With the cursor on the cell receiving the macro, you type *A* to start the Alpha command.

To write this macro in the most basic way (without the bells and whistles you'll learn about shortly), you type *FDC'TB$'RT'QU* and press Enter to move the macro into its cell. Multiplan scans down each column from left to right, running each macro it finds. The command code *'QU* (for quit) at the end of a macro ensures that Multiplan doesn't run an unrelated macro that may be in the cell directly below this one.

You can type macro characters in uppercase or lowercase. They are shown in uppercase in this book to match the way Multiplan enters keystrokes when you are in one of the special keyboard modes.

After you write the macro, you use the Name command to name it and give it a one- or two-letter run code. Then, instead of remembering and hitting six keys each time you want to switch formats, you press the Alternate key and type the run code. Multiplan replays the keys as if you were typing them at the key-board. Creating a macro to switch back to the integer format is just as easy.

THE MULTIPLAN MACRO CODES

Multiplan uses three kinds of macro codes: keycodes, command codes, and command keycodes (run codes). Figures 18-1 and 18-2 show all but the command keycodes, which are assigned by you. Though the terms are similar, these codes serve quite different purposes. Here's an overview:

Keycodes

Macros need to know not only the letters that start commands but also the keystrokes that take you through the fields in a command (such as Tab) and execute a command (such as Enter). These types of keystrokes are entered in a macro in the form of a *keycode*. A keycode is Multiplan's abbreviation for a keystroke, and consists of an apostrophe followed by two letters. As you saw in the manual/macro example, *'TB* is Tab and *'RT* is Enter (or Return).

Multiplan has macro keycodes for every cursor movement and every task available to you in non-macro operations. In standard keyboard mode, you enter the keycode by typing an apostrophe and the two letters. In the special keyboard modes (Edit Macro and Record Macro), you press the key that normally performs the action.

Command Codes

Command codes enhance the power and versatility of your macros. They include such commands as *'GO*, which directs the macro to a specific cell, and *'IF*, which branches between macros. Certain command codes, called interactive command codes, let you and your macro exchange information. When a running macro finds an interactive command code, it pauses and awaits input from the keyboard before resuming its run.

You'll find a detailed description of all the command codes later in this chapter.

Command Keycodes, or Run Codes

A command keycode runs the macro. For simplicity, let's call the command keycode the run code. A run code consists of one or two letters, typically a short version of the name you give the macro cell. For example, if you name a macro cell DOLLARSFORMAT, you can designate the run code as *D* or *DF*. When you want to run the macro, you simply hold down the Alt key and type *D* or *DF*, the run code. Other ways to run a macro are covered in the next example.

KEYCODES

Action:	Key:	Keycode:
Absolute reference	F3	'RF
Backspace	Backspace	'BS
Character left	F9	'CL
Character right	F10	'CR
Cursor left	Left Arrow	'LK
Cursor right	Right Arrow	'RK
Cursor down	Down Arrow	'DK
Cursor up	Up Arrow	'UK
Delete	Del	'DL
End	End	'EN
Enter (Return)	Enter	'RT
Escape (cancel)	Esc	'CN
Help	H or Alt-H or ?	'HP
Home	Home	'HM
Home window	Ctrl-Home	'HW
Next unlocked cell	F2	'NU
Next window	F1	'CW
Page left	Ctrl-Left Arrow	'PL
Page right	Ctrl-Right Arrow	'PR
Page down	PgDn	'PD
Page up	PgUp	'PU
Previous field or command	Shift-Tab	'PF
Previous unlocked cell	Shift-F2	'PC
Previous window	Shift-F1	'PW
Quotation marks (")	Shift-"	'QT
Recalculate	F4	'RC
Refresh links	Shift-F6	'UD
Space	Spacebar	'SP
Tab	Tab	'TB
Word left	F7	'WL
Word right	F8	'WR

FIGURE 18-1.
Multiplan macro keycodes

COMMAND CODES

Action:	Command Code:
Insert comments and reminders in a macro	'LAcomment'
Call on a macro subroutine in the specified cell	'CAcell'
End a subroutine and return to the macro	'RE
Redirect the standard run to the specified cell	'GOcell'
Branch to cells based on a test condition	'IF(test)'
Store the specified value in each specified cell	'LEcell'value'
Recalculate the specified area	'RRcell'
Go to specified cell and run the menu	'MNcell'
Go to specified cell, run menu, return to macro	'MCcell'
Pause, prompt the user for text (alpha), enter text in the specified cell	'ALprompt'cell'
Pause, prompt the user for a value, enter value in the specified cell	'VAprompt'cell'
Pause and prompt the user for input	'QEprompt'
Pause for user input (no prompt)	'?
End the macro (quit)	'QU

KEYBOARD MODES

Action:	Keystroke:
Edit Macro	F5
Single Step	Shift-F5
Record Macro	Shift-F7 or Shift-F9

FIGURE 18-2.
Multiplan macro command codes and keyboard modes

WORKING WITH MACROS

Learning something new is often easier after some solid hands-on experience. Before continuing with the nitty-gritty of Multiplan macros, let's take a short detour and write the macro shown in Figure 18-3, which produces the spreadsheet heading shown in Figure 18-4.

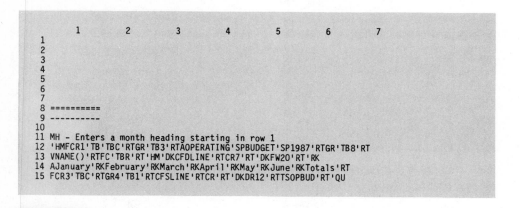

FIGURE 18-3.

The macro that produces a spreadsheet heading

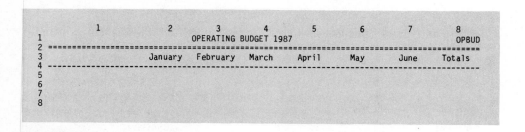

FIGURE 18-4.

The spreadsheet heading produced by a macro

Ordinarily, I wouldn't write a macro to create a spreadsheet heading because, first, this isn't a repetitive kind of activity and, second, it's a lot easier doing it the old-fashioned way—simply typing it. The advantage to doing it with a macro here is that you don't need to work with an existing spreadsheet. If you have yet to create the macros in Chapters 3 through 14, this macro demonstrates interesting techniques, scratches the itch of readers who can't wait to try macros, and produces a fireworks finale. It's a long one but stick with it.

Now fire up your computer and bring up the Multiplan screen.

Preparing for the Macro

When you are first learning how to write macros, it helps to be able to see them completely, so give the continuous format to the cells this macro will occupy: Place the cursor on R11C1 and type *FC* (Format Cells). Type *:R15C8* and press the Tab key twice. Type *C* (Cont) and press Enter.

The long lines are created by the REPT (repeat) function and an equal sign or a minus sign, enclosed in quotation marks to indicate text. Macros balk at quotation marks, so you need to enter each REPT formula in a separate cell, name it, and have the macro refer to the name. First, create the formulas: Place the cursor on R8C1 and type *V* (Value). Type *REPT(" = ",20)* and press Enter. Now place the cursor on R9C1 and type *V*. Type *REPT(" – ",20)* and press Enter. You are repeating the sign 20 times. The macro will increase the width of column 1 to 20 characters.

Now name the cells containing these formulas: Leave the cursor on R9C1 and type *N* (Name). Type *SLINE* (single line) and press Enter. Place the cursor on R8C1 and type *N*. Type *DLINE* (double line) and press Enter. This completes the preparations.

Writing the Heading Macro

The left column in the following instructions describes the actions that take place when the macro runs. The column on the right shows your keystrokes.

The left column also contains references to the Edit Macro mode (*Activate the Edit Macro mode* or *Exit the Edit Macro mode*). These references have nothing to do with the running of the macro. The Edit Macro mode, invoked and exited by pressing the F5 key, alters the operation of the keyboard. In this mode, Multiplan inserts the keycode in the macro for the keys you press. To give you the full benefit of having Multiplan do this keycode work for you, the instructions take you in and out of the Edit Macro mode.

If you make a typing error while entering the keystrokes shown in the column on the right, check the status line at the bottom of the screen before you touch any key. If you see *EM* to the right of the *Free* indicator, you are in the Edit Macro mode. If you press Backspace to erase the mistake, you will insert the keycode for Backspace in the macro. So, first press F5 to exit the Edit Macro mode, correct the mistake, press F5 again to invoke the Edit Macro mode again, and continue from where you left off.

The Heading Macro: Part 1

'HMFCR1'TB'TBC'RTGR'TB3'RTAOPERATING'SPBUDGET 'SP1987'RTGR'TB8'RT

Part 1 of the macro sends the cursor to the home position on the spreadsheet (R1C1), formats row 1 to be continuous so that the spreadsheet title will be displayed completely, enters the spreadsheet title, and moves the cursor to R1C8, the cell where Part 2 will enter the filename. Place the cursor on R12C1 and type *A* (Alpha). Press F5 to activate the Edit Macro mode.

Macro action:	Type or press:
Send the cursor home (R1C1)	Home
Start the Format command and select the Cells option	FC
Specify the row to format	R1
Move the cursor to *alignment*	Tab Tab
Select the *Cont* (continuous) option	C
Execute the Format command	Enter
Start the Goto command and select the Row-col option	GR
Move the highlight to *column*	Tab
Specify the column to go to	3
Execute the Goto command	Enter
Start the Alpha command	A
Type the spreadsheet title	OPERATING BUDGET 1987
Execute the Alpha command	Enter
Start the Goto command and select the Row-col option	GR
Move the highlight to *column*	Tab
Specify the column to go to	8
Execute the Goto command	Enter

Press F5 to exit the Edit Macro mode. There's no need to press Enter now. Simply move the cursor to R13C1, and Part 1 enters its cell.

The Heading Macro: Part 2

VNAME()'RTFC'TBR'RT'HM'DKCFDLINE'RTCR7'RT'DKFW20 'RT'RK

Part 2 uses the NAME function to generate the spreadsheet filename, right-justifies the filename, copies the REPT formula in R8C1 (DLINE) across row 2, and increases the width of column 1 to 20 characters. The cursor is on R13C1.

Macro action:	Type or press:
Start the Value command and specify the NAME function	VNAME()
Activate the Edit Macro mode	F5
Execute the Value command	Enter

Start the Format command and select the Cells option	FC
Move the highlight to *alignment*	Tab
Select the *Right* option	R
Execute the Format command	Enter
Send the cursor home	Home
Move the cursor one cell down	Down Arrow
Start the Copy command and select the From option	CF
Type the name of the cell containing the double line	DLINE
Execute the Copy command	Enter
Start the Copy command and select the Right option	CR
Specify the number of cells to copy right	7
Execute the Copy command	Enter
Move the cursor one cell down (R3C1)	Down Arrow
Start the Format command and select the Width option	FW
Specify the width of column 1	20
Execute the Format command	Enter
Move the cursor one cell to the right (R3C2)	Right Arrow

Press F5 to exit the Edit Macro mode. Again, don't bother to press Enter. Just move the cursor to R14C1, and Part 2 enters its cell.

The Heading Macro: Part 3

AJanuary'RKFebruary'RKMarch'RKApril'RKMay'RKJune'RK
Totals'RT

Part 3 enters the names of the months from January through June and the title *Totals* in R3C8. Leave the cursor on R14C1.

Macro action:	**Type or press:**
Start the Alpha command and type *January*	AJanuary
Activate the Edit Macro mode	F5
Move the cursor one cell to the right (R3C3)	Right Arrow
Type *February*	February

Move the cursor one cell to the right (R3C4)	Right Arrow
Type *March*	March
Move the cursor one cell to the right (R3C5)	Right Arrow
Type *April*	April
Move the cursor one cell to the right (R3C6)	Right Arrow
Type *May*	May
Move the cursor one cell to the right (R3C7)	Right Arrow
Type *June*	June
Move the cursor one cell to the right (R3C8)	Right Arrow
Type the title *Totals*	Totals
Execute the Alpha Command	Enter

To exit the Edit Macro mode, press F5. To enter Part 3 in its cell, move the cursor to R15C1.

The Heading Macro: Part 4

FCR3'TBC'RTGR4'TB1'RTCFSLINE'RTCR'RT'DKDR12'RT
TSOPBUD'RT'QU

Part 4 centers the month names, copies the REPT formula in R9C1 (SLINE) across row 4, moves the cursor to R5C1 so that you can start entering your titles in column 1, deletes the rows containing the macro, then stores the spreadsheet under the filename OPBUD (OPerating BUDget). The cursor is on R15C1.

Macro action:	Type or press:
Start the Format command and select the Cells option	FC
Specify the cells to format (row 3)	R3
Activate the Edit Macro mode	F5
Move the cursor to *alignment*	Tab
Specify *Ctr* (Center)	C
Execute the Format command	Enter
Start the Goto command and select the Row-Col option	GR
Specify the row to go to	4
Move the cursor to *column*	Tab
Specify the column to go to	1

Execute the Goto command	Enter
Start the Copy command and select the From option	CF
Type the name of the cell containing the single line	SLINE
Execute the Copy command	Enter
Start the Copy command and select the Right option	CR
Execute the Copy command	Enter
Move the cursor one cell down	Down Arrow
Start the Delete command and select the Row option	DR
Specify the number of rows to delete	12
Execute the Delete command	Enter
Start the Transfer command and select the Save option	TS
Type the name of the spreadsheet	OPBUD
Execute the Transfer command	Enter
Exit the Edit Macro mode	F5
Insert the Quit command code	'QU

This is the last part of the macro, so press the Enter key.

Now compare each character in each part of the macro with Figure 18-3 to make sure they agree. If something is amiss, move the cursor to that cell and type *E* (Edit). Use the F7 through F10 keys to move the highlight, then type any missing characters or press the Delete key to erase any unwanted characters.

Naming the Macro

The next step is to give the macro a descriptive name and assign a run code. A named macro is easier to remember and find on your spreadsheet. Since Multiplan runs macros downward in a column as it finds them (and stops when it reaches a 'QU code), naming the first, or top, cell in a multiple-cell macro assigns the name to the entire macro.

Place the cursor on R12C1:	Type or press:
Start the Name command	N
Name the cell	MONTHHEAD
Move the highlight to *macro: Yes (No)*	Tab Tab

Select *Yes*	Y
Move the highlight to *command key(s)*	Tab
Assign the run code	MH
Execute the command	Enter

It's always a good idea to enter the run code and a description of the macro on the spreadsheet: Place the cursor on R11C1 and type *A* (Alpha). Now, just as you see it in Figure 18-3, type *MH - Enters a month heading starting in row 1* and press Enter.

Now save the spreadsheet on disk and give it the name MHEAD: Leave the cursor where it is and type *TS* (Transfer Save). If you need to tell Multiplan which drive contains your data disk or which directory to store the file in, type the drive letter and press F6 (to produce a colon) or type the pathname. Type *MHEAD* (the filename) and press Enter.

Running the Macro

There are four ways to run a macro:

■ By using the Alt key and a run code.

■ By using the Goto command and the Macro option with a macro name. Goto Macro only runs the macro in a cell—it doesn't send the cursor to that cell.

■ By using the Goto command and the Macro option without a macro name.

■ By using a macro menu. (You'll find an example in Chapter 12.)

Let's first run the macro with its run code. Using a run code is often the best way to run a macro that isn't part of a menu. Leave the cursor where it is. Hold down the Alt key and type *MH*. Relax while the macro merrily bounces along, producing the heading, erasing its own traces, then saving the spreadsheet as OPBUD. Press the F4 key to recalculate the spreadsheet and enter the new filename in R1C8.

Next, let's use Goto Macro and the macro name. First, load the MHEAD spreadsheet: Leave the cursor where it is. Type *TL* (Transfer Load) and press a direction key to display the current directory. Move the highlight to *MHEAD* and press Enter.

Delete the OPBUD spreadsheet so that your macro can start from scratch: Type *TD* (Transfer Delete). Type *OPBUD* and press Enter. Type *Y* to confirm the deletion. Now you're set to recreate the heading.

Leave the cursor where it is:	Type or press:
Start the Goto command	G
Select the Macro option	M
Highlight the name MONTHHEAD	Right Arrow
Execute the command	Enter

This is a good way to run a macro, because you can cycle through all the macro names.

Now let's pretend the macro doesn't have a name or a run code. Before you use the other Goto Macro way to run it, load the spreadsheet again: Type *TL* (Transfer Load) and press a direction key to display the directory. Move the highlight to *MHEAD* and press Enter. Now delete the OPBUD spreadsheet again: Type *TD* (Transfer Delete). Type *OPBUD* and press Enter. Type *Y* to confirm the deletion.

When you use the Goto Macro command without a name, you tell Multiplan the cell location.

Leave the cursor where it is:	Type or press:
Start the Goto command	G
Select the Macro option	M
Identify the macro cell	R12C1
Execute the command	Enter

And again, the macro creates the heading.

If you have only a few macros, a good memory for cell locations, and no one else working on a spreadsheet, this method is satisfactory. Under most circumstances, though, finding an unnamed cell containing a macro is akin to finding the proverbial needle in a haystack. This method is not recommended.

THE COMMAND CODES

Command codes let you build long, powerful macros that perform multiple tasks. For example, you can use them to interact with a macro, to create new command menus, or to replace the Multiplan prompts with your own prompts.

Like keycodes, command codes consist of an apostrophe followed by two letters. Unlike keycodes, these letters are, in most cases, followed by the special element the command code works with followed by an ending apostrophe. This special element can contain text, a value, a test condition, or a cell reference, which can be row and column numbers or a name (R14C6 or RATE). For example, the command code that diverts a macro to cell R14C6 is:

'GOR14C6'

There are no spaces between a command code and its special element. Both the command code and the element must be in one cell, not split up. Any one cell can contain more than one command code.

When you enter a macro by using Multiplan's recording capability, you must go back and add any command codes and their special elements after you finish recording.

Here are the macro command codes and what they do, with their special elements shown in lowercase type:

'LAcomment' The *'LA* command lets you enter your own comments in a macro. Let's suppose you write a macro that formats a spreadsheet for dollars and you assign the run code *DF* (Dollars Format). You don't want to enter a description and run code in a separate cell, so you start the macro with the reminder: *'LAFormats for $'s—Run DF'*. In a long or complex macro, comments at regular intervals can document how the macro works. Comments don't appear as a screen prompt, nor do they affect the running of the macro. They are simply a nice convenience.

'CAcell' The *'CA* (call) command diverts the action of a macro to the specified cell, where it runs a subroutine. A subroutine is a macro that is called on by another macro. A subroutine can be called by more than one macro and can be called more than once. An *'RE* code embedded in the subroutine tells Multiplan to return to the macro that called for the detour. The *'CA* and *'RE* combination lets you write a macro that can nest up to 16 levels of macros.

'RE The *'RE* (return) command works in tandem with the *'CA* command and is used to end a subroutine. When Multiplan finds *'RE*, it returns to the macro that called for the detour and resumes running after the *'CA* command.

'GOcell' The *'GO* command diverts the run from the standard movement down a column to any cell that contains another macro. When Multiplan encounters *'GO*, it goes to the specified cell and runs the macro there. If the cell reference is the same as the cell that contains the *'GO* command, the macro returns to its own cell, creating what is called a *loop*. Loops can be handy macro tools. Let's say you want to change the format of certain cells to dollars and cents. You enter *FC'?'TBTB$'RT'GOR55C12'* in R55C12. The *'?* stops the run to let you type the cell locations from the keyboard. After your input, *'GOR55C12'* returns the macro to its own cell for another run. When it encounters the *'?*, it stops again so you can type more cell locations. With a loop, the macro makes repeated passes until you press the Escape key to stop it.

The *'GO* command is similar to the Goto command in the command menu, but there's a significant difference. Goto sends Multiplan to a cell that may or may not contain a macro. If the cell does contain a macro, Multiplan doesn't run it, as *'GO* does. Goto is written into a macro as *GR* (Goto command, Row-col option) followed by a cell location (for instance *GR23'TB5* to send the macro to R23C5), or *GN* (Goto command, Name option) followed by a named cell (such as *GNRATE*, which sends Multiplan to the cell named *RATE*).

'IF(test)' The *'IF* command, which is similar to the IF function, tells the macro to take one of two paths depending on the outcome of a test condition. The test compares the values enclosed in parentheses. If the test is true (is met), Multiplan continues running the macro in the same cell. If the test is false (isn't met), Multiplan moves to the next cell down and runs the macro there. To divert the macro to a cell other than the next one down, add the *'GO* command code and the cell location or the cell name (for example, *'IF(R26C2>15)' 'GOR42C7'* or *'IF(R26C2>15)' 'GORATE'*). To test multiple conditions, combine the *'IF* command code with the AND or OR logical functions. The syntax is *'IFAND(test)'* or *'IFOR(test)'*.

'LEcell'value' The *'LE* command tells the macro to store the specified value in each specified cell, union of cells, or range of cells. The value can be anything you can enter on the command line using the Value command: a number, a formula that yields a number, or a function.

'RRcell' The *'RR* (recalculate) command tells Multiplan to recalculate any formula in the area specified in the cell reference, which can be a single cell, a union of cells, or a range of cells.

'MNcell' The *'MN* (menu) command lets you create your own command menus, which appear in place of and operate the same as the standard Multiplan menu. You can have as many as 12 macros in a custom menu and more than one custom menu on a spreadsheet. The macros in a menu must be side-by-side in contiguous cells with no empty cells or cells in a continuous format between them.

A macro menu consists of three rows of information. The first row contains the command names, the second contains the text that appears on the prompt line, and the third, the macros. You select from your macro menu in the same way as you select from Multiplan's menu: You type the first letter of the command or highlight the command and press Enter. Multiplan runs the first command it finds (moving from left to right) that starts with the letter you type, so avoid having more than one command with the same first letter. Chapter 12 contains an example of a macro menu.

'MCcell' The *'MC* (menu call) command works the same as *'MN* in every way but one: Multiplan returns to the macro that called the menu when it finds the *MC* command.

'ALprompt'cell' The *'AL* (alpha) command interacts with the user. This command has three elements:

- *'AL* tells Multiplan you will be working with text.

- *prompt* is the prompt you want Multiplan to display on the message line instead of Multiplan's usual prompts. Your prompt can contain as many as 78 characters.

- *'cell'* specifies the cell (by row and column number or by name) that receives the text.

When Multiplan finds the *'AL* code, it stops the macro, displays the prompt, and awaits input from the keyboard. Multiplan puts the input text into the specified cell.

'VAprompt'cell' The *'VA* (value) command works with values in the same way that *'AL* works with text. When Multiplan finds *'VA* in a macro, it stops the macro, displays your prompt on the message line, then puts the input value into the specified cell.

'QEprompt' The *'QE* (query) command is similar to *'AL* and *'VA* in that it displays your prompt on the message line and awaits your input. Instead of entering information in a specified cell, however, *'QE* adds your input to the field highlighted in the current command. This code provides great flexibility in entering variables, and you can use as many as you want in a macro. Press the Enter key after typing your input to tell Multiplan to resume running the macro.

'? The *'?* command works the same as *'QE*, but does not provide a prompt on the message line. The *'?* is a wildcard macro character that can stand for text, a number, a formula, a cell location, or a cell name. When Multiplan finds *'?* in a macro, it pauses and awaits input from the keyboard. Since there's no prompt at the pause, you must be totally clear about what to type and when.

'QU Just as a period ends a sentence, the *'QU* (quit) command ends a macro. Without a period, you have a run-on sentence; without *'QU*, you can have a run-on macro. Let's say you have several macros, none of which ends with the *'QU* command, in contiguous cells in a column. You set the top macro in motion and Multiplan runs it. Multiplan then runs the one below, then the next one and the next one until each macro is run. With one macro split into several cells, running one part after another is fine. But if the macros are unrelated, the result can be like a dog chasing its tail, running in circles and getting nowhere. To prevent mishaps, type *'QU* at the end of every macro except subroutines, which end with *'RE*, and looping macros. If the macro is split into several cells, *'QU* belongs only at the end of the last part.

CREATING YOUR OWN MACROS

There are four phases in creating your own macros:

1. *Planning* the macro by defining what you want the macro to do and how you want the macro to do it.

2. *Writing* the macro by typing the keystrokes that will accomplish your macro goals.

3. *Naming* the macro by naming the cell containing the macro and assigning a run code.

4. *Running* the macro by pressing a few keys and watching things happen as you planned them. Clearly, this is the most satisfying phase of all.

Planning a Macro

Planning is as much a key to macro success as it is to creating a spreadsheet. Before you start, determine what you want your macro to do and which commands can accomplish your goal. If you're the least bit fuzzy about a command you plan to use, step through it manually and jot down the keys you press.

Next, look for any sequence of actions that occurs more than once in the same macro or will occur in several macros. Enter each of these routines in a separate cell where your macro can call on it as often as needed. That way, you won't have to write it into the macro over and over.

Then decide where to enter the macro. If you hit a few snags while running the macro, as many people do at the beginning, you'll find it tiresome to repeatedly move the cursor over long distances to edit the macro. So put your macro in a cell that is close to the action—in the midst of the spreadsheet if there's enough room. When things are working properly, copy the macro to a more appropriate location and blank it from the original location.

Writing a Macro

When you write a macro, you enter a sequence of keystrokes in one or more cells. Two special modes—Edit Macro and Record Macro—alter the operation of the keyboard and simplify your work.

The keystrokes that activate the Edit Macro and Record Macro modes are toggles. Pressing them once invokes the mode; pressing them again restores the keyboard to standard operation.

The Edit Macro Mode

You can insert keycodes in a macro by typing the apostrophe and two letters. The faster, more efficient way is to invoke the Edit Macro mode and have Multiplan insert the keycode for any key you press. Pressing the F5 key invokes this mode.

Let's suppose you are writing a macro to copy information from one cell to another. You type *CF* (Copy From) and press F5 to activate the Edit Macro mode. *EM* appears on the status line next to the *Free* indicator. You then press the Tab key. In standard keyboard operation, doing this would move the highlight to the *to* field. But in Edit Macro mode, this inserts 'TB, the keycode for *Tab*, in the macro.

In Edit Macro mode, Multiplan accepts your keystrokes without taking the action you've specified. So, be sure you know exactly which keys do what, and carefully plan the sequence of keystrokes in advance.

You can turn this mode on and off at will while you write the macro. When you enter a macro using the Edit Macro mode, you can have as many as 244 characters in a cell. Be sure there are no spaces anywhere in the macro except between the words in your comments and prompts.

The Record Macro Mode

The Record Macro mode tells Multiplan to record your keystrokes as you work. You turn this mode on and off by pressing either Shift-F7 or Shift-F9. In this mode, you can see every action as it occurs, just as if you were working in standard keyboard mode. In the Record Macro mode, *RM* appears to the right of the *Free* indicator on the status line.

Before you start recording, you must tell Multiplan to accumulate your keystrokes in one cell or in a range of cells. You do this by using the name RECORD in the Name command. If you specify one cell, name it RECORD. If you specify a range of cells, name the top left cell in the range RECORD. Multiplan can place as many as 64 characters in the RECORD cell. When you press Shift-F9 to turn off the recording, Multiplan automatically tacks on the 'QU command code.

If your macro fills the cell you've named RECORD, the pattern of cells Multiplan uses to hold the overflow depends on whether you defined your recording area as one cell or a range of cells. Figure 18-5 shows the pattern that Multiplan observes in each case.

When you specify one cell (say R1C15) to hold your keystrokes, Multiplan considers the recording area to be from that cell to the lower right corner of the spreadsheet. When RECORD (R1C15) is filled, Multiplan moves to the next cell down (R2C15) to record more keystrokes, and continues down the column

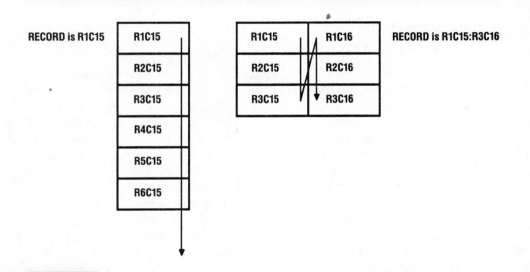

FIGURE 18-5.
Recording patterns in the *Record Macro* mode

into as many cells as needed to record all your keystrokes. If the macro reaches the bottom cell in the column, Multiplan inserts the command code 'GO at the end of that part of the macro, moves to the top cell in the next column, and continues recording there. If Multiplan encounters a cell that contains an entry, it stops recording and asks if you want to overwrite the entry. If you press *Y* to select *Yes*, it overwrites. If you press *N* to select *No*, the recording stops.

When you specify a range of cells (say R1C15:R3C16) to hold your keystrokes, your macro is strictly limited to that area. When the RECORD cell (R1C15) is filled, Multiplan moves down to R2C15 to record more keystrokes, then to R3C15, then up to R1C16, then to R2C16 and finally, to R3C16. When R3C16 is filled, Multiplan turns off recording, even if you are still typing, and doesn't add 'QU at the end. If you need to record more keystrokes, you can define a new RECORD area immediately below the last cell and resume typing, or you can add the command code 'GO where recording ended to direct Multiplan to another cell. If you specify more than one range as the RECORD area, Multiplan recognizes only the first range and ignores the others.

When you use Record Macro, you must go back and add any command codes after you finish recording. Though a bother, this is an acceptable tradeoff for the ease of recording. There's no way to shut down the recording temporarily, then pick up where you left off, so you must also go back and edit out any typing errors you may have made.

Naming a Macro

Though it's not strictly necessary to do so, macro life is a good deal simpler when you name the macro cell and assign a run code. Multiplan won't let you name a cell *R* or *C*, which could be confused with Row or Column, or use the same run code twice on a spreadsheet. You can, however, use identical letters for the cell name and run code. If you prefer pressing Alt-H to get help when you need it, don't assign the run code *H* or one that starts with *H* because pressing the Alt and H keys brings up the Help screen.

If you forget the name of a macro or its run code, you can bring up a list of all the names you've defined by starting the *Name* command and pressing an arrow key, or by using the *Print Names Macros* option in the Run Report command to print a list of all the macro names. Instead of relying on memory, especially if others are working on the spreadsheet, it's a good idea to type the run code and a brief description of how the macro works in a nearby cell or insert it in the macro by using the command code '*LAcomment*'.

RUNNING A MACRO

The cursor can be anywhere on the spreadsheet when you run a macro. The best place, though, is where you can get a bird's-eye view of the action. To cancel the macro, press the Escape key. In some situations, for instance when the macro is running, you have to press Escape more than once.

With a short, simple macro, success is virtually guaranteed at the first shot. With a long or complex macro, however, it's a good idea to test each step as you go along to make sure it works before you add the next one.

AND IF YOUR MACRO WON'T WORK

There will be times (count on it) when you create a macro that Multiplan won't accept or that doesn't work the way you intended.

When The Macro Doesn't Run as Planned

If you run a macro and Multiplan displays *Not a valid option*, check your command keystrokes closely. Your macro may have encountered a letter that is not available on the current menu.

If Multiplan displays the message *Error in Macro*, look for too few or too many apostrophes—especially too many. In most cases, you need only one apostrophe. Only when you have several command codes in succession can you legitimately end up with double apostrophes. For example, inserting your comments to flag a subroutine might look like this: *'LAStarts the update subroutine' 'GOR28C20'*. Also look for improper spaces, improper spelling of command codes, and any missing special elements needed by a command code.

Error Messages in the Cells

If you run a macro and end up with error messages in the cells, it's a safe bet that your macro upset the delicate balance between a formula and its cell references. This event is most likely to happen when your macro is shifting chunks of information during updating. But all is not lost. Just load the spreadsheet again and type *N* (for *No*) when Multiplan asks if you want to save the edits. Then rethink and rewrite the macro.

Troubleshooting in the Single Step Mode

If a macro isn't doing what you want it to do, if it stalls during its run, or if it ends prematurely with an *Error in macro* message, you can run the macro one step at a time. The Shift-F5 keys invoke the Single Step mode. Like the Edit Macro and Record Macro modes, the Single Step mode alters the operation of the keyboard (you see *ST* to the right of the *Free* indicator on the status line) and lets you carefully examine a recalcitrant macro.

After you press Shift-F5, start the macro by using either its run code or the Goto Macro command. At the first pause and at each subsequent pause, press the Enter key to run the next step. If the macro contains text, such as a spreadsheet title, hold down the Enter key, and Multiplan will type the characters on the command line. When you discover the problem, press Shift-F5 to restore the keyboard to standard operation, then edit the macro.

Editing a Macro

There's usually no need to reenter the entire macro to correct the problem. You simply edit it in the same way you would edit a formula or a title. With your cursor on the cell that needs editing, type *E* to start the Edit command. Then use the F7 through F10 keys to move the highlight to the problem. Type missing characters or press the delete key to delete unwanted characters. This is also the way to add command codes you are unable to insert in the Record Macro mode.

Ironically, the more comfortable you are with using Multiplan, the more likely you are to omit some keystrokes, simply because working with Multiplan has become automatic. Neglecting to insert an Enter keycode (*'RT*) to confirm a command seems to crop up most often. So, expect to edit a long macro a few times before things run smoothly.

If you've just finished editing a macro and Multiplan displays *Not a valid formula* when you press Enter, make sure the macro ends with quotation marks. It's easy to overlook the obvious. Perhaps you used the Backspace key instead of the F7 or F9 keys to back up the highlight. Using Backspace erases the quotes instead of jumping past them. If that's the problem, type in the quotes.

COPYING MACROS

If you create one macro, then need another that uses many of the same keystrokes, there's usually no need to retype everything. Simply copy the original to another cell, edit the copy, then name the new macro cell and assign a new run code.

When you need an existing macro on another spreadsheet, you can name it on the source spreadsheet, then transfer it by name by using the Xternal Copy command to a destination spreadsheet. You want the destination macro to remain unchanged even if you change the source macro, so be sure to keep the spreadsheets unlinked by typing *N* (for *No*) in the *linked* field of Xternal Copy.

DELETING A MACRO

You can remove a macro that outlives its usefulness by simply blanking out its cell. To keep things tidy and to allow you to reuse the run code: Start the Name command and use a direction key to display the list of cell names. Highlight the macro name, then press Tab to move the highlight to the *to refer to* field. Press Del to delete the macro's cell location and press Enter.

19

If Your Formula Won't Work

This chapter discusses formulas—those great-to-have-but-headache-when-they-don't-work phenomena that make electronic spreadsheets so valuable. The discussion is in two parts. The first part deals with the formulas you create yourself, and the second deals with the formulas in this book. You'll find both parts worthwhile reading.

CORRECTING YOUR OWN FORMULAS

When you create your own formulas, you are bound to do something on occasion that doesn't quite follow the rules. In many cases, Multiplan will both alert you to the problem and help you resolve it. For example, if a formula can't be calculated as you built it, Multiplan will display an error message on the message line or in the formula cell. However, if you enter a formula that Multiplan can calculate but the order of calculation, cell references, or other elements are wrong, you'll end up with wrong numbers. In these cases, Multiplan is doing just what you told it to do and its solution is up to you.

When Multiplan Doesn't Accept the Formula

The earliest sign of trouble is when Multiplan won't accept a formula you try to enter. When this happens Multiplan highlights the formula on the command line and displays *Not a valid formula* on the message line. All of this indicates that something is wrong with the formula's basic construction. You may be tempted to press the Escape key and start the formula from scratch, but resist the urge. In many cases, you have only to insert or delete a character.

If Multiplan can spot the problem, it highlights a specific place in the formula. When confronted by complex or numerous problems, Multiplan highlights the entire formula. Check each character carefully, particularly any place that Multiplan highlights. Here are some things to look for:

- An unequal number of open and close parentheses.

- A misspelled function name (IFF instead of IF, for example).

- A missing open parenthesis after a function name.

- Misplaced, misused, or missing operators (arithmetic, comparison, colon, and comma).

- A period instead of a comma or colon.

- The letter O instead of a zero (and vice versa).

- Extra or improper spaces.

When you find the problem, you can move the highlight left or right through the formula by pressing the edit keys—F7 (word left), F9 (character left), F8 (word right), and F10 (character right). If the entire formula is highlighted, press the F9 key to move the highlight to the first character or the F7 key to move the highlight to the first word. Type the missing character or press the Delete key to erase a character or word. After you correct the problem, press Enter.

When Multiplan Displays an Error Message

Multiplan accepts some problem formulas, but displays an error message in the formula cell, indicating that the problem is not how the formula is built but what you want it to do. For example, if you tell a formula to divide by zero, which it cannot do, you will see *#DIV/0!* in the formula cell.

When you see an error message, don't panic. Sometimes, as can happen with *#DIV/0!*, the message appears only because you haven't entered numbers in the cells that your formula references. When you enter these numbers, the error message disappears.

Other times you will see error messages all over the screen. This doesn't necessarily mean you have a slew of problem formulas. One problem formula can spawn a host of error messages simply because other formulas refer to it. When you correct the singular cause, it's likely that the widespread effect will disappear.

Types of Error Messages

Different error conditions require different approaches. The error message is your first clue. The following is a brief summary of Multiplan's error messages and some approaches to try.

#DIV/0! Your formula is attempting to divide by the contents of a cell that is empty or contains a zero. Enter a value in the cell referred to, ignore the message temporarily until the value is entered, or change the formula so it doesn't refer to the cell.

#NAME? Your formula is referring to a name that isn't assigned to any cell. Assign the name, check the spelling of the name, or change the formula so it doesn't refer to that name.

#N/A Your formula is asking for a value that isn't available. Enter a value in the cell referred to or ignore the message temporarily until the value is entered. If you use the NA() function as a flag to indicate that something still needs to be entered, the formula cell will show #N/A and all cells referring to the formula cell will show #N/A.

#NULL! Your formula is referring to an intersection of groups of cells that don't intersect. Replace the intersection operator (a space) with the union operator (a comma).

#NUM! Your formula is using illegal arithmetic or a value that is too large or too small. Check the arithmetic operators, numeric range, and formula syntax.

#REF! Your formula is referring to a deleted cell or to a non-existent cell location. Enter the cell reference again, change the formula, or correct the cell location.

#VALUE! Your formula is referring to text when a number is needed, or vice versa. Change the formula or the contents of the cell referred to.

Your formula is calculating or copying a number that is longer than can appear in the cell. Increase the width of the cell or change the cell format. (For example, reduce or eliminate the number of decimal places.)

Sorry, Wrong Number

When you suspect that your numbers are wrong, test your suspicions by having your formula work with simple numbers to which you already know the answer. This can provide valuable clues—for example, how far from the right answer the result is. It can also help you spot incremental patterns or improper negative numbers.

Next, examine the formula's construction and concept. This is when your sleuthing skills really come into play. You may have:

- Used the wrong cell reference.

- Copied the formula to a location where it's referring to the wrong cells.

- Used an absolute reference when a relative reference was called for, or vice versa.

- Typed a wrong number, operator, or cell name.

- Built the formula so that the order of calculation is wrong.

Review each element in the formula and check it against Multiplan's order of calculation. Then rethink the logic behind your formula. Your formula may be doing precisely what you told it to do, not what you meant it to do.

VIEWING YOUR FORMULAS

When you're searching for the source of a problem or when you want to change something, you can see the formulas in the following ways:

- When the cursor is on a cell containing a formula, the first 27 characters of the formula appear on the status line at the bottom of the screen.

- If the formula is too long to be seen completely on the status line, you can display it all on the command line by leaving the cursor on the formula cell and typing *E* to start the Edit command. If the formula is locked, you will have to unlock the cell first by using the Lock command.

- You can see all your formulas on screen by selecting *Yes* in the *formulas* field in Format Options. When you do so, cells display the formulas that produce the results instead of the results. To restore the spreadsheet, select *No* in the *formulas* field.

- When you select *Yes* in the *formulas* field in Print Options and then print your spreadsheet, you can see all your formulas on the printout.

- You can examine your formulas (and more) by using the Run command.

TRACKING DOWN SPREADSHEET ERRORS

Tracking down the source of a problem can be a baffling experience. Even when you study your formulas carefully, the solution can be downright elusive. This is where Multiplan's heavy hitters—the Run Audit and Run Report commands—come into play. Run Audit lets you examine your formulas on-screen, and Run Report lets you examine your spreadsheet on paper. These important error-checking and documentation tools help you better understand how your spreadsheet works.

Hitting the Audit Trail

Auditing is the process of exploring spreadsheet relationships from two angles: the cells a formula refers to and the cells that refer to a formula. Either way, Multiplan produces a good deal of information.

Let's suppose you want to audit the formula in R6C2. With the cursor on R6C2, you call up Run Audit, which offers two options: Formulas and Cells. You type *F* to select the Formulas option and press Enter. Multiplan now splits the screen into two horizontal windows, as shown in Figure 19-1.

The top window describes cell R6C2 in the following ways:

■ It contains the formula *ABS(PMT(RATE%/12,TERM * 12,LOAN))*. A highlight is on the first cell reference, the cell named RATE.

```
Formula/Value in R6C2:
ABS(PMT(RATE%/12,TERM*12,LOAN))



Value: 4363.7983242256              Displayed Value: $4,363.80
Format: Def, $(2)
Cells in RATE: R4C2



Formula/Value in R4C2:
15



Value: 15                           Displayed Value: 15.00
Format: Def, Fix(2)

RUN AUDIT FORMULAS cell: R6C2

Press arrow keys or Cancel to return to main menu
R6C2       ABS(PMT(RATE%/12,TERM*12,LO ?   98% Free      Multiplan: AMOR
```

FIGURE 19-1.
The split screen in Run Audit Formulas

■ It stores a value that is carried out to 10 decimal places.

■ It displays the stored value in dollars and cents, with a comma in the thousands place.

■ It is formatted with the default (*Def*) alignment and coded for dollars with two decimal places (*$(2)*).

■ It tells you that the cell referred to by RATE is R4C2.

The bottom window shows the location, contents, and format of R4C2, the cell reference highlighted in the top window. As you move the highlight to *TERM* and *LOAN* (the other cell references in the formula), Multiplan describes each cell in the bottom window.

You can work with ranges of cells in the same way. Let's say you're examining the range *R5C15:R6C18*. The bottom window first shows you the contents of R5C15. Multiplan's standard method for displaying cells in a range is to show all the cells in a row, then continue to the next row down. So, with the contents of R5C15 displayed, you press the Right Arrow key to see the contents of R5C16, then R5C17, then R5C18, then R6C15, then R6C16, and so on.

Key	Single Cell Reference	Range Reference
Left Arrow	Goes to previous reference	Goes to previous reference in range
Ctrl-Left	Goes to previous reference	Goes to reference immediately before range
Right Arrow	Goes to next reference	Goes to next reference in range
Ctrl-Right	Goes to next reference	Goes to reference immediately after range
PgUp	Remains where it is and sounds a "beep"	Goes to previous row in range; if none, sounds a "beep"
PgDn	Remains where it is and sounds a "beep"	Goes to next row in range; if none, sounds a "beep"
Home	Remains where it is	Goes to first cell in range
End	Remains where it is	Goes to last cell in range

FIGURE 19-2.
The keys that move the Audit highlight

```
┌─────────────────────────────────────────────────────────────────────────┐
│ ┌───────────────────────────────────────────────────────────────────┐   │
│ │Cells that use R6C2:                                               │   │
│ │███████ R8C2      R13C3     R14C3     R15C3     R16C3     R17C3     │   │
│ │R18C3   R19C3     R20C3     R21C3     R22C3     R23C3     R24C3     │   │
│ │R25C3   R26C3     R27C3     R28C3     R29C3     R30C3     R31C3     │   │
│ │R32C3   R33C3     R34C3     R35C3     R36C3     R37C3     R38C3     │   │
│ │R39C3   R40C3     R41C3     R42C3     R43C3     R44C3     R45C3     │   │
│ │R46C3   R47C3     R48C3                                            │   │
│ │Value: 4363.7983242256            Displayed Value: $4,363.80       │   │
│ │Format: Def, $(2)                                                 │   │
│ └───────────────────────────────────────────────────────────────────┘   │
│ ┌───────────────────────────────────────────────────────────────────┐   │
│ │Formula/Value in R7C2:                                            │   │
│ │PAY*12                                                            │   │
│ │                                                                  │   │
│ │                                                                  │   │
│ │                                                                  │   │
│ │Value: 52365.5798907071           Displayed Value: $52,365.58     │   │
│ │Format: Def, $(2)                                                 │   │
│ └───────────────────────────────────────────────────────────────────┘   │
│ RUN AUDIT CELLS cell: R6C2                                              │
│                                                                         │
│ Press arrow keys or Cancel to return to main menu                       │
│ R6C2      ABS(PMT(RATE%/12,TERM*12,LO ?  98% Free    Multiplan: AMOR    │
└─────────────────────────────────────────────────────────────────────────┘
```

FIGURE 19-3.
The split screen in Run Audit Cells

The highlight responds differently to your keystrokes, depending on whether you are working with a single cell reference or a range of cells. Figure 19-2 shows the results under each condition. If you've turned off the "beep" by selecting *Yes* in the *mute* field of the Options command, turn it on again.

Now let's say you select the Cells option in the Run Audit command instead of Formulas. Your screen now looks something like the one in Figure 19-3. The top window shows the cells that refer to the formula the cursor was on when you started the Run command. The bottom window shows the contents, stored value, displayed value, and format of the cell highlighted in the top window.

Pressing the Up Arrow key moves the information in the bottom window to the top window. Pressing the Down Arrow key lets you audit a previous cell. If the cell isn't referred to by any other cell, the bottom window remains empty.

Printing the Spreadsheet Reports

The reports provided by Run Report are snapshots of your spreadsheet from several angles. These reports can help uncover existing and potential problems. Run Report Print and Run Report File offer three options: Cross Ref, Names, and Summary.

```
R2C2:
Format: Def, Def(0)
Value: ==================

R6C2:
Format: Def, $(2)
Value:          $4,363.80
RATE
       R4C2
TERM
       R5C2
LOAN
       R3C2

R7C2:
Format: Def, $(2)
Value:         $52,365.58
PAY
       R6C2
       RATE
            R4C2
       TERM
            R5C2
       LOAN
            R3C2
```

FIGURE 19-4.

A report that cross references the cells on the spreadsheet

Cross Ref: A cross reference report lists the cells that contain formulas, text, and constants. This listing shows formats, contents, references to other cells, and levels of cells, as in Figure 19-4. You can choose to cross reference the cells only in a specific area or in every cell on the spreadsheet.

Names: Selecting the *All* option prints a list of all the cell names, as shown in Figure 19-5. This list identifies macro names and run codes, if any. You can also produce a list of macro names only or non-macro names only.

Summary: A summary report gives the spreadsheet statistics, including the number of cells that contain error messages, formulas that reference blank cells, cells that have formats but no value, named areas that overlap, names that are partially locked, and cells that contain a circular reference. Select the *Count* option to get a listing of cell counts only or select the *Full* option to get a listing of cell counts and a listing of the cells involved, as shown in Figure 19-6. Analysis of these summary reports can uncover subtle factors that can lead to problems, such as circular references where formulas work with each other in a looping pattern.

```
  LOAN:                      Macro - No      Command Code -  none
      R3C2

  PAY:                       Macro - No      Command Code -  none
      R6C2

  RATE:                      Macro - No      Command Code -  none
      R4C2

  TERM:                      Macro - No      Command Code -  none
      R5C2
```

FIGURE 19-5.
The names on a spreadsheet provided by Run Report

```
      0 Cells have a value of #NULL!.
      0 Cells have a value of #DIV/0!.
      0 Cells have a value of #VALUE!.
      0 Cells have a value of #REF!.
      0 Cells have a value of #NAME?.
      0 Cells have a value of #NUM!.
      0 Cells have a value of #N/A.
      0 Formulas that reference blank cells.
      1 Cells with formats but no value.
R1C3
      0 Named areas that overlap.
      0 Names are partially locked.
      0 Cells contain a Circular Reference.
```

FIGURE 19-6.
Comprehensive spreadsheet statistics provided by Run Report

EDITING YOUR FORMULA

The root of a formula problem can be syntax, cells, or concept. When you find the problem, you can rebuild the formula from scratch, but that takes time. Besides, if you attempt to rebuild a long or complex formula, a typing error or a wrong cell reference could introduce new problems. In most cases, the best approach is to edit the formula.

When you place the cursor on the formula cell and type *E* (Edit), the formula appears on the command line with a highlight after the last character.

Pressing the F7 through F10 keys moves the highlight through the formula without changing anything. The F7 (word) and F9 (character) keys move the highlight to the left. The F8 (word) and F10 (character) keys move the highlight to the right. The Backspace key moves the highlight to the left, erasing characters as it goes.

If the problem is syntax (something missing or mispelled in the formula), the highlight belongs to the left of a missing character or on top of an extra or a wrong character. With the highlight at the proper place, type any missing characters (the formula shifts to the right) or press the Delete key to erase characters or words (the formula shifts to the left).

If the problem is with a cell you selected by moving the cursor, delete the wrong cell reference first, then move the cursor to the correct cell location. When the formula has more than one problem, Multiplan will display *Not a valid formula* when you try to move the cursor. You will have to type the relative cell notation (brackets, R's, C's, and other characters) yourself before you move on to solving the other problems.

If the problem is conceptual, try to salvage as much of the formula as possible by editing with the function keys or erasing with the Backspace key. If this approach augurs more confusion than resolution, then by all means start from scratch.

When you finish editing the formula, press Enter. If the formula is used elsewhere on the spreadsheet, be sure to copy it to the other cells.

CORRECTING A FORMULA ENTERED FROM THIS BOOK

You followed the instructions in this book in every way, moved the cursor to the right cells, and typed the right characters, or so you thought. But then the instructions told you to recalculate and there they were—wrong numbers or error messages in cells containing your by-the-book formulas. One thing is certain: Your spreadsheet doesn't look like the one in this book. And here you are, trying to figure out what went wrong. Take a deep breath. Help is on the way.

The problem confronting you now is simpler than those that arise when you build your own formulas, because you are working with tested logic and concepts. So the problem has to be syntax or cell references.

When Error Messages Appear

If you get an error message in a formula cell, it is likely to be *#NAME?*. Naming is a common activity in the spreadsheet chapters, and you may have overlooked entering a name or misspelled one. Type *N* (Name) and press a direction key to bring up a listing of all the names on the spreadsheet, then press the Down Arrow key to highlight each name and show the corresponding cell locations. Compare the names on your spreadsheet to the instructions titled "Naming the Cells" in the appropriate chapter. When you find a name you overlooked, follow the naming instructions to enter it. If you find a misspelled name, first delete the cell locations that refer to it, then rename those cells.

Numbers Don't Agree

If your numbers don't agree with the spreadsheet or if you have an error message other than *#NAME?*, you inserted the wrong cell reference, typed a wrong number or symbol, or built the formula in such a way (for example, with a misplaced arithmetic operator or a parenthesis) that the order of calculation is wrong. Follow these steps to locate and correct the problem.

Step 1: Unlock the Spreadsheet

If you haven't locked the spreadsheet yet, go to Step 2. If you have a question about whether cells are locked or unlocked, hold down the F2 key. On a locked spreadsheet, the cursor jumps past the cells containing formulas or text. To make it easier to view and edit the formulas, unlock the entire spreadsheet: Leave the cursor where it is and type *LC* (Lock Cells). Press Home, then F6, then End. Pressing these keys sends the cursor to R1C1, produces a colon, and sends the cursor to the bottom right cell of the active spreadsheet. Now look at the *status* field. If *Unlocked* is in parentheses, simply press Enter. If *Locked* is in parentheses, press Tab to move the highlight to the *status* field, type *U* to select *Unlocked* and press Enter.

Step 2: Examine the Formula

Examine the formulas producing the error message or the wrong number. Move the cursor to the cell in which you first entered the formula (that is, before you may have copied it to other cells) and look at the status line at the bottom of your screen. If you can't see the entire formula, type *E* (Edit) to display it completely on the command line. Compare each character in the formula on your screen to the formula in this book. If your formula is correct, continue to the next problem formula and do the same thing.

Step 3: Correct the Formula

When you find a formula that you need to correct, edit it. If the formula is not on the command line, type *E* (Edit). A highlight appears to the right of the last character. Use F7 (word left), F8 (word right), F9 (character left), or

F10 (character right) to move the highlight to the incorrect information. Correct the formula by typing any missing characters or pressing the Delete key to delete unwanted characters or words. If a cell reference is the problem, first delete the incorrect cell reference, then move the cursor to the correct cell location. If necessary, type the relative cell notation (brackets, R's, C's, and other characters) yourself. When you finish editing the formula, press Enter. Then copy the corrected formula to any cells that need it.

Step 4: Recalculate the Spreadsheet

Press F4 to recalculate the spreadsheet. If the problem is solved, go to Step 5. If you still have an error message or a wrong number in a cell, return to Step 2 and follow the same procedure until you find each wrong formula.

Step 5: Lock the Formulas

When all is well, lock the formulas again: Leave the cursor where it is, type *LF* (Lock Formulas), and type *Y* to confirm. Then use Transfer Save to save the spreadsheet.

20
Printing Your Spreadsheet

Printing a spreadsheet turns those words and numbers that exist only behind a glass screen into tangible reality, and Multiplan makes it easy to have everything look just right on paper. You can print all or part of a spreadsheet, the results of formulas or the formulas themselves, row and column numbers, page headers and page footers, and foreign currency symbols. You can print different elements of your spreadsheet in different type styles and sizes. And if that isn't enough, you can tell Multiplan where to position the spreadsheet on the page and what kind of printer you're using. All of these features are handled by the Print command and three of its options: Options, Margins, and Heading.

PRINT OPTIONS

The print options are just that—options. You don't have to change anything because Multiplan's standard settings are often exactly what you want. But if they're not, you can change the settings to conform to your standards. The standard settings in the Print Options fields are as follows.

Area: Multiplan assumes you want to print everything on your spreadsheet, so it enters *R1:4095* in the *area* field. If you want to print only a specific area, you enter the location of the top left cell and the bottom right cell in the area, separated by a colon (for example, *R6C4:R17C12*). When you want to print a named area, you simply type in the name.

Setup: When the *setup* field is empty, Multiplan prints in standard 10-pitch type. You can use the *setup* field to send control sequences (sequences of characters) to the printer to specify other pitches and type styles, such as compressed, double-width, and boldface. For example, I typed ^[M (in English, Escape M) in the *setup* field to tell my Epson FX-compatible printer to print in 12-pitch, which my printer manual refers to as elite pitch. To do the same thing on a Hewlett Packard Laser Jet Plus printer with the Prestige Math Elite font cartridge, you would enter ^[(S12H in the *setup* field. Your printer manual contains the details on control sequences and pitches available to you.

Adapter: If you leave the standard *PRN* in the *adapter* field, Multiplan sends the spreadsheet to your printer. The *adapter* field lets you specify the device name (communication port) of the printer you want to use to print the spreadsheet.

Formulas: The standard setting tells Multiplan to print the spreadsheet values. If you want to print the formulas, select *Yes* in the *formulas* field. Multiplan then doubles the width of those columns that are 32 characters wide or less, leaves the other columns at their current widths, and prints the formulas.

Row-col numbers: Multiplan prints spreadsheets without row and column numbers. If you choose *Yes*, Multiplan prints row numbers down the left side of your spreadsheet and column numbers across the top (the same numbers you see on your screen). These numbers are invaluable when you need to troubleshoot a spreadsheet.

Currency code: An entry in the *Currency code* field tells the printer how to print a currency symbol. You need to make an entry only if your printer needs special instructions for the symbol you want.

Your option settings are saved when you save the spreadsheet. If you then create a new spreadsheet, the settings you saved on the last spreadsheet become the proposed responses on the new one. But if you quit Multiplan, all the option settings except *setup* revert to the Multiplan standards. Multiplan assumes that you want consistency, so it saves the *setup* field setting and proposes it on your next spreadsheet. This saves you the task of re-entering a control sequence. You can change the *setup* or any other Print Options setting whenever you choose.

PRINTING POINTERS

The following tips and techniques can help make printing your spreadsheets easier and more efficient.

Inserting Rows and Columns

In most cases, you can insert rows and columns to your heart's content, and Multiplan will adjust the print area to reflect those changes. But there is one exception. If you insert a new row 1 or a new column 1, the standard setting of *R1:4095* in the *area* field becomes *R2:4095* when row 1 is inserted or *C2:255* when column 1 is inserted. Therefore, any information in the new row or column won't appear on the printout unless you adjust the print area before printing, which is merely a matter of typing *R1:4095* in the *area* field.

Changing Character Sizes

When you want to print a wide spreadsheet on one page, the size of the characters ("pitch") is particularly important. The standard pitches are 10, 12, and 15 characters per horizontal inch of space. A 12-pitch character is smaller than a 10-pitch character, so you can fit more 12-pitch characters across a page. A 15-pitch character is the smallest of these three standard pitches, so you can fit more 15-pitch characters than 10- or 12-pitch characters across a page. Most dot-matrix printers can handle these pitches and more through the *setup* field. Daisywheel and laser printers can also print different pitch sizes, but you must change the daisywheel or font cartridge on the printer.

To simplify matters, every spreadsheet in this book is printed in 12-pitch type. So, if you're using a dot-matrix printer, once you enter your code for 12-pitch type, you won't have to change the *setup* field. If you're using a daisywheel printer, once you install a 12-pitch font, you won't have to switch wheels or, in the case of a laser printer, switch cartridges.

Determining the Print Width

If you're like most people, when you are in the midst of designing a spreadsheet you don't keep in mind the width of your paper when changing the widths of columns. So, when it comes time to print the spreadsheet, you can only guess its overall size. Knowing the print width helps you determine if everything will fit on one page and, if you have to split the spreadsheet into sections, where those splits should be. Print width also can help you decide what margins and pitch will produce a spreadsheet that's clear to read and pleasing to the eye.

There are two ways to determine print width: add the width of each column or print the spreadsheet, then measure it.

Adding up the column widths:

If the spreadsheet isn't big, you can determine its width column-by-column. When you place the cursor on the first column and type *FW* (Format Width), Multiplan displays the width of that column in characters. Repeat the process for the other columns that contain information, then add all the numbers. If you are printing row and column numbers, add five characters to the total. Multiplan needs those five characters for four-digit row numbers and the space between the fourth digit and the first character on the spreadsheet.

Printing and measuring:

When you use the print-and-measure method to determine print width, set the widest possible print area—a left margin of 0 and a right margin based on the pitch and paper—before you print the spreadsheet. As shown in the print margins chart in Figure 20-1, if you're printing in 10-pitch type on 8½-by-11-inch paper, set the print width to 85. If you're printing in 12-pitch type on 15-by-11-inch paper, set the print width to 163 characters. Multiplan will print page after page until the entire spreadsheet is printed. Sometimes when you print row and column numbers, characters from the last column of each row

Paper Size	Pitch	Left	Top	Maximum Print Width	Print Length	Page Length
8½" by 11"	10	0	6	85	60	66
	12	0	6	102	60	66
	15	0	6	127	60	66
11" by 8½"	10	0	6	110	45	51
	12	0	6	132	45	51
	15	0	6	165	45	51
15" by 11"	10	0	6	136	60	66
	12	0	6	163	60	66
	15	0	6	204	60	66

FIGURE 20-1.
Print margins chart

may wrap around to the left margin, making the spreadsheet appear double-spaced. Try a slightly narrower print width so that the last column prints on the next page, or eliminate the row and column numbers.

After printing, measure the spreadsheet with a ruler that shows the space increments for different pitch sizes ($\frac{1}{10}$-inch, $\frac{1}{12}$-inch, $\frac{1}{15}$-inch). These rulers are sold in computer stores and usually show line spacing (six to the inch, eight to the inch, and so on). Measuring with a standard ruler is possible, but difficult, because you have to translate the $\frac{1}{16}$-inch markings into pitch size.

The best place to measure is a dashed line that extends the full width of the spreadsheet. If you're printing row numbers, start at the point where the first digit in the four-digit number would print.

PRINT MARGINS

The print margins control where the spreadsheet starts and stops printing on the page. Multiplan provides the following margins as default (standard) settings:

Left: The left margin is five characters from the left edge of the page.

Top: The top margin is six lines (one inch) from the top edge of the page.

Print width: The print width is 70 characters per line.

Print length: The print length is 54 lines (9 inches) per page.

Page length: The page length is 66 lines (11 inches).

Indent: The indent does not relate to a spreadsheet, but sets the number of characters indented when Multiplan prints a cross-reference report. The standard setting is four characters.

Since spreadsheets come in a variety of layouts and sizes, your margins are bound to change from sheet to sheet. All you have to do is type your own numbers in the margin fields. Like the Print Options settings, all the margin settings are saved with the spreadsheet. Unlike the Print Options settings, which (except for *setup*) revert to Multiplan's standard settings when you quit Multiplan, the print margins in effect when you quit are stored in a special Multiplan file (MP.INI) so that they are in effect when you start Multiplan the next time.

The Print Margins Chart

The chart in Figure 20-1 shows the maximum print width, print length, and page length for three paper sizes and three pitches. The maximum print width is the maximum number of characters that will fit across one page when the left margin set at 0. The print length is the maximum number of lines that will print on one page when the top margin is set at 6. The page length is the maximum number of lines that will print on one page at the standard six lines to the inch.

You can position your spreadsheet anywhere on the printed page by changing the left and top margins if you keep the following in mind:

■ The left margin plus the number of characters across the spreadsheet (plus five characters if you are printing Multiplan row and column numbers) cannot exceed the maximum print width shown in Figure 20-1. The maximum print width prevents the printing from running off the paper and onto the platen. As a general rule, set the print width to the maximum shown in the table for the paper size and pitch you are using.

Suppose your spreadsheet is 90 characters wide and you are printing in 12-pitch type on 8½-by-11-inch paper. The chart shows a maximum print width of 102 characters. A print width of 102 characters minus a spreadsheet width of 90 characters is 12, so split the difference and type 6 in the *left* field and *102* in the *print width* field to center the text vertically. The spreadsheet will print on one page with equal left and right margins.

■ The top margin plus the number of spreadsheet lines (plus one line if you are printing Multiplan row and column numbers) cannot exceed the page length shown in Figure 20-1. As a general rule, keep Multiplan's top margin of six lines and set the print length to the number shown on the chart. If the spreadsheet lines exceed this print length but are less than or the same as the page length, you can set a top margin that will position the spreadsheet with equal top and bottom margins or keep the standard margins and let the spreadsheet print on consecutive pages.

Suppose your spreadsheet is 62 lines long and you are printing on 8½-by-11-inch paper. The chart shows a print length of 60 lines and a page length of 66 lines. A page length of 66 lines minus a print length of 62 lines is four lines, so split the difference and type 2 in the *top* field and *62* in the *print length* field to center the spreadsheet vertically. The spreadsheet will print on one page with equal (but small) top and bottom margins.

When your spreadsheet is wider than the maximum print width or longer than the maximum print length, Multiplan prints any leftover columns or rows on the next page.

Laser printers aren't able to print in the top half inch or the bottom half inch of a page and print six fewer lines on each page. Take this into account when you specify the print margins. Most laser printers provide special formatting codes that allow you to print the standard 66 lines per page in the available 10 inches of an 8½-by-11-inch paper. You'll find these format codes in your printer manual.

PRINTING AN OVERSIZE SPREADSHEET

Clearly, many of your spreadsheets will be too wide to print on one page. When the spreadsheet is wider than one page, you can simply tape pages together. If you can, plan the layout or change the print area so that pages start at a logical breaking point (not, for example, in the middle of a long title).

If your spreadsheet is just a tad wider than one page, here are a few ways to whittle it down to size:

■ Use a condensed type or a smaller pitch.

■ Look again at the print margins settings. Did you set the left margin to 0? Did you set the print width to the maximum for the paper size and pitch?

■ If you're printing row and column numbers, can you do without them?

■ Try reducing the width of a few columns, even "hide" a column that won't be missed by reducing its width to zero characters.

■ Take a final look at your spreadsheet. Can you create a formula to handle intermediate calculations, then delete a column? Can you abbreviate wide titles or put them in a continuous format, then reduce the width of a column?

■ Consider redesigning your spreadsheet to a vertical layout.

If your spreadsheet is a bit too long to print on one page, you have a few options to consider. You can reduce the top margin to 0 and increase the print length to 66. Or, if it doesn't crowd the spreadsheet, delete an empty row or a row of dashed lines. Then review the preceding suggestions for the wide spreadsheet. They may apply or they may trigger other ideas.

USING HEADERS AND FOOTERS

Headers and footers add flair and identity to your spreadsheet. A header is information that is printed at the top of each page; a footer is information that is printed at the bottom. Headers usually contain such things as a filename, page number, title, and date. A footer usually contains a page number.

In the Multiplan scheme of things, you enter the input for a header or footer in an out-of-the-way location on the spreadsheet, and exclude that area from the print area. Then, in the Heading option of the Print command, you tell Multiplan the location of the input information.

Multiplan prints a header immediately above the first line of the spreadsheet and a footer immediately below the last line. Your spreadsheet is likely to look better with some separation between it and a header or footer. As a general rule, when you identify the location of the input information, include one or two empty cells below the header input and one or two empty cells above the footer input. That way, the printer will leave one or two empty lines between the header and the spreadsheet, and between the spreadsheet and the footer.

Multiplan can print only the input that is displayed on your spreadsheet. So, if you have a long line of text, be sure to continue it into as many cells as needed to display it fully, and identify all those cells in the *header* field of Print Heading.

Aligning the Header and Footer

Multiplan can print your header or footer at the left, center, or right of the page. The default alignment is centered. To print the header or footer at the left margin, type the alignment code *&L* before each line of input information. To print at the right margin, type the alignment code *&R* before each line.

Alignment codes are text and can therefore share a cell with any other text input. Let's suppose your spreadsheet contains five columns of information. You want to left-justify a header that contains two lines of text. In column 6, you enter the header input in this fashion:

Column 6
&LTextline1
&LTextline2

The process is a bit different when you are working with functions such as NAME, which generates the spreadsheet filename, and NOW, which generates the serial number of the current date. NAME and NOW are considered values, so you need to separate them from the text alignment codes. You now enter the alignment codes in column 6 and the input in column 7 in this fashion:

Column 6	**Column 7**
&L	Textline
&L	NAME()
&L	NOW()

To be sure the header is printed properly at the left margin, you must reduce the width of column 6 to two characters. If column 6 is any wider, you'll end up

```
STANDARD DOT MATRIX PRINT - 10-PITCH PICA

ITALIC

ITALIC, DOUBLE STRIKE

ITALIC, DOUBLE STRIKE, EXPANDED

COMPRESSED

COMPRESSED, DOUBLE STRIKE

COMPRESSED, DOUBLE STRIKE, EXPANDED

DOUBLE-STRIKE

EMPHASIZED

EMPHASIZED, EXPANDED

EXPANDED

THIS IS A SAMPLE OF SUPERSCRIPT CHARACTERS

A SAMPLE OF SUBSCRIPT CHARACTERS

UNDERLINED CHARACTERS

THE BEAUTY OF REVERSE PRINT
```

FIGURE 20-2.
Sample type styles and sizes generated by an Epson-compatible dot matrix printer on a
Multiplan spreadsheet

with a header printed one column to the right of the left margin. If it's any narrower (a zero-width "hidden" column, for example), Multiplan will simply ignore the alignment code and center the header.

Printing Page Numbers

With a long spreadsheet that prints on successive pages, page numbers are
essential. Multiplan can show these numbers as standard Arabic numerals (1),
uppercase or lowercase Roman numerals (I or i), or uppercase or lowercase letters (A or a). When you use letters, *AA* follows *Z*.

To have Multiplan print page numbers, you use the code *&P*. In a header,
you can use *Page &P* to produce *Page 1*; in a footer, use *- &P -* to produce *- 1 -*.
If your spreadsheet is part of a report, you can tell Multiplan to start with a
page number other than 1.

PRINTING SPECIAL EFFECTS

Multiplan lets you enter printer codes directly into the cells on the spreadsheet to vary the type styles and sizes. Figure 20-2 shows several styles that can

spice up your spreadsheet. Expanded characters, for example, work well with a spreadsheet title, while emphasized characters can be effective for totals and other important numbers.

Printer codes consist of a control character and one or more letters (for example, Control-B) or an escape character and a letter (for example, Escape-E). Your printer manual is the best source of information on the special print modes available to you.

Working With a Control Character

To give you an idea of how control characters work, let's assume you are using an Epson or Epson-compatible printer and you've already entered a code in the Print Options *setup* field to print the spreadsheet in 12-pitch type. You want to print only the spreadsheet title SALES (located in R1C6) in an expanded type. According to the printer manual, Control-N sets expanded print and Control-T cancels it.

You place the cursor on R1C5, the cell to the left of the title, set the Caps Lock key, and type *A* to start the Alpha command. You now press Control-B (that is, you hold down the Control key and type *B*). Though nothing shows on screen at this point, this alerts Multiplan that the next character you type is either an escape character or a control letter. You don't have to press the Control key again. Simply type *N*. When you do so, a character resembling a crooked A appears on screen.

You now have to tell the printer where to turn off the expanded print. You move the cursor to R1C7, the cell to the right of the title. You type *A* (Alpha), press Control-B, then type *T* and press Enter. Another interesting character appears, this one resembling a paragraph symbol. When you print, Multiplan will know exactly where to start and stop the expanded type style.

Instead of occupying separate cells, printer control codes can comfortably share a cell with the text you want to affect. With the cursor on R1C6, for example, these keystrokes enter the start and stop codes and the title in one cell: Type *A*, press Control-B, type *N*, type *SALES*, press Control-B, type *T*, and press Enter.

Working with an Escape Character

Now let's suppose you want to make a row of totals on your spreadsheet stand out. Your Epson or Epson-compatible printer produces emphasized print when it receives the code Escape-E and cancels it at Escape-F.

You place the cursor on the cell to the left of the first total, set the Caps Lock key, type *A*, and press Control-B. You are now working with an escape character. What happens next is a bit different than when you work with a control character, because instead of typing only the control letter, you have to enter both the escape character and a letter.

The escape character is produced by the left bracket key, so you type [(which appears on the screen as an arrow facing left), then type *E*, and press Enter. To revert to regular type, you place the cursor on the cell to the right of the last total, again type *A*, press Control-B, then type *[F* and press Enter.

The effects produced by printer codes can be attention-grabbers that enhance the aesthetics of your spreadsheet. It's worthwhile to explore them all. As shown in Figure 20-2, you can even combine several printer codes—for example, you can print a spreadsheet title or totals in both expanded and emphasized print. Just be sure to press Control-B before typing each printer code.

PRINTING SPECIAL REPORTS

Multiplan's Run command can produce a wealth of reports that are essential for debugging and archival purposes. And it's so easy. You don't have to make any special settings or enter any control sequences. With only a few keystrokes you can tell Multiplan to print reports that:

■ Cross reference every cell that contains a formula, text, or constants, showing their contents, formats, and the way cells are listed in the order they appear in a formula.

■ List every name you assigned on the spreadsheet.

■ List only the names you assigned to macros.

■ List only the names you assigned to non-macro cells.

■ Summarize the spreadsheet and count the named cells, formulas referencing blank cells, cells containing circular references, and cells containing error messages or conditions that are likely to cause problems.

These reports add depth to your spreadsheet efforts. They are described in more detail in Chapter 19.

INDEX

RUTH K. WITKIN

A lifelong resident of New York, Ruth K. Witkin attended the City College of New York and the Long Island University Graduate School of Business Administration. Her professional business experience—in publishing, writing, advertising, and personnel—spans 25 years. Witkin has been an advertising manager as well as a writer and editor for a high-technology electronics manufacturer. She currently heads her own personnel management firm and teaches Multiplan to corporate and private clients. In addition, she is a columnist for *inCider* magazine and has written for *Business Software*.

The manuscript for this book was prepared and submitted to Microsoft Press in electronic form. Text files were processed and formatted using Microsoft Word.

Cover and interior text design by the staff of Microsoft Press
Principal typographer: Ruth Pettis
Principal production artist: Becky Geisler-Johnson

The screen displays were created on the IBM PC XT and COMPAQ Deskpro 286 and printed on the Radio Shack Daisy Wheel II and Hewlett Packard LaserJet Plus.

Text composition by Microsoft Press in Sabon with display in Helvetica Bold Condensed, using the CCI composition system and the Mergenthaler Linotron 202 digital phototypesetter.